AMERICAN ISSUES

AMERICAN ISSUES

A Primary Source Reader
in United States History

Volume II

Edited by

IRWIN UNGER

New York University

Prentice Hall, Englewood Cliffs, New Jersey 07632

Library of Congress Cataloging-in-Publication Data

American issues : a primary source reader in United States history /
  edited by Irwin Unger.
    p. cm.
  Includes bibliographical references.
  ISBN 0–13–031956–2 (v. 1). — ISBN 0–13–031964–3 (v. 2)
  1. United States—History—Sources.   I. Unger, Irwin.
  E173.A73   1994
  973—dc20   93–10920
                                                                  CIP

Acquisitions editor: Steve Dalphin
Editorial assistant: Caffie Risher
Production Coordinator: Kelly Behr
Editorial /production supervision
  and interior design: Mary McDonald
Copy editor: Sherry Babbitt
Cover design: Violet Lake Studio

Printed in the United States of America
10   9   8   7   6   5   4   3   2   1

ISBN 0-13-031964-3

Prentice-Hall International (UK) Limited, *London*
Prentice-Hall of Australia Pty. Limited, *Sydney*
Prentice-Hall Canada Inc., *Toronto*
Prentice-Hall Hispanoamericana, S.A., *Mexico*
Prentice-Hall of India Private Limited, *New Delhi*
Prentice-Hall of Japan, Inc., *Tokyo*
Simon & Schuster Asia Pte. Ltd., *Singapore*
Editora Prentice-Hall do Brasil, Ltda., *Rio de Janeiro*

Brief Contents

Contents

Preface

Americans worry about the state of education in the United States today. Recently we have been told how little students know about science, geography, mathematics, and history; we fear that our country will be unprepared to compete against the other advanced industrial societies in years to come. We are also concerned that the new generation will lack the shared civic knowledge essential for a functioning democratic system.

There is indeed reason to be dismayed by how small a stock of historical information young Americans possess. But it is important also to realize that education is not just transmission of data. It is also the fostering of critical thinking. The most encyclopedic knowledge do students little good if they cannot use it to reach valid and useful conclusions. It is this belief that has inspired *American Issues*. This two-volume work will stimulate critical thinking about American history—leading students to reject received ideas when appropriate, relate the past to their own experience, and reach conclusions on the basis of evidence. At times, no doubt, students will have to do additional reading beyond this textbook; that, of course is all to the good.

American Issues is not a compendium of scholars' views. It is constructed out of *primary documents*, the raw material of history. In its pages participants and contemporary observers express their opinions, make their observations, and reach their conclusions about events and issues of their own day that affected the nation and American society. The selections do not point in one direction on any given issue. On the contrary, they were chosen to raise questions and force the student to confront disparity, complexity, and apparent contradiction. *American Issues* avoids giving students the "straight poop." Rather, it compels them to grapple with the same ambiguous raw materials that historians process to reach their conclusions. To further the engagement process, each selection asks specific questions of the student. The approach resembles that of the 1950 Japanese movie *Rashomon*, in which an event was depicted from the perspectives of several participants and viewers were expected to reach their own conclusions. That approach, I believe, is an incomparable way to enlighten students about the rich complexity and fullness of historical reality.

The selections in Volume I and Volume II range widely in subject matter across the American past. Besides the key political questions, they deal with the social, cultural, economic, and gender problems our predecessors faced. *American Issues* is informed by the sense that America has always been a heterogeneous society whose inhabitants led their lives in many ways. Yet it does not abandon the view that all of our forebears were also part of the same American experience and shared many concerns of their era.

What can we expect from conscientious use of *American Issues?* No single text can turn a passive person into an active seeker and thinker. But *American Issues* can, I believe, engage college students' natural curiosity and tendency to differ, and encourage the habit of critical appraisal. Instructors and students alike will find *American Issues* a stimulating and challenging introduction to informed and discriminating thinking about the American past.

Irwin Unger

AMERICAN ISSUES

1

The Gilded Age City

There was a vast churning of American population after 1865. As some Americans moved west, others moved to the cities. Urban growth during the half-century following the Civil War was spectacular. In 1870 a little over a quarter of all Americans lived in cities; in 1920 over half. In sheer numbers this meant an increase from 10 million to over 54 million city dwellers.

These people came from several sources. City folk begat city folk; many urbanites were the children of urbanites. Most, however, were newcomers, people born in rural communities who moved to the cities. They came from many parts of the world. One giant contingent consisted of native-born citizens from America's own farms and villages. Most of the remainder came from Europe's farms and villages and, after about 1890, predominantly from the rural areas of southern and eastern Europe.

The mass migration to the cities was part of the great shift in the Atlantic world's economy from agriculture to commerce and industry. Most of the newcomers were drawn by the economic advantages of the cities over their rural homes. Since the movement continued over many decades, we must assume that the urban edge in jobs and living standards persisted year after year.

Yet this is not to say that the newcomers found their new urban environment ideal. The cities of America were less than perfect places to live. To use a modern phrase, they had a "deficient infrastructure," especially early in this period. Housing, sanitation, health, and transportation facilities could not meet the surging demand. The cities' institutions also were imperfect. City governments were feeble and corrupt. They lacked the power to do what was needed, and what they did do was often accomplished at high cost. The cities were also deficient in civility. Anonymity, diversity, and poverty generated crime, disorder, and social breakdown. Urban law authorities were often unable to ensure safety for life and property. Churches and philanthropic organizations tried to help but were often pushed beyond their capacities.

Yet at worst Americans had mixed feelings about their cities, for despite their drawbacks, they also had advantages. What follows is an assortment of contemporary views, pro and con, of cities and city life in the period 1870–1920.

1.1:   The Cities Acclaimed (1909, 1905)

Cities have always been problematical to country folk. Americans, moreover, even more than most other Western peoples, have long prized the Arcadian ideal of a happy, virtuous, prosperous society set in the unspoiled countryside.

But cities have also had their devotees among rural people. The first of the following selections is from a drama by the popular playwright Clyde Fitch. It concerns the Rand family, small-town people, all of whom, except the father, yearn to move to New York City. The family makes the move and suffers adversities, although George, the son, continues to defend the family's choice of the big city. What are George's claims for city life? Were the motives of the Rands, do you suppose, similar to those of most immigrants to the city during this period?

The second item is by Frederic C. Howe, a widely published journalist-reformer who flourished during the Progressive Era early in this century. The Progressives were preponderantly urban dwellers, and they did much of their work as reformers within the urban setting. It was thus natural for them to regard the cities as showcases for the virtues and values of the new, reformed society. In the following selection, what does Howe foresee for the city in the near future? Has much of what he anticipated came to pass? Have the changes he describes produced the results he expected?

A Family Debate[1]

CLYDE FITCH

Mrs. Rand: Well, I've done all, in a social way, a woman can in Middleburg, and I want to do more. . . .

Clyde Fitch, *The City*, in *Plays by Clyde Fitch*, ed., Montrose Moses and Virginia Gerson (Boston: Little Brown, 1915), IV, pp. 458–625.
[1] Footnotes deleted.

Rand: Molly, wouldn't you rather be *it* in Middleburg—than *nit* in the City? . . .

Cicely: I don't care a darn about the position, if I can only have something to do, and something to see! Who wants to smell new-mown hay, if he can breathe in gasolene *[sic]* on Fifth Avenue instead! Think of the theatres! the crowds! *Think* of being able to go out on the street and *see some one you didn't know even by sight!!* . . .

George: Middleburg and her banks are just as picayune to *me*, in comparison with the *City* and a *big career there*, as *East Middleburg and real estate* were to *you* in *1860!* . . .

Rand: You've all got an exaggerated idea of the importance of the City. This country isn't *made* or run by New York or its half dozen sisters! It's in the smaller towns,—and spread all over the country,—that you find the bone and sinew of the United States! . . . Did Lincoln need New York? Did Grant? Did a metropolis turn out McKinley, or have anything to do with forming the character and career of Grover Cleveland? . . .

[Later]

Mrs. Rand: Oh, why did we ever come here! . . . I haven't had a happy moment since I left . . . my old home. . . . I'm lonesome for my church, and if I died I wouldn't have a handful of people at my funeral. . . . Oh, what the City has done for the whole of us!

Teresa: Yes, you're right, mother. I was happy too, till I came here. It was the City that taught me to make the worst of things, instead of the best of them. . . .

Van Vranken: I agree with Tess! She and I, in a small town, would have been happy always! I'd not have been tempted like I am here. . . .

George: . . . *No!* You're all wrong! Don't blame the City. It's not her fault! It's our own! What the City does is to bring out what's strongest in us. If at heart we're good, the good in us will win! If the bad is strongest, God help us! Don't blame the City! *She* gives the man his opportunity; it is up to *him* what he makes of it! A man can live in a small town all his life, and deceive the whole place and *himself* into thinking he's got all the virtues, when at heart he's a hypocrite! . . . *But the City!!!* A man goes to the gates of the City and knocks! New York or Chicago, Boston or San Francisco, no matter *what* city so long as it's big, and busy, and selfish, and self-centred. And she comes to her gates and takes him in, and she stands him in the middle of her market place—where Wall Street and Herald Square and Fifth Avenue and the Bowery, and Harlem, and Forty-second Street all meet, and there she strips him naked of all his disguises—and all his hypocrisies,—and she paints his ambition on her fences, and lights up her skyscrapers with it! what *he wants* to be and *what he thinks he is!*—and then she says to him, Make good if you can, or to Hell with you! And what is in him comes out to clothe his nakedness, and to the City he can't lie! I *know* because *I tried!*

The Hope of Democracy

FREDERIC C. HOWE

The city is not only the problem of our civilization, it is the hope of the future. In the city democracy is awakening, it is beginning to assert itself. Here life is free and eager and countless agencies coöperate to create a warmer sympathy, a broader sense of responsibility, and a more intelligent political sense. Already the city has attained a higher degree of political responsiveness than has the commonwealth which gave it being and which jealously resents its growing independence. In many instances it is better governed than is the state or the nation at large. It is freer from the more subtle forms of corruption. For the open bribe, the loan, or even the game of poker in which the ignorant councilman is permitted to win a handsome stake are not the only means employed. Self-interest, a class-conscious feeling, the fancied advantage of party may be as powerful a motive for evil as the more vulgar methods with which we are familiar. The sinister influences bent on maintaining the *status quo*, on the prevention of necessary legislation, the control of the party, the caucus, or the convention; methods which are in vogue in national and state affairs, may be even more dangerous to democracy than the acts which violate the criminal code and which are becoming intolerable to public opinion. Moreover, in national affairs, the public is less alert, much less able to act collectively or to concentrate attention upon a given issue. The same is true in state affairs, where the divergent interests of the country and the city render united action well-nigh impossible.

The city is also being aroused to social and economic issues as well as to political ones. It is constantly taking on new activities and assuming new burdens. Everything tends to encourage this, while many things render it imperative. By necessity we are forced to meet the burdens of a complex life. We cannot live in close association without common activities, without abandoning some of our liberties to regulation. Not only do health, comfort, and happiness demand this, self-protection necessitates it.

Some of the activities which the city has assumed, or will assume, have been suggested. Through them many of the losses which the city has created will be made good. By these means the city will become fuller of opportunity than the scattered rural life which it has displaced. A conscious housing policy will be adopted. The tenement will become habitable, comfortable, and safe. Cheap and rapid transit will lure the population from the crowded slum into smaller suburban centres. For the city of the future will cover a wide area.

The same motives that have opened up breathing spots in the form of parks, as well as public baths and gymnasiums, in the crowded quarters will,

Frederic C. Howe, *The City: The Hope of Democracy* (New York: Charles Scribner's Sons, 1905), pp. 280–287, 292–293, 298–299.

in time, lead to the establishment of city clubhouses, winter recreation centres, where such advantages as are now found in the social settlement will be offered. About these centres the life of the community will focus for study, play, recreation, and political activity. Here concerts, lectures, and human intercourse will be offered. A sense of the city as a home, as a common authority, a thing to be loved and cared for, will be developed. In the city club the saloon will find a rival. From such centres charity work will be carried on. Here neglected children will be cared for, here the boys and girls will find an opportunity of escape from the street, and the mother and father a common meeting ground which is now denied them. For city life not only destroys the home of the poor, it promotes divorce. The tenement drives its dwellers to the streets and to the saloon. Private philanthropy has done much to relieve this condition through the settlement, but the service it renders is as much a public one as are the parks, the hospitals, or the schools. For the settlement is the equivalent of the outdoor park. Even from a pecuniary point of view it is a good investment to the city. The settlement promotes order, it lessens crime, it reduces petty misdemeanors, and organizes the life and energy of the slum and turns it into good channels. The uniform testimony of police officials is to the effect that a settlement or a playground is as good as a half-dozen policemen.

When the city becomes its own factory inspector, the problem of school attendance will be simplified. Then the city will be able to coördinate its administration and enforce its own ordinances. With reduced cost of transportation, through the public ownership of the means of transit, with free books and possibly free luncheons to school children, compulsory education will become a possibility. For the problem of education is largely economic or industrial. Our cities are now in the illogical position of enforcing school attendance upon those who cannot afford even the insignificant cost of the same.

These reforms will be possible through home rule, through the city-republic. With the city free in these regards it will be able to raise the educational age, adopt manual-training and trades' schools, fit its instruction to local needs, and ultimately elevate the standard of life of all classes. With the city free, the administration of our correctional institutions may be fitted to the crime. Probation courts and city farm schools may then be established and provision made for those of tender years who, in many cities, are still imprisoned with criminals, branded with the mark of crime, a brand which they can never outlive, a memory which they can never forget, an influence that can never be eradicated. Then the city will be able to discriminate between the offences of ignorance and poverty and those of instinct. Today they are all classed together. The poor who have unwittingly violated some local ordinance, such as blocking a sidewalk, driving a garbage cart without a license, failing to remove rubbish, or the like, when arrested, if unable to find bail, are cast into jail to await trial or to serve their time. An examination of the police-court blotter of the average city leads one to wonder if the offences of society against its own do not equal those of the individual against his fellows. Justice, as administered in these courts, probably hurts quite as much as it helps, and society, by its thoughtlessness, creates as much crime as it prevents. The solicitude of the common law for the occasional innocent has not been extended to the thousands of real innocents, to the children, the unfortunate, the ignorant, whom indifference punishes and, in punishing, destroys. Thousands of men and women are sent to the jails, workhouses, and penitentiary every year who should have been sent to the hospital, to an inebriate asylum, to the country, or, much better, given work. Their offence is of a negative sort. It is not wilful. It is industrial or economic; they could not catch on.

By natural processes inability to maintain life in store, factory, or sweatshop produces the outcast woman, just as sickness, irregular employment, hard times yield their unvarying harvest of vagrants, with the sequence of the lodging house, the street, and ultimately a life of petty crime. Such a career is not often taken from choice, but by misfortune. And society often arrests, sentences, and punishes, when it should help and endeavor to reclaim by work, kindness, and assistance.

We have had our public schools for so long that we accept them as a commonplace. But we do not appreciate that the high schools are raising millions of citizens to an educated estate which was known to but a limited number a few years ago. The effect of this infusion of culture into our life is beginning to make itself felt. And in the years to come, when education has, in fact, become compulsory, and the school age has been raised to a higher standard, the effect will be tremendous. Along with the schools go the public libraries. Branches and distributing agencies are extending their influence into every part of the city. Through them opportunity is offered for a continuation of study, even after the door of the school has closed.

Provision for public concerts in summer as well as in winter has already found a place in many municipal budgets. With the development of the city club there will come public orchestras, art exhibitions, and the like that will brighten the life of the community. Something like this is already being done through the libraries which are being constructed with assembly halls and meeting rooms for this purpose. Here and there the idea is taking form of utilizing the public-school buildings as local clubs. The basement, gymnasiums, and assembly rooms are being opened in the evening and during the summer months. In time there will be a modification in their architecture, equipment, and facilities, so that they will be available for a multitude of purposes instead of the limited one of education. In New York City the school buildings are already being erected with roof-gardens, where music, recreation, and a common centre for the life of the locality are offered.

These are some of the things the new city will do. It will also care for the sick, as it now does in many cities, through district physicians or visiting nurses attached to the school departments. It will find work and maintain employment agencies. It will supervise factories, mills, and work-shops. The latter function is now inadequately performed by the state at large, and the inefficiency of its performance is largely attributable to the fact that the state is attempting to supervise a matter of local concern. The regulation of the conditions of employment is as much a city function as is the preservation of the health and well-being of the community. It is also a necessary part of school administration. . . .

It is along these lines that the advance of society is to be made. It is to come about through the city. For here life is more active, while the government is close to the people. It is already manifest on every hand. Through the divorce of the city from state control this progress will be stimulated. The city will become a centre of pride and patriotism. Here art and culture will flourish. The citizen will be attached to his community just as were the burghers of the mediaeval towns. Through direct legislation the city will be democratized. Public opinion will be free to act. Then the official will be holden to a real responsibility, while national politics will no longer dominate local affairs, for the test of the candidate for office will be his citizenship in the community which he serves. . . .

. . . The city will cease to be a necessary abyss of poverty. It is our institutions and our laws, not a divine ordinance or the inherent viciousness of humankind, that are at fault. Our evils are economic, not personal. Relief is possible through a change in our laws, in an increase in the positive agencies of the government, and the taxing for the common weal of those values which are now responsible for much of the common woe. It is not personal goodness that is demanded so much as public intelligence. For the worst of the evils under which America suffers are traceable to laws creating privileges. The evils can be largely corrected through their abolition. This is most easily obtainable in the city, for it is in the city that democracy is organizing and the power of privilege most rampant.

1.2: The Cities Deplored (1885, 1890)

Post–Civil War American cities were rife with problems. One was environmental pollution, an affliction we mistakenly think is very recent.

No American city of the Gilded Age suffered as much from air pollution as did Pittsburgh. A center of the booming steel and glass industries, it relied on dirty-burning soft coal to fuel its furnaces and suffered accordingly. In the first of the following selections, William Glazier, a prominent author and lecturer, describes the city's smoky appearance in the mid-1880's, with its steady rain of soot that made tidy Pittsburgh housewives' lives a trial. But what does Glazier have to say about the health effects of the pollution? How do you explain his puzzling conclusions? When do you think we gained a better understanding of the effects of fume- and smoke-filled air?

The second item, by the Danish-born journalist Jacob Riis, focuses on the housing problems of America's growing urban centers. The cities by and large were able to meet the housing needs of the middle class. Builders constructed numerous brick, stone, and wooden homes on shady streets for the cities' professional and business families. They also began to put up large apartment buildings with spacious "flats" for those prosperous urbanites who liked to live close to the center of town.

The housing needs of wage earners were less successfully met, however. Most working-class people were unable to pay more than modest rents, and many blue-collar families and individuals were forced to live with others for financial reasons. Some had to live in cellars and the cast-off, minimally reworked former homes of the middle class who left for better neighborhoods. There was a supply of new apartments for the working class, but these were usually shoddily constructed tenements thrown up by speculative builders that often lacked heat and full interior plumbing. They quickly deteriorated into slums.

The selection below is from Riis's account of the tenements of lower Manhattan in New York City during the late 1880s. What do you deduce from his description of the causes of poverty and ill health in the slums? Did the slums cause the social and physical problems of the poor? Or did poverty cause their dreadful housing conditions? Why were the cities unable to solve the housing problem? Were all cities as deficient in housing as New York?

Pittsburgh

WILLIAM GLAZIER

By all means make your first approach to Pittsburgh in the night time, and you will behold a spectacle which has not a parallel on this continent. Darkness gives the city and its surroundings a picturesqueness which they wholly lack by daylight. It lies low down in a hollow of encompassing hills, gleaming with a thousand points of light, which are reflected from the rivers, whose waters glimmer, it may be, in the faint moonlight, and catch and reflect the shadows as well. Around the city's edge, and on the sides of the hills which encircle it like a gloomy amphitheatre, their outlines rising dark against the sky, through numberless apertures, fiery lights stream forth, looking angrily and fiercely up toward the heavens, while over all these settles a heavy pall of smoke. It is as though one had reached the outer edge of the infernal regions, and saw before him the great furnace of Pandemonium with all the lids lifted. The scene is so strange and weird that it will live in the memory forever. One pictures, as he beholds it, the tortured spirits writhing

William Glazier, *Peculiarities of American Cities* (Philadelphia, Hubbard Brothers, 1884), pp. 332–334.

in agony, their sinewy limbs convulsed, and the very air oppressive with pain and rage.

But the scene is illusive. This is the domain of Vulcan, not of Pluto. Here, in this gigantic workshop, in the midst of the materials of his labor, the god of fire, having left his ancient home on Olympus, and established himself in this newer world, stretches himself beside his forge, and sleeps the peaceful sleep which is the reward of honest industry. Right at his doorway are mountains of coal to keep a perpetual fire upon his altar; within the reach of his outstretched grasp are rivers of coal oil; and a little further away great stores of iron for him to forge and weld, and shape into a thousand forms; and at his feet is the shining river, an impetuous Mercury, ever ready to do his bidding. Grecian mythology never conceived of an abode so fitting for the son of Zeus as that which he has selected for himself on this western hemisphere. And his ancient tasks were child's play compared with the mighty ones he has undertaken to-day.

Failing a night approach, the traveler should reach the Iron City on a dismal day in autumn, when the air is heavy with moisture, and the very atmosphere looks dark. All romance has disappeared. In this nineteenth century the gods of mythology find no place in daylight. There is only a very busy city shrouded in gloom. The buildings, whatever their original material and color, are smoked to a uniform, dirty drab; their smoke sinks, and mingling with the moisture in the air, becomes a consistency which may almost be felt as well as seen. Under a drab sky a drab twilight hangs over the town, and the gas-lights, which are left burning at mid-day, shine out of the murkiness with a dull, reddish glare. Then is Pittsburgh herself. Such days as these are her especial boast, and in their frequency and dismalness, in all the world she has no rival, save London.

In truth, Pittsburgh is a smoky, dismal city, at her best. At her worst, nothing darker, dingier or more dispiriting can be imagined. The city is in the heart of the soft coal region; and the smoke from her dwellings, stores, factories, foundries and steamboats, uniting, settles in a cloud over the narrow valley in which she is built, until the very sun looks coppery through the sooty haze. According to a circular of the Pittsburgh Board of Trade, about twenty per cent, or one-fifth, of all the coal used in the factories and dwellings of the city escapes into the air in the form of smoke, being the finer and lighter particles of carbon of the coal in the air at one and the same time may be imagined. But her inhabitants do not seem to mind it; and the doctors hold that this smoke from the carbon, sulphur and iodine contained it in, is highly favorable to lung and cutaneous diseases, and is the sure death of malaria and its attendant fevers. And certainly, whatever the cause may be, Pittsburgh is one of the healthiest cities in the United States. Her inhabitants are all too busy to reflect upon the inconvenience or uncomeliness of this smoke. Work is the object of life with them. It occupies them from morning until night, from the cradle to the grave, only on Sundays, when, for the most part, the furnaces are idle, and the forges are silent. For Pittsburgh, settled by Irish-Scotch Presbyterians, is a great Sunday-keeping day. Save on this day her business men do not stop for rest or recreation, nor do they "retire" from business. They die with the harness on, and die, perhaps, all the sooner for having worn it so continuously and so long.

Pittsburgh is not a beautiful city. That stands to reason, with the heavy pall of smoke which constantly overhangs her. But she lacks beauty in other respects. She is substantially and compactly built, and contains some handsome edifices; but she lacks the architectural magnificence of some of her sister cities; while her suburbs present all that is unsightly and forbidding in appearance, the original beauties of nature having been ruthlessly sacrificed to utility.

Pittsburgh is situated in western Pennsylvania, in a narrow valley at the confluence of the Allegheny and Monongahela rivers, and at the head of the Ohio, and is surrounded by hills rising to the height of four or five hundred feet. These hills once possessed rounded outlines, with sufficient exceptional abruptness to lend them variety and picturesqueness. But they have been leveled down, cut into, sliced off, and ruthlessly marred and mutilated, until not a trace of their original outlines remain. Great black coal cars crawl up and down their sides, and plunge into unexpected and mysterious openings, their sudden disappearance lending, even in daylight, an air of mystery and diablerie to the region. Railroad tracks gridiron the ground everywhere, debris of all sorts lies in heaps, and is scattered over the earth, and huts and hovels are perched here and there, in every available spot. There is no verdure—nothing but mud and coal, the one yellow the other black. And on the edge of the city are the unpicturesque outlines of factories and foundries, their tall chimneys belching forth columns of inky blackness, which roll and whirl in fantastic shapes, and finally lose themselves in the general murkiness above.

The tranquil Monongahela comes up from the south, alive with barges and tug boats; while the swifter current of the Allegheny bears from the oil regions, at the north, slight-built barges with their freights of crude petroleum. Oil is not infrequently poured upon the troubled waters, when one of these barges sinks, and its freight, liberated from the open tanks, refuses to sink with it, and spreads itself out on the surface of the stream.

The oil fever was sorely felt in Pittsburgh, and it was a form of malaria against which the smoke-laden atmosphere was no protection. During the early years of the great oil speculation the city was in a perpetual state of excitement. Men talked oil upon the streets, in the cars and counting-houses, and no doubt thought of oil in church. Wells and barrels of petroleum, and shares of oil stock were the things most often mentioned. And though that was nearly twenty years ago, and the oil speculation has settled into a safe and legitimate pursuit, Pittsburgh is still the greatest oil mart in the world. By the means of Oil Creek and the Allegheny, the oil which is to supply all markets is first shipped to Pittsburgh, passes through the refineries there, and is then exported.

The Ohio River makes its beginning here, and in all but the season of low water and the wharves of the city are lined with boats, barges and tugs, destined for every mentionable point on the Ohio and Mississippi rivers. The Ohio River is here, as all along its course, an uncertain and capricious stream. Sometimes, in spring, or early summer, it creeps up its banks and looks menacingly at the city. At other times it seems to become weary of bearing the boats, heavily laden with merchandise, to their destined ports, and so takes a nap, as it were. The last time we beheld this water-course its bed was lying nearly bare and dry, while a small, sluggish creek, a few feet, or at most, a few yards wide, crept along the bottom, small barges being towed down steam by horses, which waded in the water. The giant was resting.

The Bend[1]

JACOB RIIS

Where Mulberry Street crooks like an elbow within hail of the old depravity of the Five Points, is "the Bend," foul core of New York's slums. . . . Never was change more urgently needed. Around "the Bend" cluster the bulk of the tenements that are stamped as altogether bad, even by the optimists of the Health Department. Incessant raids cannot keep down the crowds that make them their home. In the scores of back alleys, of stable lanes and hidden byways, of which the rent collector alone can keep track, they share such shelter as the ramshackle structures afford with every kind of abomination rifled from the dumps and ash-barrels of the city. . . .

In the street, where the city wields the broom, there is at least an effort at cleaning up. There has to be, or it would be swamped in filth overrunning from the courts and alleys where the ragpickers live. It requires more than ordinary courage to explore these on a hot day. The undertaker has to do it then, the police always. Right here, in this tenement on the east side of the street, they found little Antonia Candia, victim of fiendish cruelty, "covered," says the account found in the records of the Society for the Prevention of Cruelty to Children, "with sores, and her hair matted with dried blood." Abuse is the normal condition of "the Bend," murder its everyday crop, with the tenants not always the criminals. In this block between Bayard, Park, Mulberry, and Baxter Streets, "the Bend" proper, the late Tenement House Commission counted 155 deaths of children in a specimen year (1882). Their percentage of the total mortality in the block was 68.28, while for the whole city the proportion was only 46.20. The infant mortality in any city or place as compared with the whole number of deaths is justly considered a good barometer of its general sanitary condition. Here, in this tenement, No. 59½, next to Bandit's Roost, fourteen persons died that year, and eleven

Jacob Riis, *How the Other Half Lives: Studies among the Tenements of New York* (New York: Charles Scribner's Sons, 1903), pp. 55, 61, 65.

[1] Footnotes deleted.

of them were children; in No. 61 eleven, and eight of them not yet five years old. According to the records in the Bureau of Vital Statistics only thirty-nine people lived in No. 59½ in the year 1888, nine of them little children. There were five baby funerals in that house the same year. Out of the alley itself, No. 59, nine dead were carried in 1888, five in baby coffins. . . . The general death-rate for the whole city that year was 26.27.

These figures speak for themselves, when it is shown that in the model tenement across the way at Nos. 48 and 50, where the same class of people live in greater swarms (161, according to the record), but under good management, and in decent quarters, the hearse called that year only twice, once for a baby. The agent of the Christian people who built that tenement will tell you that Italians are good tenants, while the owner of the alley will oppose every order to put his property in repair with the claim that they are the worst of a bad lot. Both are right, from their different stand-points. It is the stand-point that makes the difference—and the tenant.

What if I were to tell you that this alley, and more tenement property in "the Bend," all of it notorious for years as the vilest and worst to be found anywhere, stood associated on the taxbooks all through the long struggle to make its owners responsible, which has at last resulted in a qualified victory for the law, with the name of an honored family, one of the "oldest and best," rich in possessions and in influence, and high in the councils of the city's government? It would be but the plain truth. Nor would it be the only instance by very many that stand recorded on the Health Department's books of a kind that has come near to making the name of landlord as odious in New York as it has become in Ireland.

.   .   .   .

Well do I recollect the visit of a health inspector to one of these tenements on a July day when the thermometer outside was climbing high in the nineties; but inside, in that awful room, with half a dozen persons washing, cooking, and sorting rags, lay the dying baby alongside the stove, where the doctor's thermometer ran up to 115°! Perishing for the want of a breath of fresh air in this city of untold charities! Did not the manager of the Fresh Air Fund write to the pastor of an Italian Church only last year that "no one asked for Italian children," and hence he could not send any to the country?

.   .   .   .

. . . In the stifling July nights, when the big barracks are like fiery furnaces, their very walls giving out absorbed heat, men and women lie in restless, sweltering rows, panting for air and sleep. Then every truck in the street, every crowded fire-escape, becomes a bedroom, infinitely preferable to any the house affords. A cooling shower on such a night is hailed as a heaven-sent blessing in a hundred thousand homes.

Life in the tenements in July and August spells death to an army of little ones whom the doctor's skill is powerless to save. When the white badge of mourning flutters from every second door, sleepless mothers walk the streets in the gray of the early dawn, trying to stir a cooling breeze to fan the brow of the sick baby. There is no sadder sight than this patient devotion striving against fearfully hopeless odds. Fifty "summer doctors," especially trained to this work, are then sent into the tenements by the Board of Health, with free advice and medicine for the poor. Devoted women follow in their track with care and nursing for the sick. Fresh-air excursions run daily out of New York on land and water; but despite all efforts the grave-diggers in Calvary work over-time, and little coffins are stacked mountain-high on the deck of the Charity Commissioners' boat when it makes its semi-weekly trips to the city cemetery.

Under the most favorable circumstances, an epidemic, which the well-to-do can afford to make light of as a thing to be got over or avoided by reasonable care, is excessively fatal among the children of the poor, by reason of the practical impossibility of isolating the patient in a tenement. The measles, ordinarily a harmless disease, furnishes a familiar example. Tread it ever so lightly on the avenues, in the tenements it kills right and left. . . . The records showed that respiratory diseases, the common heritage of the grippe and the measles, had caused death in most cases, discovering the trouble to be, next to the inability to check the contagion in those crowds, in the poverty of the parents and the wretched home conditions that made proper care of the sick impossible. . . .

That ignorance plays its part, as well as poverty and bad hygienic surroundings, in the sacrifice of life is of course inevitable. They go usually hand in hand.

1.3:   City Government (1905, 1902)

Historians have been of two minds about city government in the late nineteenth and early twentieth centuries. On the one hand, it was corrupt and inefficient, providing poor services at high cost. On the other hand, in the absence of formal welfare agencies, these corrupt governments, ruled by political machines, were more generous, more compassionate, and more effective than the reform administrations that periodically, and temporarily, replaced them.

The first selection below is an account of how a precinct captain ("ward heeler"), early in this century, helped build and retain voter loyalty for Tammany Hall, the venal machine of the Democratic Party in New York City. Some of it comes from the diary of George Washington Plunkitt, a Tammany leader, but most is comment by the journalist William L. Riordan, who interviewed Plunkitt extensively.

How would you characterize the way Plunkitt goes about his job? Judging from this description, could the Tammany machine, with a little stretching, be characterized as a social welfare organization? Were there other agencies at this time that performed these same functions? Does Plunkitt's account suggest anything significant about the relations of immigrants to the city machines? Did city dwellers pay an excessively high price for the machine's help?

The second selection is from Lincoln Steffens's famous muckraking exposé series on city corruption first published in McClure's Magazine *early in this century and later collected as* The Shame of the Cities. *Steffens, who is writing of St. Louis, takes a dimmer view of the city machines than does Plunkitt. In the first selection a connection is implied between immigrants and corrupt machines. What is Steffens's alternative explanation for urban corruption? Which explanation of why the city machines flourished is the more valid?*

Strenuous Life of the Tammany District Leader[1]

WILLIAM L. RIORDAN

The life of the Tammany district leader is strenuous. To his work is due the wonderful recuperative power of the organization.

One year it goes down to defeat and the prediction is made that it will never again raise its head. The district leader undaunted by defeat, collects his scattered forces, organizes them as only Tammany knows how to organize, and in a little while the organization is as strong as ever.

No other politician in New York or elsewhere is exactly like the Tammany district leader or works as he does. As a rule, he has no business or occupation other than politics. He plays politics every day and night in the year, and his headquarters bears the inscription, "Never closed."

Everybody in the district knows him. Everybody knows where to find him, and nearly everybody goes to him for assistance of one sort or another, especially the poor of the tenements.

He is always obliging. He will go to the police courts to put in a good word for the "drunks and disorderlies" or pay their fines, if a good word is not effective. He will attend christenings, weddings, and funerals. He will feed the hungry and help bury the dead.

A philanthropist? Not at all. He is playing politics all the time.

Brought up in Tammany Hall, he has learned how to reach the heart of the great mass of voters. He does not bother about reaching their heads. It is

William L. Riordan, *Plunkitt of Tammany Hall: Plain Talks and Practical Politics* (New York: McClure Phillips and Company, 1905), pp. 167–183, *passim.*
[1] This chapter is based on extracts from [George Washington] Plunkitt's Diary and on my daily observation of the work of the district leader.—*W.L.R.*

his belief that arguments and campaign literature have never gained votes.

He seeks direct contact with the people, does them good turns when he can, and relies on their not forgetting him on election day. His heart is always in his work, too, for his subsistence depends on its results.

If he holds his district and Tammany is in power, he is amply rewarded by a good office and the opportunities that go with it. What these opportunities are has been shown by the quick rise to wealth of so many Tammany district leaders. With the examples before him of Richard Croker, once leader of the Twentieth District; John F. Carroll, formerly leader of the Twenty-ninth; Timothy ("Dry Dollar") Sullivan, late leader of the Sixth, and many others, he can always look forward to riches and ease while he is going through the drudgery of his daily routine.

This is a record of a day's work by Plunkitt:

2 A.M.: Aroused from sleep by the ringing of his door bell; went to the door and found a bartender, who asked him to go to the police station and bail out a saloon-keeper who had been arrested for violating the excise law. Furnished bail and returned to bed at three o'clock.

6 A.M.: Awakened by fire engines passing his house. Hastened to the scene of the fire, according to the custom of the Tammany district leaders, to give assistance to the fire sufferers, if needed. Met several of his election district captains who are always under orders to look out for fires, which are considered great vote-getters. Found several tenants who had been burned out, took them to a hotel, supplied them with clothes, fed them, and arranged temporary quarters for them until they could rent and furnish new apartments.

8:30 A.M.: Went to the police court to look after his constituents. Found six "drunks." Secured the discharge of four by a timely word with the judge, and paid the fines of two.

9 A.M.: Appeared in the Municipal District Court. Directed one of his district captains to act as counsel for a widow against whom dispossess proceedings had been instituted and obtained an extension of time. Paid the rent of a poor family about to be dispossessed and gave them a dollar for food.

11 A.M.: At home again. Found four men waiting for him. One had been discharged by the Metropolitan Railway Company for neglect of duty, and wanted the district leader to fix things. Another wanted a job on the road. The third sought a place on the Subway and the fourth, a plumber, was looking for work with the Consolidated Gas Company. The district leader spent nearly three hours fixing things for the four men, and succeeded in each case.

3 P.M.: Attended the funeral of an Italian as far as the ferry. Hurried back to make his appearance at the funeral of a Hebrew constituent. Went conspicuously to the front booth in the Catholic church and the synagogue, and later attended the Hebrew confirmation ceremonies in the synagogue.

7 P.M.: Went to district headquarters and presided over a meeting of election district captains. Each captain submitted a list of all the voters in his dis-

trict, reported on their attitude toward Tammany, suggested who might be won over and how they could be won, told who were in need, and who were in trouble of any kind and the best way to reach them. District leader took notes and gave orders.

8 P.M.: Went to a church fair. Took chances on everything, bought ice-cream for the young girls and the children. Kissed the little ones, flattered their mothers and took their fathers out for something down at the corner.

9 P.M.: At the club-house again. Spent $10 on tickets for a church excursion and promised a subscription for a new church-bell. Bought tickets for a base-ball game to be played by two nines from his district. Listened to the complaints of a dozen push-cart peddlers who said they were persecuted by the police and assured them he would go to Police Headquarters in the morning and see about it.

10:30 P.M.: Attended a Hebrew wedding reception and dance. Had previously sent a handsome wedding present to the bride.

12 P.M.: In bed.

That is the actual record of one day in the life of Plunkitt. He does some of the same things every day, but his life is not so monotonous as to be wearisome.

Sometimes the work of a district leader is exciting, especially if he happens to have a rival who intends to make a contest for the leadership at the primaries. In that case, he is even more alert, tries to reach the fires before his rival, sends our runners to look for "drunks and disorderlies" at the police stations, and keeps a very close watch on the obituary columns of the newspapers.

A few years ago there was a bitter contest for the Tammany leadership of the Ninth District between John C. Sheehan and Frank J. Goodwin. Both has had long experience in Tammany politics and both understood every move of the game.

Every morning their agents went to their respective headquarters before seven o'clock and read through the death notices in all the morning papers. If they found that anybody in the district had died, they rushed to the homes of their principals with information and then there was a race to the house of the deceased to offer condolences, and, if the family were poor, something more substantial.

One the day of the funeral there was another contest. Each faction tried to surpass the other in the number and appearance of the carriages it sent to the funeral, and more than once they almost came to blows at the church or in the cemetery.

On one occasion the Goodwinites played a trick on their adversaries which has since been imitated in other districts. A well-known liquor dealer who had a considerable following died, and both Sheehan and Goodwin were eager to become his political heir by making a big showing at the funeral.

Goodwin managed to catch the enemy napping. He went to all the livery stables in the district, hired all the carriages for the day, and gave orders to two hundred of his men to be on hand as mourners.

Sheehan had never had any trouble about getting all the carriages that he wanted, so he let the matter go until the night before the funeral. Then he found that he could not hire a carriage in the district.

He called his district committee together in a hurry and explained the situation to them. He could get all the vehicles he needed in the adjoining district, he said, but if he did that, Goodwin would rouse the voters of the Ninth by declaring that he (Sheehan), had patronized foreign industries.

Finally, it was decided that there was nothing to do but go over to Sixth and Broadway for carriages. Sheehan made a fine turnout at the funeral, but the deceased was hardly in his grave before Goodwin raised the cry of "Protection to home industries," and denounced his rival for patronizing livery-stable keepers outside of his district. The cry had its effect in the primary campaign. At all events, Goodwin was elected leader.

A recent contest for the leadership of the Second District illustrated further the strenuous work of the Tammany district leaders. The contestants were Patrick Divver, who had managed the district for years, and Thomas F. Foley.

Both were particularly anxious to secure the large Italian vote. They not only attended all the Italian christenings and funerals, but also kept a close lookout for the marriages in order to be on hand with wedding presents.

At first, each had his own reporter in the Italian quarter to keep track of the marriages. Later, Foley conceived a better plan. He hired a man to stay all day at the City Hall marriage bureau, where most Italian couples go through the civil ceremony, and telephone to him at his saloon when anything was doing at the bureau.

Foley had a number of presents ready for use and, whenever he received a telephone message from his man, he hastened to the City Hall with a ring or a watch or a piece of silver and handed it to the bride with his congratulations. As a consequence, when Divver got the news and went to the home of the couple with the present, he always found that Foley had been ahead of him. Toward the end of that campaign, Divver also stationed a man at the marriage bureau and then there were daily foot races and fights between the two leaders.

Sometimes the rivals come into conflict at the death-bed. One night a poor Italian peddler died in Roosevelt Street. The news reached Divver and Foley about the same time, and as they knew the family of the man was destitute, each went to an undertaker and brought him to the Roosevelt tenement.

The rivals and the undertakers met at the house and an altercation ensued. After much discussion the Divver undertaker was selected. Foley had more carriages at the funeral, however, and he further impressed the Italian voters by paying the widow's rent for a month, and sending her half a ton of coal and a barrel of flour.

The rivals were put on their mettle toward the end of the campaign by the wedding of a daughter of one of the original Cohens of the Baxter Street region. The Hebrew vote in the district is nearly as large as the Italian vote, and Divver and Foley set out to capture the Cohens and their friends.

They stayed up nights thinking what they would give the bride. Neither knew how much the other was prepared to spend on a wedding present, or what form it would take; so spies were employed by both sides to keep watch on the jewelry stores, and the jewelers of the district were bribed by each side to impart the desired information.

At last Foley heard that Divver had purchased a set of silver knives, forks, and spoons. He at once bought a duplicate set and added a silver tea service. When the presents were displayed at the home of the bride Divver was not in a pleasant mood and he charged his jeweler with treachery. It may be added that Foley won at the primaries.

One of the fixed duties of a Tammany district leader is to give two outings every summer, one for the men of his district and the other for the women and children, and a beefsteak dinner and a ball every winter. The scene of the outings is, usually, one of the groves along the [Long Island] Sound.

The ambition of the district leader on these occasions is to demonstrate that his men have broken all records in the matter of eating and drinking. He gives out the exact number of pounds of beef, poultry, butter, etc., that they have consumed and professes to know how many potatoes and ears of corn have been served.

According to his figures, the average eating record of each man at the outing is about ten pounds of beef, two or three chickens, a pound of butter, a half peck of potatoes, and two dozen ears of corn. The drinking records, as given out, are still more phenomenal. For some reason, not yet explained, the district leader thinks that his popularity will be greatly increased if he can show that his followers can eat and drink more than the followers of any district leader.

The same idea governs the beefsteak dinners in the winter. It matters not what sort of steak is served or how it is cooked; the district leader considers only the question of quantity, and when he excels all others in this particular, he feels, somehow, that he is a bigger man, and deserves more patronage than his associates in the Tammany Executive Committee.

As to the balls, they are the events of the winter in the extreme East Side and West Side society. Mamie and Maggie and Jennie prepare for them months in advance, and their young men save up for the occasion just as they save for the summer trips to Coney Island.

The district leader is in his glory at the opening of the ball. He leads the cotillion with the prettiest woman present—his wife, if he has one, permitting—and spends almost the whole night shaking hands with his constituents. The ball costs him a pretty penny, but he has found that the investment pays.

By these means the Tammany district leader reaches out into the homes of his district, keeps watch not only on the men, but also on the women and children; knows their needs, their likes and dislikes, their troubles and their hopes, and places himself in a position to use his knowledge for the benefit of his organization and himself. Is it any wonder that scandals do not permanently disable Tammany and that it speedily recovers from what seems to be crushing defeat?

Corruption in St. Louis[1]

LINCOLN STEFFENS

The corruption of St. Louis came from the top. The best citizens—the merchants and big financiers—used to rule the town, and they ruled it well. . . . But a change occurred. Public spirit became private spirit, public enterprise became private greed.

Along about 1890, public franchises and privileges were sought not only for legitimate profit and common convenience, but for loot. Taking but slight and always selfish interest in the public councils, the big men misused politics. The riff-raff, catching the smell of corruption, rushed into the Municipal Assembly, drove out the remaining respectable men, and sold the city—its streets, it wharves, its markets, and all that it had—to the now greedy business men and bribers. In other words, when the leading men began to devour their own city, the herd rushed into the trough and fed also. . . .

[A grand jury said:] "Our investigation, covering more or less fully a period of ten years, shows that, with few exceptions, no ordinance has been passed wherein valuable privileges or franchises are granted until those interested have paid the legislators the money demanded for action in the particular case. Combines in both branches of the Municipal Assembly are formed by members sufficient in number to control legislation. . . . So long has this practice existed, that such members have come to regard the receipt of money for action on pending measures as a legitimate perquisite of a legislator."

One legislator consulted a lawyer with the intention of suing a firm to recover an unpaid balance on a fee for the grant of a switch way. . . . In order to insure a regular and indisputable revenue, the combine of each house drew up a schedule of bribery prices for all possible sorts of grants, just such a list as a commercial traveler takes out on the road with him. There was a price for a grain elevator, a price for a short switch; side tracks were charged by the linear foot . . . ; street improvement cost so much. . . .

Claude Wetmore and Lincoln Steffens, "Tweed Days in St. Louis," *McClure's Magazine,* October 1902, pp. 577–579.
[1] Footnotes deleted.

As there was a scale for favorable legislation, so there was one for defeating bills. It made a difference in the price if there was opposition, and it made a difference whether the privilege asked was legitimate or not. But nothing was passed free of charge. Many of the legislators were saloon keepers—it was in St. Louis that a practical joker nearly emptied the House of Delegates by getting a boy to rush into a session and call out, "Mister, your saloon is on fire,"—but even the saloon keepers of a neighborhood had to pay to keep in their inconvenient locality a market which public interest would have moved. . . .

The blackest years were 1898, 1899, and 1900. . . . Franchises worth millions were granted without one cent of cash to the city, and with provision for only the smallest future payment; several companies which refused to pay blackmail had to leave; citizens were robbed more and more boldly, pay-rolls were padded with the names of non-existent persons; work on public improvements was neglected, while money for them went to the boodlers.

2

Populism

Agriculture made an important contribution to the economic surge of the post–Civil War years. From the nation's farms, plantations, and ranches poured an ever-widening flood of wheat, corn, cotton, fruit, vegetables, beef, pork, and dairy products. Many Americans—and people around the world—benefited from this torrent of food and fiber. Yet the farmers were not happy. As production rose, farm prices fell, farm debt soared, and land values stagnated. Many farmers and farm leaders denounced the economic and political arrangements they believed had contributed to their plight.

During the 1870s farm discontent expressed itself through the Granger Movement that blamed agriculture's troubles on "monopolies," especially those in transportation and farm machinery manufacture, and advocated marketing by farmers themselves rather than through various middlemen. The Grangers organized independent farmers' parties in the midwest and helped enact state laws regulating railroads and other business groups that distributed farm products.

By the late 1880s, with farm prices still declining, the Grangers gave way to the Alliances, farmers' organizations, mainly in the South and the Plains, which sought to check deflation and provide relief to farm debtors through manipulation of the money supply. In early 1892 a number of insurgent groups, including the Alliances, the Knights of Labor, and various independent reformers, joined to form the People's Party, usually called the Populists.

The new party embraced the Alliance programs but with special emphasis on "free silver"—that is, the U.S. Treasury's coinage into dollars of all silver bullion brought to it, with sixteen ounces of silver to equal one ounce of gold. Free silver, said the reformers, would pump up the money supply and so increase prices, make credit cheaper, and relieve debtors of their crippling burdens.

In 1892 the People's Party challenged the two major parties at the polls, running candidates for state offices and for Congress and president. The Populist national ticket of James B. Weaver and James G. Field garnered over a million popular votes, about 9 per cent of the total, and won the electoral vote of several western states.

The year 1892 was the high-water mark of the People's Party; thereafter its support declined, but not its influence. The Populists gave voice to a widespread mood of the day that economic inequality and the dominance of wealth had progressed too far and should be reversed. Following the Panic of 1893, Populist ideas invaded the Democratic Party, especially in the West and South, where it expressed in part festering sectional resentment against the power centers of the East.

In the selections below you will encounter the views of Populists and Populist-influenced Democrats as well as their opponents. Consider, as previously, the spirit as well as the logic behind the arguments advanced.

2.1:   The Financial Conspiracy (1892)

Many, though not all, Populist leaders targeted the "money question" as the ultimate source of the nation's ills. One classic statement of this position was the widely circulated pamphlet Seven Financial Conspiracies Which Have Enslaved the American People, *by the Kansas People's Party leader Sarah Emery.*

Consider the tone of Emery's indictment. Is it moderate and balanced? Populist arguments such as hers have been called paranoid by their critics. Does Emery's description seem unduly suspicious and overwrought to you? Some scholars have also seen signs of anti-Semitism in Populist manifestos that emphasize money issues, such as Seven Financial Conspiracies. *Does Emery's essay suggest this in any way? Do you know if the other side in the "money battle," the "Gold Bugs," also exaggerated the significance of the monetary system and demonized their opponents?*

Financial Conspiracies

SARAH EMERY

The system of American government as instituted by our fathers afforded little if any opportunity for robbery and oppression . . . . Thirty years ago the American laborer was a prospective lord. He saw within his reach a home of

Sarah Emery, *Seven Financial Conspiracies Which Have Enslaved the American People* (Lansing, MI: D. A. Reynolds, 1892), pp. 10–70 *passim.*

plenty for his family, and an old age of comfort for himself. The bright picture before him inspired industry, economy, and sobriety, and the laborer was a peaceful, sober, respected citizen . . . . But today what is the outlook for the wage-worker of this country? He sees before him only toil, unremitting, half-requited toil; hope dies out in his bosom, despondency takes possession of his heart; and unless sustained by a strong faith and a giant will he breaks beneath the weight of oppression, seeks relief in a suicide's grave, or worse still, attempts to drown his grief in the intoxicating cup and finally drifts into the great army of inebriates.

We are now led to the question, wherefore this amazing change in the condition of the working classes of this country? There is a solution to this problem. As I have stated before the American system of government afforded little or no opportunity for robbery and oppression, but the vast plains and teeming valleys of this grand republic . . . was [sic] a coveted prize long sought by civilized brigandage. To obtain possession of this vast wealth and reduce an intelligent people to the position of slaves, was by no means an easy task. But the promptings of avarice were not to be silenced, and greed was ever on the alert to seize the coveted prize. The fatal opportunity at last presented itself . . . . [Emery describes the coming of the Civil War and how Wall Street welcomed the war.] Now do you ask why this exaltation over a prospective civil war? Do you ask why the money-kings of Wall Street . . . were so anxious, and positively joyous, when the guns were turned upon Fort Sumpter [sic] . . . . Do you suppose the story of Uncle Tom and Little Eva had touched their hearts and they had sworn vengeance on the perpetrators of such cruelty? No, no; the money-kings of Wall Street . . . were not the men whose hearts were touched with pity by the cries of their distress. Their love of gain had stifled the finer instincts of their nature, and they rejoiced because they saw in the preparation for war their long-coveted opportunity for plunder. The calamity of war must bring its necessities, and through these necessities they determined to subjugate their unsuspecting brother men. To accomplish this it became necessary to obtain possession of the national finances. As blood, the circulating medium of the body, is the life of the body, so they knew that money, the circulating medium of the country, was the life of the country. Its industry, its education, its morality, in truth, its very life depended on the medium of exchange. Controlling it, they could send the warm life current through the channels of trade, dispensing peace, happiness, and prosperity, or they could check its flow, and completely paralyze the industries of the country. They knew their opportunity was at hand, and the tidings of war that blanched the cheek and sent terror to the hearts of the multitude was [sic] to their ears sweeter than the music of the spheres . . . .

The necessities of war required vast sums of money; but the treasury was empty, the gold and silver of the country had fled. What was to be done? . . . [W]e learn that the money-kings of Wall Street graciously tendered loans to the government in her distress at from 24 to 36 per cent interest—these same money-kings whom today we hear quoted as those *generous, patriotic, capitalists* . . . .

But the great leader, Lincoln, was not to be baffled; he loved the people better than Shylock, and justice better than oppression. . . . [1]

The issuance of this money at once brought relief to the country. . . . Light began to break through the darkness that spread over the country, the destitution of the soldier's family gave way to moderate comfort. . . . With an abundance of money, not even the blight of war could check the prosperity of the country . . . . Commerce, industry, and education received a new impetus, and flourished as never before in the history of the country.

But Shylock was sullen and disconsolate. Having failed in his scheme to rob the people through exorbitant rates of interest, he immediately entered upon another scheme of brigandage which even the adroit Lincoln seemed unable to fathom. Having hoarded the gold and silver of the country, it was through this channel . . . he must despoil the country. . . . We find that only four days after passage of the legal tender act to supply the country with government money, a bankers' convention was held in Washington. . . . Shylock was alarmed; he saw in the legal tender act a friend to the people, that it would transfer the monopoly of money from his hands to the control of the people; he saw it as a precedent which, if established, would forever after enable the government to relieve itself and the people without submitting to his usurious extortions. . . . This, then, was plainly the object of that notable bankers' convention, *to create a demand for Shylock's hoarded gold.* . . .

The next scheme for robbing the people was the national bank act passed in 1863. Of all the villainous schemes of robbery ever practiced upon our people the national banking system stands preeminent. By it Shylock was permitted to invest his greenbacks in government bonds at face value; upon these bonds he not only drew gold interest in advance but by means of the banks scheme he actually had 90 per cent of their value returned to him. . . . None but the wealthy classes are able to enter upon this profitable banking business. If it is proper for the government to make the business of the wealthy thus lucrative, is it not equally just to give like advantages to the poorer classes?

A wise government will look to the interests of its wealth producers who constitute the great toiling masses, and a just government would make the way to prosperity as easy for its humblest as for its most wealthy citizen. If this system is good for banking it ought to be good for every other legitimate enterprise, and every other law-abiding citizen is entitled to like consideration. . . .

The third scheme of robbery was that of *contracting the currency* by destroying the greenbacks. In pursuance of this plan the act of April 12, 1866, was passed, whereby it was provided that a regular and systematic cremation of greenbacks should take place. . . .

---

[1] He authorized the issuance of millions of dollars of paper money, the so-called greenbacks—ED.

The fourth act in Shylock's tragedy, by which the government and this great people were sacrificed, is familiarly known as the *credit-strengthening act,* by which the 5–20 bonds were made payable in coin.[2] This act . . . added to the burdens of the people more than six hundred millions of dollars. . . . Those who opposed the measures were denounced as repudiators, and in his inaugural address [President Ulysses] Grant warned his party that no repudiator of one farthing of the public debt would be trusted in public place . . . . The Republican party [had] nominated U. S. Grant at the urgent solicitation and petition of forty capitalists in New York City.

August Belmont was chairman of the Democratic national committee [in 1868]; he was also agent of the Rothschilds, who were in possession of several hundred millions of the 5–20 bonds, and particularly interested in the credit-strengthening act. As early as March 13, 1868, Baron James Rothschild instructed August Belmont that unless the Democratic party went in for paying the 5–20 bonds in gold it *must be defeated* . . . . This action had the effect for which undoubtedly it was intended, that of demoralizing the Democratic party on the eve of the election, thus ensuring the election of Grant, who had pledged himself to the money power . . . .

The next and fifth step in the infernal scheme was that of refunding the national debt. Few people ever comprehended the enormity of that crime, and never was there a deeper laid plot to reduce the people to abject and hopeless servitude . . . .

The object of funding our debt was to establish a bond system on the same plan of England's bonded debt. England's debt, which commenced with the same infamous banking system which we have adopted, was established two centuries ago. The interest on her debts supports a few idle aristocrats, but it has reduced to ignorance and degradation millions of her toiling people. Another object of funding our debt was to build up a moneyed oligarchy, and an aristocracy of wealth to compete with that of our ancient foe.

Having refunded and made payable in coin the bonds which had not cost their holders more than sixty cents on the dollar, the casual observer is satisfied that the last robbery has been perpetrated. But the busy brain of avarice is ever reaching out . . . for gain, *gain,* GAIN; and we next find these civilized brigands have consummated a scheme for the *demonetization of silver.* This act, passed in 1873, destroyed the monetary quality of silver, and thus produced a farther [*sic*] contraction of the currency . . . .

Shylock, with his hoarded millions, could rest on beds of down. Neither fire, flood, mildew, nor blight brought anxiety to him . . . . Indeed, the entire country had become sponsor for his wealth, for under the law every

---

[2]The so-called 5–20 bonds were securities issued by the Union government during the Civil War to raise money for war purposes. Purchasers could pay for them in paper greenbacks while receiving the interest in gold. The question of how the principle should be repaid when it became due was left unclear, and the measure mentioned here was designed to end the ambiguity—ED.

producer and millions of wage-workers had been instituted a vigilance committee to look after his welfare . . . . The government held that property in safe keeping and did not charge a cent for the favor; it collected his interest and paid it over to him free of charge; it paid his gold interest in advance and exempted him from taxation; the insurance agent and the tax gatherer were strangers to him, they did not molest him or make him afraid, and being thus fortified, he was content to let the producers of wealth eke out a miserable existence while he fared sumptuously every day. But it was not the American capitalist alone who entered into this murderous scheme for demonetizing silver. In the *Banker's Magazine* of August 1873, we find the following on this subject:

> In 1872, silver being demonetized in France, England and Holland, a capital of $500,000 was raised and Ernest Seyd of London was sent to this country with this fund, as agent of the foreign bond holders and capitalists, to effect the same object (demonetization of silver), which was accomplished.

There you have it, a paid agent of English capitalists sent to this country with $500,000 to buy the American Congress and rob the American people . . . .

Not only did the demonetization of silver prevent, or at least retard, the payment of the bonds, but it added to the value of the gold in which these bonds were then to be paid. Every dollar taken from the circulation adds to the value of that which is left, hence the demonetization of silver increases the value of gold . . . .

Would to God that the record of atrocities against this nation might end here! But no, with the people crushed and staggering beneath the burdens imposed upon them through the preceding robberies, we next find these vampires in Congress inflicting [still another] scourge upon the people by means of the resumption act.

This act . . . authorized the secretary of the treasury to destroy the fractional [paper] currency, and issue silver coin in like denomination to take its place. The people have found the fractional currency convenient . . . for small remittances in trade. The destruction of this money was a serious injury to the business men of the country . . . .

We have now completed a brief outline of . . . atrocious conspiracies against this government; conspiracies which for boldness of purpose and cruelty of design, are without parallel in the annals of crime, and all perpetrated within the brief period of thirteen years; thirteen years in which the powers of darkness sat enthroned in our national capitol; thirteen years of utter disregard for the rights of the people; thirteen years in which class-legislation gave birth to more moneyed and monopolistic powers than ever before cursed any civilized people.

The people having slept until this machinery was perfected, have at last awakened from their dreams of freedom to find their liberties fettered, and themselves in the grasp of a system of monopolies whose titanic enginery is crushing out not only liberty, but life itself. And when we consider the fact that representatives of these monopolies sit in our congressional halls and practically control the United States Senate, that highest law-making power in the land, who does not tremble for the safety not only of our Republic, but of our civilization . . . .

History proves that nothing has been so disastrous to nations as the enactment of laws which favor the few at the expense of the many. There is no robbery so suicidal as that sanctioned by law; for it not only destroys the morality of the legalized robber, starves and kills the victimized masses, but it degrades the law-maker himself to a level with the most notorious highwayman . . . . And history proves that such legislation destroys nations, degrades humanity, and is a mockery against the most high God. Against the Eternal Judge who will not hold guiltless him who lends a voice to such iniquitous legislation . . . a legislation that destroys both soul and body of the toiling millions.

2.2:   The Populist Party Platform (1892)

Meeting at Omaha in July 1892, the People's Party adopted a platform that went beyond the demands of the dirt farmers' leaders to express the concerns of social critics and reformers who foresaw imminent social catastrophe for America if something were not done soon. The preamble of this platform was written by Ignatius Donnelly, novelist, journalist, intellectual, and former Republican congressman from Minnesota.

How do you explain the platform's apocalyptic tone? In what ways does it seek to create a farmer-labor alliance? It has been said that Populism foreshadowed twentieth-century liberalism. Is there anything in the platform that reminds you of later Progressive and New Deal policies and programs?

The Preamble of the Platform of the People's Party

Assembled upon the 116th anniversary of the Declaration of Independence, the People's Party of America, in their first national convention, invoking upon their action the blessing of Almighty God, puts forth, in the name and on behalf of the people of this country, the following preamble and declaration of principles:—The conditions which surround us best justify our cooperation: we meet in the midst of a nation brought to the verge of moral, political, and material ruin. Corruption dominates the ballot-box, the legisla-

Edward McPherson, *A Handbook of Politics for 1892* (Washington, DC: James J. Chapman, 1892), pp. 269–271.

tures, the Congress, and even touches the ermine of the bench. The people are demoralized; most of the states have been compelled to isolate the voters at the polling-places to prevent universal intimidation or bribery. The newspapers are largely subsidized or muzzled; public opinion silenced; business prostrated; our homes covered with mortgages; labor impoverished; and the land concentrating in the hands of the capitalists. The urban workmen are denied the right of organization for self-protection; imported pauperized labor beats down their wages; a hireling standing army, unrecognized by our laws, is established to shoot them down, and they are rapidly degenerating into European conditions. The fruits of the toil of millions are boldly stolen to build up colossal fortunes for a few, unprecedented in the history of mankind; and the possessors of these, in turn, despise the Republic and endanger liberty. From the same prolific womb of governmental injustice we breed two great classes—tramps and millionaires.

The national power to create money is appropriated to enrich bondholders; a vast public debt, payable in legal tender currency, has been funded into gold bearing bonds, thereby adding millions to the burdens of the people. Silver, which has been accepted as coin since the dawn of history, has been demonetized to add to the purchasing power of gold by decreasing the value of all forms of property as well as human labor; and the supply of currency is purposely abridged to fatten usurers, bankrupt enterprise, and enslave industry. A vast conspiracy against mankind has been organized on two continents, and it is rapidly taking possession of the world. If not met and overthrown at once, it forebodes [*sic*] terrible convulsions, the destruction of civilization, or the establishment of an absolute despotism.

We have witnessed for more than a quarter of a century the struggles of the two great political parties for power and plunder, while grievous wrongs have been inflicted upon the suffering people. We charge that the controlling influences dominating both these parties have permitted the existing dreadful conditions to develop without serious effort to prevent or restrain them. Neither do they now promise us any substantial reform. They have agreed together to ignore in the coming campaign every issue but one. They propose to drown the outcries of a plundered people with the uproar of a sham battle over the tariff, so that capitalists, corporations, national banks, rings, trusts, watered stock, the demonetization of silver, and the oppressions of the usurers may all be lost sight of. They propose to sacrifice our homes, lives and children on the altar of mammon; to destroy the multitude in order to secure corruption funds from the millionaires.

Assembled on the anniversary of the birthday of the nation, and filled with the spirit of the grand general and chieftain who established our independence, we seek to restore the government of the Republic to the hands of "the plain people," with whose class it originated. We assert our purposes to be identical with the purposes of the National Constitution, "to form a more perfect union and establish justice, insure domestic tranquility, provide for the common defence, promote the general welfare, and secure the blessings of liberty for ourselves and our posterity." We declare that this republic can only endure as a free government while built upon the love of the whole people for each other and for the nation; that it cannot be pinned together by bayonets; that the civil war is over, and that every passion and resentment which grew out of it must die with it; and that we must be in fact, as we are in name, one united brotherhood of freemen.

Our country finds itself confronted by conditions for which there is no precedent in the history of the world; our annual agricultural productions amount to billions of dollars in value, which must in a few weeks or months, be exchanged for billions of dollars of commodities consumed in their production; the existing currency supply is wholly inadequate to make this exchange; the results are falling prices, the formation of combines and rings, the impoverishment of the producing class. We pledge ourselves, if given power, we will labor to correct these evils by wise and reasonable legislation, in accordance with the terms of our platform. We believe that the powers of government—in other words, of the people—should be expanded (as in the case of the postal service) as rapidly and as far as the good sense of an intelligent people and the teachings of experience shall justify, to the end that oppression, injustice, and poverty shall eventually cease in the land.

While our sympathies as a party of reform are naturally upon the side of every proposition which will tend to make men intelligent, virtuous, and temperate, we nevertheless regard these questions—important as they are—as secondary to the great issues now pressing for solution, and upon which not only our individual prosperity but the very existence of free institutions depends; and we ask all men to first help us to determine whether we are to have a republic to administer before we differ as to the conditions upon which it is to be administered; believing that the forces of reform this day organized will never cease to move forward until every wrong is remedied, and equal rights and equal privileges securely established for all the men and women of this country.

We declare, therefore,—

First—That the union of the labor forces of the United States this day consummated shall be permanent and perpetual; may its spirit enter all hearts for the salvation of the republic and the uplifting of mankind!

Second—Wealth belongs to him who creates it, and every dollar taken from industry without an equivalent is robbery. "If any will not work, neither shall he eat." The interests of rural and civic labor are the same; their enemies are identical.

Third—We believe that the time has come when the railroad corporations will either own the people or the people must own the railroads; and, should the government enter upon the work of owning and managing all railroads, we should favor an amendment to the Constitution by which all persons engaged in the government service shall be placed under a civil service regulation of the most rigid character, so as to prevent the increase of the power of the national administration by the use of such additional government employees.

First, *Money*—We demand a national currency, safe, sound, and flexible, issued by the general government only, a full legal tender for all debts, public and private, and that, without the use of banking corporations, a just, equitable, and efficient means of distribution direct to the people, at a tax not to exceed two per cent per annum, to be provided as set forth in the sub-treasury plan of the Farmers' Alliance, or a better system; also, by payments in discharge of its obligation for public improvements.

a. We demand free and unlimited coinage of silver and gold at the present legal ratio of sixteen to one.
b. We demand that the amount of circulating medium be speedily increased to not less than fifty dollars per capita.
c. We demand a graduated income tax.
d. We believe that the money of the country should be kept as much as possible in the hands of the people, and hence we demand that all state and national revenues shall be limited to the necessary expenses of the government economically and honestly administered.
e. We demand that postal savings banks be established by the government for the safe deposit of the earnings of the people and to facilitate exchange.

Second, *Transportation*—Transportation being a means of exchange and a public necessity, the government should own and operate the railroads in the interest of the people.

Third, *Land*—The land, including all the natural sources of wealth, is the heritage of the people, and should not be monopolized for speculative purposes, and alien ownership of land should be prohibited. All land now held by railroads and other corporations in excess of their actual needs, and all lands now owned by aliens, should be reclaimed by the government and held for actual settlers only.

Resolutions

Whereas, Other questions have been presented for our considerations, we hereby submit the following, not as part of the platform of the People's party, but as resolutions of the sentiment of this convention.

1. *Resolved*, That we demand a free ballot and a fair count in all elections, and pledge ourselves to secure it to every legal voter without federal intervention, through the adoption by the States of the unperverted Australian or secret ballot system.

2. *Resolved*, That the revenue derived from a graduated income tax should be applied to the reduction of the burden of taxation now resting upon the domestic industries of this country.

3. *Resolved*, That we pledge our support to fair and liberal pensions to ex-Union soldiers and sailors.

4. *Resolved*, That we condemn the fallacy of protecting American labor under the present system, which opens our ports to the pauper and criminal classes of the world, and crowds out our wage-earners; and we denounce the present ineffective laws against contract labor, and demand the further restriction of undesirable immigration.

5. *Resolved*, That we cordially sympathize with the efforts of organized workingmen to shorten the hours of labor, and demand a rigid enforcement of the existing eight-hour law on government work, and ask that a penalty clause by added to said law.

6. *Resolved*, That we regard the maintenance of a large standing army of mercenaries, known as the Pinkerton system, as a menace to our liberties, and we demand its abolition; and we condemn the recent invasion of the Territory of Wyoming by the hired assassins of the plutocracy, assisted by federal officials.

7. *Resolved*, That we commend to the favorable consideration of the people and the reform press the legislative system known as the initiative and referendum.

8. *Resolved*, That we favor a constitutional provision limiting the office of President and Vice-President to one term, and providing for the election of senators of the United States by a direct vote of the people.

9. *Resolved*, That we oppose any subsidy or national aid to any private corporation for any purpose.

10. *Resolved*, That this convention sympathizes with the Knights of Labor and their righteous contest with the tyrannical combine of clothing manufacturers of Rochester, and declares it to be the duty of all who hate tyranny and oppression to refuse to purchase the goods made by said manufacturers, or to patronize any merchants who sell such goods.

2.3:   William Allen White
and the Kansas Populists (1896)

In 1896, when he wrote the article below, William Allen White was the twenty-eight-year-old editor of the Emporia Gazette, *a newspaper in a small city in Kansas. The son of a doctor, White would later become a champion of social and political reform, but at this point he despised the home-grown reformers who called themselves Populists. The following essay was published during the heat of the presidential contest between William Jenning Bryan and William McKinley and immediately attracted national attention as a biting critique of midwestern Populism by a midwesterner. Republican newspapers by the score promptly reprinted the essay, and the McKinley campaign people distributed it as an anti-Bryan broadside.*

What are White's chief complaints about the Kansas Populists? Were his charges valid? What social factors in White's background might explain why this son of Kansas was so hostile to the farmers' party of his state?

What's the Matter with Kansas?

WILLIAM ALLEN WHITE

Today the Kansas Department of Agriculture sent out a statement which indicates that Kansas has gained less than two thousand people in the past year. There are about two hundred and twenty-five thousand families in this state, and there were ten thousand babies born in Kansas, and yet so many people have left the state that the natural increase is cut down to less than two thousand net.

William Allen White, *The Autobiography of William Allen White* (New York: The Macmillan Company, 1946), pp. 280–283. Reprinted with permission of Barbara White Walker.

This has been going on for eight years.

If there had been a high brick wall around the state eight years ago, and not a soul had been admitted or permitted to leave, Kansas would be a half million souls better off than she is today. And yet the nation has increased in population. In five years ten million people have been added to the national population, yet instead of gaining a share of this—say, half a million—Kansas has apparently been a plague spot and, in the very garden of the world, has lost population by ten thousands every year.

Not only has she lost population, but she has lost money. Every moneyed man in the state who could get out without loss has gone. Every month in every community sees someone who has a little money pack up and leave the state. This has been going on for eight years. Money has been drained out all the time. In towns where ten years ago there were three or four or half a dozen money-lending concerns, stimulating industry by furnishing capital, there is now none, or one or two that are looking after the interest and principal already outstanding.

No one brings any money into Kansas any more. What community knows over one or two men who have moved in with more than $5,000 in the past three years? And what community cannot count half a score of men in that time who have left, taking all the money they could scrape together?

Yet the nation has grown rich; other states have increased in population and wealth—other neighboring states. Missouri has gained over two million, while Kansas has been losing half a million. Nebraska has gained in wealth and population while Kansas has gone downhill. Colorado has gained every way, while Kansas has lost every way since 1888.

What's the matter with Kansas?

There is no substantial city in the state. Every big town save one has lost in population. Yet Kansas City, Omaha, Lincoln, St. Louis, Denver, Colorado Springs, Sedalia, the cities of the Dakotas, St. Paul and Minneapolis and Des Moines—all cities and towns in the West—have steadily grown.

Take up the government blue book [which lists federal officeholders] and you will see that Kansas is virtually off the map. Two or three little scrubby consular places in yellow-fever-stricken communities that do not aggregate ten thousand dollars a year is all the recognition that Kansas has. Nebraska draws about one hundred thousand dollars; little old North Dakota draws about fifty thousand dollars; Oklahoma doubles Kansas; Missouri leaves her a thousand miles behind; Colorado is almost seven times greater than Kansas—the whole west is ahead of Kansas.

Take it by any standard you please, Kansas is not in it.

Go east and you hear them laugh at Kansas; go west and they sneer at her; go south and they "cuss" her; go north and they have forgotten her. Go into any crowd of intelligent people gathered anywhere on the globe, and you will find the Kansas man on the defensive. The newspaper columns and magazines once devoted to praise of her, to boastful facts and startling figures concerning her resources, are now filled with cartoons, jibes and

Pefferian speeches. Kansas just naturally isn't in it. She has traded places with Arkansas and Timbuctoo.

What's the matter with Kansas?

We all know; yet here we are at it again. We have an old mossback Jacksonian who snorts and howls because there is a bathtub in the State House; we are running that old jay for Governor. We have another shabby, wild-eyed, rattle-brained fanatic who has said openly in a dozen speeches that "the rights of the user are paramount to the rights of the owner"; we are running him for Chief Justice, so that capital will come tumbling over itself to get into the state. We have raked the old ash heap of failure in the state and found an old human hoop skirt who has failed as a businessman, who has failed as an editor, who has failed as a preacher, and we are going to run him for Congressman-at-Large. He will help the looks of the Kansas delegation at Washington. Then we have discovered a kid without a law practice and have decided to run him for Attorney General. Then, for fear some hint that the state had become respectable might percolate through the civilized portions of the nation, we have decided to send three or four harpies out lecturing, telling the people that Kansas is raising hell and letting the corn go to weed.

Oh, this is a state to be proud of! We are a people who can hold up our heads! What we need is not more money, but less capital, fewer white shirts and brains, fewer men with business judgment, and more of those fellows who boast that they are "just ordinary clodhoppers, but they know more in a minute about finance than John Sherman"; we need more men who are "posted," who can bellow about the crime of '73, who hate prosperity, and who think, because a man believes in national honor, he is a tool of Wall Street. We have had a few of them—some hundred fifty thousand—but we need more.

We need several thousand gibbering idiots to scream about the "Great Red Dragon" of Lombard Street [a term for the British Wall Street]. We don't need population, we don't need wealth, we don't need well-dressed men on the streets, we don't need cities on the fertile prairies; you bet we don't! What we are after is the money power. Because we have become poorer and ornerier and meaner than a spavined, distempered mule, we, the people of Kansas, propose to kick; we don't care to build up, we wish to tear down.

"There are two ideas of government," said our noble [William Jennings] Bryan at Chicago. "There are those who believe that if you legislate to make the well-to-do prosperous, this prosperity will leak through on those below. The Democratic idea has been that if you legislate to make the masses prosperous their prosperity will find its way up and through every class and rest upon them."

That's the stuff! Give the prosperous man the dickens! Legislate the thriftless man into ease, whack the stuffing out of the creditors and tell the debtors who borrowed the money five years ago when money "per capita" was greater than it is now, that the contraction of currency gives him a right to repudiate.

Whoop it up for the ragged trousers; put the lazy, greasy fizzle, who can't pay his debts on the altar, and bow down and worship him. Let the state ideal be high. What we need is not the respect of our fellow men, but the chance to get something for nothing.

Oh, yes, Kansas is a great state. Here are people fleeing from it by the score every day, capital going out of the state by the hundreds of dollars; and every industry but farming paralyzed, and that crippled, because its products have to go across the ocean before they can find a laboring man at work who can afford to buy them. Let's don't stop this year. Let's drive all the decent, self-respecting men out of the state. Let's keep the old clodhoppers who know it all. Let's encourage the man who is "posted." He can talk, and what we need is not mill hands to eat our meat, nor factory hands to eat our wheat, nor cities to oppress the farmer by consuming his butter and eggs and chickens and produce. What Kansas needs is men who can talk, who have large leisure to argue the currency question while their wives wait at home for a nickel's worth of bluing.

What's the matter with Kansas?

Nothing under the shining sun. She is losing her wealth, population and standing. She has got her statesmen, and the money power is afraid of her. Kansas is all right. She has started in to raise hell as Mrs. [Mary Ellen] Lease advised, and she seems to have an over-production. But that doesn't matter. Kansas never did believe in diversified crops. Kansas is all right. There is absolutely nothing wrong with Kansas. "Every prospect pleases and only man is vile."

2.4:   The American Federation of Labor and the Populists (1892)

One national labor group, the Knights of Labor, endorsed the Populist candidates in 1892. But the Knights were in precipitous decline by this date, and by itself their endorsement meant little. The most robust part of the American trade union movement in the early 1890s was the American Federation of Labor, headed by Samuel Gompers, who preached "pure and simple" trade unionism. According to Gompers, organized labor had to focus on collective bargaining and employ only the traditional trade union weapons of strikes, picketing, and boycotts to improve the wages and reduce the hours of working people. Political agitation was a mistake.

Why does Gompers reject the Populist Party? What does he have to say about organized labor's political activities generally? Do you know if wage earners in large numbers actually supported the Populists?

Organized Labor in the 1892 Presidential Campaign

SAMUEL GOMPERS

It is with some trepidation that I begin writing this article, for while it may be true that I have as good opportunities as any other man in the country of conjecturing the probable action of the workingmen of America, and particularly those affiliated with the American Federation of Labor in the coming Presidential campaign, I am certain that my article will please but very few. I have had to say and write some things in my more than twenty-five years' connection with the labor movement for which I have incurred the displeasure of some very earnest, though, in my opinion, mistaken men who differ with our movement and myself, as one of its representatives, as to methods, but not as to the ultimate end and aim of the social, economic and political struggle of the toiling masses.

I feel sure that this production will in nowise tend to lessen this difference of opinion, but if it will tend to give a clearer understanding to a number of friends and foes as to what the trade unions really are; that their methods are within the range of reason; that their work is being crowned with success as far as conditions will permit; that they are the natural organization of the wage-earning masses; and that it is their mission to secure the amelioration as well as the emancipation of labor—then I shall feel my conscience eased, and be amply rewarded, in venturing to write an article upon the probable action of the American Federation of Labor in the coming Presidential campaign.

Why should its attitude be different in the coming Presidential campaign from what it has been in the past? In what way does the coming campaign differ from those of 1876, 1880, 1884 or 1888? Is there any particular principle involved in the party issues in which the wageworkers have a deep or keen interest? There is indeed none. . . .

The members of the organizations affiliated with the Federation will no doubt, in a large measure, as citizens, vote for the candidate of the party of their own political predilections. But the number is ever on the increase who disenthral themselves from partisan voting and exercise their franchise to reward or chastise those parties and candidates, that deserve either their friendship or resentment. With us it is not a question of parties or men; it is a question of measures.

That there exists a feeling of dissatisfaction with, and bitter antagonism to, both the Republican and Democratic parties is not to be gainsaid. Broken promises to labor, insincere, half-hearted support and even antagonism of legislation in the interest of the toilers on the one hand, and the alacrity and devotion with which the interests of the corporations and the wealth-possessing class are nurtured, protected and advanced on the other,

Samuel Gompers, "Organized Labor in the Campaign," *North American Review*, July 1892, pp. 91–93.

have had their effect, and the result is that many toilers have forever severed their connection with the old parties. That the number will continue to grow larger year by year I have not the slightest doubt. To me this party defection of the wageworkers is one of the signs of the dawn of a healthier public opinion, a sturdier manhood and independence, and a promise to maintain the liberties that the people now enjoy, as well as to ever struggle on to attain that happy goal towards which, throughout its entire history, the human family have been perpetually pushing forward.

But in leaving the old parties, to whom, to what shall former Democratic or Republican workmen turn? To the People's Party? Are such changes and improvements promised there that the workers can with any degree of assurance throw in their political fortunes with that party? Of course, acting upon the principle "of all evils choose the least," they will more generally coöperate with the People's Party than with any similar party heretofore gracing the Presidential political arena.

As a matter of fact, however, to support the People's Party under the belief that it is a *labor* party is to act under misapprehension. It is not and cannot, in the nature of its make-up, be a labor party, or even one in which the wageworkers will find their haven. Composed, as the People's Party is, mainly of *employing* farmers without any regard to the interests of the *employed* farmers of the country districts or the mechanics and laborers of the industrial centers, there must of necessity be a divergence of purposes, methods, and interests.

In speaking thus frankly of the composition of the People's Party there is no desire to belittle the efforts of its members, or even to withhold the sympathy due them in their agitation to remedy the wrongs which they suffer from corporate power and avarice; on the contrary, the fullest measure of sympathy and all possible encouragement should and will be given them; for they are doing excellent work in directing public attention to the dangers which threaten the body politic of the republic. But, returning to the consideration of the entire coöperation or amalgamation of the wage-workers' organizations with the People's Party, I am persuaded that all who are more than superficial observers, or who are keen students of the past struggles of the proletariat of all countries, will with one accord unite in declaring the union impossible, because it is unnatural. Let me add that, before there can be any hope of the unification of labor's forces of the field, farm, factory, and workshop, the people who work on and in them for wages must be organized to protect their interests against those who pay them wages for that work.

2.5:   Populism and the Democrats (1896)

Even if the Populists were not able to transform themselves into a major national party, they did succeed in infusing both Democrats and

Republicans with some of their concerns and ideas. In the Plains states, both major parties adopted Populist rhetoric and policies; in many places in the "solid" Democratic South, Populist-influenced politicians success-fully challenged the conservative "Bourbon" wing of the dominant party for control.

In 1893 a financial panic struck the nation, ushering in four years of depression. In the cities business failures threw thousands out of work; on the farms plummeting prices for crops led to a torrent of mortgage foreclosures. The response of President Grover Cleveland's administra-tion to the hard times seemed to many Americans both callous and too slavishly accommodating to the business community.

It was in this setting that western Democrats staged a revolt against the eastern, Cleveland wing of the party. The agent of the revolt was a Nebraska lawyer and two-term congressman, William Jennings Bryan. At the 1896 Democratic presidential nominating convention in Chicago, Bryan rose to denounce the party's eastern wing and to proclaim a cru-sade for the "toilers" and the "producing masses" against their oppres-sors. His electrifying "cross of gold" speech, excerpted below, won him the nomination, and with it control of the party by its western and southern wings.

What does Bryan's speech reveal about the sectional and occupational identity of the Democrats who supported free silver? Aside from free silver, what else is Bryan proposing? Bryan invokes the precedents of Andrew Jackson and Thomas Jefferson to support his position on banks. Is his claim historically valid? Conservatives attacked the Bryan speech as radical rabble-rousing. Was it?

The Cross of Gold

WILLIAM JENNINGS BRYAN

Speech Concluding Debate on the Chicago Platform

Mr. Chairman and Gentlemen of the Convention: I would be presumptuous, indeed, to present myself against the distinguished gentlemen to whom you have listened if this were a mere measuring of abilities; but this is not a con-test between persons. The humblest citizen in all the land, when clad in the armor of a righteous cause, is stronger than all the hosts of error. I come to speak to you in defense of a cause as holy as the cause of liberty—the cause of humanity.

William Jennings Bryan, *The First Battle: The Story of the Campaign of 1896* (Chicago: W. B. ConKrey Company, n.d.), pp. 199–206.

When this debate is concluded, a motion will be made to lay upon the table the resolution offered in commendation of the administration, and also the resolution offered in condemnation of the administration. We object to bringing this question down to the level of persons. The individual is but an atom; he is born, he acts, he dies; but principles are eternal; and this has been a contest over a principle.

Never before in the history of this country has there been witnessed such a contest as that through which we have just passed. Never before in the history of American politics has a great issue been fought out as this issue has been, by the voters of a great party. On the fourth of March, 1895, a few Democrats, most of them members of Congress, issued an address to the Democrats of the nation, asserting that the money question was the paramount issue of the hour; declaring that a majority of the Democratic party had the right to control the action of the party on this paramount issue; and concluding with the request that the believers in the free coinage of silver in the Democratic party should organize, take charge of, and control the policy of the Democratic party. Three months later, at Memphis, an organization was perfected, and the silver Democrats went forth openly and courageously proclaiming their belief, and declaring that, if successful, they would crystallize into a platform the declaration which they had made. Then began the conflict. With a zeal approaching the zeal which inspired the crusaders who followed Peter the Hermit, our silver Democrats went forth from victory unto victory until they are now assembled, not to discuss, not to debate, but to enter up the judgment already rendered by the plain people of this country. In this contest brother has been arrayed against brother, father against son. The warmest ties of love, acquaintance and association have been disregarded; old leaders have been cast aside when they have refused to give expression to the sentiments of those whom they would lead, and new leaders have sprung up to give direction to this cause of truth. Thus has the contest been waged, and we have assembled here under as binding and solemn instructions as were ever imposed upon representatives of the people. . . .

The gentleman who preceded me [ex-Governor William E. Russell] spoke of the State of Massachusetts; let me assure him that not one present in all this convention entertains the least hostility to the people of the State of Massachusetts, but we stand here representing people who are the equals, before the law, of the greatest citizens in the State of Massachusetts. When you [turning to the gold delegates] come before us and tell us that we are about to disturb your business interests, we reply that you have disturbed our business interests by your course.

We say to you that you have made the definition of a business man too limited in its application. The man who is employed for wages is as much a business man as his employer; the attorney in a country town is as much a business man as the corporation counsel in a great metropolis; the merchant at the cross-roads store is as much a business man as the merchant of New York; the farmer who goes forth in the morning and toils all day—who begins in the spring and toils all summer—and who by the application of brain and muscle to the natural resources of the country creates wealth, is as much a business man as the man who goes upon the board of trade and bets upon the price of grain; the miners who go down a thousand feet into the earth, or climb two thousand feet upon the cliffs, and bring forth from their hiding places the precious metals to be poured into the channels of trade are as much business men as the few financial magnates who, in a back room, corner the money of the world. We come to speak for this broader class of business men.

Ah, my friends, we say not one word against those who live upon the Atlantic coast, but the hardy pioneers who have braved all the dangers of the wilderness, who have made the desert to blossom as the rose—the pioneers away out there [pointing to the West], who rear their children near to Nature's heart, where they can mingle their voices with the voices of the birds—out there where they have erected schoolhouses for the education of their young, churches where they praise their Creator, and cemeteries where rest the ashes of their dead—these people, we say, are as deserving of the consideration of our party as any people in this country. It is for these that we speak. We do not come as aggressors. Our war is not a war of conquest; we are fighting in the defense of our homes, our families, and posterity. We have petitioned, and our petitions have been scorned; we have entreated, and our entreaties have been disregarded; we have begged, and they have mocked when our calamity came. We beg no longer; we entreat no more; we petition no more. We defy them.

The gentleman from Wisconsin has said that he fears a Robespierre. My friends, in this land of the free you need not fear that a tyrant will spring up from among the people. What we need is an Andrew Jackson to stand, as Jackson stood, against the encroachments of organized wealth.

They tell us that this platform was made to catch votes. We reply to them that changing conditions make new issues; that the principles upon which Democracy rests are as everlasting as the hills, but that they must be applied to new conditions as they arise. Conditions have arisen, and we are here to meet those conditions. They tell us that the income tax ought not to be brought in here; that it is a new idea. They criticise us for our criticism of the Supreme Court of the United States. My friends, we have not criticised; we have simply called attention to what you already know. If you want criticism, read the dissenting opinions of the court. There you will find criticisms. They say that we passed an unconstitutional law; we deny it. The income tax law was not unconstitutional when it was passed; it was not unconstitutional when it went before the Supreme Court for the first time; it did not become unconstitutional until one of the judges changed his mind, and we cannot be expected to know when a judge will change his mind. The income tax is just. It simply intends to put the burdens of government justly upon the backs of the people. I am in favor of an income tax. When I find a man who is not willing to bear his share of the burdens of the government which protects him, I find a man who is unworthy to enjoy the blessings of a government like ours.

They say that we are opposing national bank currency; it is true. If you will read what Thomas Benton said, you will find he said that, in searching history, he could find but one parallel to Andrew Jackson; that was Cicero, who destroyed the conspiracy of Cataline and saved Rome. Benton said that Cicero only did for Rome what Jackson did for us when he destroyed the bank conspiracy and saved America. We say in our platform that we believe that the right to coin and issue money is a function of government. We believe it. We believe that it is a part of sovereignty, and can no more with safety be delegated to private individuals than we could afford to delegate to private individuals the power to make penal statutes or levy taxes. Mr. Jefferson, who was once regarded as good Democratic authority, seems to have differed in opinion from the gentleman who has addressed us on the part of the minority. Those who are opposed to this proposition tell us that the issue of paper money is a function of the bank, and that the Government ought to go out of the banking business. I stand with Jefferson rather than with them, and tell them, as he did, that the issue of money is a function of government, and that the banks ought to go out of the governing business.

They complain about the plank which declares against life tenure in office. They have tried to strain it to mean that which it does not mean. What we oppose by that plank is the life tenure which is being built up in Washington, and which excludes from participation in official benefits the humbler members of society.

Let me call your attention to two or three important things. The gentleman from New York says that he will propose an amendment to the platform providing that the proposed change in our monetary system shall not affect contracts already made. Let me remind you that there is no intention of affecting those contracts which according to present laws are made payable in gold; but if he means to say that we cannot change our monetary system without protecting those who have loaned money before the change was made, I desire to ask him where, in law or in morals, he can find justification for not protecting the debtors when the act of 1873 was passed, if he now insists that we must protect the creditors.

He says he will also propose an amendment which will provide for the suspension of free coinage if we fail to maintain the parity within a year. We reply that when we advocate a policy which we believe will be successful, we are not compelled to raise a doubt as to our own sincerity by suggesting what we shall do if we fail. I ask him, if he would apply his logic to us, why he does not apply it to himself. He says he wants this country to try to secure an international agreement. Why does he not tell us what he is going to do if he fails to secure an international agreement? There is more reason for him to do that than there is for us to provide against the failure to maintain the parity. Our opponents have tried for twenty years to secure an international agreement, and those are waiting for it most patiently who do not want it at all.

And now, my friends, let me come to the paramount issue. If they ask us why it is that we say more on the money question than we say upon the tariff question, I reply that, if protection has slain its thousands, the gold standard has slain its tens of thousands. If they ask us why we do not embody in our platform all the things that we believe in, we reply that when we have restored the money of the Constitution all other necessary reforms will be possible; but that until this is done there is no other reform that can be accomplished.

Why is it that within three months such a change has come over the country? Three months ago, when it was confidently asserted that those who believe in the gold standard would frame our platform and nominate our candidates, even the advocates of the gold standard did not think that we could elect a president. And they had good reason for their doubt, because there is scarcely a State here today asking for the gold standard which is not in the absolute control of the Republican party. But note the change. Mr. McKinley was nominated at St. Louis upon a platform which declared for the maintenance of the gold standard until it can be changed into bimetallism by international agreement. Mr. McKinley was the most popular man among the Republicans, and three months ago everybody in the Republican party prophesied his election. How is today? Why, the man who was once pleased to think that he looked like Napoleon—that man shudders today when he remembers that he was nominated on the anniversary of the battle of Waterloo. Not only that, but as he listens he can hear with ever-increasing distinctness the sound of the waves as they beat upon the lonely shores of St. Helena.

Why this change? Ah, my friends, is not the reason for the change evident to any one who will look at the matter? No private character, however pure, no personal popularity, however great, can protect from the avenging wrath of an indignant people a man who will declare that he is in favor of fastening the gold standard upon this country, or who is willing to surrender the right of self-government and place the legislative control of our affairs in the hands of foreign potentates and powers.

We go forth confident that we shall win. Why? Because upon the paramount issue of this campaign there is not a spot of ground upon which the enemy will dare to challenge battle. If they tell us that the gold standard is a good thing, we shall point to their platform and tell them that their platform pledges the party to get rid of the gold standard and substitute bimetallism. If the gold standard is a good thing, why try to get rid of it? I call your attention to the fact that some of the very people who are in this convention today and who tell us that we ought to declare in favor of international bimetallism—thereby declaring that the gold standard is wrong and that the principle of bimetallism is better—these very people four months ago were open and avowed advocates of the gold standard, and were then telling us that we could not legislate two metals together, even with the aid of all the world. If the gold standard is a good thing, we ought to declare in favor of its retention and not in favor of abandoning it; and if the gold standard is a bad thing why should we wait until other nations are willing to help us to let go? Here is the line of battle, and we care not upon which issue they force the fight; we are prepared to meet them on either issue or on both. If they tell us that the gold standard is the standard of civilization, we reply to them that this, the most enlightened of all the nations of the earth, has never declared for a gold standard and that both the great parties this year are declaring against it. If the gold standard is the standard of civilization, why, my friends, should we not have it? If they come to meet us on that issue we can present the history of our nation. More than that; we can tell them that they will search the pages of history in vain to find a single instance where the common people of any land have ever declared themselves in favor of the gold standard. They can find where the holders of fixed investments have declared for a gold standard, but not where the masses have.

Mr. Carlisle[1] said in 1878 that this was a struggle between "the idle holders of idle capital" and "the struggling masses, who produce the wealth and pay the taxes of the country;" and, my friends, the question we are to decide is: Upon which side will the Democratic party fight; upon the side of "the idle holders of idle capital" or upon the side of "the struggling masses?" That is the question which the party must answer first, and then it must be answered by each individual hereafter. The sympathies of the Democratic party, as shown by the platform, are on the side of the struggling masses who have ever been the foundation of the Democratic party. There are two ideas of government. There are those who believe that, if you will only legislate to make the well-to-do prosperous, their prosperity will leak through on those below. The Democratic idea, however, has been that if you legislate to make the masses prosperous, their prosperity will find its way up through every class which rests upon them.

You come to us and tell us that the great cities are in favor of the gold standard; we reply that the great cities rest upon our broad and fertile prairies. Burn down your cities and leave our farms, and your cities will spring up again as if by magic; but destroy our farms and the grass will grow in the streets of every city in the country.

My friends, we declare that this nation is able to legislate for its own people on every question, without waiting for the aid or consent of any other nation on earth; and upon that issue we expect to carry every State in the Union. I shall not slander the inhabitants of the fair State of Massachusetts nor the inhabitants of the State of New York by saying that, when they are confronted with the proposition, they will declare that this nation is not able to attend to its own business. It is the issue of 1776 over again. Our ancestors, when but three millions in number, had the courage to declare their political independence of every other nation; shall we, their descendants,

[1] John G. Carlisle, a hard-money Kentucky Democrat and Cleveland's secretary of the Treasury—ED.

when we have grown to seventy millions, declare that we are less independent than our forefathers? No, my friends, that will never be the verdict of our people. Therefore, we care not upon what lines the battle is fought. If they say bimetallism is good, but that we cannot have it until other nations help us, we reply that, instead of having a gold standard because England has, we will restore bimetallism, and then let England have bimetallism because the United States has it. If they dare to come out in the open field and defend the gold standard as a good thing, we will fight them to the uttermost. Having behind us the producing masses of this nation and the world, supported by the commercial interests, the laboring interests, and the toilers everywhere, we will answer their demand for a gold standard by saying to them: You shall not press down upon the brow of labor this crown of thorns, you shall not crucify mankind upon a cross of gold.

2.6:   A Reformer Repudiates Free Silver (1896)

Meeting in St. Louis at their own convention soon after the Democrats adjourned, the Populists accepted Bryan as their 1896 presidential candidate and adopted free silver as the key plank of their platform. Not all Populists endorsed this free silver strategy, however. One dissenter was the journalist-reformer Henry Demarest Lloyd who, although a college-educated easterner, supported the party's broader campaign against inequality. In the following letter to the economist Richard Ely, Lloyd expresses his dismay over what he considers the opportunism of the Populist delegates who accepted Bryan and his platform.

What are Lloyd's chief objections to the proceedings at the Populists' St. Louis convention? What does he mean by saying that free silver is "the cow-bird of the Reform movement"? Did free silver actually come to grips with the political and economic inequality that concerned the Populists, or was it an illusion, as some said?

Silver Issue a "Cow-bird" of Reform

HENRY DEMAREST LLOYD

I didn't answer your letter because I was too sore about the whole business. The People's Party Convention at St. Louis was the most discouraging experience of my life. It was not so much that the leaders tricked and bulldozed and betrayed, but that the people submitted. The craze for success "this time" had full possession of all of them. It was in the main a splendid body of men, but, withal, there was lacking in them that grasp of fundamental

Caro Lloyd, *Henry Demarest Lloyd: A Biography* (New York: G. P. Putnam's Sons, 1912), vol. 1, pp. 263–264.

principle which alone keeps parties together. No party can cohere unless its members have some common article of faith so completely engrained in the very texture of their minds that they spontaneously and without the necessity of conference will take practically the same views of the same questions. The People's party is a fortuitous collection of the dissatisfied. If it had been organized around a clear cut *principle*, of which its practical proposals were merely external expressions, it could never have been seduced into fusion, nor induced even to consider the nomination of a man like Bryan who rejects its own bottom doctrine. Such a party will have to be built up by conscious effort or evolved by the sharp pressure of events.

The Free Silver movement is a fake. Free Silver is the cow-bird of the Reform movement. It waited until the nest had been built by the sacrifices and labour of others, and then it laid its eggs in it, pushing out the others which lie smashed on the ground. It is now flying around while we are expected to do the incubating. I for one decline to sit on the nest to help any such game.

. . . The People's party has been betrayed . . . but after all it is its own fault. No party that does not lead its leaders will ever succeed. Lincoln had to be pulled along by his party every step he took. There was a *principle* there that had taken possession of 4,000,000 men and if it could not have found effectuation in one man it would have done it through another.

I may vote for Bryan as the Knight of the Disinherited, like Ivanhoe, but he will not be the next President, and I am content.

3

Outward Thrust

For a time during the closing years of the nineteenth century, the United States joined the big power race for overseas markets and colonies. Although the country had acquired Alaska and several small islands soon after the Civil War, until the 1890s most of its expansionist energies had been expended on settling and exploiting the broad expanse within its own national boundaries. Numerous, rich, and aggressive, Americans had not been averse to bullying weaker neighbors and forcibly dispossessing the Native Americans. Still, they had avoided acquiring territory detached from the North American continent. Nor had they been particularly interested in overseas investment or, with the notable exception of the South's cotton, in overseas markets. All told, as the nation entered the post-Reconstruction era, the inward-looking United States was a relatively minor player on world economic and political stages.

These attitudes soon changed. The documents that follow address the issues of why this occurred. They suggest why the self-satisfied and prosperous republic abandoned its inward focus and, at least for a time, dreamed of an empire. In the selections below you will encounter a range of opinion on America's outward thrust of the 1890s that culminated in the Spanish-American War and the acquisition of the Philippines, Puerto Rico, Hawaii, and other lands beyond the nation's continental borders.

3.1: Racial Destiny (1885)

Darwinian survival-of-the-fittest ideas not only sanctioned laissez-faire (free market) economics but also encouraged American expansionism. Nations and races, like individuals, differed in natural talent and abili-

ties, many Darwinists believed. Some nations and races were superior, and, like superior individuals, deserved to rule the rest. Writing in 1885, the Congregational minister Josiah Strong depicted in Darwinian terms the triumph of the American branch of the Anglo-Saxon race over all its competitors and its ultimate dominion over much of the world. Historians note that in his book Our Country, *which is excerpted below, Strong put into words what many educated Americans implicitly believed in this period.*

Is it surprising that a Protestant minister should announce views such as those Strong expressed? Are they Christian beliefs? Would it be fair to liken the notion of Anglo-Saxon superiority that Strong asserts to the views of Aryan supremacy that German Nazis disseminated during the 1930s and 1940s? What do you suppose foreigners thought of Strong's vision of an American-dominated world? It is interesting that Strong was a part of the reformist Social Gospel trend in organized Protestantism, which sought to improve social conditions for the poor and for labor. Do his statements seem compatible with this position? How could he maintain the two perspectives simultaneously?

Why the Anglo-Saxons Will Triumph

JOSIAH STRONG

It is not necessary to argue to those for whom I write that the two great needs of mankind, that all men may be lifted up into the light of the highest Christian civilization, are, first, a pure, spiritual Christianity, and, second, civil liberty. Without controversy, these are the forces which, in the past, have contributed most to the elevation of the human race, and they must continue to be, in the future, the most efficient ministers to its progress. It follows, then, that the Anglo-Saxon, as the great representatives of these two ideas, the depositary of these two greatest blessings, sustains peculiar relations to the world's future, is divinely commissioned to be, in a peculiar sense, his brother's keeper. Add to this the fact of his rapidly increasing strength in modern times, and we have well nigh a demonstration of his destiny. . . .

There can be no reasonable doubt that North America is to be the great home of the Anglo-Saxon, the principal seat of his power, the center of his life and influence. Not only does it constitute seven-elevenths of his possessions, but his empire is unsevered, while the remaining four-elevenths are fragmentary and scattered over the earth. . . .

But we are to have not only the larger portion of the Anglo-Saxon race for generations to come, we may reasonably expect to develop the highest type

Josiah Strong, *Our Country* (New York: Baker and Taylor, for the Home Missionary Society, 1885), pp. 161, 165, 168, 170–171, 172–175.

of Anglo-Saxon civilization. If human progress follows a law of development, if

"Time's noblest offspring is the last,"

our civilization should be the noblest; for we are

"The heirs of all the ages in the foremost files of time,"

and not only do we occupy the latitude of power, but *our land is the last to be occupied in that latitude.* There is no other virgin soil in the North Temperate Zone. If the consummation of human progress is not to be looked for here, if there is yet to flower a higher civilization, where is the soil that is to produce it? . . .

Mr. Darwin is not only disposed to see, in the superior vigor of our people, an illustration of his favorite theory of natural selection, but even intimates that the world's history thus far has been simply preparatory for our future, and tributary to it. He says: "There is apparently much truth in the belief that the wonderful progress of the United States, as well as the character of the people, are the results of natural selection; for the more energetic, restless and courageous men from all parts of Europe have emigrated during the last ten or twelve generations to that great country, and have there succeeded best. Looking at the distant future, I do not think that the Rev. Mr. Zincke takes an exaggerated view when he says: 'All other series of events—as that which resulted in the culture of mind in Greece, and that which resulted in the Empire of Rome—only appear to have purpose and value when viewed in connection with, or rather as subsidiary to, the great stream of Anglo-Saxon emigration to the West.'"

There is abundant reason to believe that the Anglo-Saxon race is to be, is, indeed, already becoming, more effective here than in the mother country. . . .

It may be easily shown, and is of no small significance, that the two great ideas of which the Anglo-Saxon is the exponent are having a fuller development in the United States than in Great Britain. There the union of Church and State tends strongly to paralyze some of the members of the body of Christ. Here there is no such influence to destroy spiritual life and power. Here, also, has been evolved the form of government consistent with the largest possible civil liberty. Furthermore, it is significant that the marked characteristics of this race are being here emphasized most. Among the most striking features of the Anglo-Saxon is his money-making power—a power of increasing importance in the widening commerce of the world's future. . . . [A]lthough England is by far the richest nation of Europe we have already outstripped her in the race after wealth, and we have only begun the development of our vast resources.

Again, another marked characteristic of the Anglo-Saxon is what may be called an instinct of genius for colonizing. His unequaled energy, his indomitable perseverance, and his personal independence, made him a pioneer. He excels all others in pushing his way into new countries. It was those in whom this tendency was strongest that came to America, and this inherited tendency has been further developed by the westward sweep of successive generations across the continent. So noticeable has this characteristic become that English visitors remark it. Charles Dickens once said that the typical American would hesitate to enter heaven unless assured that he could go further west.

Again, nothing more manifestly distinguishes the Anglo-Saxon than his intense and persistent energy; and he is developing in the United States an energy which, in eager activity and effectiveness, is peculiarly American. This is due partly to the fact that Americans are much better fed than Europeans, and partly to the undeveloped resources of a new country, but more largely to our climate, which acts as a constant stimulus. Ten years after the landing of the Pilgrims, the Rev. Francis Higginson, a good observer, wrote: "A sup of New England air is better than a whole flagon of English ale." Thus early had the stimulating effect of our climate been noted. Moreover, our social institutions are stimulating. In Europe the various ranks of society are, like the strata of the earth, fixed and fossilized. There can be no great change without a terrible upheaval, a social earthquake. Here society is like the waters of the sea, mobile; as General [James] Garfield said, and so signally illustrated in his own experience, that which is at the bottom today may one day flash on the crest of the highest wave. Every one is free to become whatever he can make of himself; free to transform himself from a rail-splitter or a tanner or a canal-boy, into the nation's President. Our aristocracy, unlike that of Europe, is open to all comers. Wealth, position, influence, are prizes offered for energy; and every farmer's boy, every apprentice and clerk, every friendless and penniless immigrant, is free to enter the lists. Thus many causes co-operate to produce here the most forceful and tremendous energy in the world.

What is the significance of such facts? These tendencies infold the future; they are the mighty alphabet with which God writes his prophecies. May we not, by a careful laying together of the letters, spell out something of his meaning? It seems to me that God, with infinite wisdom and skill, is training the Anglo-Saxon race for an hour sure to come in the world's future. Heretofore there has always been in the history of the world a comparatively unoccupied land westward, into which the crowded countries of the East have poured their surplus populations. But the widening waves of migration, which millenniums ago rolled east and west from the valley of the Euphrates, meet today on our Pacific coast. There are no more new worlds. The unoccupied arable lands of the earth are limited, and will soon be taken. The time is coming when the pressure of population on the means of subsistence will be felt here as it is now felt in Europe and Asia. Then will the world enter upon a new stage of its history—*the final competition of races, for which the Anglo-Saxon is being schooled.* Long before the thousand millions are here, the mighty *centrifugal* tendency, inherent in this stock and strengthened in the United States, will assert itself. Then this race of unequaled energy, with all the majesty of numbers and the might of wealth behind it—the representative, let us hope, of the largest liberty, the purest Christianity, the highest civilization—having developed peculiarly aggressive traits calculated to impress its institutions upon mankind, will spread itself over the earth. If I read not amiss, this powerful race will move down upon Mexico, down upon Central and South America, out upon the islands of the sea, over upon Africa and beyond. And can any one doubt that the result of this competition of races will be the "survival of the fittest"?

3.2:   Manhood and Imperialism (1899)

One of the most vigorous proponents of American expansion was the young politician Theodore Roosevelt. During the early 1880s he had tried his hand at ranching in the Dakotas. In 1897 he became assistant secretary of the navy under President William McKinley and in that capacity in 1898 dispatched the American Pacific fleet to the Philippines to prepare for war with Spain. During the Spanish-American War Roosevelt quit his navy post to organize a cavalry regiment, known as the Rough Riders, for service in Cuba. TR returned from Cuba a war hero and in 1899 ran successfully for governor of New York. Eventually, of course, he became president of the United States.

In the selection below, written before he was elected to high office, Roosevelt expresses views that would influence how many Americans regarded the rest of the world. How would you characterize these attitudes? Can you see any connection between these opinions and Roosevelt's interest in ranching? Can you guess what a modern feminist might say about the source of Roosevelt's views? Why does TR believe that unpatriotic attitudes were especially widespread among the educated? Can Roosevelt's opinions be found among Americans today?

Manhood and Foreign Policy

THEODORE ROOSEVELT

It is a matter of serious concern to every college man, and, indeed, to every man who believes in the good effects of a liberal education, to see the false views which seem to obtain among so many of the leaders of educated thought, not only upon the Monroe Doctrine, but upon every question

Theodore Roosevelt, *American Ideals* (New York: G. P. Putnam's Sons, 1897), pp. 240–245.

which involves the existence of a feeling of robust Americanism. Every educated man who puts himself out of touch with the current of American thought, and who on conspicuous occasions assumes an attitude hostile to the interest of America, is doing what he can to weaken the influence of educated men in American life. The crude, ill-conditioned jealousy of education, which is so often and so lamentably shown by large bodies of our people, is immensely stimulated by the action of those prominent educated men in whom education seems to have destroyed the strong, virile virtues and especially the spirit of Americanism.

.   .   .   .

There are many upright and honorable men who take the wrong side, that is, the anti-American side, of the Monroe Doctrine because they are too short-sighted or too unimaginative to realize the hurt to the nation that would be caused by the adoption of their views. There are other men who take the wrong view simply because they have not thought much of the matter, or are in unfortunate surroundings, by which they have been influenced to their own moral hurt. There are yet other men in whom the mainspring of the opposition to that branch of American policy known as the Monroe Doctrine is sheer timidity. This is sometimes the ordinary timidity of wealth. Sometimes, however, it is peculiarly developed among educated men whose education has tended to make them over-cultivated and over-sensitive to foreign opinion. They are generally men who undervalue the great fighting qualities, without which no nation can ever rise to the first rank.

The timidity of wealth is proverbial, and it was well illustrated by the attitude taken by too many people of means at the time of the Venezuela trouble.[1] Many of them, including bankers, merchants, and railway magnates, criticized the action of the President and the Senate, on the ground that it had caused business disturbance. Such a position is essentially ignoble. When a question of national honor or of national right or wrong, is at stake, no question of financial interest should be considered for a moment. Those wealthy men who wish the abandonment of the Monroe Doctrine because its assertion may damage their business, bring discredit to themselves, and, so far as they are able, discredit to the nation of which they are a part.

It is an evil thing for any man of education to forget that education should intensify patriotism, and that patriotism must not only be shown by striving to do good to the country from within, but by readiness to uphold its interests and honor, at any cost, when menaced from without. Educated men owe to the community the serious performance of this duty. We need not concern ourselves with the *emigré* educated man, the American who deliberately takes up his permanent abode abroad, whether in London or Paris; he is usually a man of weak character, unfitted to do good work either abroad or at home, who does what he can for his country by relieving it of

---

[1] A confrontation between the U.S. and Britain in 1895 over the Venezuela-British Guiana boundary—ED.

his presence. But the case is otherwise with the American who stays at home and tries to teach the youth of his country to disbelieve in the country's rights, as against other countries, and to regard it as the sign of an enlightened spirit to decry the assertion of those rights by force of arms. This man may be inefficient for good; but he is capable at times of doing harm, because he tends to make other people inefficient likewise. In our municipal politics there has long been evident a tendency to gather in one group the people who have no scruples, but who are very efficient, and in another group the amiable people who are not efficient at all. This is but one manifestation of the general and very unwholesome tendency among certain educated people to lose the power of doing efficient work as they acquire refinement. Of course in the long run a really good education will give not only refinement, but also an increase of power, and of capacity for efficient work. But the man who forgets that a real education must include the cultivation of the fighting virtues is sure to manifest this tendency to inefficiency. It is exhibited on a national scale by the educated men who take the anti-American side of international questions. There are exceptions to the rule; but as a rule the healthy man, resolute to do the rough work of the world, and capable of feeling his veins tingle with pride over the great deeds of the men of his own nation, will naturally take the American side of such a question as the Monroe Doctrine. Similarly the anæmic man of refinement and cultivation, whose intellect has been educated at the expense of his character, and who shrinks from all these struggles through which alone the world moves on to greatness, is inclined to consider any expression of the Monroe Doctrine as truculent and ill advised.

.   .   .   .

. . . No triumph of peace is quite so great as the supreme triumphs of war. The courage of the soldier, the courage of the statesman who has to meet storms which can be quelled only by soldierly qualities—this stands higher than any quality called out merely in time of peace. It is by no means necessary that we should have war to develop soldierly attributes and soldierly qualities; but if the peace we enjoy is of such a kind that it causes their loss, then it is far too dearly purchased, no matter what may be its attendant benefits. It may be that some time in the dim future of the race the need for war will vanish; but that time is yet ages distant. As yet no nation can hold its place in the world, or can do any work really worth doing, unless it stands ready to guard its rights with an armed hand. . . .

.   .   .   .

. . . It is very important that we should, as a race, keep the virile fighting qualities and should be ready to use them at need; but it is not at all important to use them unless there is need. . . .

.   .   .   .

. . . Every man among us is more fit to meet the duties and responsibilities of citizenship because of the perils over which, in the past, the nation has triumphed; because of the blood and sweat and tears, the labor and anguish, through which, in the days that have gone, our forefathers moved on to triumph. There are higher things in this life than the soft and easy enjoyment of material comfort. It is through strife, or the readiness for strife, that a nation must win greatness. We ask for a great navy, partly because we think that the possession of such a navy is the surest guaranty of peace, and partly because we feel that no national life is worth having if the nation is not willing, when the need shall arise, to stake everything on the supreme arbitrament of war, and to pour out its blood, its treasure, and its tears like water, rather than submit to the loss of honor and renown.

3.3:   Trade and Markets (1900)

If most Americans in 1898 felt Spain's brutality against the Cuban people and its apparent sabotage of the American battleship Maine [1] *in Havana harbor were ample justifications for war, the American business community, just pulling out of the mid-1890s depression, felt otherwise. War, many business leaders feared, would create further economic uncertainty. Yet America's quick victory over Spain changed the minds of many industrialists and bankers. Perhaps, they now felt, an emerging American empire would create new trade opportunities, especially in east Asia, and save the nation from market saturation at home. Particularly intriguing were the possibilities of the formerly Spanish-ruled Philippines, just a few hundred miles off the East Asian coast, which had fallen into American hands soon after the declaration of war.*

Albert Beveridge, a young Republican Senator from Indiana, was not a businessman, but he believed that the Philippines were a potentially valuable economic asset for America. In the following selection, Beveridge argues for retaining the islands rather than surrendering them or permitting them to become an independent country. What were the supposed economic advantages of retaining the Philippines? Has history shown Beveridge to be correct regarding the important commercial role of the Philippines? What other arguments for keeping the islands in American hands does he marshal? The senator seems uneasy about fitting colonies into the American constitutional system. Why would new colonies challenge American constitutional precedents?

---

[1] An American naval commission investigated the *Maine* disaster and concluded that the explosion came from outside the vessel's hull. Although the commission could not fix blame for the tragedy, most Americans assumed that a deliberately set Spanish mine was responsible.

Why We Must Keep the Philippines

ALBERT BEVERIDGE

Mr. President, I address the Senate at this time because Senators and Members of the House on both sides have asked that I give to Congress and the country my observations in the Philippines and the far East, and the conclusions which those observations compel. . . .

Mr. President, the times call for candor. The Philippines are ours forever, "territory belonging to the United States," as the Constitution calls them. And just beyond the Philippines are China's illimitable markets. We will not retreat from either. We will not repudiate our duty in the archipelago. We will not abandon our opportunity in the Orient. We will not renounce our part in the mission of our race, trustee, under God, of the civilization of the world. And we will move forward to our work, not howling out regrets like slaves whipped to their burdens, but with gratitude for a task worthy of our strength, and thanksgiving to Almighty God that He has marked us as His chosen people, henceforth to lead in the regeneration of the world.

This island empire is the last land left in all the oceans. If it should prove a mistake to abandon it, the blunder once made would be irretrievable. If it proves a mistake to hold it, the error can be corrected when we will. Every other progressive nation stands ready to relieve us.

But to hold it will be no mistake. Our largest trade henceforth must be with Asia. The Pacific is our ocean. More and more Europe will manufacture the most it needs, secure from its colonies the most it consumes. Where shall we turn for consumers of our surplus"? Geography answers the question. China is our natural customer. She is nearer to us than to England, Germany, or Russia, the commercial powers of the present and the future. They have moved nearer to China by securing permanent bases on her borders. The Philippines give us a base at the door of all the East.

Lines of navigation from our ports to the Orient and Australia; from the Isthmian Canal to Asia; from all Oriental ports to Australia, converge at and separate from the Philippines. They are a self-supporting, dividend-paying fleet, permanently anchored at a spot selected by the strategy of Providence, commanding the Pacific. And the Pacific is the ocean of the commerce of the future. Most future wars will be conflicts for commerce. The power that rules the Pacific, therefore, is the power that rules the world. And, with the Philippines, that power is and will forever be the American Republic. . . .

Nothing is so natural as trade with one's neighbors. The Philippines make us the nearest neighbors of all the East. Nothing is more natural than to trade with those you know. This is the philosophy of all advertising. The Philippines bring us permanently face to face with the most sought-for cus-

Congressional Globe, 56th Cong., 1st sess., 1900, 33, pt. O: 704–712.

tomers of the world. National prestige, national propinquity, these and commercial activity are the elements of commercial success. The Philippines give the first; the character of the American people supply the last. It is a providential conjunction of all the elements of trade, of duty, and of power. If we are willing to go to war rather than let England have a few feet of frozen Alaska, which affords no market and commands none, what should we not do rather than let England, Germany, Russia, or Japan have all the Philippines? And no man on the spot can fail to see that this would be their fate if we retired. . . .

Here, then, Senators, is the situation. Two years ago there was no land in all the world which we could occupy for any purpose. Our commerce was daily turning toward the Orient, and geography and trade developments made necessary our commercial empire over the Pacific. And in that ocean we had no commercial, naval, or military base. To-day we have one of the three great ocean possessions of the globe, located at the most commanding commercial, naval, and military points in the eastern seas, within hail of India, shoulder to shoulder with China, richer in its own resources than any equal body of land on the entire globe, and peopled by a race which civilization demands shall be improved. Shall we abandon it? That man little knows the common people of the Republic, little understands the instincts of our race, who thinks we will not hold it fast and hold it forever, administering just government by simplest methods. We may trick up devices to shift our burden and lessen our opportunity; they will avail us nothing but delay. We may tangle conditions by applying academic arrangements of self-government to a crude situation; their failure will drive us to our duty in the end. . . .

But, Senators, it would be better to abandon this combined garden and Gibraltar of the Pacific, and count our blood and treasure already spent a profitable loss, than to apply any academic arrangement of self-government to these children. They are not capable of self-government. How could they be? They are not of a self-governing race. They are Orientals, Malays, instructed by Spaniards in the latter's worst estate.

They know nothing of practical government except as they have witnessed the weak, corrupt, cruel, and capricious rule of Spain. What magic will anyone employ to dissolve in their minds and characters those impressions of governors and governed which three centuries of misrule has created? What alchemy will change the oriental quality of their blood and set the self-governing currents of the American pouring through their Malay veins? How shall they, in the twinkling of an eye, be exalted to the heights of self-governing peoples which required a thousand years for us to reach, Anglo-Saxon though we are? . . .

Mr. President, self-government and internal development have been the dominant notes of our first century; administration and the development of other lands will be the dominant notes of our second century. And administration is as high and holy a function as self-government, just as the care of a trust estate is as sacred an obligation as the management of our own concerns. Cain was the first to violate the divine law of human society which makes of us our brother's keeper. And administration of good government is the first lesson in self-government, that exalted estate toward which all civilization tends. . . .

The Declaration of Independence does not forbid us to do our part in the regeneration of the world. If it did, the Declaration would be wrong, just as the Articles of Confederation, drafted by the very same men who signed the Declaration, was found to be wrong. The Declaration has no application to the present situation. It was written by self-governing men for self-governing men. . . .

Senators in opposition are estopped from denying our constitutional power to govern the Philippines as circumstances may demand, for such power is admitted in the case of Florida, Louisiana, Alaska. How, then, is it denied in the Philippines? Is there a geographical interpretation to the Constitution? Do degrees of longitude fix constitutional limitations? Does a thousand miles of ocean diminish constitutional power more than a thousand miles of land? . . .

No; the oceans are not limitations of the power which the Constitution expressly gives Congress to govern all territory the nation may acquire. The Constitution declares that "Congress shall have power to dispose of and make all needful rules and regulations respecting the territory belonging to the United States." Not the Northwest Territory only; not Louisiana or Florida only; not territory on this continent only, but any territory anywhere belonging to the nation. The founders of the nation were not provincial. Theirs was the geography of the world. They were soldiers as well as landsmen, and they knew that where our ships should go our flag might follow. They had the logic of progress, and they knew that the Republic they were planting must, in obedience to the laws of our expanding race, necessarily develop into the greater Republic which the world beholds to-day, and into the still mightier Republic which the world will finally acknowledge as the arbiter, under God, of the destinies of mankind. And so our fathers wrote into the Constitution these words of growth, of expansion, of empire, if you will, unlimited by geography or climate or by anything but the vitality and possibilities of the American people: "Congress shall have power to dispose of and make all needful rules and regulations respecting the territory belonging to the United States. . . . "

Mr. President, this question is deeper than any question of party politics; deeper than any question of the isolated policy of our country even; deeper even than any question of constitutional power. It is elemental. It is racial. God has not been preparing the English-speaking and Teutonic peoples for a thousand years for nothing but vain and idle self-contemplation and self-admiration. No! He has made us the master organizers of the world to establish system where chaos reigns. He has given us the spirit of progress to overwhelm the forces of reaction throughout the earth. He has made us adepts in government that we may administer government among savage and senile peoples. Were it not for such a force as this the world would relapse into barbarism and night. And of all our race He has marked the American people as His chosen nation to finally lead in the regeneration of the world. This is the divine mission of America, and it holds for us all the profit, all the glory, all the happiness possible to man. We are trustees of the world's progress, guardians of its righteous peace. The judgment of the Master is upon us: "Ye have been faithful over a few things; I will make you ruler over many things."

What shall history say of us? Shall it say that we renounced that holy trust, left the savage to his base condition, the wilderness to the reign of waste, deserted duty, abandoned glory, forget our sordid profit even, because we feared our strength and read the charter of our powers with the doubter's eye and the quibbler's mind? Shall it say that, called by events to captain and command the proudest, ablest, purest race of history in history's noblest work, we declined that great commission? Our fathers would not have had it so. No! They founded no paralytic government, incapable of the simplest acts of administration. They planted no sluggard people, passive while the world's work calls them. They established no reactionary nation. They unfurled no retreating flag. . . .

Blind indeed is he who sees not the hand of God in events so vast, so harmonious, so benign. Reactionary indeed is the mind that perceives not that this vital people is the strongest of the saving forces of the world; that our place, therefore, is at the head of the constructing and redeeming nations of the earth; and that to stand aside while events march on is a surrender of our interests, a betrayal of our duty as blind as it is base. Craven indeed is the heart that fears to perform a work so golden and so noble; that dares not win a glory so immortal. . . .

Mr. President and Senators, adopt the resolution offered, that peace may quickly come and that we may begin our saving, regenerating, and uplifting work. . . . Reject it, and the world, history, and the American people will know where to forever fix the awful responsibility for the consequences that will surely follow such failure to do our manifest duty. How dare we delay when our soldiers' blood is flowing? [Applause in the galleries].

3.4: The Anti-Imperialists (1899)

Most Americans undoubtedly supported the decision to go to war with Spain in 1898. But what transpired in the Philippines after the American occupation did not seem very different from Spanish rule in Cuba. The Filipinos quickly came to resent the American presence and rose up against the new oppressor. For two years Americans and Filipinos fought a nasty and brutal guerrilla war to determine the islands' fate. In the end American troops put down the Filipino fighters and imposed

U.S. rule on the archipelago. But the Philippine Insurrection made a mockery of benevolent American claims.

Many Americans strongly opposed their nation's role in the Philippines, and in November 1898 a group of reformers, journalists, academics, clergy, business leaders, and maverick politicians formed the Anti-Imperialist League to resist the colonialist drift. The League initially campaigned to defeat the annexation of the Philippines. Once the annexation treaty was ratified, however, it turned its efforts against the cruel war to subdue the Filipinos. The following selection is the platform adopted by the Anti-Imperialist League in 1899.

What is the League leaders' intellectual strategy in appealing to the American people? Is their statement effective propaganda? Do you know whether views such as theirs influenced the way Americans responded to the Filipinos? What future course did Filipino-American relations take? What are those relations like now?

We Must Perfect Imperialism

ANTI-IMPERIALIST LEAGUE

We hold that the policy known as imperialism is hostile to liberty and tends toward militarism, an evil from which it has been our glory to be free. We regret that it has become necessary in the land of Washington and Lincoln to reaffirm that all men, of whatever race or color, are entitled to life, liberty, and the pursuit of happiness. We maintain that governments derive their just powers from the consent of the governed. We insist that the subjugation of any people is "criminal aggression" and open disloyalty to the distinctive principles of our government.

We earnestly condemn the policy of the present National Administration in the Philippines. It seeks to extinguish the spirit of 1776 in those islands. We deplore the sacrifice of our soldiers and sailors, whose bravery deserves admiration even in an unjust war. We denounce the slaughter of the Filipinos as a needless horror. We protest against the extension of American sovereignty by Spanish methods.

We demand the immediate cessation of the war against liberty, begun by Spain and continued by us. We urge that Congress be promptly convened to announce to the Filipinos our purpose to concede to them the independence for which they have so long fought and which of right is theirs.

The United States have always protested against the doctrine of international law which permits the subjugation of the weak by the strong. A self-governing state cannot accept sovereignty over an unwilling people. The

The text of the platform is included in Carl Schurz, "The Policy of Imperialism." In Frederic Bancroft, ed. *Speeches, Correspondence, and Political Papers of Carl Schurz* (New York: G. P. Putnam's Sons, 1913), pp. 77–79.

United States cannot act upon the ancient heresy that might makes right.

Imperialists assume that with the destruction of self-government in the Philippines by American hands, all opposition here will cease. This is a grievous error. Much as we abhor the war of "criminal aggression" in the Philippines, greatly as we regret the blood of the Filipinos is on American hands, we more deeply resent the betrayal of American institutions at home. The real firing line is not in the suburbs of Manila. The foe is of our own household. The attempt of 1861 was to divide the country. That of 1899 is to destroy its fundamental principles and noblest ideals.

Whether the ruthless slaughter of the Filipinos shall end next month or next year is but an incident in a contest that must go on until the Declaration of Independence and the Constitution of the United States are rescued from the hands of their betrayers. Those who dispute about standards of value while the Republic is undermined will be listened to as little as those who would wrangle about the small economies of the household while the house is on fire. The training of a great people for a century, the aspiration for liberty of a vast immigration are forces that will hurl aside those who in the delirium of conquest seek to destroy the character of our institutions.

We deny that the obligation of all citizens to support their Government in times of grave National peril applies to the present situation. If an Administration may with impunity ignore the issues upon which it was chosen, deliberately create a condition of war anywhere on the face of the globe, debauch the civil service for spoils to promote the adventure, organize a truth-suppressing censorship and demand of all citizens a suspension of judgment and their unanimous support while it chooses to continue the fighting, representative government itself is imperiled.

We propose to contribute to the defeat of any person or party that stands for the forcible subjugation of any people. We shall oppose for reelection all who in the White House or in Congress betray American liberty in pursuit of un-American gains. We still hope that both of our great political parties will support and defend the Declaration of Independence in the closing campaign of the century.

We hold, with Abraham Lincoln, that "no man is good enough to govern another man without that man's consent. When the white man governs himself, that is self-government, but when he governs himself and also governs another man, that is more than self-government—that is despotism." "Our reliance is in the love of liberty which God has planted in us. Our defense is in the spirit which prizes liberty as the heritage of all men in all lands. Those who deny freedom to others deserve it not for themselves, and under a just God cannot long retain it."

We cordially invite the cooperation of all men and women who remain loyal to the Declaration of Independence and the Constitution of the United States.

4

The Progressive Impulse

During the first two decades of the twentieth century, as the country shifted from rural to urban, its political structure also altered. More prosperous than ever, many Americans nevertheless felt uneasy over the rapid economic and social changes taking place. Their discomfort with the unfamiliar spawned a many-sided reform movement we call Progressivism.

Progressivism has long been a puzzle to scholars. Its shape seems fuzzy and changing, including within its boundaries a wide range of views, programs, and personnel. Its origins too seem unclear. Who favored reform during the early twentieth century? Were they the same people who had supported Populist political insurgency during the 1890s? And why did the movement appear when it did?

The selections below represent different and often competing aspects of Progressive thought. As you read these, you might consider whether there is a single thread connecting all of them, or whether Progressivism is just a convenient name for a grab bag of reformist demands that fortuitously surfaced together in the decade preceding World War I.

4.1: The Danger of Concentrated Wealth (1912, 1913)

The wave of business combinations formed between 1898 and 1903 was a response to the single national market that emerged following completion of the transportation and communications network. Deprived of

local monopoly power and forced into cutthroat competition with aggres-
sive distant firms, business leaders sought to consolidate their operations.
In the six-year period straddling the turn of the century, there were 234
industrial mergers representing some $6 billion in capital.

The merger movement dismayed the public. How could small produc-
ers survive in an era of huge trusts? How severely would consumers be
hurt by price fixing when competition waned? How could representative
government fend off giant business firms when they sought favors?

The four selections below reflect various views of business consolida-
tion. The first two, by Theodore Roosevelt and Woodrow Wilson, repre-
sent different Progressive responses. The third, by the J. P. Morgan firm,
is the reply of the leading American investment bankers to the conclu-
sions of the Pujo Committee, a subcommittee of the House of
Representatives that, in its report of 1913, had declared that financial
power was dangerously concentrated in the hands of a small number of
northeastern banks. The last selection is by another Progressive, Walter
Weyl, who emphasizes the dangers to consumers from the monopoly power
of big business.

As you read the Roosevelt and Wilson pieces, consider the differences
in approach of the two political leaders, who were both within the
Progressive orbit. Do they have identical attitudes toward concentrated
business power? How are their prescriptions for cure related to their long-
term party allegiances? Has the passage of eighty years since the speeches
were delivered demonstrated which of the formulas for dealing with con-
centrated economic power is more effective in protecting the public inter-
est? As for the remarks of J. P. Morgan, should we reject his position out
of hand? He was, after all, the chief target of the Pujo investigators.

The selection by Progressive journalist Walter Weyl is especially inter-
esting. We know that a consumer movement first appeared during the
Progressive Era. Two important measures—the Pure Food and Drug Act
and the Meat Inspection Act (both passed in 1906)—attest to the
Progressives' concern for consumer welfare. But Weyl makes a larger
point than the mere need for consumer protection measures, for he sees
consumer concerns as the common thread that bound diverse Progressives
and distinguished them from their Populist predecessors. How might con-
sumer concerns have united various reform groups during these years?
What other aspects of the Progressive program besides the 1906 measures
had consumer relevance? According to Weyl, what other element in the
American economy, in addition to big business, threatened consumer
interests? Is his analysis valid?

Republican Anti-Trust

THEODORE ROOSEVELT

Again and again while I was President, from 1902 to 1908, I pointed out that under the anti-trust law[1] alone it was neither possible to put a stop to business abuses nor possible to secure the highest efficiency in the service rendered by business to the general public. The anti-trust law must be kept on our statute books, and, as hereafter shown, must be rendered more effective in the cases where it is applied. But to treat the anti-trust law as an adequate, or as by itself a wise, measure of relief and betterment is a sign not of progress, but of Toryism and reaction. It has been of benefit so far as it has implied the recognition of a real and great evil, and the at least sporadic application of the principle that all men alike must obey the law. But as a sole remedy, universally applicable, it has in actual practice completely broken down; as now applied it works more mischief than benefit. It represents the waste of effort—always damaging to a community—which arises from the attempt to meet new conditions by the application of outworn remedies instead of fearlessly and in common-sense fashion facing the new conditions and devising the new remedies which alone can work effectively for good.

The anti-trust law, if interpreted as the Baltimore platform[2] demands it shall be interpreted, would apply to every agency by which not merely industrial but agricultural business is carried on in this country; under such an interpretation it ought in theory to be applied universally, in which case practically all industries would stop; as a matter of fact, it is utterly out of the question to enforce it universally, and, when enforced sporadically, it causes continual unrest, puts the country at a disadvantage with its trade competitors in international commerce, hopelessly puzzles honest business men and honest farmers as to what their rights are, and yet, as has just been shown in the cases of the Standard Oil and the Tobacco Trusts, it is no real check on the great trusts at which it was in theory aimed, and, indeed, operates to their benefit. Moreover, if we are to compete with other nations in the markets of the world as well as to develop our own material civilization at home, we must utilize those forms of industrial organization that are indispensable to the highest industrial productivity and efficiency.

An important volume entitled "Concentration and Control" has just been issued by President Charles R. Van Hise of the University of Wisconsin. The University of Wisconsin has been more influential than any other agency in making Wisconsin what it has become, a laboratory for wise social and indus-

New York Times, August 7, 1912.

[1] The Sherman Anti-Trust Act of 1890, which sought to outlaw "every contract, combination . . . , or conspiracy in restraint of trade or commerce"—ED.

[2] The platform that the Democratic Party adopted in Baltimore in June 1912—ED.

trial experiment in the betterment of conditions. President Van Hise is one of those thoroughgoing but sane and intelligent radicals from whom much of leadership is to be expected in such a matter. The sub-title of his book shows that his endeavor is to turn the attention of his countrymen toward practically solving the trust problem of the United States.

In his preface he states that his aim is to suggest a way to gain the economic advantages of the concentration of industry and at the same time to guard the interests of the public and to assist in the rule of enlightenment, reason, fair play, mutual consideration, and toleration. In sum, he shows that unrestrained competition as an economic principle has become too destructive to be permitted to exist, and that the small men must be allowed to co-operate under penalty of succumbing before their big competitors; and yet such co-operation, vitally necessary to the small man, is criminal under the present law. He says:

> With the alternative before the business men of co-operation or failure, we may be sure that they will co-operate. Since the law is violated by practically every group of men engaged in trade from one end of the country to the other, they do not feel that in combining they are doing a moral wrong. The selection of the individual or corporation for prosecution depends upon the arbitrary choice of the Attorney General, perhaps somewhat influenced by the odium which attaches to some of the violators of the law. They all take their chance, hoping that the blow will fall elsewhere. With general violation and sporadic enforcement of an impracticable law, we cannot hope that our people will gain respect for it.
>
> In conclusion, there is presented as the solution of the difficulties of the present industrial situation, concentration, co-operation, and control. Through concentration we may have the economic advantages coming from magnitude of operations. Through co-operation we may limit the wastes of the competitive system. Through control by commission we may secure freedom for fair competition, elimination of unfair practices, conservation of our natural resources, fair wages, good social conditions, and reasonable prices.
>
> Concentration and co-operation in industry in order to secure efficiency are a world-wide movement. The United States cannot resist it. If we isolate ourselves and insist upon the subdivision of industry below the highest economic efficiency, and do not allow co-operation, we shall be defeated in the world's markets. We cannot adopt an economic system less efficient than our great competitors, Germany, England, France, and Austria. Either we must modify our present obsolete laws regarding concentration and co-operation so as to conform with the world movement, or else fall behind in the race for the world's markets. Concentration and co-operation are conditions imperatively essential for industrial advance; but if we allow concentration and co-operation there must be control in order to protect the people, and adequate control is only possible through the administrative commission. Hence concentration, co-operation, and control are the keywords for a scientific solution of the mighty industrial problem which now confronts this Nation. . . .

We Progressives stand for the rights of the people. When these rights can best be secured by insistence upon States' rights, then we are for States' rights; when they can best be secured by insistence upon National rights, then we are for National rights. Inter-State commerce can be effectively controlled only by the Nation. The States cannot control it under the Constitution, and to amend the Constitution by giving them control of it would amount to a dissolution of the Government. The worst of the big trusts have always endeavored to keep alive the feeling in favor of having the States themselves, and not the Nation, attempt to do this work, because they know that in the long run such effort would be ineffective. There is no surer way to prevent all successful effort to deal with the trusts than to insist that they be dealt with by the States rather than by the Nation, or to create a conflict between the States and the Nation on the subject. The well-meaning ignorant man who advances such a proposition does as much damage as if he were hired by the trusts themselves, for he is playing the game of every big crooked corporation in the country. The only effective way in which to regulate the trusts is through the exercise of the collective power of our people as a whole through the Governmental agencies established by the Constitution for this very purpose.

Grave injustice is done by the Congress when it fails to give the National Government complete power in this matter; and still graver injustice by the Federal courts when they endeavor in any way to pare down the right of the people collectively to act in this matter as they deem wise; such conduct does itself tend to cause the creation of a twilight zone in which neither the Nation nor the States have power. Fortunately, the Federal courts have more and more of recent years tended to adopt the true doctrine, which is that all these matters are to be settled by the people themselves, and that the conscience of the people, and not the preferences of any servants of the people, is to be the standard in deciding what action shall be taken by the people. As Lincoln phrased it: "The [question] of National power and State rights as a principle is no other than the principle of generality and locality. Whatever concerns the whole should be confided to the whole—to the General Government; while whatever concerns only the State should be left exclusively to the State."

It is utterly hopeless to attempt to control the trusts merely by the anti-trust law, or by any law the same in principle, no matter what the modifications may be in detail. In the first place, these great corporations cannot possibly be controlled merely by a succession of lawsuits. The administrative branch of the Government must exercise such control. The preposterous failure of the Commerce Court has shown that only damage comes from the effort to substitute judicial for administrative control of great corporations. In the next place, a loosely drawn law which promises to do everything would reduce business to complete ruin if it were not also so drawn as to accomplish almost nothing. . . .

Contrast what has actually been accomplished under the inter-State commerce law with what has actually been accomplished under the anti-trust law. The first has, on the whole, worked in a highly efficient manner and achieved real and great results; and it promises to achieve even greater results, (although I firmly believe that if the power of the Commissioners grows greater it will be necessary to make them and their superior, the

President, even more completely responsible to the people for their acts). The second has occasionally done good, has usually accomplished nothing, but generally left the worst conditions wholly unchanged, and has been responsible for a considerable amount of downright and positive evil.

What is needed is the application to all industrial concerns and all co-operating interests engaged in inter-State commerce in which there is either monopoly or control of the market of the principles on which we have gone in regulating transportation concerns engaged in such commerce. The anti-trust law should be kept on the statute books and strengthened so as to make it genuinely and thoroughly effective against every big concern tending to monopoly or guilty of anti-social practices.

At the same time, a National industrial commission should be created which should have complete power to regulate and control all the great industrial concerns engaged in inter-State business—which practically means all of them in this country. This commission should exercise over these industrial concerns like powers to those exercised over the railways by the Inter-State Commerce Commission, and over the National banks by the Controller of the Currency, and additional powers if found necessary. The establishment of such a commission would enable us to punish the individual rather than merely the corporation, just as we now do with banks, where the aim of the Government is not to close the bank but to bring to justice personally any bank official who has gone wrong.

This commission should deal with all the abuses of the trusts—all the abuses such as those developed by the Government suit against the Standard Oil and Tobacco Trusts—as the Inter-State Commerce Commission now deals with rebates. It should have complete power to make the capitalization absolutely honest and put a stop to all stock watering. Such supervision over the issuance of corporate securities would put a stop to exploitation of the people by dishonest capitalists desiring to declare dividends on watered securities, and would open this kind of industrial property to ownership by the people at large. It should have free access to the books of each corporation and power to find out exactly how it treats its employees, its rivals, and the general public. It should have power to compel the unsparing publicity of all the acts of any corporation which goes wrong.

The regulation should be primarily under the administrative branch of the Government and not by lawsuit. It should prohibit and effectually punish monopoly achieved through wrong, and also actual wrongs done by industrial corporations which are not monopolies, such as the artificial raising of prices, the artificial restriction on productivity, the elimination of competition by unfair or predatory practices, and the like; leaving industrial organizations free within the limits of fair and honest dealing to promote through the inherent efficiency of organization the power of the United States as a competitive Nation among Nations, and the greater abundance at home that will come to our people from that power wisely exercised.

Democratic Anti-Trust

WOODROW WILSON

A trust is formed in this way: a few gentlemen "promote" it—that is to say, they get it up, being given enormous fees for their kindness, which fees are loaded on to the undertaking in the form of securities of one kind or another. The argument of the promoters is, not that every one who comes into the combination can carry on his business more efficiently than he did before; the argument is: we will assign to you as your share in the pool twice, three times, four times, or five times what you could have sold your business for to an individual competitor who would have to run it on an economic and competitive basis. We can afford to buy it at such a figure because we are shutting out competition. We can afford to make the stock of the combination half a dozen times what it naturally would be and pay dividends on it, because there will be nobody to dispute the prices we shall fix.

Talk of that as sound business? Talk of that as inevitable? It is based upon nothing except power. It is not based upon efficiency. It is no wonder that the big trusts are not prospering in proportion to such competitors as they still have in such parts of their business as competitors have access to; they are prospering freely only in those fields to which competition has no access. Read the statistics of the Steel Trust, if you don't believe it. Read the statistics of any trust. They are constantly nervous about competition, and they are constantly buying up new competitors in order to narrow the field. The United States Steel Corporation is gaining in its supremacy in the American market only with regard to the cruder manufactures of iron and steel, but wherever, as in the field of more advanced manufactures of iron and steel, it has important competitors, its portion of the product is not increasing, but is decreasing, and its competitors, where they have a foothold, are often more efficient than it is.

Why? Why, with unlimited capital and innumerable mines and plants everywhere in the United States, can't they beat the other fellows in the market? Partly because they are carrying too much. Partly because they are unwieldy. Their organization is imperfect. They bought up inefficient plants along with efficient, and they have got to carry what they have paid for, even if they have to shut some of the plants up in order to make any interest on their investments; or, rather, not interest on their investments, because that is an incorrect word,—on their alleged capitalization. Here we have a lot of giants staggering along under an almost intolerable weight of artificial burdens, which they have put on their own backs, and constantly looking about lest some little pigmy with a round stone in a sling may come out and slay them.

Woodrow Wilson, *The New Freedom* (New York: Doubleday, Page and Company, 1913), pp. 167–175, 176–177, 179–181.

For my part, I want the pigmy to have a chance to come out. And I foresee a time when the pigmies will be so much more athletic, so much more astute, so much more active, than the giants, that it will be a case of Jack the giant-killer. Just let some of the youngsters I know have a chance and they'll give these gentlemen points. Lend them a little money. They can't get any now. See to it that when they have got a local market they can't be squeezed out of it. . . . For I'll undertake to put a water-logged giant out of business any time, if you will give me a fair field and as much credit as I am entitled to, and let the law do what from time immemorial law has been expected to do,—see fair play. . . .

I take my stand absolutely, where every Progressive ought to take his stand, on the proposition that private monopoly is indefensible and intolerable. And there I will fight my battle. And I know how to fight it. Everybody who has even read the newspapers knows the means by which these men built up their power and created these monopolies. Any decently equipped lawyer can suggest to you statutes by which the whole business can be stopped. What these gentlemen do not want is this: they do not want to be compelled to meet all comers on equal terms. I am perfectly willing that they should beat any competitor by fair means; but I know the foul means they have adopted, and I know that they can be stopped by law. If they think that coming into the market upon the basis of mere efficiency, upon the mere basis of knowing how to manufacture goods better than anybody else and to sell them cheaper than anybody else, they can carry the immense amount of water that they have put into their enterprises in order to buy up rivals, then they are perfectly welcome to try it. But there must be no squeezing out of the beginner, no crippling his credit; no discrimination against retailers who buy from a rival; no threats against concerns who sell supplies to a rival; no holding back of raw material from him; no secret arrangements against him. All the fair competition you choose, but no unfair competition of any kind. And then when unfair competition is eliminated, let us see these gentlemen carry their tanks of water on their backs. All that I ask and all I shall fight for is that they shall come into the field against merit and brains everywhere. If they can beat other American brains, then they have got the best brains.

But if you want to know how far brains go, as things now are, suppose you try to match your better wares against these gentlemen, and see them undersell you before your market is any bigger than the locality and make it absolutely impossible for you to get a fast foothold. If you want to know how brains count, originate some invention which will improve the kind of machinery they are using, and then see if you can borrow enough money to manufacture it. You may be offered something for your patent by the corporation,—which will perhaps lock it up in a safe and go on using the old machinery; but you will not be allowed to manufacture. I know men who have tried it, and they could not get the money, because the great money lenders of this country are in the arrangement with the great manufacturers of this country, and they do not propose to see their control of the market interfered with by outsiders. And who are outsiders? Why, all the rest of the people of the United States are outsiders.

They are rapidly making us outsiders with respect even of the things that come from the bosom of the earth, and which belong to us in a peculiar sense. Certain monopolies in this country have gained almost complete control of the raw material, chiefly in the mines, out of which the great body of manufactures are carried on, and they now discriminate, when they will, in the sale of that raw material between those who are rivals of the monopoly and those who submit to the monopoly. We must soon come to the point where we shall say to the men who own these essentials of industry that they have got to part with these essentials by sale to all citizens of the United States with the same readiness and upon the same terms. Or else we shall tie up the resources of this country under private control in such fashion as will make our independent development absolutely impossible.

There is another injustice that monopoly engages in. The trust that deals in the cruder products which are to be transformed into the more elaborate manufactures often will not sell these crude products except upon the terms of monopoly—that is to say, the people that deal with them must buy exclusively from them. And so again you have the lines of development tied up and the connections of development knotted and fastened so that you cannot wrench them apart.

Again, the manufacturing monopolies are so interlaced in their personal relationships with the great shipping interests of this country, and with the great railroads, that they can often largely determine the rates of shipment. . . .

And when you reflect that the twenty-four men who control the United States Steel Corporation, for example, are either presidents or vice-presidents or directors in 55 per cent of the railways of the United States, reckoning by the valuation of those railroads and the amount of their stock and bonds, you know just how close the whole thing is knitted together in our industrial system, and how great the temptation is. These twenty-four gentlemen administer that corporation as if it belonged to them. The amazing thing to me is that the people of the United States have not seen that the administration of a great business like that is not a private affair; it is a public affair. . . .

The big trusts, the big combinations, are the most wasteful, the most uneconomical, and, after they pass a certain size, the most inefficient, way of conducting the industries of this country.

A notable example is the way in which Mr. Carnegie was bought out of the steel business. Mr. Carnegie could build better mills and make better steel rails and make them cheaper than anybody else connected with what afterward became the United States Steel Corporation. They didn't dare leave him outside. He had so much more brains in finding out the best processes; he had so much more shrewdness in surrounding himself with the most successful assistants; he knew so well when a young man who came into his employ was fit for promotion and was ripe to put at the head of some branch of his business and was sure to make good, that he could undersell every mother's son of them in the market for steel rails. And they bought him out at a price that amounted to three or four times,—I believe actually five times,—the estimated value of his properties and of his business, because they couldn't beat him in competition. And then in what they charged afterward for their product,—the product of his mills included,— they made us pay the interest on the four or five times the difference.

That is the difference between a big business and a trust. A trust is an arrangement to get rid of competition, and a big business is a business that has survived competition by conquering in the field of intelligence and economy. A trust does not bring efficiency to the aid of business; it *buys efficiency out of business*. I am for big business, and I am against the trusts. Any man who can survive by his brains, any man who can put the others out of the business by making the thing cheaper to the consumer at the same time that he is increasing its intrinsic value and quality, I take off my hat to, and I say: "You are the man who can build up the United States, and I wish there were more of you." . . .

Shall we try to get the grip of monopoly away from our lives, or shall we not? Shall we withhold our hand and say monopoly is inevitable, that all that we can do is to regulate it? Shall we say that all that we can do is to put government in competition with monopoly and try its strength against it? Shall we admit that the creature of our own hands is stronger than we are? We have been dreading all along the time when the combined power of high finance would be greater than the power of the government. Have we come to a time when the President of the United States or any man who wishes to be the President must doff his cap in the presence of this high finance, and say, "You are our inevitable master, but we will see how we can make the best of it?"

We are at the parting of the ways. We have, not one or two or three, but many, established and formidable monopolies in the United States. We have, not one or two, but many, fields of endeavor into which it is difficult, if not impossible, for the independent man to enter. We have restricted credit, we have restricted opportunity, we have controlled development, and we have come to be one of the worst ruled, one of the most completely controlled and dominated, governments in the civilized world—no longer a government by free opinion, no longer a government by conviction and the vote of the majority, but a government by the opinion and the duress of small groups of dominant men.

If the government is to tell big business men how to run their business, then don't you see that big business men have to get closer to the government even than they are now? Don't you see that they must capture the government, in order not to be restrained too much by it? Must capture the government? They have already captured it. Are you going to invite those inside to stay inside? They don't have to get there. They are there. Are you going to own your own premises, or are you not? That is your choice. Are you going to say: "You didn't get into the house the right way, but you are in there, God bless you; we will stand out here in the cold and you can hand us out something once in a while"?

At the least, under the plan I am opposing, there will be an avowed partnership between the government and the trusts. I take it that the firm will be ostensibly controlled by the senior member. For I take it that the government of the United States is at least the senior member, though the younger member has all along been running the business. But when all the momentum, when all the energy, when a great deal of the genius, as so often happens in partnerships the world over, is with the junior partner, I don't think that the superintendence of the senior partner is going to amount to very much. And I don't believe that benevolence can be read into the hearts of the trusts by the superintendence and suggestions of the federal government; because the government has never within my recollection had its suggestions accepted by the trusts. On the contrary, the suggestions of the trusts have been accepted by the government.

There is no hope to be seen for the people of the United States until the partnership is dissolved. And the business of the party now entrusted with power is going to be to dissolve it.

The "Monopolists" Respond

J. P. MORGAN AND COMPANY

To Honorable A. P. Pujo, Chairman,
Committee on Banking and Currency
House of Representatives,
Washington, D.C.

Dear Sir:

You have invited us to supplement the recent inquiry of your committee by presenting "such considerations as may occur to you (us) bearing upon the question of concentration and control of money and credit." . . .

We would suggest, . . . with the utmost respect, that a large part of the valuable time of your Committee, in our belief, has been consumed in an endeavor to piece out a certain theory as to money and credit, which theory it will be impossible ever to demonstrate; for its establishment is, and always will be, prevented by economic laws which have operated ever since the beginnings of barter and trade.

We suggest to you that such ills—and they are neither few nor trifling—as are existent in this country's financial affairs are the outcome of a clumsy and outworn banking system rather than of the schemes of men; and that to eradicate such ills at their source, there is needed not legislation upon some

Letter from Messrs. J. P. Morgan and Company (New York: privately printed, February 25, 1913), pp. 1–13 *passim.*

one or more isolated symptoms, but rather a careful diagnosis of our whole banking system; a study of the successful system of other countries which for decades have been free from periodic panics which have distressed this country; and finally cooperation among all committees in Congress which consider this subject to the one end of wise and comprehensive—as contrasted with piecemeal—legislation. . . . such "concentration" as has taken place in New York and other financial centres has been due, not to the purposes and activities of men, but primarily to the operation of our antiquated banking system which automatically compels interior banks to concentrate in New York City hundreds of millions of reserve funds; and next, to economic laws which in every country create some one city as the great financial centre, and which draw to it, in enormous volume, investment funds for the development of industrial enterprises throughout the country. . . .

We lay especial stress upon this point of economic rule, for the reason that not only the Resolution (H. Res. 504) under which your Committee acts, but many questions to witnesses, indicated a belief that for their own selfish ends certain men, or a group of them, have succeeded in transcending the laws of supply and demand (which operate all over the world) and in establishing new economic laws. . . .

If any one man, or group of men had the ability and resources—which they do not—to withhold credits in any one market like New York, the situation would ordinarily be promptly relieved by the automatic inflow of credits from some altogether foreign source. . . .

For the maintenance of such an impossible economic theory there have been spread before your Committee elaborate tables of so-called interlocking directorates from which exceedingly mistaken inferences have been publicly drawn. In these tables it is shown that 180 bankers and bank directors serve upon the boards of corporations having resources aggregating twenty-five billion dollars, and it is implied that this vast aggregate of the country's wealth is at the disposal of these 180 men. But such an implication rests solely upon the untenable theory that these men, living in different parts of the country, in many cases personally unacquainted with each other, and in most cases associated only in occasional transactions, vote always for the same policies and control with united purpose the directorates of the 132 corporations on which they serve. The testimony failed to establish any concerted policy or harmony of action binding these 180 men together, and as a matter of fact no such policy exists. The absurdity of the assumption of such control becomes more apparent when one considers that on the average these directors represent only one quarter of the memberships of their boards. It is preposterous to suppose that every "interlocking" director has full control in every organization with which he is connected, and that the majority of directors who are not "interlocking" are mere figureheads, subject to the will of a small minority of their boards. . . .

Such growth in the size of banks in New York and Chicago has frequently been erroneously designated before your Committee as "concentration," whereas we have hitherto pointed out the growth of banking resources in New York City has been less rapid than that of the rest of the country. But increase of capital and merger of two or more banks into one institution (with the same resources as the aggregate of the banks merging into it) has [sic] been frequent, especially since January 1, 1908.

These mergers, however, are a development due simply to the demand for larger banking facilities to care for the growth of the country's business. As our cities double and treble in size and importance, as railroads extend and industrial plants expand, not only is it natural, but it is necessary that our banking institutions should grow in order to care for the increased demands put upon them. Perhaps it is not known as well as it should be that in New York City the largest banks are far inferior in size to banks in the commercial capitals of other and much smaller countries. . . . [The letter then points out that it takes either large banks to finance large enterprises or cooperation between several smaller ones.]

For a private banker to sit upon . . . a directorate is in most instances a duty, not a privilege. Inquiry will readily develop the fact that the members of the leading banking houses in this country—and it was the leading houses only against which animadversions were directed—are besought continually to act as directors in various corporations, whose securities they handle, and that in general they enter only those boards which the opinion of the investing public requires them to enter, as an evidence of good faith that they are willing to have their names publicly associated with the management.

Yet, before your Committee, this natural and eminently desirable relationship was made to appear almost sinister and no testimony whatever was adduced to show the actual working of such relationships. . . . [The letter concludes with an explanation as to why banks felt it necessary to sell securities, appoint fiscal agents, and maintain such close scrutiny over corporations, and a comment that unlimited liability and the force of public opinion prevented most banks from malpractice.]

Respectfully submitted,
(Signed) J. P. MORGAN & CO.
New York City
February 25, 1913.

The Consumer Factor

WALTER WEYL

The plutocracy is more and more opposed by an ever larger number of social groups and individuals, not only for what it does and for what it is, but for the deeper economic tendencies which it represents. Different men are arrayed against the plutocracy for different reasons. While, however, such common hostility is a sufficient stimulus to an aggressive campaign, it is not

Walter Weyl, *The New Democracy* (New York: Macmillan, 1912), pp. 249–254.

a basis broad enough for a constructive program. Unless the opponents of the plutocracy have some common positive aim, their antagonism will dissipate itself in abortive assaults and waste heat, without permanent influence upon social conditions.

There exists, however, such a common aim. This aim, which holds together the opponents of an intrenched plutocracy, is the attainment of a common share in the conquered continent, in the material and moral accumulations of a century. When the trust raises prices, obtains valuable franchises or public lands, escapes taxation, secures bounties, lowers wages, evades factory laws, or makes other profitable maneuvers, it is diverting a part of the social surplus from the general community to itself. The public pays the higher prices, loses the franchises or lands, pays higher taxes, suffers in wages (and pays for the ill effects of low wages), and generally makes up dollar for dollar for all such gains. In all these things the people have a perceivable interest. The great mass is injured in its capacity of wage earner, salary earner, taxpayer, and consumer.

Of these capacities that of the consumer is the most universal, since even those who do not earn wages or pay direct taxes consume commodities. In America to-day the unifying economic force, about which a majority, hostile to the plutocracy, is forming, is the common interest of the citizen as a consumer of wealth, and incidentally as an owner of (undivided) national possessions. The producer (who is only the consumer in another rôle) is highly differentiated. He is banker, lawyer, soldier, tailor, farmer, shoeblack, messenger boy. He is capitalist, workman, money lender, money borrower, urban worker, rural worker. The consumer, on the other hand, is undifferentiated. All men, women, and children who buy shoes (except only the shoe manufacturer) are interested in cheap good shoes. The consumers of most articles are overwhelmingly superior in numbers to the producers.

Despite this overwhelming superiority in numbers, the consumer, finding it difficult to organize, has often been worsted in industrial battles. In our century-long tariff contests, a million inaudible consumers have often counted less than has a petty industry in a remote district. The consumer thought of himself as a producer, and he united only with men of his own productive group. For a time there was a certain reason for such an alignment. It was a period of falling prices, of severe competition, in which the whole organization of industry favored the consumer. In fact, the unorganized and ruthless consumer was blamed—and rightly blamed (as he is still rightly blamed to-day)—for many of the evils of industry. The curse of the sweat-shop and of the starving seamstress, sewing by candle-light, was fairly brought to the doors of the bargain-hunting housewife. The consumer, though acting singly, felt himself secure.

Even when prices began to rise, consumers remained quiescent. There was greater difficulty in resisting price advances, because the loss to each individual from each increase was so infinitesimal. The reverse of the overwhelming numbers of the consumers was the small individual interest of each in each transaction. Wages affected a man far more sensibly than did prices. If a motorman's wages were reduced one cent an hour he might lose thirty dollars a year; a rise of ten cents in the price of shoes, on the other hand, meant a loss of, at most, two dollars a year. A man could not spend his lifetime fighting ten-cent increases. The cure for high prices was high wages.

As prices continue to rise, however, as a result (among other causes) of our gradually entering into a monopoly period, a new insistence is laid upon the rights of the consumer, and political unity is based upon him. Where formerly production seemed to be the sole governing economic fact of a man's life, to-day many producers have no direct interest in their product. It is a very attenuated interest which the Polish slag-worker has in the duty on steel billets, but the Polish slag-worker and the Boston salesgirl and the Oshkosh lawyer have a similar interest (and a common cause of discontent) as consumers of the national wealth. The universality of the rise of prices has begun to affect the consumer as though he were attacked by a million gnats. The chief offense of the trust becomes its capacity to injure the consumer. Therefore the consumer, disinterred from his grave, reappears in the political arena as the "common man," the "plain people," the "strap-hanger," "the man on the street," "the taxpayer," the "ultimate consumer." Men who voted as producers are now voting as consumers.

We are now beginning to appeal to the "ultimate consumer," the man who actually eats, wears, or uses the article. A generation ago we legislated for the penultimate shopkeeper, or the ante-penultimate manufacturer. Our contest for railroad rate regulation was formerly waged in the interest of the producer or shipper, and not primarily in the interest of the consumer. The rates in question were freight, not passenger, rates, and the great problem was not so much low freight rates (which more immediately benefited the consumer) as equal freight rates, in which the competing manufacturer was primarily interested.

It is difficult for the consumer to act industrially in concert. The "rent strikes" on the East Side of New York have always been unsuccessful. The meat strikes have been equally without result. The work of the Consumers' Leagues has been chiefly a humanitarian labor for the benefit of producers, and we have never successfully developed in America great coöperative associations of workingmen consumers, like those of England, Belgium, France, and Germany. The appeal to the consumer has therefore been made on the political field. . . .

Of all the hard blows which the course of American political and economic development has dealt the traditional system of political ideas and institutions, perhaps the hardest is this demand for discrimination on behalf of union labor. It means that the more intelligent and progressive American workingmen are coming to believe that the American political and economic organization does not sufficiently secure the material improvement of the wage-earner. This conviction may be to a large extent erroneous. Certain it is that the wages of unorganized farm laborers have been increasing as rapidly during the past thirty years as have the wages of the organized mechanics. But whether erroneous or not, it is widespread and deep-rooted; and whatever danger it possesses is derived from the fact that it affords to a substantially revolutionary purpose a large and increasing popular following. The other instances of organization for special purposes which have been remarked have superficially, at least, been making for conservatism. The millionaire and the professional politician want above all things to be let alone, and to be allowed to enjoy the benefit of their conquests. But the labor organizations cannot exercise the power necessary in their opinion to their interests without certain radical changes in the political and economic order; and inasmuch as their power is likely to increase rather than diminish, the American people are confronted with the prospect of persistent, unscrupulous, and increasing agitation on behalf of an economic and political reorganization in favor of one class of citizens.

The large corporations and the unions occupy in certain respects a similar relation to the American political system. Their advocates both believe in associated action for themselves and in competition for their adversaries. They both demand governmental protection and recognition, but resent the notion of efficient governmental regulation. They have both reached their existing power, partly because of the weakness of the state governments, to which they are legally subject, and they both are opposed to any interference by the Federal government—except exclusively on their own behalf. Yet they both have become so very powerful that they are frequently too strong for the state governments, and in different ways they both traffic for their own benefit with the politicians, who so often control those governments. Here, of course, the parallelism ends and the divergence begins. The corporations have apparently the best of the situation, because existing institutions are more favorable to the interests of the corporations than to the interests of the unionists; but on the other hand, the unions have the immense advantage of a great and increasing numerical strength. They are beginning to use the suffrage to promote a class interest, though how far they will travel on this perilous path remains doubtful. In any event, it is obvious that the development in this country of two such powerful and unscrupulous and well-organized special interests has created a condition which the founders of the Republic never anticipated, and which demands as a counterpoise a more effective body of national opinion, and a more powerful organization of the national interest.

4.2:   Conservation and Efficiency (1908, 1912)

A recent school of historians has emphasized the importance of "efficiency" in the Progressive agenda. Progressives were not so much defenders of the weak against the strong, they say, as missionaries for applying expert knowledge to administration—even if the weak suffered.

This aspect of Progressivism can, in fact, be detected in several realms—business regulation, scientific management, and municipal government, for example. But it appeared most clearly in the conservation movement, where the mainstream, led by Roosevelt and his friend and ally Gifford Pinchot, emphasized the use of the nation's natural endowment in a prudent and effective manner to maximize its commercial returns and extend its life.

These "utilitarian" conservationists competed with a wing of the natural resources movement moved by a different rationale and set of goals. "Preservationists" cherished unspoiled nature for its aesthetic and "spiritual" values and wished to keep it inviolate for future generations, even if this meant forgoing economic advantage. The most prominent preservationist was John Muir, a Scottish-born naturalist whose experiences in California in the late 1860s stimulated his love of nature. The differences between the preservationists and utilitarians did not prevent Muir and Roosevelt from being friends.

The two selections below bracket the utilitarian-preservationist controversy. The first is a statement composed by a conference of governors in 1908. The second, by Muir, is an attack on the plans of San Francisco officials to dam the Tuolumne River in the Sierras in order to supply water to the fast-growing Bay City. (The city won.)

What are the differences in tone and emphasis between the two statements? In what ways does the first document express the utilitarian conservationist viewpoint? How does the battle over the Tuolumne dam reveal the strain between the two positions on the nation's natural endowment? In what ways do the documents reveal a tension between the "efficiency" and the moral dimensions of Progressivism? Which of the two positions comes closest to the philosophy of the ecology movement of today?

Conservation Statement

GOVERNORS OF THE STATES

Declaration

We the Governors of the States and Territories of the United States of America, in Conference assembled, do hereby declare the conviction that the great prosperity of our country rests upon the abundant resources of the land chosen by our forefathers for their homes and where they laid the foundation of this great Nation.

Proceedings of a Conference of Governors in The White House May 13–15, 1908 (Washington: Government Printing Office, 1909), pp. 192–193.

We look upon these resources as a heritage to be made use of in establishing and promoting the comfort, prosperity, and happiness of the American People, but not to be wasted, deteriorated, or needlessly destroyed.

We agree that our country's future is involved in this; that the great natural resources supply the material basis on which our civilization must continue to depend, and on which the perpetuity of the Nation itself rests.

We agree, in the light of facts brought to our knowledge and from information received from sources which we can not doubt, that this material basis is threatened with exhaustion. Even as each succeeding generation from the birth of the Nation has performed its part in promoting the progress and development of the Republic, so do we in this generation recognize it as a high duty to perform our part; and this duty in large degree lies in the adoption of measures for the conservation of the natural wealth of the country.

We declare our firm conviction that this conservation of our natural resources is a subject of transcendent importance, which should engage unremittingly the attention of the Nation, the States, and the People in earnest cooperation. These natural resources include the land on which we live and which yields our food; the living waters which fertilize the soil, supply power, and form great avenues of commerce; the forests which yield the materials for our homes, prevent erosion of the soil, and conserve the navigation and other uses of our streams; and the minerals which form the basis of our industrial life, and supply us with heat, light, and power.

We agree that the land should be so used that erosion and soil-wash shall cease; that there should be reclamation of arid and semi-arid regions by means of irrigation, and of swamp and overflowed regions by means of drainage; that the waters should be so conserved and used as to promote navigation, to enable the arid regions to be reclaimed by irrigation, and to develop power in the interests of the People; that the forests which regulate our rivers, support our industries, and promote the fertility and productiveness of the soil should be preserved and perpetuated; that the minerals found so abundantly beneath the surface should be so used as to prolong their utility; that the beauty, healthfulness, and habitability of our country should be preserved and increased; that the sources of national wealth exist for the benefit of the People, and that monopoly thereof should not be tolerated.

We commend the wise forethought of the President in sounding the note of warning as to the waste and exhaustion of the natural resources of the country, and signify our high appreciation of his action in calling this Conference to consider the same and to seek remedies therefore through cooperation of the Nation and the States.

We agree that this cooperation should find expression in suitable action by the Congress within the limits of and coextensive with the national jurisdiction of the subject, and, complementary thereto, by the legislatures of the several States within the limits of and coextensive with their jurisdiction.

We declare the conviction that in the use of the natural resources our independent States are interdependent and bound together by ties of mutual benefits, responsibilities and duties.

We agree in the wisdom of future conferences between the President, Members of Congress, and the Governors of States on the conservation of our natural resources with a view of continued cooperation and action on the lines suggested; and to this end we advise that from time to time, as in his judgment may seem wise, the President call the Governors of the States and Members of Congress and others into conference.

We agree that further action is advisable to ascertain the present condition of our natural resources and to promote the conservation of the same; and to that end we recommend the appointment by each State of a Commission on the Conservation of Natural Resources, to cooperate with each other and with any similar commission of the Federal Government.

We urge the continuation and extension of forest policies adapted to secure the husbanding and renewal of our diminishing timber supply, the prevention of soil erosion, the protection of headwaters, and the maintenance of the purity and navigability of our streams. We recognize that the private ownership of forest lands entails responsibilities in the interests of all the People, and we favor the enactment of laws looking to the protection and replacement of privately owned forests.

We recognize in our waters a most valuable asset of the People of the United States, and we recommend the enactment of laws looking to the conservation of water resources for irrigation, water supply, power, and navigation, to the end that navigable and source streams may be brought under complete control and fully utilized for every purpose. We especially urge on the Federal Congress the immediate adoption of a wise, active, and thorough waterway policy, providing for the prompt improvement of our streams and the conservation of their watersheds required for the uses of commerce and the protection of the interests of our People.

We recommend the enactment of laws looking to the prevention of waste in the mining and extraction of coal, oil, gas, and other minerals with a view to their wise conservation for the use of the People, and to the protection of human life in the mines.

Let us conserve the foundations of our prosperity.

Respectfully submitted,

[Signatures]

Hetch Hetchy

JOHN MUIR

Yosemite[1] is so wonderful that we are apt to regard it as an exceptional creation, the only valley of its kind in the world; but Nature is not so poor as to

John Muir, *The Yosemite* (New York: The Century Company, 1912), pp. 249–262.

[1] The Yosemite is the beautiful Sierra Valley in California set aside as a national park in 1890 through the efforts of Muir and others—ED.

have only one of anything. Several other yosemites have been discovered in the Sierra that occupy the same relative positions on the Range and were formed by the same forces in the same kind of granite. One of these, the Hetch Hetchy Valley, is in the Yosemite National Park about twenty miles from Yosemite and is easily accessible to all sorts of travelers by road and trail. . . .

I have always called it the "Tuolomne Yosemite," for it is a wonderfully exact counterpart of the Merced Yosemite not only in its sublime rocks and waterfalls but in the gardens, groves and meadows of its flowery park-like floor. . . .

Imagine yourself in Hetch Hetchy on a sunny day in June, standing waist-deep in grass and flowers . . . while the great pines sway dreamily with scarcely perceptible motion. Looking northward across the Valley you see a plain, gray granite cliff arising abruptly out of the gardens and groves to a height of 1800 feet, and in front of it Tueeulala's silvery scarf burning with irised sun-fire. In the first white outburst at the head there is an abundance of visible energy, but it is speedily hushed and concealed in divine repose, and its tranquil progress to the base of the cliff is like that of a downy feather in a still room. Now observe the fineness and marvelous distinctiveness of the various sun-illumined fabrics into which the water is woven; they sift and float from form to form down the face of that grand gray rock in so leisurely and unconfused a manner that you can examine their texture, and patterns of and tones of color as you would a piece of embroidery held in the hand. Toward the top of the fall you see groups of booming, comet-like masses, their solid white heads separate, their tails like combed silk interlacing among delicate gray and purple shadows, ever forming and dissolving, worn out by friction in their rush through the air. . . . Near the bottom the width of the fall has increased from about twenty-five feet to a hundred feet. Here it is composed of even finer tissues, and is still without a trace of disorder— air, water and sunlight woven into stuff that spirits might wear. . . .

It appears, therefore, that Hetch Hetchy Valley, far from being a plain, common, rock-bound meadow, as many who have not seen it seem to sup-pose, is a grand landscape garden, one of Nature's rarest and most precious mountain temples. As in Yosemite, the sublime rocks of its walls seem to glow with life, whether leaning back in repose or standing erect in thought-ful attitudes, giving welcome to storms and calms alike, their brows in the sky, their feet set in the groves and gay flowery meadows, while birds, bees and butterflies help the river and waterfalls to stir all the air into music— things frail and fleeting and types of permanence meeting here and blend-ing, just as they do at Yosemite, to draw her lovers into close and confiding communion with her.

Sad to say, this most precious and sublime feature of the Yosemite National Park, one of the greatest of all our natural resources for the uplift-ing joy and peace and health of the people, is in danger of being dammed and made into a reservoir to help supply San Francisco with water and light, thus flooding it from wall to wall and burying its gardens and groves one or two hundred feet deep. This grossly destructive commercial scheme has long been planned and urged (though water as pure and abundant can be got from sources outside of the people's park, in a dozen different places), because of the comparative cheapness of the dam and of the territory which it is sought to divert from the great uses to which it was dedicated in the Act of 1890 establishing the Yosemite National Park.

The making of gardens and parks goes on with civilization all over the world, and they increase both in size and number as their value is recognized. Everybody needs beauty as well as bread, places to play in and pray in, where Nature may heal and cheer and give strength to body and soul alike. This natural beauty-hunger is made manifest in the little window-sill gardens of the poor, though perhaps only a geranium slip in a broken cup, as well as in the carefully tended rose and lily gardens of the rich, the thousands of spacious city parks and botanical gardens, and in our magnificent National parks—the Yellowstone, Yosemite, Sequoia, etc.—Nature's sublime wonder-lands, the admiration and joy of the world. Nevertheless, like anything else worth while, from the very beginning, however well guarded, they have always been subject to attack by despoiling gain-seekers and mischief-makers of every degree from Satan to Senators, eagerly trying to make everything immediately and selfishly commercial, with schemes disguised in smug-smiling philanthropy, industriously, shampiously crying, "Conservation, conservation, panutilization," that man and beast may be fed and the dear Nation made great. Thus long ago a few enterprising merchants utilized the Jerusalem temple as a place of business instead of a place of prayer, changing money, buying and selling cattle and sheep and doves; and earlier still, the first forest reservation, including only one tree, was likewise despoiled. Ever since the establishment of the Yosemite National Park, strife has been going on around its borders and I suppose this will go on as part of the universal battle between right and wrong, however much its boundaries may be shorn, or its wild beauty destroyed.

The first application to the Government by the San Francisco Supervisors for the commercial use of Lake Eleanor and the Hetch Hetchy Valley was made in 1903, and on December 22nd of that year it was denied by the Secretary of the Interior, Mr. Hitchcock, who truthfully said:

> Presumably the Yosemite National Park was created such by law because of the natural objects of varying degrees of scenic importance located within its boundaries, inclusive alike of its beautiful small lakes, like Eleanor, and its majestic wonders, like Hetch Hetchy and Yosemite Valley. It is the aggregation of such natural scenic features that makes the Yosemite Park a wonderland which the Congress of the United States sought by law to reserve for all coming time as nearly as practicable in the condition fashioned by the hand of the Creator—a worthy object of National pride and a source of healthful pleasure and rest for the thousands of people who may annually sojourn there during the heated months.

In 1907 when Mr. Garfield became Secretary of the Interior the application was renewed and granted; but under his successor, Mr. Fisher, the matter has been referred to a Commission, which as this volume goes to press still has it under consideration. . . .

That any one would try to destroy such a place seems incredible; but sad experience shows that there are people good enough and bad enough for anything. The proponents of the dam scheme bring forward a lot of bad arguments to prove that the only righteous thing to do with the people's parks is to destroy them bit by bit as they are able. Their arguments are curiously like those of the devil, devised for the destruction of the first garden—so much of the very best Eden fruit going to waste; so much of the best Tuolumne water and Tuolumne scenery going to waste. Few of their statements are even partly true, and all are misleading.

Thus, Hetch Hetchy, they say, is a "low-lying meadow." On the contrary, it is a high-lying natural landscape garden, as the photographic illustrations show.

"It is a common minor feature, like thousands of others." On the contrary it is a very uncommon feature; after Yosemite, the rarest and in many ways the most important in the National Park.

"Damming and submerging it 175 feet deep would enhance its beauty by forming a crystal-clear lake." Landscape gardens, places of recreation and worship, are never made beautiful by destroying and burying them. The beautiful sham lake, forsooth, would be only an eyesore, a dismal blot on the landscape, like many others to be seen in the Sierra. For, instead of keeping it at the same level all the year, allowing Nature centuries of time to make new shores, it would, of course, be full only a month or two in the spring, when the snow is melting fast; then it would be gradually drained, exposing the slimy sides of the basin and shallower parts of the bottom, with the gathered drift and waste, death and decay of the upper basins, caught here instead of being swept on to decent natural burial along the banks of the river or in the sea. Thus the Hetch Hetchy dam-lake would be only a rough imitation of a natural lake for a few of the spring months, an open sepulcher for the others.

"Hetch Hetchy water is the purest of all to be found in the Sierra, unpolluted, and forever unpollutable." On the contrary, excepting that of the Merced below Yosemite, it is less pure than that of most of the other Sierra streams, because of the sewerage of camp grounds draining into it, especially of the Big Tuolumne Meadows camp ground, occupied by hundreds of tourists and mountaineers, with their animals, for months every summer, soon to be followed by thousands from all the world.

These temple destroyers, devotees of ravaging commercialism, seem to have a perfect contempt for Nature, and, instead of lifting their eyes to the God of the mountains, lift them to the Almighty Dollar.

Dam Hetch Hetchy! As well dam for water-tanks the people's cathedrals and churches, for no holier temple has ever been consecrated by the heart of man.

4.3: Social Justice Progressivism (1892, 1912)

Although efficient administration may have been the core issue for some Progressives, others were moved by broader social sympathies. These social justice reformers were particularly numerous among the settlement house workers—middle-class men and women who established community centers in the urban slums where the poor, many of them foreign born, could learn skills, absorb American ways, and find refuge from the harsh city environment. The settlements were actually precursors of Progressivism. May were established in the 1890s, but their impact on the larger society awaited the stirring of the urban middle class in the new century.

The social justice Progressives did not confine their labors to the settlement houses. Many were active in city-wide good-government movements and efforts on the state and national levels to shelter women and child workers from exploitation, reduce the hazards of dangerous occupations, improve protection for consumers, and make government machinery more responsive to voter majorities than to special interests.

The first selection below, by Jane Addams, describes the activities of Hull House, the settlement she founded in the Chicago slums in 1889. It has been said that the white middle-class settlement workers patronized the people they sought to help and failed to respect their values and traditions. Does this attitude come through in Addams's description? Or does she seem alert to this danger and seek to avoid it? Did most slum dwellers in early twentieth-century America themselves want to assimilate middle-class "American" values?

The second selection is the 1912 platform of the Progressive Party of America, known as the "Bull Moose Party." Organized by the social justice Progressives when the regular Republicans denied their hero, Teddy Roosevelt, the presidential nomination, the Bull Moose Party was the high-water mark of Progressive zeal to remake America. What are the platform's most advanced features? Does their program foreshadow later national reform programs? Which ones? Do you know if any of the social policies endorsed here had already been tried in the states? How well did Roosevelt and his party do in the 1912 presidential election?

Hull House, Chicago: An Effort toward Social Democracy[1]

JANE ADDAMS

Hull House, Chicago's first Social Settlement, was established in September, 1889. It . . . was opened by two women, supported by many friends, in the belief that the mere foothold of a house, easily accessible, ample in space, hospitable and tolerant in spirit, situated in the midst of the large foreign colonies which so easily isolate themselves in American cities, would be in itself a serviceable thing for Chicago. . . . It was opened on the theory that the dependence of classes on each other is reciprocal; and that as "the social relation is essentially a reciprocal relation, it gave a form of expression that has peculiar value." . . .

Hull House is an ample old residence, well built and somewhat ornately decorated after the manner of its time, 1856. . . . It once stood in the suburbs, but the city has steadily grown up around it and its site now has corners on three or four distinct foreign colonies. Between Halsted Street and the river live about ten thousand Italians. . . . To the south on Twelfth Street are many Germans, and side streets are given over almost entirely to Polish and Russian Jews. Further south, these Jewish colonies merge into a huge Bohemian colony, so vast that Chicago ranks as the third Bohemian city in the world. To the northwest are many Canadian-French, . . . and to the north are many Irish and first-generation Americans. . . .

The streets are inexpressibly dirty, the number of schools inadequate, factory legislation unenforced, the street-lighting bad, and paving miserable, . . . and the stables defy all laws of sanitation. . . . The Hebrews and Italians do the finishing for the great clothing-manufacturers. . . . As the design of the sweating system is the elimination of rent from the manufacture of clothing, the "outside work" is begun after the clothing leaves the cutter. For this work no basement is too dark, no stable loft too foul, no rear shanty too provisional, no tenement room too small, as these conditions imply low rental. Hence these shops abound in the worst of the foreign districts, where the sweater easily finds his cheap basement and his home finishers. . . .

This site for a Settlement was selected . . . because of its diversity and the variety of activity for which it presented an opportunity. It has been the aim of the residents to respond to all sides of the neighborhood life. . . . One thing seemed clear in regard to entertaining these foreigners: to preserve and keep for them whatever of value their past life contained and to bring them into contact with a better type of Americans. For two years, every Saturday evening, our Italian neighbors were our guests; entire families came . . . and the house became known as a place where Italians were welcome and where national holidays were observed. They came to us with their

Jane Addams, "Hull House, Chicago: An Effort toward Social Democracy," *Forum*, vol. 14 (October 1892), pp. 226–241.

[1]Footnotes deleted.

petty law-suits, sad relics of the *vendetta*, with their incorrigible boys, with their hospital cases, with their aspirations for American clothes, and with their needs for an interpreter. . . .

But our social evenings are by no means confined to foreigners. Our most successful clubs are entirely composed of English speaking and American-born young people. . . . The boys who are known as the Young Citizens' Club are supposed to inform themselves on municipal affairs. . . . The gymnasium is a somewhat pretentious name for a building next door which was formerly a saloon, but which we rented last fall, repaired, and fitted up with simple apparatus. . . . The more definite humanitarian effect of Hull House has taken shape in a day nursery. . . . During two months of this summer the reports sent in from Hull House to the Municipal Order League and through it to the Health Department were one thousand and thirty-seven, . . . and a marked improvement has taken place in the scavenger service and in the regulation of the small stables of the ward. . . .

Last May twenty girls from a knitting factory who struck because they were docked for loss of time when they were working by the piece, came directly from the factory to Hull House. . . . They had heard that we "stood by working people." We were able to have the strike arbitrated . . . and we had the satisfaction of putting on record one more case of arbitration in the slowly growing list. . . . It is difficult to classify the Working Peoples' Social Science Club, which meets weekly at Hull House. It is social, educational, and civic in character, the latter because it strongly connects the house with the labor problems in their political and social aspects. . . .

I am always sorry to have Hull House regarded as philanthropy, although it doubtless has strong philanthropic tendencies. . . . Working people live in the same streets with those in need of charity, but they themselves require and want none of it. As one of their number has said, they require only that their aspirations be recognized and stimulated and the means of attaining them put at their disposal. Hull House makes a constant effort to secure these means, but to call that effort philanthropy is to use the word unfairly and to underestimate the duties of good citizenship.

Progressive Party Platform of 1912: What the New Party Stands For

The conscience of the people, in a time of grave national problems, has called into being a new party, born of the nation's sense of justice. We of the Progressive party here dedicate ourselves to the fulfillment of the duty laid upon us by our fathers to maintain the government of the people, by the people and for the people whose foundations they laid. . . .

The Old Parties

Political parties exist to secure responsible government and to execute the will of the people.

Kirk Harold Porter and Donald Bruce Johnson, *National Party Platforms, 1840–1956* (Urbana: University of Illinois Press, 1956), pp. 334–336.

From these great tasks both of the old parties have turned aside. Instead of instruments to promote the general welfare, they have become the tools of corrupt interests which use them impartially to serve their selfish purposes. Behind the ostensible government sits enthroned an invisible government owing no allegiance and acknowledging no responsibility to the people.

To destroy this invisible government, to dissolve the unholy alliance between corrupt business and corrupt politics is the first task of the statesmanship of the day.

The deliberate betrayal of its trust by the Republican party, the fatal incapacity of the Democratic party to deal with the new issues of the new time, have compelled the people to forge a new instrument of government through which to give effect to their will in laws and institutions.

Unhampered by tradition, uncorrupted by power, undismayed by the magnitude of the task, the new party offers itself as the instrument of the people to sweep away old abuses, to build a new and nobler commonwealth. . . .

The Rule of the People

. . . In particular, the party declares for direct primaries for the nomination of State and National officers, for nation-wide preferential primaries for candidates for the presidency; for the direct election of United States Senators by the people; and we urge on the States the policy of the short ballot, with responsibility to the people secured by the initiative, referendum and recall. . . .

Equal Suffrage

The Progressive party, believing that no people can justly claim to be a true democracy which denies political rights on account of sex, pledges itself to the task of securing equal suffrage to men and women alike.

Corrupt Practices

We pledge our party to legislation that will compel strict limitation of all campaign contributions and expenditures, and detailed publicity of both before as well as after primaries and elections.

Publicity and Public Service

We pledge our party to legislation compelling the registration of lobbyists; publicity of committee hearings except on foreign affairs, and recording of all votes in committee; and forbidding federal appointees from holding office in State or National political organizations, or taking part as officers or delegates in political conventions for the nomination of elective State or National officials.

The Courts

The Progressive party demands such restriction of the power of the courts as shall leave to the people the ultimate authority to determine fundamental questions of social welfare and public policy. To secure this end, it pledges itself to provide:

1. That when an Act, passed under the police power of the State, is held unconstitutional under the State Constitution, by the courts, the people, after an ample interval for deliberation, shall have an opportunity to vote on the question whether they desire the Act to become law, notwithstanding such decision.
2. That every decision of the highest appellate court of a State declaring an Act of the Legislature unconstitutional on the ground of its violation of the Federal Constitution shall be subject to the same review by the Supreme Court of the United States as is now accorded to decisions sustaining such legislation.

Administration of Justice

. . . We believe that the issuance of injunctions in cases arising out of labor disputes should be prohibited when such injunctions would not apply when no labor disputes existed.

We believe also that a person cited for contempt in labor disputes, except when such contempt was committed in the actual presence of the court or so near thereto as to interfere with the proper administration of justice, should have a right to trial by jury.

Social and Industrial Justice

The supreme duty of the Nation is the conservation of human resources through an enlightened measure of social and industrial justice. We pledge ourselves to work unceasingly in State and Nation for:

Effective legislation looking to the prevention of industrial accidents, occupational diseases, overwork, involuntary unemployment, and other injurious effects incident to modern industry;

The fixing of minimum safety and health standards for the various occupations, and the exercise of the public authority of State and Nation, including the Federal Control over interstate commerce, and the taxing power, to maintain such standards;

The prohibition of child labor;

Minimum wage standards for working women, to provide a "living wage" in all industrial occupations;

The general prohibition of night work for women and the establishment of an eight hour day for women and young persons;

One day's rest in seven for all wage workers;

The eight hour day in continuous twenty-four-hour industries;

The abolition of the convict contract labor system; substituting a system of prison production for governmental consumption only; and the application of prisoners' earnings to the support of their dependent families;

Publicity as to wages, hours and conditions of labor; full reports upon industrial accidents and diseases, and the opening to public inspection of all tallies, weights, measures and check systems on labor products;

Standards of compensation for death by industrial accident and injury and trade disease which will transfer the burden of lost earnings from the families of working people to the industry, and thus to the community;

The protection of home life against the hazards of sickness, irregular employment and old age through the adoption of a system of social insurance adapted to American use;

The development of the creative labor power of America by lifting the last load of illiteracy from American youth and establishing continuation schools for industrial education under public control and encouraging agricultural education and demonstration in rural schools;

The establishment of industrial research laboratories to put the methods and discoveries of science at the service of American producers;

We favor the organization of the workers, men and women, as a means of protecting their interests and of promoting their progress. . . .

Currency

. . . The issue of currency is fundamentally a Government function and the system should have as basic principles soundness and elasticity. The control should be lodged with the Government and should be protected from domination or manipulation by Wall Street or any special interests.

We are opposed to the so-called Aldrich currency bill,[1] because its provisions would place our currency and credit system in private hands, not subject to effective public control. . . .

Conservation

. . . We believe that the remaining forests, coal and oil lands, water powers and other natural resources still in State or National control (except agricultural lands) are more likely to be wisely conserved and utilized for the general welfare if held in the public hands.

In order that consumers and producers, managers and workmen, now and hereafter, need not pay toll to private monopolies of power and raw material, we demand that such resources shall be retained by the State or Nation, and opened to immediate use under laws which will encourage development and make to the people a moderate return for benefits conferred.

[1] A measure proposed by a Senate Committee headed by Nelson W. Aldrich of Rhode Island to reform the old National Bank system that had performed so poorly during the Panic of 1907.

5

Race and Ethnicity

The two decades on either side of 1900 witnessed a vast turnover of nationalities and races in America. As noted, sometime in the 1890s the source of immigrants to America shifted decisively from western and northern Europe to eastern and southern Europe. Particularly after 1900, far fewer proportionately of the newcomers came from Britain, Germany, Ireland, and Scandinavia and far more from Poland, Russia, Austria-Hungary, Greece, and Italy. Meanwhile, in the years just preceding World War I, there began a migration to northern cities of African-American people, until then tied overwhelmingly, as during slavery days, to the rural South.

There were important differences between these two human streams. The people from the southern countryside who came to New York, Chicago, Philadelphia, and Cleveland were English-speaking, Protestant, American citizens. The transatlantic arrivals were, of course, foreigners, who spoke alien tongues, and were predominantly Catholic, Greek Orthodox, or Jewish. The migrants from the rural South were black; the newcomers from Europe were white. Race would make a difference.

But there were also significant overlaps between the two groups. Both were rural peoples, new to city life and city ways. Both were predominantly unskilled workers who found their economic niches in the mines, factories, and construction sites doing the hard, dirty, menial labor the industrial society of the day required. Both met prejudice and bigotry from old-stock white Americans already on the scene, although African-Americans undoubtedly suffered more than immigrants.

The selections that follow depict how the post-1890 newcomers to northern cities were perceived and received. The new arrivals were not uniformly scorned. There remained among old-stock white Americans a residue of good will toward immigrants and black people based on the nation's democratic, egalitarian traditions. Many business leaders welcomed the newcomers, especially the white immigrants, as a source of cheap labor. Still, the balance was clearly tipped against a generous toleration, as the documents below suggest.

5.1:   The Great Migration:
The Dark Side (1905, 1919)

Southern black people began to move north in substantial numbers in the earliest years of this century. The trickle became a torrent after 1915, when World War I blocked the normal flow of European immigrants and created major labor shortages in northern industry.

Jobs, however, were not the only magnet drawing rural African-Americans northward. The North also promised to be freer and less repressive than Dixie, where segregation by race, known as "Jim Crow," remained entrenched, and violence against blacks had accelerated.

One of the black newcomers' favorite destinations was booming Chicago, where the stockyards and the city's many industrial plants provided employment. By 1920 the Windy City had almost 110,000 African-American residents, almost four times the number in 1900.

The first selection below describes the Chicago "Black Belt" shortly after the turn of the century. Even in this early period some of the major problems that would continue to plague black urban dwellers in the North had surfaced. What are some of these? What does the reference to "strike-breakers" suggest? What are some of the hopeful aspects of life in the "Black Belt" as described here? What are some of the sources of racial tension?

The second selection depicts the savage Chicago race riot of 1919, fourteen years after the scene described in the previous document. This was one of a dozen shameful racial disorders that erupted in the first two decades of the twentieth century. Can you deduce from the account the causes of the barbaric behavior described? Group antagonisms have been very widespread in America, but they were seldom so brutal and destructive as those between whites and blacks in the cities, especially in the early part of this century. What explains this ferocity? Did race riots continue long past this period? Have recent racial disorders been similar to the Chicago riot of 1919?

Social Bonds in the "Black Belt" of Chicago: Negro Organizations and the New Spirit Pervading Them[1]

FANNIE BARRIER WILLIAMS

The last federal census [1900] showed the Negro population of Chicago to be about 35,000. The present population is estimated to be over 50,000, an

Fannie Barrier Williams, "Social Bonds in the 'Black Belt' of Chicago: Negro Organizations and the New Spirit Pervading Them," *Charities*, October 7, 1905, pp. 40–44.

[1] Footnotes deleted.

increase of about forty per cent in five years. The colored people who are thus crowding into Chicago come mostly from the states of Kentucky, Tennessee, Alabama, Mississippi, Louisiana, Arkansas, and Missouri. . . . [The] many industrial strikes . . . in the last ten years have brought thousands of colored people to Chicago, either for immediate work as strikebreakers, or with the prospect of employment for both skilled and unskilled workers . . . ; thousands of Negro men and women are now employed in the stockyards and other large industrial plants where ten years ago this would not have been thought of.

This increase of Negro population has brought with it problems that directly affect the social and economic life of the newcomers. Prevented from mingling easily and generally with the rest of the city's population, according to their needs and deservings, but with no preparation made for segregation . . . they have been subject to more social ills than any other nationality among us. . . . The real problem of the social life of the colored people in Chicago, as in all northern cities, lies in the fact of their segregation. While they do not occupy all the worst streets and live in all the unsanitary houses in Chicago, what is known as the "Black Belt" is altogether forbidding and demoralizing. . . .

The organizations created and maintained by them in Chicago are numerous and touch almost every phase of our social life. . . . First in importance is the Negro church. There are 25 regularly organized colored churches. This number includes 9 Methodist, 8 Baptist, 1 Catholic, 1 Episcopal, 1 Christian and 1 Presbyterian. In addition to these there are numerous missions in various parts of the "Black Belt." . . . Most of these churches are burdened with oppressive indebtedness, and because of this their usefulness as agents of moral up-lift is seriously handicapped. . . . Thousands of Negroes know and care for no other entertainment than that furnished by the church. . . .

Next to the Negro church, in importance, as affecting the social life of the people are the secret orders, embracing such organizations as the Masons, Odd Fellows, Knights of Pythias, True Reformers, the United Brotherhood, . . . the Ancient Order of Foresters, and the Elks. Nearly all of these secret orders have auxiliary associations composed of women. . . .

In the matter of employment, the colored people of Chicago have lost in the last ten years nearly every occupation of which they once had almost a monopoly. There is now scarcely a Negro barber left in the business district. Nearly all the janitor work in the large buildings has been taken away from them by the Swedes. White men and women as waiters have supplanted colored men in nearly all the first-class hotels and restaurants. Practically all the shoe polishing is now done by Greeks. Negro coachmen and expressmen and teamsters are seldom seen in the business districts. It scarcely need be stated that colored young men and women are almost never employed as clerks and bookkeepers in business establishments. . . .

The increase of the Negro population in Chicago . . . has not tended to liberalize public sentiment; in fact hostile sentiment has been considerably intensified by the importation from time to time of colored men as strike-breakers. Then again a marked increase of crime among the Negro population has been noted in recent years. All these things have tended to put us in a bad light, resulting in an appreciable loss of friends and well-wishers.

Chicago Commission on Race Relations: Causes of the Race Riot

Sunday afternoon, July 27, 1919, hundreds of white and Negro bathers crowded the lake-front beaches at Twenty-sixth and Twenty-ninth streets. This is the eastern boundary of the thickest Negro residence area. At Twenty-sixth Street Negroes were in great majority; at Twenty-ninth Street there were more whites. An imaginary line in the water separating the two beaches had been generally observed by the two races. Under the prevailing relations, aided by wild rumors and reports, this line served virtually as a challenge to either side to cross it. Four Negroes who attempted to enter the water from the "white" side were driven away by the whites. They returned with more Negroes, and there followed a series of attacks with stones, first one side gaining the advantage, then the other.

Eugene Williams, a Negro boy of seventeen, entered the water from the side used by Negroes and drifted across the line supported by a railroad tie. He was observed by the crowd on the beach and promptly became a target for stones. He suddenly released the tie, went down and was drowned. Guilt was immediately placed on Stauber, a young white man, by Negro witnesses who declared that he threw the fatal stone.[1]

White and Negro men dived for the boy without result. Negroes demanded that the policeman present arrest Stauber. He refused; and at this crucial moment arrested a Negro on a white man's complaint. Negroes then attacked the officer. These two facts, the drowning and the refusal of the policeman to arrest Stauber, together marked the beginning of the riot.

Two hours after the drowning, a Negro, James Crawford, fired into a group of officers summoned by the policeman at the beach and was killed by a Negro policeman. Reports and rumors circulated rapidly, and new crowds began to gather. Five white men were injured in clashes near the beach. As darkness came Negroes in white districts to the west suffered severely. Between 9:00 P.M. and 3:00 A.M. twenty-seven Negroes were beaten, seven stabbed, and four shot. Monday morning was quiet, and Negroes went to work as usual.

Returning from work in the afternoon many Negroes were attacked by white ruffians. Street-car routes, especially at transfer points, were the cen-

Chicago Commission on Race Relations: The Negro in Chicago (Chicago: University of Chicago Press, 1927), pp. 596–598. © University of Chicago Press.

[1] A jury later determined that Williams had drowned because he was kept from coming ashore by the white stone-throwers – ED.

ters of lawlessness. Trolleys were pulled from the wires, and Negro passengers were dragged into the street, beaten, stabbed, and shot. The police were powerless to cope with these numerous assaults. During Monday, four Negro men and one white assailant were killed, and thirty Negroes were severely beaten in street-car clashes. Four white men were killed, six stabbed, five shot, and nine severely beaten. It was rumored that the white occupants of the Angelus Building at Thirty-fifth Street and Wabash Avenue had shot a Negro. Negroes gathered about the building. The white tenants sought police protection, and one hundred policemen, mounted and on foot, responded. In a clash with the mob the police killed four Negroes and injured many.

Raids into the Negro residence area then began. Automobiles sped through the streets, the occupants shooting at random. Negroes retaliated by "sniping" from ambush. At midnight surface and elevated car service was discontinued because of a strike for wage increases, and thousands of employees were cut off from work.

On Tuesday, July 29, Negro men en route on foot to their jobs through hostile territory were killed. White soldiers and sailors in uniform, aided by civilians, raided the "Loop" business section, killing two Negroes and beating and robbing several others. Negroes living among white neighbors in Englewood, far to the south, were driven from their homes, their household goods were stolen, and their houses were burned or wrecked. On the West Side an Italian mob, excited by a false rumor that an Italian girl had been shot by a Negro, killed Joseph Lovings, a Negro.

Wednesday night at 10:30 Mayor [William] Thompson yielded to pressure and asked the help of the three regiments of militia which had been stationed in nearby armories during the most severe rioting, awaiting the call. They immediately took up positions throughout the South Side. A rainfall Wednesday night and Thursday kept many people in their homes, and by Friday the rioting had abated. On Saturday incendiary fires burned forty-nine houses in the immigrant neighborhood west of the Stock Yards. Nine hundred and forty-eight people, mostly Lithuanians, were made homeless, and the property loss was about $250,000. Responsibility for the fires was never fixed.

The total casualties of this reign of terror were thirty-eight deaths—fifteen white, twenty-three Negro—and 537 people injured. Forty-one per cent of the reported clashes occurred in the white neighborhood near the Stock Yards between the south branch of the Chicago River and Fifty-fifth Street, Wentworth Avenue and the city limits, and 34 per cent in the "Black Belt" between Twenty-second and Thirty-ninth streets, Wentworth Avenue and Lake Michigan. Others were scattered.

Responsibility for many attacks was definitely placed by many witnesses upon the [white] "athletic clubs," including "Ragen's Colts," the "Hamburgers," "Aylwards," "Our Flag," the "Standard," the "Sparklers," and several others. The mobs were made up for the most part of boys between fifteen and twenty-two. Older persons participated, but the youth of the rioters was conspicuous in every clash. Little children witnessed the brutalities and frequently pointed out the injured when the police arrived.

5.2:   Black Americans Respond (1905, 1923)

People of good will, black and white, were appalled by what one Progressive called "the race war in the North." In 1909, soon after a shocking race riot in Springfield, Illinois, a group of reformers established the National Association for the Advancement of Colored People (NAACP) to work for better black-white relations and for improved economic conditions for black workers.

The NAACP represented a union of two elements: white Progressives and a new African-American leadership, northern-born and northern-educated. Many of the latter were members of the Niagara Movement, a black defense group established in 1905 that rejected the acquiescence in segregation and second-class citizenship associated with Booker T. Washington, head of Tuskegee Institute in Alabama.[1] The leading figure in the Niagara Movement was W.E.B. Du Bois, a brilliant black scholar who had earned a doctorate in history at Harvard and gone on to a successful academic career. Du Bois became the head of publicity and research for the NAACP and remained with it as a leading militant voice for over twenty years.

The first selection below is a statement composed by Du Bois for the Niagara Movement. What changes in the treatment of black Americans does it demand? How does Du Bois seek to awaken the support of the white majority? Why would contemporaries have considered a statement like this a bold departure from the past? Why does it end with a pledge that blacks themselves will seek to fulfill certain obligations?

The second selection is by Marcus Garvey, a black West Indian who came to the United States in 1916 with his plan for a Universal Negro Improvement Association. Garvey was a nationalist who sought to awaken black racial pride, establish ties between blacks of the Americas and Africa, and encourage the independence of black Africa, then almost totally under European colonial dominion. He too opposed Booker T. Washington's timid approach to race improvement, but his alternative was different from Du Bois's.

---

[1] Washington was author of the so-called Atlanta Compromise that pledged black Americans to abandon claims to suffrage rights and social equality in exchange for economic opportunity. Its pronouncement at the 1895 Cotton States Exposition in Atlanta won wide applause from the white community and made Washington a "leader" of his race in the eyes of whites.

In the United States Garvey proved an effective voice of black pride, and thousands of urban blacks joined the Universal Negro Improvement Association and contributed to several of Garvey's black run commercial and political ventures. Eventually opposition from established black leaders, including Du Bois, and from the federal government led to Garvey's conviction for mail fraud. He died in obscurity in London in 1940.

How would you characterize the essential differences between the Du Bois and the Garvey responses to racial oppression? Whose recent views do Garvey's foreshadow? Were Garvey's plans practical ones? Why did they appeal to black city dwellers in the 1920s?

What Black Americans Want

W.E.B. DU BOIS

We believe that [Negro-American] citizens should protest emphatically and continually against the curtailment of their political rights. We believe in manhood suffrage: we believe that no man is so good, intelligent or wealthy as to be entrusted wholly with the welfare of his neighbor.

We believe also in protest against the curtailment of our civil rights. All American citizens have the right to equal treatment in places of public entertainment according to their behavior and deserts.

We especially complain against the denial of equal opportunities to us in economic life; in the rural districts of the south this amounts to peonage and virtual slavery; all over the south it tends to crush labor and small business enterprises: and everywhere American prejudice, helped often by iniquitous laws, is making it more difficult for Negro-Americans to earn a decent living.

Common school education should be free to all American children and compulsory. High school training should be adequately provided for all, and college training should be the monopoly of no class or race in any section of our common country. We believe that in defense of its own institutions, the United States should aid common school education, particularly in the south, and we especially recommend concerted agitation to this end. We urge an increase in public high school facilities in the south, where the Negro-Americans are almost wholly without such provisions. We favor well-equipped trade and technical schools for the training of artisans, and the need of adequate and liberal endowment for a few institutions of higher education must be patent to sincere well-wishers of the race.

We demand upright judges in courts, juries selected without discrimination on account of color and the same measure of punishment, and the same efforts at reformation for black as for white offenders. We need

The Cleveland Gazette, July 22, 1905.

orphanages and farm schools for dependent children, juvenile reformatories for delinquents, and the abolition of the dehumanizing convict-lease system. . . .

We hold up for public execration the conduct of two opposite classes of men; the practice among employers of importing ignorant Negro-American laborers in emergencies, and then affording them neither protection nor permanent employment; and the practice of labor unions of proscribing and boycotting and oppressing thousands of their fellow-toilers, simply because they are black. These methods have accentuated and will accentuate the war of labor and capital, and they are disgraceful to both sides. . . .

We regret that this nation has never seen fit adequately to reward the black soldiers who in its five wars, have defended their country with their blood, and yet have been systematically denied the promotions which their abilities deserve. And we regard as unjust, the exclusion of black boys from the military and navy training schools. . . .

The Negro race in America, stolen, ravished and degraded, struggling up through difficulties and oppression, needs sympathy and receives criticism, needs help and is given hindrance, needs protection and is given mob-violence, needs justice and is given charity, needs leadership and is given cowardice and apology, needs bread and is given a stone. This nation will never stand justified before God until these things are changed.

Especially are we surprised and astonished at the recent attitude of the church of Christ — on the increase of a desire to bow to racial prejudice, to narrow the bounds of human brotherhood, and to segregate black men in some outer sanctuary. This is wrong, unchristian and disgraceful to twentieth century civilization. . . .

And while we are demanding, and ought to demand, and will continue to demand the rights enumerated above, God forbid that we should ever forget to urge corresponding duties upon our people.

The duty to vote.
The duty to respect the rights of others.
The duty to work.
The duty to obey the laws.
The duty to be clean and orderly.
The duty to send our children to school.
The duty to respect ourselves, even as we respect others.

Black Pride

MARCUS GARVEY

I saw the injustice done my race because it was black, and I became dissatisfied on that account. I went traveling to South and Central America and parts of the West Indies to find out if it was so elsewhere, and I found the

Marcus Garvey, "The Negro's Greatest Enemy." Reprinted with permission from *Current History* magazine (18, September 1923), pp. 951–957. © 1923, Current History, Inc.

same situation. I set sail for Europe to find out if it was different there, and again I found the same stumbling block —"You are black." I read of the conditions in America. I read "Up From Slavery," by Booker T. Washington, and then my doom — if I may call it — of being a race leader dawned upon me in London after I had traveled through almost half of Europe.

I asked, "Where is the black man's Government?" "Where is his King and his kingdom?" "Where is his President, his country, and his ambassador, his army, his navy, his men of big affairs?" I could not find them, and then I declared, "I will help to make them."

Becoming naturally restless for the opportunity of doing something for the advancement of my race, I was determined that the black man would not continue to be kicked about by all the other races and nations of the world, as I saw in the West Indies, South and Central America and Europe and as I read of it in America. My young and ambitious mind led me into flights of great imagination. I saw before me, even as I do now, a new world of black men, not peons, serfs, dogs and slaves, but a nation of sturdy men making their impress upon civilization and causing a new light to dawn upon the human race. My brain was afire. There was a world of thought to conquer. I had to start ere it became too late and the work be not done. Immediately I boarded a ship at Southampton [England] for Jamaica, where I arrived on July 15, 1914. The Universal Negro Improvement Association and African Communities (Imperial) League was founded and organized five days after my arrival with the program of uniting all the negro peoples of the world into one great body to establish a country and Government absolutely their own. . . .

Being black, I have committed an unpardonable offense against the very light colored negroes in America and the West Indies by making myself famous as a negro leader of millions. In their view no black man must rise above them, but I still forge ahead determined to give to the world the truth about the new negro who is determined to make and hold for himself a place in the affairs of men. The Universal Negro Improvement Association has been misrepresented by my enemies. They have tried to make it appear that we are hostile to other races. This is absolutely false. We love all humanity. We are working for the peace of the world which we believe can only come about when all races are given their due.

We feel that there is absolutely no reason why there should be any differences between the black and white races, if each stop to adjust and steady itself. We believe in the purity of both races. We do not believe the black man should be encouraged in the idea that his highest purpose in life is to marry a white woman, but we do believe that the white man should be taught to respect the black woman in the same way as he wants the black man to respect the white woman. It is a vicious and dangerous doctrine of social equality to urge, as certain colored leaders do, that black and white should get together, for that would destroy the racial purity of both.

We believe that the black people should have a country of their own where they should be given the fullest opportunity to develop politically, socially and industrially. The black people should not be encouraged to remain in white people's countries and expect to be Presidents, Governors, Mayors, Senators, Congressmen, Judges and social and industrial leaders. We believe that with the rising ambition of the negro, if a country is not provided for him in another 50 or 100 years, there will be a terrible clash that will end disastrously to him and disgrace our civilization. We desire to prevent such a clash by pointing the negro to a home of his own. We feel that all well disposed and broad minded white men will aid in this direction. It is because of this belief no doubt that my negro enemies, so as to prejudice me further in the opinion of the public, wickedly state that I am a member of the Ku Klux Klan, even though I am a black man.[1]

I have been deprived of the opportunity of properly explaining my work to the white people of America through the prejudice worked up against me by jealous and wicked members of my own race. My success as an organizer was much more than rival negro leaders could tolerate. They, regardless of consequences, either to me or to the race, had to destroy me by fair means or foul. The thousands of anonymous and other hostile letters written to the editors and publishers of the white press by negro rivals to prejudice me in the eyes of public opinion are sufficient evidence of the wicked and vicious opposition I have had to meet from among my own people, especially among the very lightly colored. But they went further than the press in their attempts to discredit me. They organized clubs all over the United States and the West Indies, and wrote both open and anonymous letters to city, State and Federal officials of this and other Governments to induce them to use their influence to hamper and destroy me. No wonder, therefore, that several Judges, District Attorneys and other high officials have been against me without knowing me. No wonder, therefore, that the great white population of this country and of the world has a wrong impression of the aims and objects of the Universal Negro Improvement Association and of the work of Marcus Garvey.

The Struggle of the Future

Having had the wrong education as a start in his racial career, the negro has become is own greatest enemy. Most of the trouble I have had in advancing the cause of the race has come from negroes. Booker Washington aptly described the race in one of his lectures by stating that we were like crabs in a barrel, that none would allow the other to climb over, but on any such attempt all would continue to pull back into the barrel the one crab that would make the effort to climb out. Yet, those of us with vision cannot desert the race, leaving it to suffer and die.

---

[1] Garvey was accused of cooperating with the Klan because he favored separation of the races, a position the Klan endorsed, though for different purposes from Garvey's — ED.

Looking forward a century or two, we can see an economic and political death struggle for the survival of the different race groups. Many of our present-day national centres will have become over-crowded with vast surplus populations. The fight for bread and position will be keen and severe. The weaker and unprepared group is bound to go under. That is why, visionaries as we are in the Universal Negro Improvement Association, we are fighting for the founding of a negro nation in Africa, so that there will be no clash between black and white and that each race will have a separate existence and civilization all its own without courting suspicion and hatred or eyeing each other with jealousy and rivalry within the borders of the same country.

White men who have struggled for and built up their countries and their own civilizations are not disposed to hand them over to the negro or any other race without let or hindrance. It would be unreasonable to expect this. Hence any vain assumption on the part of the negro to imagine that he will one day become President of the Nation, Governor of the State, or Mayor of the city in the countries of white men, is like waiting on the devil and his angels to take up their residence in the Realm on High and direct there the affairs of Paradise.

5.3:   The New Immigration and American Toleration (1911, 1912)

Although individual immigrants sometimes endured physical attack and intimidation, intolerance toward European immigrants in the early twentieth century primarily took verbal, economic, and legislative forms. Groups such as the Immigration Restriction League agitated for laws excluding immigrants unable to read and write (in any language) in the expectation that many from the newer regions of immigration would be disqualified. Other anti-immigrant organizations demanded laws capping the total admitted each year and setting quotas on specific nationality groups.

Americans had always worried that foreign newcomers would be difficult to assimilate culturally. But by the 1890s there were racial fears as well. The latest wave of foreigners, said many immigration restrictionists, derived from inferior human stock and so could never become a desirable element of American society, no matter how many classes they took in American civics or in the English language.

The selections below touch on several issues that concerned native-born Americans—and the immigrants as well—during the years 1890–1930. The first is an excerpt from the Dillingham Commission's report of 1911. The commission was authorized by Congress to investigate the problems created by the new arrivals. Supposedly guided by objec-

tive principles, it produced a report in forty-two volumes that was strong-
ly colored by the common cultural and racial prejudices of the day.

What were the commission members' complaints against the newcom-
ers? In what ways did they distinguish between recent immigrants and
those of the earlier nineteenth century? Can you detect a political reality
behind sparing the earlier arrivals from criticism? How is the commis-
sion's reasoning flawed?

The second selection is from the autobiography of Mary Antin, a
young Jewish woman born in Polotzk, Poland, who came to the United
States with her family in 1894 at the age of thirteen and became a writer
and social worker. In what way does she challenge the views of the
Dillingham Commission? Do you think her experience was typical of that
of the new immigrants in general? What role was the school system
expected to play in the process of assimilating the immigrants? Is there
any indication that her teacher encouraged Antin to retain any of her
family heritage? Was her experience in school different from that of immi-
grants of our own day? Does the role of Antin's teacher tell us anything
about the attitudes of some native-born Americans toward the new-
comers?

Dillingham Commission Report

Brief Statement of the Investigations

Plan and Scope of the Inquiry

Briefly stated, the plan of work adopted by the Commission included a study
of the sources of recent immigration in Europe, the general character of
incoming immigrants, the methods employed here and abroad to prevent
the immigration of persons classed as undesirable in the Unites States immigration law, and finally a thorough investigation into the general status of
the more recent immigrants as residents of the United States, and the effect
of such immigration upon the institutions, industries, and people of this
country. As above suggested, the chief basis of the Commission's work was
the changed character of the immigration movement to the United States
during the past twenty-five years.

During the fiscal year 1907, in which the Commission was created, a total
of 1,285,349 immigrants were admitted to the United States. Of this number
1,207,619 were from Europe, including Turkey in Asia, and of these 979,661,
or 81 per cent, came from the southern and eastern countries, comprising
Austria-Hungary, Bulgaria, Greece, Italy, Montenegro, Poland, Portugal,

Abstracts of Reports of the Immigration Commission (Dillingham Commission) (Washington, DC:
Government Printing Office, 1911), pp. 3 ff.

Roumania, Russia, Servia, Spain, Turkey in Europe, and Turkey in Asia.

Twenty-five years earlier, in the fiscal year 1882, 648,186 European immigrants came to the United States, and of these only 84,973, or 13.1 per cent, came from the countries above enumerated, while 563,213, or 86.9 per cent, were from Belgium, Great Britain and Ireland, France, Germany, the Netherlands, Scandinavia, and Switzerland, which countries furnished about 95 per cent of the immigration movement from Europe to the United States between 1819 and 1883.

During the entire period for which statistics are available — July 1, 1819, to June 30, 1910 — a total of 25,528,410 European immigrants, including 106,481 from Turkey in Asia, were admitted to the United States. Of these, 16,052,900, or 62.9 per cent, came from the northern and western countries enumerated, and 9,475,510, or 37.1 per cent, from southern and eastern Europe and Turkey in Asia. For convenience the former movement will be referred to in the Commission's reports as the "old immigration" and the latter as the "new immigration." The old and the new immigration differ in many essentials. The former was, from the beginning, largely a movement of settlers who came from the most progressive sections of Europe for the purpose of making for themselves homes in the New World. They entered practically every line of activity in nearly every part of the country. Coming during a period of agricultural development, many of them entered agricultural pursuits, sometimes as independent farmers, but more often as farm laborers, who, nevertheless, as a rule soon became landowners. They formed an important part of the great movement toward the West during the last century, and as pioneers were most potent factors in the development of the territory between the Allegheny Mountains and the Pacific coast. They mingled freely with the native Americans and were quickly assimilated, although a large proportion of them, particularly in later years, belonged to non–English-speaking races. This natural bar to assimilation, however, was soon overcome by them, while the racial identity of their children was almost entirely lost and forgotten.

On the other hand, the new immigration has been largely a movement of unskilled laboring men who have come, in large part temporarily, from the less progressive and advanced countries of Europe in response to the call for industrial workers in the eastern and middle western States. They have almost entirely avoided agricultural pursuits, and in cities and industrial communities have congregated together in sections apart from native Americans and the older immigrants to such an extent that assimilation has been slow as compared to that of the earlier non–English-speaking races.

The new immigration as a class is far less intelligent than the old, approximately one-third of all those over 14 years of age when admitted being illiterate. Racially they are for the most part essentially unlike the British, German, and other peoples who came during the period prior to 1880, and generally speaking they are actuated in coming by different ideals, for the old immigration came to be a part of the country, while the new, in a large measure, comes with the intention of profiting, in a pecuniary way, by the superior advantages of the new world and then returning to the old country.

The old immigration movement, which in earlier days was the subject of much discussion and the cause of no little apprehension among the people of the country, long ago became thoroughly merged into the population, and the old sources have contributed a comparatively small part of the recent immigrant tide. Consequently the Commission paid but little attention to the foreign-born element of the old immigrant class and directed its efforts almost entirely to an inquiry relative to the general status of the newer immigrants as residents of the United States.

In pursuance of this policy the Commission began its study of the subject in the countries of Europe which are the chief sources of the new immigration, and followed the emigration movement to ports of embarkation, across the ocean in the steerage, and finally to every part of the United States and into practically every line of activity in which the new immigrants were to be found. . . .

The old immigration movement was essentially one of permanent settlers. The new immigration is very largely one of individuals a considerable proportion of whom apparently have no intention of permanently changing their residence, their only purpose in coming to America being to temporarily take advantage of the greater wages paid for industrial labor in this country. This, of course, is not true of all the new immigrants, but the practice is sufficiently common to warrant referring to it as a characteristic of them as a class. From all data that are available it appears that nearly 40 per cent of the new immigration movement returns to Europe and that about two-thirds of those who go remain there. This does not mean that all of these immigrants have acquired a competence and returned to live on it. Among the immigrants who return permanently are those who have failed, as well as those who have succeeded. Thousands of those returning have, under unusual conditions of climate, work, and food, contracted tuberculosis and other diseases; others are injured in our industries; still others are widows and children of aliens dying here. These, with the aged and temperamentally unfit, make up a large part of the aliens who return to their former homes to remain.

The old immigration came to the United States during a period of general development and was an important factor in that development, while the new immigration has come during a period of great industrial expansion and has furnished a practically unlimited supply of labor to that expansion.

As a class the new immigrants are largely unskilled laborers coming from countries where their highest wage is small compared with the lowest wage in the United States. Nearly 75 per cent of them are males. About 83 per cent are between the ages of 14 and 45 years, and consequently are producers rather than dependents. They bring little money into the country and send or take a considerable part of their earnings out. More than 35 per cent are illiterate, as compared with less than 3 per cent of the old immigrant class. Immigration prior to 1882 was practically unregulated, and consequently many were not self-supporting, so that the care of alien paupers in several States was a serious problem. The new immigration has for the most part been carefully regulated so far as health and likelihood of pauperism are concerned, and, although drawn from classes low in the economic scale, the new immigrants as a rule are the strongest, the most enterprising, and the best of their class.

Causes of the Movement

While social conditions affect the situation in some countries, the present immigration from Europe to the United States is in the largest measure due to economic causes. It should be stated, however, that emigration from Europe is not now an absolute economic necessity, and as a rule those who emigrate to the United States are impelled by a desire for betterment rather than by the necessity of escaping intolerable conditions. This fact should largely modify the natural incentive to treat the immigration movement from the standpoint of sentiment and permit its consideration primarily as an economic problem. In other words, the economic and social welfare of the United States should now ordinarily be the determining factor in the immigration policy of the Government.

Unlike Canada, Argentina, Brazil, Australia, and other immigrant-receiving countries, the United States makes no effort to induce immigration. A law for the encouragement of immigration by guaranteeing in this country labor contracts made abroad was enacted in 1864 but repealed in 1868. Later legislation has tended to prevent the introduction of contract laborers and assisted or induced immigration, the purpose of the Government being that the movement should be a natural one. The law respecting assisted immigration, however, does not deny the right of a person already in this country to send for an otherwise admissible relative or friend, and a large part of the present movement, especially from southern and eastern Europe, is made possible through such assistance. The immediate incentive of the great bulk of present-day immigration is the letters of persons in this country to relatives or friends at home. Comparatively few immigrants come without some reasonably definite assurance that employment awaits them, and it is probable that as a rule they know the nature of that employment and the rate of wages. A large number of immigrants are induced to come by quasi labor agents in this country, who combine the business of supplying laborers to large employers and contractors with the so-called immigrant banking business and the selling of steamship tickets.

Another important agency in promoting emigration from Europe to the United States is the many thousands of steamship-ticket agents and subagents operating in the emigrant-furnishing districts of southern and eastern Europe. Under the terms of the United States immigration law, as well as the laws of most European countries, the promotion of emigration is forbidden, but nevertheless the steamship-agent propaganda flourishes everywhere. It does not appear that the steamship lines as a rule openly direct the operations of these agents, but the existence of the propaganda is a matter of common knowledge in the emigrant-furnishing countries and, it is fair to assume, is acquiesced in, if not stimulated, by the steamship lines as well. With the steamship lines the transportation of steerage passengers is purely a commercial matter; moreover, the steerage business which originates in southern and eastern Europe is peculiarly attractive to the companies, as many of the immigrants travel back and forth, thus insuring east-bound as well as west-bound traffic. . . .

Immigration of Criminals

While control of the immigration movement so far as physical and mental defectives are concerned has reached a high degree of efficiency, no adequate means have been adopted for preventing the immigration of criminals, prostitutes, and other morally undesirable aliens. The control of the latter classes is a much more difficult matter. In spite of the stringent law, criminals or moral defectives of any class, provided they pass the medical inspection, can usually embark at European ports and enter the United States without much danger of detection. A considerable number of criminals or aliens with criminal records are debarred annually at United States ports, but this results from the vigilance of immigrant inspectors or from chance information rather than from our system of regulation.

While it does not appear from available statistics that criminality among the foreign-born increases the volume of crime in proportion to the total population, nevertheless the coming of criminals and persons of criminal tendencies constitutes one of the serious social effects of the immigration movement. The present immigration law is not adequate to prevent the immigration of criminals, nor is it sufficiently effective as regards the deportation of alien criminals who are in this country. . . .

The Padrone System

In the case of the earlier immigration of several southern and eastern European races to the United States the control of some individuals in this country by padrones has occurred. Under this system persons have taken advantage of their better knowledge of our language and conditions to control the labor of the new immigrants of the same race. The system was somewhat prevalent in the case of the earlier Italian immigrants and in such case the padrones controlled the labor of their fellow-countrymen in construction and other work. Later a good many Syrian peddlers were controlled by padrones who furnished them with stocks in trade and profited unduly by their labor. With the development of immigration of any such race, however, and the establishment of such races as factors in the population of the country, the padrone system has substantially disappeared. At the present time practically the only aliens under the control of padrones in any considerable numbers are the Greek boys employed in shoe-shining establishments or in peddling flowers, fruit, or vegetables in the larger cities. This evil became so prevalent that when the immigration law of 1907 was enacted the following were included in the debarred classes:

> All children under 16 years of age unaccompanied by one of both of their parents at the discretion of the Secretary of Commerce and Labor, or under such regulations as he may from time to time prescribe.

Under this provision the importation of boys by padrones has been curtailed and the Bureau of Immigration makes persistent and continual efforts to stamp out the evil. While this condition in the case of the Greeks may continue for some time, it seems altogether probable that as persons of that race progress in the United States the influence of the padrones will largely disappear, as has been the case with other European races. . . .

Immigration and Crime

It is impossible from existing data to determine whether the immigrant population in this country is relatively more or less criminal than the native-born population. Statistics show that the proportion of convictions for crimes according to the population is greater among the foreign-born than among the native-born. It must be remembered, however, that the proportion of persons of what may be termed the criminal age is greater among the foreign-born than among natives, and when due allowance is made for this fact it appears that criminality, judged by convictions, is about equally prevalent in each class. It is obviously impossible to determine whether the proportion of unpunished criminals is relatively greater among the foreign- or among the native- born. It is sometimes stated that the detection and conviction of criminals, especially for higher crimes, is more difficult in the case of the foreign-born. Probably this is true of certain localities and perhaps generally true in the case of certain nationalities, but there is no proof that this condition applies to the foreign-born elements as a whole in the country at large. It is possible that in some localities prejudice against or sympathy for foreigners influences convictions or acquittals. In large cities a part of the apparent criminality of the foreign-born consists merely of violations of ordinances, which are offenses only because the persons who commit them are not naturalized. Prominent in this class of offenses is street peddling without a license in cities where such licenses are granted only to citizens.

The proportion of the more serious crimes of homicide, blackmail, and robbery, as well as the least serious offenses, is greater among the foreign-born. The disproportion in this regard is due principally to the prevalence of homicides and other crimes of personal violence among Italians and to the violation of city ordinances previously mentioned.

The Promised Land

MARY ANTIN

The public school has done its best for us foreigners, and for the country, when it has made us into good Americans. I am glad it is mine to tell how the miracle was wrought in one case. You should be glad to hear of it, you born Americans; for it is the story of the growth of your country; of the flocking of your brothers and sisters from the far ends of the earth to the flag you love; of the recruiting of your armies of workers, thinkers, and leaders. And you will be glad to hear of it, my comrades in adoption; for it is a rehearsal of your own experience, the thrill and wonder of which your own hearts have felt.

How long would you say, wise reader, it takes to make an American? By the middle of my second year in school I had reached the sixth grade. When, after the Christmas holidays, we began to study the life of Washington, running through a summary of the Revolution, and the early days of the Republic, it seemed to me that all my reading and study had been idle until then. The reader, the arithmetic, the song book, that had so fascinated me until now, became suddenly sober exercise books, tools wherewith to hew a way to the source of inspiration. When the teacher read to us out of a big book with many bookmarks in it, I sat rigid with attention in my little chair, my hands tightly clasped on the edge of my desk; and I painfully held my breath, to prevent sighs of disappointment escaping, as I saw the teacher skip the parts between bookmarks. When the class read, and it came my turn, my voice shook and the book trembled in my hands. I could not pronounce the name of George Washington without a pause. Never had I prayed, never had I chanted the songs of David, never had I called upon the Most Holy, in such utter reverence and worship as I repeated the simple sentences of my child's story of the patriot. I gazed with adoration at the portraits of George and Martha Washington, till I could see them with my eyes shut. And whereas formerly my self- consciousness had bordered on conceit, and I thought myself an uncommon person, parading my schoolbooks through the streets, and swelling with pride when a teacher detained me in conversation, now I grew humble all at once, seeing how insignificant I was beside the Great.

As I read about the noble boy who would not tell a lie to save himself from punishment, I was for the first time truly repentant of my sins. Formerly I had fasted and prayed and made sacrifice on the Day of Atonement, but it was more than half play, in mimicry of my elders. I had no real horror of sin, and I knew so many ways of escaping punishment. I am sure my family, my neighbors, my teachers in Polotzk—all my world, in fact—strove together, by example and precept, to teach me goodness. Saintliness had a new incarnation in about every third person I knew. I did

Mary Antin, *The Promised Land* (Boston: Houghton Mifflin Company, 1912), pp. 222–228.

respect the saints, but I could not help seeing that most of them were a little bit stupid, and that mischief was much more fun than piety. Goodness, as I had known it, was respectable, but not necessarily admirable. The people I really admired, like my Uncle Solomon, and Cousin Rachel, were those who preached the least and laughed the most. My sister Frieda was perfectly good, but she did not think the less of me because I played tricks. What I loved in my friends was not inimitable. One could be downright good if one really wanted to. One could be learned if one had books and teachers. One could sing funny songs and tell anecdotes if one travelled about and picked up such things, like one's uncles and cousins. But a human being strictly good, perfectly wise, and unfailingly valiant, all at the same time, I had never heard or dreamed of. This wonderful George Washington was as inimitable as he was irreproachable. Even if I had never, never told a lie, I could not compare myself to George Washington; for I was not brave—I was afraid to go out when snowballs whizzed—and I could never be the First President of the United States.

So I was forced to revise my own estimate of myself. But the twin of my new-born humility, paradoxical as it may seem, was a sense of dignity I had never known before. For if I found that I was a person of small consequence, I discovered at the same time that I was more nobly related than I had ever supposed. I had relatives and friends who were notable people by the old standards,—I had never been ashamed of my family,—but this George Washington, who died long before I was born, was like a king in greatness, and he and I were Fellow Citizens. There was a great deal about Fellow Citizens in the patriotic literature we read at this time; and I knew from my father how he was a Citizen, through the process of naturalization, and how I also was a citizen, by virtue of my relation to him. Undoubtedly I was a Fellow Citizen, and George Washington was another. It thrilled me to realize what sudden greatness had fallen on me; and at the same time it sobered me, as with a sense of responsibility. I strove to conduct myself as befitted a Fellow Citizen.

Before books came into my life, I was given to stargazing and daydreaming. When books were given me, I fell upon them as a glutton pounces on his meat after a period of enforced starvation. I lived with my nose in a book, and took no notice of the alternations of the sun and stars. But now, after the advent of George Washington and the American Revolution, I began to dream again. I strayed on the common after school instead of hurrying home to read. I hung on fence rails, my pet book forgotten under my arm, and gazed off to the yellow-streaked February sunset, and beyond, and beyond. I was no longer the central figure of my dreams; the dry weeds in the lane crackled beneath the tread of Heroes.

What more could America give a child? Ah, much more! As I read how the patriots planned the Revolution, and the women gave their sons to die in battle, and the heroes led to victory, and the rejoicing people set up the Republic, it dawned on me gradually what was meant by *my country*. The people all desiring noble things, and striving for them together, defying their oppressors, giving their lives for each other—all this it was that made *my country*. It was not a thing that I *understood;* I could not go home and tell Frieda about it, as I told her other things I learned at school. But I knew one could say "my country" and *feel* it, as one felt "God" or "myself." My teacher, my schoolmates, Miss Dillingham, George Washington himself could not mean more than I when they said "my country," after I had once felt it. For the Country was for all the Citizens, and *I was a Citizen*. And when we stood up to sing "America," I shouted the words with all my might. I was in very earnest proclaiming to the world my love for my new-found country.

> *I love thy rocks and rills,*
> *Thy woods and templed hills.*

Boston Harbor, Crescent Beach, Chelsea Square—all was hallowed ground to me. As the day approached when the school was to hold exercises in honor of Washington's Birthday, the halls resounded at all hours with the strains of patriotic songs; and I, who was a model of the attentive pupil, more than once lost my place in the lesson as I strained to hear, through closed doors, some neighboring class rehearsing "The Star-Spangled Banner." If the doors happened to open, and the chorus broke out unveiled—

> *O! say, does that Star-Spangled Banner yet wave*
> *O'er the land of the free, and the home of the brave?—*

delicious tremors ran up and down my spine, and I was faint with suppressed enthusiasm.

Where had been my country until now? What flag had I loved? What heroes had I worshipped? The very names of these things had been unknown to me. Well I knew that Polotzk was not my country. It was *goluth* — exile. On many occasions in the year we prayed to God to lead us out of exile. The beautiful Passover service closed with the words, "Next year, may we be in Jerusalem." On childish lips, indeed, those words were no conscious aspiration; we repeated the Hebrew syllables after our elders, but without their hope and longing. Still not a child among us was too young to feel in his own flesh the lash of the oppressor. We knew what it was to be Jews in exile, from the spiteful treatment we suffered at the hands of the smallest urchin who crossed himself; and thence we knew that Israel had good reason to pray for deliverance. But the story of the Exodus was not history to me in the sense that the story of the American Revolution was. It was more like a glorious myth, a belief in which had the effect of cutting me off from the actual world, by linking me with a world of phantoms. Those moments of exaltation which the contemplation of the Biblical past afforded us, allowing us to call ourselves the children of princes, served but to tinge with a more poignant sense of disinheritance the long humdrum stretches of our life. In very truth we were a people without a country. Surrounded by mocking foes and detractors, it was difficult for me to realize the persons of my people's heroes or the events in which they moved. Except in moments of abstraction from the world around me, I scarcely understood that Jerusalem was an actual spot on the earth, where once the Kings of the Bible, real people, like my neighbors in Polotzk, ruled in puissant majesty. For the conditions of our civil life did not permit us to cultivate a spirit of nationalism. The freedom of worship that was grudgingly granted within the narrow limits of the Pale by no means included the right to set up openly any ideal of a Hebrew State, any hero other than the Czar. What we children picked up of our ancient political history was confused with the miraculous story of the Creation, with the supernatural legends and hazy associations of Bible lore. As to our future, we Jews in Polotzk had no national expectations; only a lifeworn dreamer here and there hoped to die in Palestine. If Fetchke and I sang, with my father, first making sure of our audience, "Zion, Zion, Holy Zion, not forever is it lost," we did not really picture to ourselves Judæa restored.

So it came to pass that we did not know what *my country* could mean to a man. And as we had no country, so we had no flag to love. It was by no far-fetched symbolism that the banner of the House of Romanoff became the emblem of our latter-day bondage in our eyes. Even a child would know how to hate the flag that we were forced, on pain of severe penalties, to hoist above our housetops, in celebration of the advent of one of our oppressors. And as it was with country and flag, so it was with heroes of war. We hated the uniform of the soldier, to the last brass button. On the person of a Gentile, it was the symbol of tyranny; on the person of a Jew, it was the emblem of shame.

So a little Jewish girl in Polotzk was apt to grow up hungry-minded and empty-hearted; and if, still in her outreaching youth, she was set down in a land of outspoken patriotism, she was likely to love her new country with a great love, and to embrace its heroes in a great worship. Naturalization, with us Russian Jews, may mean more than the adoption of the immigrant by America. It may mean the adoption of America by the immigrant.

6

World War I

In the summer of 1914 the great powers of Europe went to war. In a matter of weeks the armies and navies of two great coalitions, the Central Powers (Germany, Austria-Hungary, and later Turkey) and the Entente, or Allies (France, Great Britain, Russia, and later Italy), were locked in murderous combat in Europe and around the world.

For two and a half years the United States remained on the sidelines, the largest and most powerful neutral in a world at war. President Woodrow Wilson initially urged his compatriots to remain "impartial in thought as well as in action," but from the outset this proved impossible. Too many Americans were tied by sentiment or culture to one side or the other. Moreover, the United States, with its great industrial and financial resources, could not easily detach itself economically from Europe's confrontation.

Both sides sought to mold American policy for their own ends. The Allies saw the United States as a source of credit, supplies, and munitions and tried to insure free access to these resources. Beyond this, some Allied leaders hoped to draw the great American republic into the war as an actual military partner. The Central Powers also could not ignore the United States. Unable themselves to procure American goods through the Allied blockade and with no expectation of American alliance, they limited their goals to keeping the United States neutral and preventing the Allies from taking full advantage of America's financial, industrial, and military might.

Inevitably, America's relations with the belligerents were colored by disagreements over neutral rights in time of war. The Wilson administration defended the right of Americans under international law to trade a wide range of goods with whomever they wished, and to travel wherever and however they wished.

Neither the Allies nor Central Powers accepted America's broad definition of neutral rights, but the British and French benefited more from free trade with the United States than did the Germans and Austro-Hungarians, and so clashed with America less. Indeed, the Germans soon sought to block American trade with the Allies in the only way they could: by use of the U-boat, a torpedo-armed submarine that could sink without warning any merchant vessel suspected of carrying war material to the enemy. The tactic was often brutal. Crews and passengers could not be saved by the small, vulnerable U-boats and so often perished. To charges of inhumanity, the Germans responded that the Allied blockade of food to German civilians was as barbarous as submarine warfare.

Americans disagreed over which policies to pursue toward the warring powers during 1914–17. Their views were affected by ethnicity, ideology, patriotism, politics, culture, material interest, and other considerations. These differing attitudes and the motives behind them are suggested in the documents that follow.

6.1:   The Submarine Dimension (1915)

No belligerent action during World War I set off as explosive a response in the United States as did the German submarine campaign against Allied and neutral shipping. In February 1915 the German government announced that all merchant vessels, whether neutral or enemy, found in a broad zone surrounding the British Isles would be sunk on sight, even if this meant injury or death to crews and passengers. This "unrestricted" U-boat warfare violated the traditional usages of war, and the American government threatened to hold the Imperial German government "to a strict accountability" for any loss of American lives and property under the order. The first selection below is the note sent by Secretary of State William Jennings Bryan to the German government conveying the American position. In fact, Bryan correctly stated the normal practices of war, but the Germans felt they had no choice.

The second selection is the response of the German foreign minister, Gottlieb von Jagow, to the American protest against the sinking in May 1915 of the British passenger liner the Lusitania, *with the loss of 1,200 civilian lives, including 128 American. American opinion was outraged, and the attack had been almost universally condemned. But is it fair to see the Germans as barbarians, indifferent to human life? Does the German foreign minister make a convincing case for his country's use of the submarine weapon in the instances he describes? Why was the American government, do you suppose, so unsympathetic to German arguments? Was the American government ever willing, in later years, to limit the travel of its citizens in dangerous war zones?*

Protesting Unrestricted U-Boat Warfare

WILLIAM JENNINGS BRYAN

Washington, February 10, 1915

Please address a note immediately to the Imperial German Government to the following effect:

The Government of the United States, having had its attention directed to the proclamation of the German Admiralty issued on the 4th of February, . . . feels it to be its duty to call the attention of the Imperial German Government, with sincere respect and the most friendly sentiments but very candidly and earnestly, to the very serious possibilities of the course of action apparently contemplated under that proclamation.

The Government of the United States views those possibilities with such grave concern that it feels it to be its privilege, and indeed its duty in the circumstances, to request the Imperial German Government to consider before action is taken the critical situation in respect of the relations between this country and Germany which might arise were the German naval forces, in carrying out the policy foreshadowed in the Admiralty's proclamation, to destroy any merchant vessel of the United States or cause the death of American citizens.

It is of course not necessary to remind the German Government that the sole right of a belligerent in dealing with neutral vessels on the high seas is limited to visit and search, unless a blockade is proclaimed and effectively maintained, which this Government does not understand to be proposed in this case. To declare or exercise a right to attack and destroy any vessel entering a prescribed area of the high seas without first certainly determining its belligerent nationality and the contraband character of its cargo would be an act so unprecedented in naval warfare that this Government is reluctant to believe that the Imperial Government of Germany in this case contemplates it as possible. The suspicion that enemy ships are using neutral flags improperly can create no just presumption that all ships traversing a prescribed area are subject to the same suspicion. It is to determine exactly such questions that this Government understands the right of visit and search to have been recognized.

This Government has carefully noted the explanatory statement issued by the Imperial German Government at the same time with the proclamation

[U.S. Department of State], *Papers Relating to the Foreign Relations of the United States, 1915. Supplement: The World War* (Washington: Government Printing Office, 1928), pp. 98–100.

of the German Admiralty, and takes this occasion to remind the Imperial German Government very respectfully that the Government of the United States is open to none of the criticisms for unneutral action to which the German Government believe the governments of certain other neutral nations have laid themselves open; that the Government of the United States has not consented to or acquiesced in any measures which may have been taken by the other belligerent nations in the present war which operate to restrain neutral trade, but has, on the contrary, taken in all such matters a position which warrants it in holding those governments responsible in the proper way for any untoward effects upon American shipping which the accepted principles of international law do not justify; and that it, therefore, regards itself as free in the present instance to take with a clear conscience and upon accepted principles the position indicated in this note.

If the commanders of German vessels of war should act upon the presumption that the flag of the United States was not being used in good faith and should destroy on the high seas an American vessel or the lives of American citizens, it would be difficult for the Government of the United States to view the act in any other light than as an indefensible violation of neutral rights which it would be very hard indeed to reconcile with the friendly relations now so happily subsisting between the two Governments.

If such a deplorable situation should arise, the Imperial German Government can readily appreciate that the Government of the United States would be constrained to hold the Imperial German Government to a strict accountability for such acts of their naval authorities and to take any steps it might be necessary to take to safeguard American lives and property and to secure to American citizens the full enjoyment of their acknowledged rights on the high seas.

The Government of the United States, in view of these considerations, which it urges with the greatest respect and with the sincere purpose of making sure that no misunderstanding may arise and no circumstance occur that might even cloud the intercourse of the two Governments, expresses the confident hope and expectation that the Imperial German Government can and will give assurance that American citizens and their vessels will not be molested by the naval forces of Germany otherwise than by visit and search, though their vessels may be traversing the sea area delimited in the proclamation of the German Admiralty.

It is added for the information of the Imperial Government that representations have been made to His Britannic Majesty's Government in respect to the unwarranted use of the American flag for the protection of British ships.

[Secretary of State William Jennings] Bryan

The Germans Defend Their Submarine Policy

GOTTLIEB VON JAGOW

Berlin, May 28, 1915

The Imperial Government has subjected the statements of the Government of the United States to a careful examination and has the lively wish on its part also to contribute in a convincing and friendly manner to clear up any misunderstandings which may have entered into the relations of the two Governments through the events mentioned by the American Government.

With regard firstly to the cases of the American steamers *Cushing* and *Gulflight*, the American Embassy has already been informed that it is far from the German Government to have any intention of ordering attacks by submarines or flyers on neutral vessels in the zone which have not been guilty of any hostile act; on the contrary, the most explicit instructions have been repeatedly given the German armed forces to avoid attacking such vessels. If neutral vessels have come to grief through the German submarine war during the past few months, by mistake, it is a question of isolated and exceptional cases which are traceable to the misuse of flags by the British Government in connection with carelessness or suspicious actions on the part of [the] captains of the vessels. In all cases where a neutral vessel through no fault of its own has come to grief through the German submarine or flyers according to the facts as ascertained by the German Government, this Government has expressed its regret at the unfortunate occurrence and promised indemnification where the facts justified it. The German Government will treat the cases of the American steamers *Cushing* and *Gulflight* according to the same principles. An investigation of these cases is in progress. Its results will be communicated to the Embassy shortly. The investigation might, if thought desirable, be supplemented by an international commission of inquiry, pursuant to Title III of the Hague Convention of October 18, 1907, for the pacific settlement of international disputes.

In the case of the sinking of the English steamer *Falaba*, the commander of the German submarine had the intention of allowing passengers and crew ample opportunity to save themselves. It was not until the captain disregarded the order to lay to and took to flight, sending up rocket signals for help, that the German commander ordered the crew and passengers by signals and megaphone to leave the ship within ten minutes. As a matter of fact he allowed them twenty-three minutes and did not fire the torpedo until suspicious steamers were hurrying to the aid of the *Falaba*.

With regard to the loss of life when the British passenger steamer *Lusitania* was sunk, the German Government has already expressed its deep regret to the neutral Governments concerned that nationals of those countries lost their lives on that occasion. The Imperial Government must state

[U.S. Department of State]. *Papers Relating to the Foreign Relations of the United States, 1915. Supplement: The World War* (Washington: Government Printing Office, 1928), pp. 419–421.

for the rest the impression that certain important facts most directly connected with the sinking of the *Lusitania* may have escaped the attention of the Government of the United States. It therefore considers it necessary in the interest of the clear and full understanding aimed at by either Government primarily to convince itself that the reports of the facts which are before the two Governments are complete and in agreement.

The Government of the United States proceeds on the assumption that the *Lusitania* is to be considered as an ordinary unarmed merchant vessel. The Imperial Government begs in this connection to point out that the *Lusitania* was one of the largest and fastest English commerce steamers, constructed with Government funds as auxiliary cruisers, and is expressly included in the navy list published by British Admiralty. It is moreover known to the Imperial Government from reliable information furnished by its officials and neutral passengers that for some time practically all the more valuable English merchant vessels have been provided with guns, ammunition, and other weapons, and reinforced with a crew specially practiced in manning guns. According to reports at hand here, the *Lusitania* when she left New York undoubtedly had guns on board which were mounted under decks and masked.

The Imperial Government furthermore has the honor to direct the particular attention of the American Government to the fact that the British Admiralty by a secret instruction of February of this year advised the British merchant marine not only to seek protection behind neutral flags and markings, but even when so disguised to attack German submarines by ramming them. High rewards have been offered by the British Government as a special incentive for the destruction of the submarines by merchant vessels, and such rewards have already been paid out. In view of these facts, which are satisfactorily known to it, the Imperial Government is unable to consider English merchant vessels any longer as "undefended territory" in the zone of maritime war designated by the Admiralty Staff of the Imperial German Navy, the German commanders are consequently no longer in a position to observe the rules of capture otherwise usual and with which they invariably complied before this. Lastly, the Imperial Government must specially point out that on her last trip the *Lusitania*, as on earlier occasions, had Canadian troops and munitions on board, including no less than 5,400 cases of ammunition destined for the destruction of brave German soldiers who are fulfilling with self-sacrifice and devotion their duty in the service of the Fatherland. The German Government believes that it acts in just self-defense when it seeks to protect the lives of its soldiers by destroying ammunition destined for the enemy with the means of war at its command. The English steamship company must have been aware of the dangers to which passengers on board the *Lusitania* were exposed under the circumstances. In taking them on board in spite of this the company quite deliberately tried to use the lives of American citizens as protection for the ammunition carried, and violated the clear provisions of American laws which expressly prohibit, and provide punishment for, the carrying of passengers on ships which have explosives on board. The company thereby wantonly caused the death of so many passengers. According to the express report of the submarine commander concerned, which is further confirmed by all other reports, there can be no doubt that the rapid sinking of the *Lusitania* was primarily due to the explosion of the cargo of ammunition caused by the torpedo. Otherwise, in all human probability, the passengers of the *Lusitania* would have been saved.

The Imperial Government holds the facts recited above to be of sufficient importance to recommend them to a careful examination by the American Government. The Imperial Government begs to reserve a final statement of its position with regard to the demand made in connection with the sinking of the *Lusitania* until a reply is received from the American Government.

[Foreign Minister Gottlieb] von Jagow

6.2: Voices for Intervention (1915)

There was never any serious support in the United States for entering the war on the side of the Central Powers. But from the beginning some Americans sought to align the United States militarily with Britain and France. There have been many explanations for this tilt to the Allies. Below are three contemporary documents that suggest reasons for American sympathy for the Allied side and for the military support for Britain and France America finally provided.

The first is an excerpt from the Bryce Report of 1915, a British indictment of German behavior toward civilians in the German-occupied regions of France and Belgium. James Bryce, chief author of the report, was the former British ambassador to the United States, a respected figure who had written a famous book about America a generation before.

The Bryce Report was part of a concerted Allied propaganda campaign to influence American public opinion. Do the statements of the report ring true? Is it clear that the brutality against civilians described was deliberate German policy? How do Bryce and his colleagues link the Belgian and French atrocities to German, or "Prussian," militarism?

The second item is a memo from the private papers of Robert Lansing, the man who succeeded William Jennings Bryan as secretary of state in 1915. Although he represented an officially neutral nation, clearly Lansing himself was not neutral. What were the bases for his pro-Allies feelings? Were they shared by other influential Americans? Were his views of German policies and goals valid?

The third selection is a letter by Lansing to President Wilson on the issue of extending financial credits to the Allies to allow them to continue to buy American munitions and other war supplies. Earlier, in 1914, the American government had sought to discourage American loans to any of the belligerents as an unneutral act. Lansing's proposal represents a *retreat from that policy. By April 1917 U.S. investors had bought $2.3 billion of Allied bonds.*

Critics of American intervention in World War I have said that the liberal loan policy of the Wilson administration created an economic stake in Allied victory that powerfully influenced American policy. What were Lansing's reasons for wanting to liberalize American loan policies? Are his arguments convincing? Did America have an economic stake in the Allied cause and was this a significant factor in drawing the United States into the war in 1917?

British Report on German Atrocities in Belgium

AMBASSADOR JAMES BRYCE

In the minds of Prussian officers War seems to have become a sort of sacred mission, one of the highest functions of the omnipotent State, which is itself as much an Army as a State. Ordinary morality and the ordinary sentiment of pity vanish in its presence, superseded by a new standard which justifies to the soldier every means that can conduce to success, however shocking to a natural sense of justice and humanity, however revolting to his own feelings. The Spirit of War is deified. Obedience to the State and its War Lord leaves no room for any other duty or feeling. Cruelty becomes legitimate when it promises victory. Proclaimed by the heads of the army, this doctrine would seem to have permeated the officers and affected even the private soldiers, leading them to justify the killing of non-combatants as an act of war, and so accustoming them to slaughter that even women and children become at last the victims. It cannot be supposed to be a national doctrine, for it neither springs from nor reflects the mind and feelings of the German people as they have heretofore been known to other nations. It is a specifically military doctrine, the outcome of a theory held by a ruling caste who have brooded and thought, written and talked and dreamed about War until they have fallen under its obsession and been hypnotised by its spirit.

The doctrine is plainly set forth in the German Official Monograph on the usages of War on land, issued under the direction of the German staff. This book is pervaded throughout by the view that whatever military needs suggest becomes thereby lawful, and upon this principle, as the diaries show, the German officers acted. . . .

(a) Killing of Non-Combatants

The killing of civilians in Belgium has been already described sufficiently. Outrages on the civilian population of the invaded districts, the burning of villages, the shooting of innocent inhabitants and the taking of hostages, pillage and destruction continued as the German armies passed into France. . . .

Report of the Committee on Alleged German Outrages (London: His Majesty's Stationary Office, 1915), pp. 44–61.

A proclamation (a specimen of which was produced to the Committee) issued at Reims, and placarded over the town, affords a clear illustration of the methods adopted by the German Higher Command. The population of Reims is warned that on the slightest disturbance part or the whole of the city will be burnt to the ground and all the hostages taken from the city (a long list of whom is given in the proclamation) immediately shot. . . .

Naturally soldiers in a foreign country, with which they were unacquainted, cannot be expected always to give accurately the names of villages through which they passed on their marches, but this does not prevent their evidence from being definite as to what they actually saw in the farms and houses where the German troops had recently been. Many shocking outrages are recorded. [Several] examples here may suffice, . . . A sergeant who had been through the retreat from Mons, and then taken part in the advance from the Marne, and who had been engaged in driving out some German troops from a village, states that his troop halted outside a bakery just inside the village. It was a private house where baking was done, "not like our bakeries here." Two or three women were standing at the door. The women motioned them to come into the house, as did also three civilian Frenchmen who were there. They took them into a garden at the back of the house. At the end of the garden was the bakery. They saw two old men— between 60 and 70 years of age—and one old woman lying close to each other in the garden. All three had the scalps cut right through and the brains were hanging out. They were still bleeding. Apparently they had only just been killed. The three French civilians belonged to this same house. One of them spoke a few words of English. He gave them to understand that these three had been killed by the Germans because they had refused to bake bread for them. . . .

A lance-corporal in the Rifles, who was on patrol duty with five privates during the retirement of the Germans after the Marne, states that they entered a house in a small village and took ten Uhlans prisoners and then searched the house and found two women and two children. One was dead, but the body not yet cold. The left arm had been cut off just below the elbow. The floor was covered with blood. The woman's clothing was disarranged. The other woman was alive but unconscious. Her right leg had been cut off above the knee. There were two little children, a boy about 4 or 5 and a girl of about 6 or 7. The boy's left hand was cut off at the wrist and the girl's right hand at the same place. They were both quite dead. The same witness states that he saw several women and children lying dead in various other places, but says he could not say whether this might not have been accidentally caused in legitimate fighting.

The evidence before us proves that, in the parts of France referred to, murder of unoffending civilians and other acts of cruelty, including aggravated cases of rape, carried out under threat of death, and sometimes actually followed by murder of the victim, were committed by some of the German troops.

(b)   The Treatment of Women and Children

The evidence shows that the German authorities, when carrying out a policy of systematic arson and plunder in selected districts, usually drew some distinction between the adult male population on the one hand and the women and children on the other. It was a frequent practice to set apart the adult males of the condemned district with a view to the execution of a suitable number—preferably of the younger and more vigorous—and to reserve the women and children. . . .

We find many well-established cases of the slaughter (often accompanied by mutilation) of whole families, including not infrequently that of quite small children. In two cases it seems to be clear that preparations were made to burn a family alive. These crimes were committed over a period of many weeks and simultaneously in many places, and the authorities must have known or ought to have known that cruelties of this character were being perpetrated, nor can anyone doubt that they could have been stopped by swift and decisive action on the part of the heads of the German army. . . .

The cases of violation, sometimes under threat of death, are numerous and clearly proved. . . . They were often accompanied with cruelty, and the slaughter of women after violation is more than once credibly attested.

It is quite possible that in some cases where the body of a Belgian or a French woman is reported as lying in the roadside pierced with bayonet wounds or hanging naked from a tree, or else as lying gashed and mutilated in a cottage kitchen or bedroom, the woman in question gave some provocation. She may by act or word have irritated her assailant, and in certain instances evidence has been supplied both as to the provocation offered and as to the retribution inflicted:—

> "Just before we got to Melen," says a witness, who had fallen into the hands of the Germans on August 5th, "I saw a woman with a child in her arms standing on the side of the road on our left-hand side watching the soldiers go by. Her name was G . . . , aged about sixty-three, and a neighbour of mine. The officer asked the woman for some water in good French. She went inside her son's cottage to get some and brought it immediately he had stopped. The officer went into the cottage garden and drank the water. The woman then said, when she saw the prisoners, 'Instead of giving you water you deserve to be shot.' The officer shouted to us, 'March.' We went on, and immediately I saw the officer draw his revolver and shoot the woman and child. One shot killed both." . . .

In considering the question of provocation it is pertinent to take into account the numerous cases in which old women and very small children have been shot, bayoneted, and even mutilated. Whatever excuse may be offered by the Germans for the killing of grown-up women, there can be no possible defence for the murder of children, and if it can be shown that infants and small children were not infrequently bayoneted and shot it is a fair inference that many of the offences against women require no explanation more recondite than the unbridled violence of brutal or drunken criminals. . . .

Conclusions

From the foregoing pages it will be seen that the Committee have come to a definite conclusion upon each of the heads under which the evidence has been classified.

It is proved—

i. That there were in many parts of Belgium deliberate and systematically organised massacres of the civil population, accompanied by many isolated murders and other outrages.
ii. That in the conduct of the war generally innocent civilians, both men and women, were murdered in large numbers, women violated, and children murdered.
iii. That looting, house burning, and the wanton destruction of property were ordered and countenanced by the officers of the German Army, that elaborate provision had been made for systematic incendiarism at the very outbreak of the war, and that the burnings and destruction were frequent where no military necessity could be alleged, being indeed part of a system of general terrorization.
iv. That the rules and usages of war were frequently broken, particularly by the using of civilians, including women and children, as a shield for advancing forces exposed to fire, to a less degree by killing the wounded and prisoners, and in the frequent abuse of the Red Cross and the White Flag.

Sensible as they are of the gravity of these conclusions, the Committee conceive that they would be doing less than their duty if they failed to record them as fully established by the evidence. Murder, lust, and pillage prevailed over many parts of Belgium on a scale unparalleled in any war between civilised nations during the last three centuries.

Our function is ended when we have stated what the evidence establishes, but we may be permitted to express our belief that these disclosures will not have been made in vain if they touch and rouse the conscience of mankind, and we venture to hope that as soon as the present war is over, the nations of the world in council will consider what means can be provided and sanctions devised to prevent the recurrence of such horrors as our generation is now witnessing.

Germany Must Not Be Allowed to Win the War

ROBERT LANSING

July 11, 1915

I have come to the conclusion that the German Government is utterly hostile to all nations with democratic institutions because those who compose it

Private Memoranda Books, The Papers of Robert Lansing, Manuscripts Division, Library of Congress, Washington, DC.

see in democracy a menace to absolutism and the defeat of the German ambition for world domination. Everywhere German agents are plotting and intriguing to accomplish the supreme purpose of their Government.

Only recently has the conviction come that democracy throughout the world is threatened. Suspicions of the vaguest sort only a few months [ago] have been more and more confirmed. From many sources evidence has been coming until it would be folly to close one's eyes to it.

German agents have undoubtedly been at work in Mexico arousing anti-American feeling and holding out false hopes of support. The proof is not conclusive but is sufficient to compel belief. Germans also appear to be operating in Haiti and San Domingo and are probably doing so in other Latin American republics.

I think that this is being done so that this nation will have troubles in America and be unable to take part in the European War if a repetition of such outrages as the LUSITANIA sinking should require us to act. It may even go further and have in mind the possibility of a future war with this Republic in case the Allies should be defeated.

In these circumstances the policies we adopt are vital to the future of the United States and, I firmly believe to the welfare of mankind, for I see in the perpetuation of democracy the one hope of universal peace and progress for the world. Today German absolutism is the great menace to democracy.

I think that we should, therefore, adopt the following for the present and pursue these policies until conditions materially change:

1. The settlement for the time being at least of present submarine controversy because the American people are still much divided on the merits of the war. As it progresses, I believe, that the real objects of the German Government will be disclosed and there will be united opposition. Meanwhile we should get ready to meet the worst.

2. A rigorous and continuing prosecution of all plots in this country and a vigilant watch on Germans and their activities here.

3. Secret investigations of German activities in Latin America, particularly Mexico, and the adoption of means to frustrate them.

4. The cultivation of a Pan American doctrine with the object of alienating the American republics from European influence, especially the German influence. . . .

8. The actual participation of this country in the war in case it becomes evident that Germany will be the victor. A triumph for German imperialism *must not be.* We ought to look forward to this possibility and make ready to meet it.

There is a future possibility which does not change the foregoing policies but which emphasizes the last one. It is that the war may end in a draw or with the German Empire dominant over their enemies.

The argument could then be made by the German Government that, in spite of the fact that the world was arrayed against it, it succeeded in preventing the defeat of the Empire, and that having thus proved its superior efficiency it should be continued and supported as the agency best fitted to restore the German nation to a state of prosperity.

I believe that this argument would be potent with the German people, who are in the habit of unquestioning obedience to their rulers in thought as well as action. Of course the terrible cost of the war, when the time to consider that arrives, will weaken the argument for the people will ask what is the recompense for the great sacrifices they have made, the great sufferings which they have endured, and the Government will have nothing to show. The nation may then rise and demand a change to a political system in which their voice will be supreme. But, if the argument should prevail and the present military oligarchy should be perpetuated, then what?

My judgment is that the German Government, cherishing the same ambition of world empire which now possesses it, would with its usual vigor and thoroughness prepare to renew its attack on democracy. I think, however, that it would not pursue the course taken in this war which had failed because it would realize that the democratic nations would be more watchful and less trustful and better prepared to resist. It would probably endeavor to sow dissentions [*sic*] among the nations with liberal institutions and seek an alliance with other governments based to a more or less degree on the principle of absolutism.

The two powers, which would probably be approached by Germany, would be Russia and Japan, which are almost as hostile to democracy as Germany and which have similar ambitions of territorial expansion.

These three great empires would constitute an almost irresistable [*sic*] coalition against the nations with republican and liberal monarchical institutions. It would be the old struggle of absolutism against democracy, an even greater struggle than the one now in progress. The outcome would be doubtful, with, as it seems to me, the chances in favor of the autocratic allies.

The success of these three empires would mean a division for the time being at least of the world among them. I imagine that Germany would be master of Western Europe, of Africa and probably of the Americas; that Russia would dominate Scandinavia, and Western and Southern Asia; and Japan would control the Far East, the Pacific and possibly the West Coast of North America.

Their success would mean the overthrow of democracy in the world, the suppression of individual liberty, the setting up of evil ambitions, the subordination of the principles of right and justice to physical might directed by arbitrary will, and the turning back of the hands of human progress two centuries.

These, I believe, would be the consequences of the triumph of this triple alliance of autocratic empires, a triumph which even the most optimistic cannot deny to be a reasonable expectation.

The remedy seems to me to be plain. It is that Germany must not be permitted to win this war and to break even, though to prevent it this country is forced to take an active part. This ultimate necessity must be constantly in our minds in all our controversies with the belligerents. American public opinion must be prepared for the time, which may come, when we will have to cast aside our neutrality and become one of the champions of democracy.

We must in fact risk everything rather than leave the way open for a new combination of powers, stronger and more dangerous to liberty than the Central Allies are today.

Lending the Allies Money

ROBERT LANSING

Washington, September 6, 1915

My dear Mr. President:

Doubtless Secretary [William] McAdoo has discussed with you the necessity of floating government loans for the belligerent nations, which are purchasing such great quantities of goods in this country, in order to avoid a serious financial situation which will not only affect them but this country as well.

Briefly, the situation, as I understand it, is this: Since December 1st, 1914, to June 30, 1915, our exports have exceeded our imports by nearly a billion dollars, and it is estimated that the excess will be from July 1st to December 31, 1915, a billion and three quarters. Thus for the year 1915 the excess will be approximately two and [a] half billions of dollars.

It is estimated that the European banks have about three and [a] half billions of dollars in gold in their vaults. To withdraw any considerable amount would disastrously affect the credit of the European nations, and the consequence would be a general state of bankruptcy.

If the European countries cannot find means to pay for the excess of goods sold to them over those purchased from them, they will have to stop buying and our present export trade will shrink proportionately. The result would be restriction of outputs, industrial depression, idle capital and idle labor, numerous failures, financial demoralization, and general unrest and suffering among the laboring classes.

Probably a billion and three quarters of the excess of European purchases can be taken care of by the sale of American securities held in Europe and by the transfer of trade balances of oriental countries, but that will leave three quarters of a billion to be met in some other way. Furthermore, even if that is arranged, we will have to face a more serious situation in January, 1916, as the American securities held abroad will have been exhausted.

I believe that Secretary McAdoo is convinced and I agree with him that there is only one means of avoiding this situation which would so seriously affect economic conditions in the country, and that is the flotation of large bond issues by the belligerent governments. Our financial institutions have the money to loan and wish to do so. On account of the great balance of trade in our favor the proceeds of these loans would be expended here. The result would be a maintenance of the credit of the borrowing nations based on their gold reserve, a continuance of our commerce at its present volume and industrial activity with the consequent employment of capital and labor and national prosperity.

The difficulty is—and this is what Secretary McAdoo came to see me about—that the Government early in the war announced that it considered "war loans" to be contrary to "the true spirit of neutrality." A declaration to this effect was given to the press about August 15, 1914, by Secretary Bryan. The language is as follows: "In the judgment of this Government loans by American bankers to any foreign nation at war is inconsistent with the true spirit of neutrality."

In October, 1914, after a conference with you, I gave my "impressions" to certain New York bankers in reference to "credit loans," but the general statement remained unaffected. In drafting the letter of January 20, 1915, to Senator Stone I sought to leave out a broad statement and to explain merely the reasons for distinguishing between "general loans" and "credit loans." However, Mr. Bryan thought it well to repeat the August declaration and it appears in the first sentence of division 13 of the letter, a copy of which I enclose.

On March 31, 1915, another press statement was given out from the Department which read as follows:

> "The State Department has from time to time received information directly or indirectly to the effect that belligerent nations had arranged with Banks in the United States for credits in various sums. While loans to belligerents have been disapproved, this Government has not felt that it was justified in interposing objection to the credit arrangements which have been brought to its attention. It has neither approved these nor disapproved—it has simply taken no action in the premises and expressed no opinion."

Manifestly the Government has committed itself to the policy of discouraging general loans to belligerent governments. The practical reasons for the policy at the time we adopted it were sound, but basing it on the ground that loans are "inconsistent with the true spirit of neutrality" is now a source of embarrassment. This latter ground is as strong today as it was a year ago, while the practical reasons for discouraging loans have largely disappeared. We have more money than we can use. Popular sympathy has become crystallized in favor of one or another of the belligerents to such an extent that the purchase of bonds would in no way increase the bitterness of partisanship or cause a possibly serious situation.

Now, on the other hand, we are face to face with what appears to be a critical economic situation, which can only be relieved apparently by the investment of American capital in foreign loans to be used in liquidating the enormous balance of trade in favor of the United States.

Can we afford to let a declaration as to our conception of "the true spirit of neutrality" made in the first days of the war stand in the way of our national interests which seem to be seriously threatened?

If we cannot afford to do this, how are we to explain away the declaration and maintain a semblance of consistency?

My opinion is that we ought to allow the loans to be made for our own good, and I have been seeking some means of harmonizing our policy, so unconditionally announced, with the flotation of general loans. As yet I have found no solution to the problem.

Secretary McAdoo considers that the situation is becoming acute and that something should be done at once to avoid the disastrous results which will follow a continuance of the present policy.

Faithfully yours,

Robert Lansing

6.3:   Opponents of Intervention (1917)

From the outset several groups opposed American intervention in the European war. First there were the pacifists, whether members of "peace churches," like the Quakers and Mennonites, or adherents of various secular pacifist groups. Many Socialists also opposed U.S. intervention, although on political, not moral, grounds. Ethnic considerations also played a role in opposing going to war. Many German-Americans and Irish-Americans either favored the Central Powers or disliked the Allies. Finally, some midwestern Progressives were "isolationists" who denied that America had any vital interest in European affairs and urged their fellow citizens to steer clear of overseas entanglements.

The antiwar forces were unable to keep America neutral, however. Soon after the German government announced resumption of unrestricted U-boat warfare in early 1917, the United States declared war on the Central Powers. The first selection below is a statement issued by the Socialist Party of America in early April, several days after the U.S. war declaration, expressing their opposition to the war. What were the bases of the Socialist position? Were they consistent with Socialist analyses of the nature of contemporary society? From this statement, can you deduce the Socialist attitude toward national loyalty and traditional patriotism?

The second selection is an excerpt from Wisconsin Senator Robert La Follette's remarks during the war-declaration debate in Congress. It is representative of the views of many midwestern Progressives. What is La Follette's analysis of the origins of the war? How does it differ from that of the Socialists? How does his analysis influence his view of the war's justice? Do his remarks betray national biases and prejudices? La Follette's own state, Wisconsin, was home to a very large German-American population. Could the senator's views have been colored by that fact?

Socialist Party Convention: The Socialists Protest the War

The Socialist Party and the War[1]

The Socialist Party of the United States in the present grave crisis, solemnly reaffirms its allegiance to the principle of internationalism and working class solidarity the world over, and proclaims its unalterable opposition to the war just declared by the government of the United States.

Modern wars as a rule have been caused by the commercial and financial rivalry and intrigues of the capitalist interests in the different countries. Whether they have been frankly waged as wars of aggression or have been hypocritically represented as wars of "defense," they have always been made by the classes and fought by the masses. Wars bring wealth and power to the ruling classes, and suffering, death and demoralization to the workers.

They breed a sinister spirit of passion, unreason, race hatred and false patriotism. They obscure the struggles of the workers for life, liberty and social justice. They tend to sever the vital bonds of solidarity between them and their brothers in other countries, to destroy their organizations and to curtail their civic and political rights and liberties.

The Socialist Party of the United States is unalterably opposed to the system of exploitation and class rule which is upheld and strengthened by military power and sham national patriotism. We, therefore, call upon the workers of all countries to refuse support to their governments in their wars. The wars of the contending national groups of capitalists are not the concern of the workers. The only struggle which would justify the workers in taking up arms is the great struggle of the working class of the world to free itself from economic exploitation and political oppression, and we particularly warn the workers against the snare and delusion of so-called defensive warfare. As against the false doctrine of national patriotism we uphold the ideal of international working-class solidarity. In support of capitalism, we will not willingly give a single life or a single dollar; in support of the struggle of the workers for freedom we pledge our all.

The mad orgy of death and destruction which is now convulsing unfortunate Europe was caused by the conflict of capitalist interests in the European countries.

In each of these countries, the workers were oppressed and exploited. They produced enormous wealth but the bulk of it was withheld from them

The American Labor Yearbook, vol. 2 (1917–18), pp. 50–52.

[1]Majority report adopted at the St. Louis Convention of the Socialist Party, April 7–14, 1917, and ratified by referendum.

by the owners of the industries. The workers were thus deprived of the means to repurchase the wealth which they themselves had created.

The capitalist class of each country was forced to look for foreign markets to dispose of the accumulated "surplus" wealth. The huge profits made by the capitalists could no longer be profitably reinvested in their own countries, hence, they were driven to look for foreign fields of investment. The geographical boundaries of each modern capitalist country thus became too narrow for the industrial and commercial operations of its capitalist class.

The efforts of the capitalists of all leading nations were therefore centered upon the domination of the world markets. Imperialism became the dominant note in the politics of Europe. The acquisition of colonial possessions and the extension of spheres of commercial and political influence became the object of diplomatic intrigues and the cause of constant clashes between nations.

The acute competition between the capitalist powers of the earth, their jealousies and distrusts of one another and the fear of the rising power of the working class forced each of them to arm to the teeth. This led to the mad rivalry of armament, which, years before the outbreak of the present war, had turned the leading countries of Europe into armed camps with standing armies of many millions, drilled and equipped for war in times of "peace."

Capitalism, imperialism and militarism had thus laid the foundation of an inevitable general conflict in Europe. The ghastly war in Europe was not caused by an accidental event, nor by the policy or institutions of any single nation. It was the logical outcome of the competitive capitalist system.

The six million men of all countries and races who have been ruthlessly slain in the first thirty months of this war, the millions of others who have been crippled and maimed, the vast treasures of wealth that have been destroyed, the untold misery and sufferings of Europe, have not been sacrifices exacted in a struggle for principles or ideals, but wanton offerings upon the altar of private profit.

The forces of capitalism which have led to the war in Europe are even more hideously transparent in the war recently provoked by the ruling class of this country.

When Belgium was invaded, the government enjoined upon the people of this country the duty of remaining neutral, thus clearly demonstrating that the "dictates of humanity," and the fate of small nations and of democratic institutions were matters that did not concern it. But when our enormous war traffic was seriously threatened, our government calls upon us to rally to the "defense of democracy and civilization."

Our entrance into the European war was instigated by the predatory capitalists in the United States who boast of the enormous profit of seven billion dollars from the manufacture and sale of munitions and war supplies and from the exportation of American food stuffs and other necessaries. They are also deeply interested in the continuance of war and the success of the allied arms through their huge loans to the governments of the allied powers and through other commercial ties. It is the same interests which strive for imperialistic domination of the Western Hemisphere.

The war of the United States against Germany cannot be justified even on the plea that it is a war in defense of American rights or American "honor." Ruthless as the unrestricted submarine war policy of the German government was and is, it is not an invasion of the rights of the American people, as such, but only an interference with the opportunity of certain groups of American capitalists to coin cold profits out of the blood and sufferings of our fellow men in the warring countries of Europe.

It is not a war against the militarist regime of the Central Powers. Militarism can never be abolished by militarism.

It is not a war to advance the cause of democracy in Europe. Democracy can never be imposed upon any country by a foreign power by force of arms.

It is cant and hypocrisy to say that the war is not directed against the German people, but against the Imperial Government of Germany. If we send an armed force to the battlefields of Europe, its cannon will mow down the masses of the German people and not the Imperial German Government.

Our entrance into the European conflict at this time will serve only to multiply the horrors of the war, to increase the toll of death and destruction and to prolong the fiendish slaughter. It will bring death, suffering and destitution to the people of the United States and particularly to the working class. It will give the powers of reaction in this country the pretext for an attempt to throttle our rights and to crush our democratic institutions, and to fasten upon this country a permanent militarism.

The working class of the United States has no quarrel with the working class of Germany or of any other country. The people of the United States have no quarrel with the people of Germany or any other country. The American people did not want and do not want this war. They have not been consulted about the war and have had no part in declaring war. They have been plunged into this war by the trickery and treachery of the ruling class of the country through its representatives in the National Administration and National Congress, its demagogic agitators, its subsidized press, and other servile instruments of public expression.

We brand the declaration of war by our government as a crime against the people of the United States and against the nations of the world.

In all modern history there has been no war more unjustifiable than the war in which we are about to engage.

No greater dishonor has ever been forced upon a people than that which the capitalist class is forcing upon this nation against its will.

A Progressive Opposes the Declaration of War

ROBERT LA FOLLETTE

Mr. LA FOLLETTE. Mr. Chairman, when history records the truth about this awful act we are about to commit here, which means the maiming and dismembering of thousands of our noble boys and the deaths of thousands more, it will record that the Congress of the United States made this declaration of war under a misapprehension of the facts inexcusable in itself and that the people at large acquiesced in it on the theory that the Congress should have the facts, and would not make a declaration of war not justified by every rule of equity and fair dealing between nations, impartially applied by this country to all belligerents, and that after our following that course one of these contesting nations, despite our impartial action, had wantonly destroyed our legitimate commerce and destroyed the lives of some of our people.

I say the people acquiesce in our actions here to-day on exactly that false assumption of the facts. We have not treated, as a Government, these belligerents with any degree of impartiality; but, on the contrary, have demanded of one of them absolute obedience to our ideas and interpretations of international law, and have allowed at least one of the other belligerents to override at will the established rules and practice of all the civilized nations of the world for a hundred years with but feeble protest, and, in many cases, with no protest at all.

We surrendered to Great Britain practically all we contested for in the War of 1812. It is true, as far as we know, that she has not impressed our seamen, but she has seized and appropriated to her own use entire cargoes and the ships that carried them. Not carriers in European trade, but carriers to South America.

One of the underlying causes of the awful holocaust in Europe was because Germany had by her systematized reductions in cost of manufacturing, by subsidization of transportation lines and methods of credits made such serious inroads on Great Britain's trade in South America as to seriously disturb her equanimity and threaten her prestige as well as attendant profits.

Mr. Chairman, this war now devastating Europe so ruthlessly is not a war of humanity, but a war of commercialism, and there is not a student of economic conditions within the sound of my voice but knows that to be the fundamental cause of that war, although there are many primary and intermediate questions entering into it. But I digress, Mr. Chairman. I have said that Great Britain has seized our ships engaged in peaceful commerce on the Western Hemisphere, surrounded by all the hallowed shades of the Monroe doctrine, which we are about to abrogate; has taken them to England and

Congressional Record, 65th Cong., 1st sess. (1917), pp. 371–372.

impressed them into her own service, and apparently without protest from our Government now demanding a strict accounting by Germany.

Mr. Chairman, there is no doubt in my mind but that Germany's action in regard to her submarine warfare is reprehensible, is wrong, and would merit punishment; but, Mr. Chairman, can we consistently declare war on Germany and enter into an alliance with "perfidious Albion,"[2] who, without regard to international law, laid down a prescribed zone in the Atlantic Ocean and the North Sea sowing those waters with deadly contact mines. Three of our vessels were sunk in this prescribed zone with attendant loss of life; many other vessels were likewise destroyed without protest by our Government, which by indisputable evidence has, to some extent at least, suppressed the facts in regard to the matter.

Mr. Chairman, is a life lost by the destruction of a vessel, coming in contact with a floating mine less dear than one lost on a vessel sunk by a torpedo fired by a submarine? Is the water less cold or wet?

Mr. Chairman, the highwayman who holds you up is less culpable than the coward who sends you a bomb by express or through the mail or sets a spring gun. The floating mine, in my judgment, is more despicable than the submarine, whose operators are at least taking some chances of losing their own lives. We are asked to go into partnership with the belligerent who prescribed a zone and sowed it full of mines to help it destroy the belligerent who prescribed a zone and in that zone uses submarines. Oh, consistency, thou art a jewel! . . .

The President of the United States in his message of the 2d of April [1917] said that the European war was brought on by Germany's rulers without the sanction or will of the people. For God's sake, what are we doing now? Does the President of the United States feel that the will of the American people is being consulted in regard to this declaration of war? The people of Germany surely had as much consideration as he has given the people of the United States. He has heard the cry of the Shylocks calling for their pound of flesh; later on he will hear the cry of Rachel weeping for her children and mourning because they are not, sacrificed to make good the pound of flesh in the name of liberty. The exclamation "O Liberty! Liberty! how many crimes are committed in thy name!" was well made.

Ours is the greatest Nation on the face of the globe. We have had a chance, if we had maintained a strict neutrality, to have bound up the wounds of the oppressed and to have upheld the tenets of the highest civilization throughout the world. But, no; we are asked to go into partnership with the country that has never allowed justice and right to have any weight with her when conquest and gold were placed in the balance. In India, which she held by right of conquest, as a punishment to those natives of that country who desired to be free of England's yoke and rebelled, even as did we in our Revolutionary period, she mercifully tied many of the rebels to the

---

[2]A hostile name for England—ED.

mouths of her cannon and humanely blew them to atoms as a sample of English Christianity. She destroyed the Boer Republic by intrigue and force of arms; she forced, for love of gold, the opium trade on China. Christian England, our would-be partner! In the Napoleonic wars she, by force of arms, confiscated the entire shipping of small but neutral nations to her own use, just as she has in a smaller degree appropriated ships of our citizens to her own use within the past two years. During the Civil War she fell over herself to recognize the Confederacy, and gave it every encouragement possible. Now we are asked to become her faithful ally against a country that, whatever her faults, surely has no blacker record than that of Christian England; to contribute our money and our people in the holy name of liberty to destroy one belligerent, which the President designates as Prussian militarism, a menace of the world; but English navalism, which is surely as great a menace, we enter into partnership with. George Washington said, "Avoid European entanglements," but we are recklessly entering a path to the end of which no man can foresee or comprehend, at the behest of, in many cases, a venal press and of a pacifist President.

God pity our country, gentlemen of the House of Representatives, if you desire that this cup be placed to our country's lips to quaff for crimes committed by a country for unneutral actions and that we enter into an alliance with another country which has been much less neutral. You may do so; I can not so vote at this time. . . .

Mr. Chairman, throughout the country patriotic meetings are being held to encourage enlistments of our young men and boys into the Army to engage in this war in advance of our declaration.

Mr. Chairman, I suggest a resolution, which should be passed and adhered to by the young men of our country and by our soldiers who are asked to enter the trenches of Europe:

"I hereby pledge myself to the service of my country and will guarantee to go and uphold its honor and its flag as soon as the sons of all the newspaper editors who have stood out for our entering the war, and who are of age for enlistment, have enlisted for the cause and the proprietors and editors themselves have patriotically enlisted, on the theory that they should feel it their duty to do so as instigators of the act."

Likewise, Mr. Chairman, the sons of manufacturers of ammunition and war supplies, and all stockholders making profits from such trade. They should freely offer their sons on the altar of their country and, in case of their being under military age, go themselves. Likewise, Mr. Chairman, the J. Pierpont Morgans and their associates, who have floated war loans running into millions which they now want the United States to guarantee by entering the European war; after they and all the holders of such securities have offered their sons and themselves, when of military age, on the altar of their country, and, Mr. Chairman, when the above-mentioned persons have no sons and are too old themselves to accept military service, then they shall, to make good their desire for the upholding of American honor and American rights, donate in lieu of such service of selves or sons one-half of all their worldly goods to make good their patriotic desire for our entering the European war in the name of liberty and patriotism.

Mr. Chairman, it will be fitting for those who have really nothing at stake in this war but death to enter into it and give their lives in the name of liberty and patriotism, after the persons covered by the above resolution have done their part as above suggested and many thousands of our citizens will see it that way ere long.

7

The Twenties Culture War

The 1920s have come down to us as the Jazz Age, a time when Americans, buoyed by prosperity, abandoned social concerns and gave themselves up to moneymaking and personal gratification. The conventional icons of the era include the Charleston, the flapper, the speakeasy, fast cars, the Greenwich Village bohemian, the real estate speculator, and the Wall Street bull market.

But this picture of a carefree, hedonistic society distorts reality. If economic and class conflict in the 1920s were muted by the bright glow of prosperity, cultural conflict was not. Indeed, few eras in our history witnessed such bitter clashes of contending values, credos, and loyalties. Although the battles were often confused, in general they pitted politically conservative, traditional, white Protestant rural and small-town Americans against various groups defined as outsiders by virtue of their liberal-to-radical politics, their religious or ethnic deviation, their urban cosmopolitanism, or sometimes all three.

The selections below illustrate three of the major cultural battlegrounds of the 1920s: political radicalism, religious and racial tolerance, and prohibition. There were other cultural struggles during the twenties as well as clashes over such issues as Darwinian evolution, sexual behavior, and the deportment of the young. All, however, were really aspects of the same cultureal and ideological confrontation.

Keep in mind that the following documents refer to only a few facets of the twenties "culturel war" and do not present the full range of positions even on the controversies they discuss. As you read the selections, consider why the 1920s brought out cultural conflict in so lacerating a way.

2.1: Sacco-Vanzetti (1927, 1927)

In May 1920 two Italian-born anarchists, Nicola Sacco and Bartolomeo Vanzetti, were arrested for the murder of two shoe factory employees in the course of a payroll robbery in South Braintree, Massachusetts. The two men were tried and, in July 1921, convicted and sentenced to death.

The case erupted into a cause célèbre and became the focus of suspicion, anger, and guilt. Many of the nation's liberal and radical intellectuals considered the trial a travesty of justice. The accused men, they said, had been railroaded by a prosecutor and judge hostile to their nationality and their political radicalism. Some of America's brightest and most talented men and women, operating through Sacco-Vanzetti defense committees, demanded a new trial to reverse the convictions. The far left staged protest rallies in major cities around the world to demand the convicted men's exoneration.

In 1927 the friends of the two anarchists prevailed on Massachusetts governor Alvan T. Fuller to review the trial. Fuller appointed a committee headed by A. Lawrence Lowell, president of Harvard University, to examine the trial record to see if an injustice had been done. On the basis of this report the governor decided to let the sentences stand. On August 23, 1927, the two men went to their deaths in the electric chair still protesting their innocence. To this day questions of their guilt and of the fairness of their trial arouse passionate feelings among people who can still identify with the opposing sides as they took shape seventy years ago.

The first selection is from Governor Fuller's message rejecting the charge of unfairness and refusing to order a new trial. It is true that this was an immensely complicated case, but is it possible to say anything valid about the probable fairness of the trial from Fuller's remarks as transcribed here?

The second selection is from a pamphlet by the poet Edna St. Vincent Millay written a few months after the executions. It obviously reflects the poet's own passionate commitment to the cause that had excited such powerful emotions. Why do you suppose a person like Millay might have been swept up in the Sacco-Vanzetti controversy? Are poets more sensitive to injustice than others? Were the creative people of this era more alienated from mainstream American life than figures such as Governor Fuller and A. Lawrence Lowell? Is there any sign of such alienation in Millay's pamphlet? How do you explain her linkage of the execution of Sacco and Vanzetti with the first World War?

Trial of Sacco-Vanzetti Held to Be Fair

ALVAN T. FULLER

Boston, Massachusetts, August 3, 1927

On April 15th, 1920, a paymaster and his guard were held up, robbed and brutally murdered at South Braintree, Massachusetts. On May 5th, 1920,

Alvan T. Fuller, *Decision of Gov. Alvan T. Fuller in the Matter of the Appeal of Bartolomeo Vanzetti and Nicola Sacco . . .* (Boston: 1928), pp. 3–8.

Nicola Sacco and Bartolomeo Vanzetti were arrested; they were later tried and found guilty of the murder. The verdict was followed by seven motions for a new trial and two appeals to the Supreme Court for the Commonwealth, all of which were heard and later denied. Prior to the trial of the two men in this case, Vanzetti had been arrested, tried and convicted of an attempted holdup on December 24, 1919, at Bridgewater, Massachusetts, and sentenced to fifteen years imprisonment.

The appeal to the Governor was presented by counsel for the accused on May 3rd of the present year. It was my first official connection with the case. . . .

The inquiry that I have conducted has had to do with the following questions:—

Was the jury trial fair?
Were the accused entitled to a new trial?
Are they guilty or not guilty?

As to the first question, complaint has been made that the defendants were prosecuted and convicted because they were anarchists. As a matter of fact, the issue of anarchy was brought in by them as an explanation of their suspicious conduct. Their counsel, against the advice of Judge Thayer, decided to attribute their actions and conduct to the fact that they were anarchists, suggesting that they were armed to protect themselves, that they were about to start out, at ten o'clock at night, to collect radical literature, and that the reason they lied was to save their friends.

I have consulted with every member of the jury now alive, eleven in number. They considered the judge fair; that he gave them no indication of his own opinion of the case. Affidavits have been presented claiming that the judge was prejudiced. I see no evidence of prejudice in his conduct of the trial. That he had an opinion as to the guilt or innocence of the accused after hearing the evidence is natural and inevitable.

The allegation has been made that conditions in the court room were prejudicial to the accused. After careful inquiry of the jury and others I find no evidence to support this allegation. I find the jurors were thoroughly honest men and that they were reluctant to find these men guilty but were forced to do so by the evidence. I can see no warrant for the assertion that the jury trial was unfair.

The charge of the judge was satisfactory to the counsel for the accused and no exceptions were taken to it. The Supreme Judicial Court for the Commonwealth has considered such of the more than 250 exceptions taken during the course of the trial as counsel for the accused chose to argue and over-ruled them all, thus establishing that the proceedings were without legal flaw.

I have read the record and examined many witnesses and the jurymen to see from a layman's standpoint whether the trial was fairly conducted. I am convinced that it was.

The next question is whether newly discovered evidence was of sufficient merit to warrant a new trial.

After the verdict against these men, their counsel filed and argued before Judge Thayer seven distinct supplementary motions for a new trial six of them on the ground of newly discovered evidence, all of which were denied. I have examined all of these motions and read the affidavits in support of them to see whether they presented any valid reason for granting the accused men a new trial. I am convinced that they do not and I am further convinced that the presiding judge gave no evidence of bias in denying them all and refusing a new trial. The Supreme Judicial Court for the Commonwealth, which had before it appeals on four of the motions and had the opportunity to read the same affidavits which were submitted to Judge Thayer, declined to sustain the contentions of counsel for the accused. In my own investigations on the question of guilt, I have given these motions and their supporting affidavits and the witnesses every consideration. . . .

It has been a difficult task to look back six years through other people's eyes. Many of the witnesses told me their story in a way I felt was more a matter of repetition than the product of their memory. Some witnesses replied that during the six years they had forgotten; they could not remember; that it was a disagreeable experience and they had tried to forget it. I could not hope to put myself in the position of a juryman and have the advantage of seeing the witness on the stand and listening to the evidence and judging the spoken word. The motions for a new trial, however, were all made from affidavits and therefore they could be reviewed under the same circumstances as prevailed when the Judge heard them.

The next question, and the most vital question of all, is that of the guilt or innocence of the accused. In this connection I reviewed the Bridgewater attempted holdup for which Vanzetti had previously been tried before another jury and found guilty. At this trial Vanzetti did not take the witness stand in his own defense. He waived the privilege of telling his own story to the jury, and did not subject himself to cross examination. Investigating this case, I talked to the counsel for Vanzetti at the Plymouth trial, the jurymen, the trial witnesses, new witnesses, present counsel and Vanzetti. I have talked with the government witnesses who saw the Bridgewater holdup and who identified Vanzetti, and I believe their testimony to be substantially correct. I believe with the jury that Vanzetti was guilty and that his trial was fair. I found nothing unusual about this case except, as noted above, that Vanzetti did not testify.

In the Bridgewater case, practically everyone who witnessed the attempted holdup and who could have identified the bandits identified Vanzetti.

The South Braintree crime was particularly brutal. The murder of the paymaster (Parmenter) and the guard (Berardelli) was not necessary to the robbery. The murders were accomplished first, the robbery afterward. The first shot laid Berardelli low in the roadway, and after Parmenter was shot, he dropped the money box in the road and ran across the street. The money could then have been taken but the murderers pursued Parmenter across the road and shot him again, and then returned and fired three more shots into Berardelli, four in all, leaving his lifeless form in the roadway. The plan was evidently to kill the witnesses and terrorize the bystanders. The murderers escaped in an automobile driven by one of their confederates, the automobile being afterward located in the woods at Bridgewater, 18 miles distant.

Vanzetti when arrested on May 5th had in his hip pocket a fully loaded revolver. Sacco had a loaded pistol tucked into the front of his trousers and 20 loose carridges which fitted his pistol. Upon being questioned by the police, both men told what they afterward admitted was a tissue of lies. Sacco claimed to have been working at Kelly's shoe factory on April 15th, the date of the South Braintree crime. Upon investigation, it was proven that he was not at work on that day. He then claimed to have been at the Italian Consulate in Boston on that date but the only confirmation of this claim is the memory of a former employee of the Consulate who made a deposition in Italy that Sacco among forty others was in the office that day. This employee had no memorandum to assist his memory.

As the result of my study of the record and my personal investigation of the case, including my interviews with a large number of witnesses, I believe, with the jury, that Sacco and Vanzetti were guilty and that the trial was fair.

This crime was committed seven years ago. For six years, through dilatory methods, one appeal after another, every possibility for delay has been utilized, all of which lends itself to attempts to frighten and coerce witnesses, to influence changes in testimony, to multiply by the very years of time elapsed the possibilities of error and confusion.

It might be said that by undertaking this investigation I have contributed to the elaborate consideration accorded these men. My answer is that there was a feeling on the part of some people that the various delays that had dragged this case through the courts for six years were evidence that a doubt existed as to the guilt of these two men. The feeling was not justified. The persistent, determined efforts of an attorney of extraordinary versality and industry, the judge's illness, the election efforts of three District Attorneys, and dilatoriness on the part of most of those concerned are the principal causes of delay. The delays that have dragged this case out for six years are inexcusable.

This task of review has been a laborious one and I am proud to be associated in this public service with clear eyed witnesses, unafraid to tell the truth, and with jurors who discharged their obligations in accordance with their convictions and their oaths.

As a result of my investigation I find no sufficient justification for executive intervention.

I believe with the jury, that these men, Sacco and Vanzetti, were guilty, and that they had a fair trial. I furthermore believe that there was no justifiable reason for giving them a new trial.

(*Signed*) Alvan T. Fuller

Fear

EDNA ST. VINCENT MILLAY

There are two names you would not have me mention, for you are sick of the sound of them. All men must die, you say, and these men have died, and would that their names might die with them; would that their names were as names written in the sands, you say, to be dissipated by the next incoming tide! For you long to return to your gracious world of a year ago, where people had pretty manners and did not raise their voices; where people whom you knew, whom you had entertained in your houses, did not shout and weep and walk the streets vulgarly carrying banners, because two quite inconsequential people, two men who could not even speak good English, were about to be put forever out of mischief's way. *Do* let us forget, you say; after all, what *does* it matter?

You are right; it does not matter very much. In a world more beautiful than this it would have mattered more. On the surface of a Christianity already so spotted and defaced by the crimes of the Church this stain does not show very dark. In a freedom already so riddled and gashed by the crimes of the state this ugly rent is with difficulty to be distinguished at all.

And you are right; it is well to forget that men die. So far we have devised no way to defeat death, or to outwit him, or to buy him over. At any moment the cloud may split above us and the golden spear of death leap at the heart; at any moment the earth crack and the hand of death reach up from the abyss to grasp our ankles; at any moment the wind rise and sweep the roofs from our houses, making one dust of our ceilings and ourselves. And if not, we shall die soon, anyhow. It is well to forget that this is so.

But that man before his time, wantonly and without sorrow, is thrust from the light of the sun into the darkness of the grave by his brother's blindness or fear it is well to remember, at least until it has been shown to the satisfaction of all that this too is beyond our power to change.

Two months ago, in Massachusetts, these men whom I do not name were efficiently despatched out of the sunlight into the darkness of the grave. The executions of the death sentence upon them went forward without interference; there were no violent demonstrations. Whatever of agitation there was has steadily decreased since that night. Today things are very quiet. From time to time some small newspaper remarks editorially that the hysteria

Edna St. Vincent Millay, *Fear* (New York: The Sacco-Vanzetti National League, n.d. [1927])

which swept the country has abated, and congratulates its readers upon having escaped disintegration. Aside from this there is little comment. The general opinion is that the affair has pretty well blown over. And the world sleeps easy on its pillow.

Yet if all is quiet today, it is more for this reason than for any other; that though you sit in the same room with a man you cannot hear his thoughts. And the tumult is in the mind; the shouting and rioting are in the thinking mind. Nothing has abated; nothing has changed; nothing is forgotten. It is as if the two months which have elapsed were but the drawing of a breath. In very truth, for those who sat in silence on that night of the 22nd of August, waiting for news from the prison, and in silence when the news came, it is still the night of the 22nd of August, for there has been no dawn.

I do not call these men by name, for I know how nervous and irritable you become at the sight of these names on the printed page; how your cheek flushes and you cluck with exasperation; how you turn to your family with words on your tongue which in former days you would not have used at all—"vipers, vermin, filth." This is because you were just dozing off nicely again after the shocking uproar of two months ago, and do not wish to be disturbed. You are as cross as an old dog asleep on the hearth if I shake you and try to get you out into the rainy wind. This is because what you most want out of life is not to be disturbed. You wish to lie peacefully asleep for a few years yet, and then to lie peacefully dead.

If you should rouse yourself for a moment and look about you at the world, you would be troubled, I think, and feel less peaceful and secure, seeing how it is possible for a man as innocent as yourself of any crime to be cast into prison and be killed. For whether or not these men whom I do not name were guilty of the crime of murder, it was not for murder that they died. The crime for which they died was the crime of breathing upon the frosty window and looking out.

"These Anarchists!" you say; "shall I never hear the last of them?"

Indeed, I fear it will be some time before you hear the last of them. I do not mean by this what you think I mean. I do not mean that plotting mischief is afoot, that thousands of people hitherto gentle and retired are now grimly engaged in fashioning engines of death to plant beneath the State House floor. This is not what I mean, although you will say it is what I meant.

It is of your children I was thinking, your young sons and daughters, your grandsons and granddaughters, these young people with whom you have already so much difficulty, because, as you say, they have so few illusions. How often already have they not stood looking at you coldly while with warm cheek and faltering accent you presented your pretty concepts: duty, honor, courage, purity, sacrifice—those fragile dolls of yours, that are always dressed for summer, no matter what the sky?

Your children heard you discussing the case in question. "Anarchists, murderers, Anarchists, Anarchists." This was your discussion of the case. They looked at you, yawned, and left the room.

Their minds are dark to you. But they are busy. Out of your sight they read, they ponder, they work things out. In your presence they often sit in a not too respectful silence, interrupting suddenly your placid remarks by their brisk utterance of some untidy truth never mentioned in your house before.

They are frankly occupied chiefly with the real business of life, which, as everybody knows, is having your own way, and getting as much as possible for as little as possible. It is you who have taught them this angular truth; you have failed only in that you have not been able to impart to them as well the ruffles and passementerie with which you are accustomed to adorn it. They were just beginning to look about them at life when war broke out and surrounded them with death. They know how important it is to have a good time while you can; in the next war it is they who will be taken.

As for their illusions, well, they have seen you at war, and they are beginning to understand why you went to war; they have seen you engaged in many another dubious and embarrassing activity; and now they have seen this. They who have been chidden time and again for having so little softness in them see how their parents, for all their gentle voices and courteous ways, more hard, more unscrupulous, more relentless, than themselves in their most iron moods. It is from these children, I fear, that you are likely to hear again on the subject, though not in so many words.

But, you say, what we did was done for the good of the country, to protect its honor, its institutions, the glory of its flag.

What is this honor, that a breath can tarnish? This glory, that a whisper can bring it low? What are these noble institutions, that a wind from any quarter can set to trembling like towers of jelly?

You do not know exactly what they are. For you do not live with them. They are not trees to shade you, water to quench your thirst. They are golden coins, hidden under the mattress in a very soiled wallet. The only pleasure they afford you is the rapturous dread lest some one may be taking them away. And some one is taking them away. But not the one you think.

Unkindness, hypocrisy, and greed—these are the forces that shall bring us low and enslave our children. Yet we quarter their troops in our houses without a murmur. We show them where the treasure is hid. But they know it already.

This is the way you look at it: These men were Anarchists, and they are well out of the way; you are fortunate to have escaped destruction at their hands; they were probably murderers; but, in any case, they are well out of the way. It was that word Anarchist which brought them to the chair; that word, and your ignorance of its meaning.

For you do not at all know what an Anarchist is. And all through this trial in which the word Anarchist has played such an important part you have not even looked up the word in the dictionary, your position being that, in the first place, you know quite well enough, and, in the second place, you would think shame to know.

An Anarchist, you insist, is a man who makes bombs and puts them under the State House, and that is that. On the contrary, that is by no means that. The person you have in mind is not an Anarchist, he is a bomber. You will find him everywhere—among Anarchists, among Fascists, among dry-law enforcers, among Modernists, among Fundamentalists, and freely distributed throughout the Ku Klux Klan. He is that person who, when he does not like a thing, lynches it, tars and feathers it, lays a curse upon it, or puts a bomb under it. His name is legion, and you will find him in every party.

An Anarchist, according to the dictionary, is a person who believes that human beings are naturally good, and that if left to themselves they would, by mutual agreement, govern themselves much better and much more peaceably than they are being governed now by a government based on violence. An interesting theory. Nonsense, of course, because man is not naturally good; man is naturally cruel, selfish and vain, and what he would be if left to his own devices it is horrible to contemplate. Still, it is an interesting concept, very idealistic, very pretty.

Of those who hold with the theory of Anarchism, the dictionary further tells us, there is one group whose members "occasionally resort to an act of violence against representatives of oppression to express a protest against, or to draw public attention to, existing social wrongs." (It is in this group that your bombers are happy and at home.) But "generally speaking," says the dictionary, "Anarchism repudiates violent methods, and hopes for a gradual evolution towards its goal."

Ah, you will say, but these men belonged to the violent group!

Their history would indicate otherwise. Up to the time of their detention for the crime for which they were later sentenced to die no slightest act of violence had ever been attributed to either of them. There are those who would have given much to be able to bring to light against them such an act of violence, and were unable to do so; it is to the counsel for the prosecution that I refer. "Throughout the entire trial" (I quote the uncontested statement of one who was in a position to know the facts)—"not one word of testimony was introduced against their character for honesty, peace, and good order."

I am going into this in some detail because I find it interesting. You, I fear, find it not only uninteresting, but vaguely and uncomfortably obscene. Yet, after all, you have very plentifully had your say on the subject—that action of yours, you know, that spoke so much louder than any words.

These men were castaways upon our shore, and we, an ignorant and savage tribe, have put them to death because their speech and their manners were different from our own, and because to the untutored mind that which is strange is in its infancy ludicrous, but in its prime evil, dangerous, and to be done away with.

These men were put to death because they made you nervous; and your children know it. The minds of your children are like clear pools, reflecting faithfully whatever passes on the bank; whereas in the pool of your own mind, whenever an alien image bends above, a fish of terror leaps to meet it, shattering its reflection.

I am free to say these things because I am not an Anarchist, although you will say that I am. It is unreasonable to you that a person should go to any trouble in behalf of another person unless the two are members of the same family, or of the same fraternity, or, at the remotest, of the same political party. As regards yourself and the man who lives next door to you, you wish him well, but not so very well. Even if he is a member of the same church as yourself, you do not wish him so inordinately well. Whereas if he does not belong to the same church as yourself, and if, in addition, he does things a little out of the ordinary, such as walk in the street without a hat, you do not wish him well at all. In any case, as regards your neighbor and yourself, although you have no desire to see his house burn down or his children killed in a motor accident, a most modest worldly success will do very well for him, as far as you are concerned. For these and other reasons sufficiently naive and self-revealing, you take it as a matter of course that, of the many persons involved in the recent agitation in Boston, those who were not in the ring for what they could get out of it were revolutionists of the most flagrant dye. It is impossible for you to conceive that men could weep in public and women permit themselves to be thrown in jail because (as it seemed to them) the blue hem of Justice was being dragged in the mire. In the world in which you live Justice is a woman of stone above a courthouse door.

As I said before, I am not sufficiently idealistic to share the political opinions of these men with whose fate I am concerned. It is impossible for me to be an Anarchist, for I do not believe in the essential goodness of man; man is quite patently, to my sight, the worm of the Moody and Sankey hymns.[1] Except for this fact, I should of course think twice before writing as I do. For, although I was born in this country, and am possessed of that simple right of the citizen to hold any opinions he may hold, yet to avail one's self of this right and express opinions contrary to the opinions of the majority may become, as we have lately seen, a folly punishable by the extreme correction. For surely you are not still insisting that these two poor wretches were put to death solely for the crime of murder? You and I both know that we must be careful, not only what we do, but also what we say, and even what we think, if we would not have one day our sleep brutally broken in upon and ourselves rudely forced to enter a place where we do not at all wish to go. And surely you will not deny that, if you would remain undisturbed, it is more important to be on the side of the established order of things than to be innocent of even the grossest crime?

As I said before, I dare say these things because I am not an Anarchist; but I dare say them for another reason, too: because my personal physical freedom, my power to go in and out when I choose, my personal life even, is no longer quite as important to me as it once was. Death even, that outrageous intrusion, appears to me at moments, and more especially when I think of what happened in Boston two months ago, death appears to me somewhat as

[1] Dwight Moody and Ira Sankey were two Protestant evangelists who wrote hymns—ED.

a darkened room, in which one might rest one's battered temples out of the world's way, leaving the sweeping of the crossings to those who still think it important that the crossings be swept. As if indeed it mattered the least bit in the world whether the crossings be clean or foul, when of all the people passing to and from there in the course of an eight-hour day not one out of ten thousand has a spark of true courage in his heart, or any love at all, beyond the love of a cat for the fire, for any earthly creature other than himself. The world, the physical world, and that once was all in all to me, has at moments such as these no road through a wood, no stretch of shore, that can bring me comfort. The beauty of these things can no longer at such moments make up to me at all for the ugliness of man, his cruelty, his greed, his lying face.

7.2:   The Ku Klux Klan (1924, 1921)

The most extreme expression of traditional America's hostility to "alien" trends and "alien" groups was the Ku Klux Klan. The Klan of the 1920s aped the Klan of the Reconstruction period, but it had both a broader agenda and a wider geographical range than its predecessor. With its program of racial and religious intolerance, cultural conformity, and superpatriotism, the Klan in the twenties spread beyond the South and for a time threatened to become a decisive force in American politics on a national level.

The first selection below includes statements from two local Klan organizations, the first from New Jersey, the second from Louisiana. What are the essential ingredients of the Klan philosophy as expressed in these documents? Although they do not mention blacks and do not deal with political viewpoints, what do you suppose, judging from these documents, the Klan felt about black Americans and political dissenters?

The second selection is a brief letter written in 1921 by the famous editor of the Emporia Gazette, *the Progressive journalist, William Allen White. White despised the Klan in no uncertain terms. What tradition does he fall back on for his denunciation? Why would you expect a man like White to be proof against the appeal of the Klan? How could an editor like White have influenced the attitudes of the people of Emporia, Kansas, toward the Klan?*

Statements from the Ku Klux Klan

The New Jersey Klan Speaks Out

The Rising of the Ku Klux Klan—The New Reformation

"On account of the abuses of religion by the Roman Catholic hierarchy, civilization had reached a universal crisis in the sixteenth century; and Martin Luther, the chosen instrument of God, was placed in the breach to prevent the wheels of progress from being reversed and the world from being plunged into greater darkness than that of the Dark Ages.

"The thousand years preceding the Reformation, known by religious historians as Satan's Millennium, was brought on by the Romish Church with her paganistic worship and practices, during which time millions of men and women poured out their blood as martyrs of the Christian religion. . . .

The White-Robed Army

"Now come the Knights of the Ku Klux Klan in this crucial hour of our American history to contend for the faith of our fathers who suffered and died in behalf of freedom. At the psychological moment they have arrived to encourage the hearts of those who have been battling heroically for the rights and privileges granted them under the Constitution of the United States.

"How our hearts have been thrilled at the sight of this army! Words fail to express the emotions of the soul at the appearance of this mighty throng upon the battle-field, where a few faithful followers of the lowly Nazarene have been contending for the faith once delivered to the Saints, against Papal mobs who have torn down gospel tabernacles, wrecked buildings and imprisoned Protestant worshipers.

Our National Peril

"The World War was the signal for greater alarm than the average American has been willing to admit. Notwithstanding the sacrifices that had to be made at home and the thousands of our young men who crossed the sea and laid down their lives on the battlefields of the Old World, it has taken the Ku Klux Klan to awaken even a portion of the population of the United States to our national peril. Our religious and political foes are not only within our gates, but are coming by the hundreds of thousands, bringing the chaos and ruin of old European and Asiatic countries to un-Americanize and destroy our nation, and to make it subserve the purposes of the Pope in his aspirations for world supremacy.

Rome Would Overthrow Public Schools

"One of the great efforts of the Roman hierarchy toward this end is to get control of our public schools by placing Roman Catholics on school boards and in the schoolrooms and taking the Bible out of the schools. In the event of their success in their efforts to overthrow our present school system there would be a string of beads around every Protestant child's neck and a Roman Catholic catechism in his hand. 'Hail Mary, Mother of God,' would be on every child's lips, and the idolatrous worship of dead saints a part of the daily programme.

The Jewish and Catholic Alliance

"The money-grasping Jew, who has no use for the Christ of Calvary, does all in his power to bring discredit on Christianity, and would be pleased to see the whole structure broken down, and in this way get rid of his responsibility for crucifying the Christ on Calvary and bringing the curse on his race, which they have had to suffer since the beginning of the Christian era. The sons of Abraham have therefore become a strong ally to the Papacy, not because they have anything in common with it in religion, but in their political propaganda against American institutions and principles.

"While no true Christian has anything against the Jew, it must be admitted that this alliance with the Papacy is a dangerous menace to our flag and country. The Jew is insoluble and indigestible; and when he grows in numbers and power till he becomes a menace to Christianity and the whole moral fabric, drastic measures will have to be taken to counteract his destructive work, and more especially when he is in alliance with the old Papal religio-political machine."

The Louisiana Klan's Manifesto

Awake! Americans, Awake!

"Awake, Americans! You descendants of the patriots of the Revolution! You sons of the Pilgrim Fathers who fought back the hordes of the Tyrant! Gird on the armor of God who led you out of bondage and chased slavery from out of our land! There is an enemy without our gates ten thousand times more dangerous than the redcoats ever were!

"Catholic politicians are filling the air with propaganda which would lead you to believe that old Ship of State has broken loose from her moorings and is drifting far to sea. They cry out in tones of agony that people are growing intolerant and Protestants are seeking to abridge religious liberty. Catholics will prescribe our religion and forbid a Protestant funeral in a Catholic Church. Forbid Catholics attendance at Masonic funerals and then lay claim to a corner on tolerance. Now when Rome is caught red handed in her designs to make American Catholics and Protestants interfere, she cries intolerance and would have you believe that liberty is crushed and bleeding.

"When Protestants exercise a right guaranteed to all under the Constitution, when Americans meet in peaceable assembly, Catholics arm themselves with bludgeons and blunderbusses and try to beat down honest men and murder American citizens. Only fools resort to force to settle a dispute and bricks and rocks are only used by savages. Rome not having any grounds on which to fight in the realm of reason seeks to unite State and Church by the use of sandbags and billies. Reason and enlightenment with them are taboo. Blind passion is appealed to and ignorance is made a virtue. Intellectual darkness for the masses is sought by Rome as surely as a robber seeks the shadows. For when the bright light of reason shines upon her, priests lose their power, and her influence crumbles as hastily as would a snowbank in the nether regions.

"Catholic politicians, if intrusted with power, would pass laws to force American organizations out of existence and shackle liberty, as they have done in every clime wherein they have reigned supreme.

"There are men seeking high office in Louisiana to-day who if elected in numbers sufficient would jail Americans for assembling in peaceful meetings and give to Rome the revenue of our State. Take the Eagle from off the dollar and in its stead place a likeness of the unholy face of [Pope] Pius. Strip the stripes from the American Flag and rend the Stars asunder, and make for us a National banner with background dark and gloomy, and mount upon it a cluster of garlic to commemorate the odor that permeates the Vatican. Turn back the march of civilization and chain the Bible to a box. Tether the intellects of man and enslave reason. Place a statue of a priest where now stands the Goddess of Liberty and place in his hand the torch of intolerance. Demolish our free institutions of learning and imprison those bold enough to preach freedom of the masses. Have black-robed nuns who know only slavery teach our children and drown our art in miasmic ignorance.

"Not all Catholics are of this stripe, but those who seek high office are tainted woefully with Catholic teachings and some have been so bold as to proclaim no Protestant is fit for office and Catholics are the only hope of liberty."

Letter on the Ku Klux Klan

WILLIAM ALLEN WHITE

September 17, 1921

An organizer of the Ku-Klux Klan was in Emporia the other day, and the men whom he invited to join his band at ten dollars per join turned him down. Under the leadership of Dr. J. B. Brickell and following their own judgment after hearing his story, the Emporians told him that they had no time for him. The proposition seems to be:

Anti foreigners
Anti Catholics
Anti Negroes.

There are, of course, bad foreigners and good ones, good Catholics and bad ones, and all kinds of Negroes. To make a case against a birthplace, a religion, or a race is wickedly un-American and cowardly. The whole trouble with the Ku-Klux Klan is that it is based upon such deep foolishness that it is bound to be a menace to good government in any community. Any man fool enough to be Imperial Wizard would have power without responsibility and both without any sense. That is social dynamite.

American institutions, our courts, our legislators, our executive officers are strong enough to keep the peace and promote justice and good will in the community. If they are not, then the thing to do is to change these institutions and do it quickly, but always legally. For a self-constituted body of moral idiots, who would substitute the findings of the Ku-Klux Klan for the processes of law to try to better conditions, would be a most un-American outrage which every good citizen should resent.

It is to the everlasting credit of Emporia that the organizer found no suckers with $10 each to squander here. Whatever Emporia may be otherwise, it believes in law and order, and absolute freedom under the constitution for every man, no matter what birth or creed or race, to speak and meet and talk and act as a free law-abiding citizen. The picayunish cowardice of a man who would substitute Klan rule and mob law for what our American fathers have died to establish and maintain should prove what a cheap screw outfit the Klan is.

7.3:   Wets versus Drys (1915, 1924)

Another 1920s cultural fault line ran between supporters of nationwide prohibition ("drys") and defenders of the right to drink ("wets"). National prohibition had long been a goal of moral reformers and Protestant evangelicals, and, aided by wartime sentiment against German-American brewers and by public concern for the moral safety of soldiers, these groups induced Congress to pass the Eighteenth Amendment prohibiting the manufacture, sale, and transportation of alcoholic beverages anywhere in the United States. On January 16, 1920, the United States became officially "dry."

Many Americans disliked prohibition and refused to comply with the law. Opponents emphasized its denial of personal liberty. They claimed it encouraged bootlegging, rumrunning, and other criminal activities. Some insisted that it deprived working people of an innocent pleasure just to suit the prejudices of prudes and puritans. The drys fought back, defending the Eighteenth Amendment as "a noble experiment," an expression of decency, prudence, and wise concern for the health and well-being of the American people.

The first selection below, written while the debate over a prohibition amendment was reaching a crescendo, is a defense of moderate drinking that highlights many of the cultural and moral differences between wets and drys. As Percy Andreae sees it, what motivates the prohibitionists? What is the author referring to when he mentions "great wealth-produc-

ing industries"? What was the intellectual and cultural connection between the prohibitionists and the more conservative Protestant denominations?

The second selection is a resolution adopted by a pro-Eighteenth Amendment group in 1924, four years after national prohibition, as expressed through the Volstead Act,[1] had been put into effect. Clearly the prohibitionists were now on the defensive. From their statement, what seems to be the vulnerable points of the dry position? How did the drys hope to make the law more effective? Do you know what finally happened to the "noble experiment"?

A Glimpse Behind the Mask of Prohibition

PERCY ANDREAE

I have met many active prohibitionists, . . . all of them thoroughly in earnest. In some instances I have found that their allegiance to the cause of prohibition took its origin in the fact that some near relative or friend had succumbed to overindulgence in liquor. In one or two cases the man himself had been the victim of this weakness, and had come to the conclusion, firstly, that every one else was constituted as he was; and secondly, that unless one were prevented from drinking, he would not be secure from the temptation to do so himself.

This is one class of prohibitionists. The other, and by far the larger class, is made up of religious zealots, to whom prohibition is a word having at bottom a far wider application than that which is generally attributed to it. The liquor question . . . is merely put forth by them as a means to an end, an incidental factor in a fight which has for its object the supremacy of a certain form of religious faith. The belief of many of these people is that the Creator frowns upon enjoyment of any and every kind, and that he has merely endowed us with certain desires and capacities for pleasure in order to give us an opportunity to please Him by resisting them. They are, of course, perfectly entitled to this belief. . . . But are they privileged to force that belief on their fellow beings? That, in substance, is the question that is involved in the present-day prohibition movement. . . .

Prohibition is merely the title of the movement. Its real purpose is of a religious, sectarian character. . . . If any one doubts the truth of the statement, let me put this to him: How many Roman Catholics are prohibitionists? How many Jews, the most temperate race on earth, are to be found in

[1]Passed in October 1919, the Volstead Act spelled out the specifics of the anti-alcohol legislation permitted by the Eighteenth Amendment.

Percy Andreae, *The Prohibition Movement in Its Broader Bearings upon Social, Commercial, and Religious Liberties* (Chicago: Felix Mendelsohn, 1915), pp. 9–19.

the ranks of prohibition? Or Lutherans? Or German Protestants generally? What is the proportion of Episcopalians to that of Methodists, Baptists, and Presbyterians . . . in the active prohibition army? The answer to these questions will, I venture to say, prove conclusively the assertion that the fight for prohibition is synonymous with the fight of a certain religious sect, or group of sects, for the supremacy of its ideas. . . .

[T]he suppression of liquor . . . is [not] the ultimate end they have in view. . . . It is . . . part and parcel of their lugubrious notion of Godworship [sic] which they eventually hope to impose upon the rest of humanity; a Sunday without a smile, no games, no recreation, no pleasures, no music, card-playing tabooed, dancing anathematized, the beauties of art decried as impure—in short, this world reduced to a barren, forbidding wilderness in which we, its inhabitants, are to pass our time contemplating the joys of the next. . . .

Now if the habit of drinking to excess were a growing one, as our prohibitionist friends claim that it is, we should to-day . . . not be here at all to argue it; for the evil . . . has existed for so many ages that, if it were as general and contagious as is claimed, and its results as far-reaching as they are painted, the human race would have been destroyed by it long ago. Of course, the contrary is the case. The world has progressed in this as in all other respects. Compare, for instance, the drinking to-day with the drinking of a thousand years ago, nay, of only a hundred odd years ago, when a man, if he wanted to ape his so-called betters, did so be contriving to be carried to bed every night "drunk as a lord." Has that condition of affairs been altered by legislative measures restricting the right of the individual to control himself? No. It has been altered by that far greater power, the moral force of education and the good example which teaches mankind the very thing that prohibition would take from it: the virtue of self-control and moderation in all things. . . . Prohibition . . . is the direct negation of the term self-control. In order to save the small percentage of men who are too weak to resist their animal desires, it aims to put chains on every man, the weak and the strong alike. And if this is proper in one respect, why not in all respects? Yet what would one think of a proposition to keep all men locked up because a certain number have a propensity to steal . . . ?

I consider the danger which threatens civilized society from the growing power of a sect whose views on prohibition are merely an exemplification of their generally low estimate of man's ability to rise to higher things by his own volition to be of infinitely greater consequence than the danger that, in putting their narrow theories to the test, a few billions of invested property will be destroyed, a number of great wealth-producing industries wiped out, the rate of individual taxation largely increased, and a million or so of struggling wage earners doomed to face starvation. These latter considerations, of course, must appeal to every thinking man, but what are they compared with the greater questions involved? Already the government of our State [Illinois], and indeed of a good many other States, has passed practically into the hands of a few preacher politicians of a certain creed. With the machine they have built up, by appealing to the emotional weaknesses of the more or less unintelligent masses, they have lifted themselves on to a pedestal of power that has enabled them to dictate legislation or defeat it at their will. . . .

And what does it all mean? It means that government by emotion is to be substituted for government by reason, and government by emotion . . . is . . . the most dangerous and pernicious of all forms of government. It has already crept into the legislative assemblies of most of the States of the Union, and is being craftily fostered by those who know how easily it can be made available for their purposes. . . . Prohibition is but one of its fruits, and the hand that is plucking this fruit is the same hand of intolerance that drove forth certain of our forefathers from the land of their birth to seek the sheltering freedom of these shores.

What a strange reversal of conditions! The intolerants of a few hundred years ago are the upholders of liberty to-day, while those they once persecuted, having multiplied by grace of the very liberty that has so long sheltered them here, are now planning to impose the tyranny of their narrow creed upon the descendants of their persecutors of yore.

Let the greater public, which is, after all, the arbiter of the country's destinies, pause and ponder these things before they are allowed to progress too far. Prohibition, though it must cause, and is already causing, incalculable damage, may never succeed in this country; but that which is behind it, as the catapults and the cannon were behind the battering rams in the battles of olden days, is certain to succeed unless timely measures of prevention are resorted to; and if it does succeed, we shall witness the enthronement of a monarch in this land of liberty compared with whose autocracy the autocracy of the Russian Czar is a mere trifle.

The name of this monarch is Religious Intolerance.

Citizenship Conference to the American People: Have Faith in Prohibition

1. We challenge those who are opposed to the Eighteenth Amendment to come out into the open, and have the courage to repeal the Amendment if they can and the manhood to observe it until they can. Hip-pocket guardians of liberty and defenders of the Constitution are teaching the doctrine of qualified allegiance. The man who upholds the Constitution must uphold the whole of it.

2. The Volstead Act must never be amended by its enemies. That way lies nullification. If it is ever to be amended, the amending must be done by its friends, not its foes. It must be amended not to prevent enforcement, but to perfect enforcement after a reasonable trial has demonstrated the way.

"Message of the Citizenship Conference to the American People," in Ethan R. Shaw, *Prohibition: Going or Coming?* (Berwyn, IL: Shaw Publishing Company, 1924), pp. 423–28.

3. The time has arrived when the American people should see to it that only those are elected to public office who, in the words of Lincoln, will neither violate in the slightest particular the laws of the land, nor tolerate their violation by others. The state or federal official who does not respect the sanctity of his oath to support the federal Constitution should resign his office and give place to one who will neither violate his oath nor betray the confidence of the people. Too often members of Congress and of State Legislatures are violating the laws that they themselves have made. They should be retired to private life. Law-makers should not be law-breakers.

4. We emphasize the grave responsibility which rests upon the courts to compel obedience on the part of those who by open violation are bringing the administration of justice into disrepute. There is increasing evidence that after three years the judges are beginning to realize that the imposition of fines, which amount to nothing more than a small license tax on the vast profits of the illegal liquor traffic, is ineffectual to stop the criminal. We commend those judges who are promoting efficient enforcement of the Eighteenth Amendment by imposing jail sentences, and who, in injunction proceedings, are depriving offenders of the use of their property for saloons and other unlawful purposes.

Official tests show that over ninety per cent of the liquor seized in all sections of the country contains poison in greater or less degree and this iminent menace to life and health must be given increasing consideration by the Courts and juries in cases against illicit makers and sellers.

We urge upon the federal and state judges the need of more stringent action on the part of the courts to prevent the law's delays, and of extreme penalties for persistent offenders to compel the law-breaker to cease his lawlessness and arouse in the cynical and indifferent a new respect for law.

5. When the press of the country carried a report, although incorrect, that an incoming ocean liner had been blocked by the rum fleet in entering New York Harbor, it shocked the moral sense and wounded the pride of the American people. They are impatient at the disgrace which attends the successful operations of the rum runners. They will not believe that the most powerful nation in the world is impotent to prevent the landing of illicit liquor on American soil.

In this juncture we look with confidence to the President of the United States. We ask him to place every available craft and every available agency which may lawfully be used for the purpose, to police our shores. We assure him of our support in using every power at his command to compel respect for constituted authority. An expectant nation looks to him to assert and maintain the majesty of the law.

6. The Eighteenth Amendment places equal responsibility for law enforcement on state and nation. We demand that every Governor of every state shall fully co-operate with the President in securing the enforcement of the Eighteenth Amendment and the Volstead Act. The states with many times the number of officers that the federal government has at its command, should face the responsibility of doing their share in this vital law

enforcement work. With only 1,522 federal agents, and over 250,000 state and local agents, it must manifest that the citizens of the states must hold to greater responsibility their own officers.

7. Realizing the powerful influence of the press, and its vast opportunity through its editors, artists and reporters to mould public opinion, we earnestly ask that it will not permit its news columns, its editorial pages, or its cartoons and illustrations to be used to promote disrespect for law or to hold up to ridicule and contempt our Constitution and our laws.

8. A democracy has been truly defined as "government by public opinion." On the people of this country rests the ultimate responsibility for law enforcement. Public officials can go only so far as we will go with them.

Our final appeal is to the people. Our homes, our schools, and our universities must instill a respect for law into the hearts and minds of the youth of today who are to be the citizens of tomorrow. Our churches must preach the gospel of loyalty. Every liberty-loving, law-abiding citizen must stand up and be counted. When the supremacy of law is challenged, silence is acquiescence. Propaganda must be answered by truth. Complacency must give place to a militant spirit which shall awaken the conscience of the country.

"This is my covenant, saith the Lord, that I will put my laws in the hearts of the people and write them in their minds."

Inspired by this promise, we press on to achieve the realization of the aspiration of Lincoln that "reverence for law may become the political religion of the nation."

8

The New Deal

In October 1929 the stock market boom collapsed, triggering the longest and steepest economic slide in American history. At the Depression's worst, in the winter of 1932–33, the nation's total output was 31 percent below its 1929 peak; unemployment reached 25 percent of the labor force. During that appalling period millions of citizens wondered whether the existing social order could long survive the economic collapse.

In their desperation Americans might have turned for salvation to extremist leaders outside the liberal tradition, as many did in Europe under similar pressures. Instead they chose as their president, Franklin Roosevelt, the standard-bearer of the party out of power at the time of the crash. What followed was the New Deal, a legislative program more sweeping and comprehensive than any in our history.

The New Deal was many things simultaneously. It was a relief program to provide jobs and income to millions of unemployed men and women. It was a drive to stimulate the stalled economy and get private production moving again. It was a bid to reform the nation's financial institutions, provide insurance against social hazards, encourage trade union organization, and revitalize natural resource management. It was inconsistent and changeable. Roosevelt and his advisers had no clear idea of exactly what was wrong with the economy and no certain formula for fixing it. Their policies and programs were often improvised, although their reform agenda drew heavily on early twentieth-century Progressivism for inspiration.

Frightened by the devastating economic and financial breakdown, at first most Americans were willing to give Roosevelt and the Democrats a blank check for change. By 1934, however, many old conservatives had regained their confidence and were beginning to take aim at the president and his policies. The left too rallied, and Marxists and various neo-Populists were soon attacking FDR as a friend of big business and even a covert fascist.

In the selections below you will encounter both defenders and opponents of the New Deal. But the voices are not simply pro and con. In their support or opposition the authors have individual perspectives that reward analysis.

8.1:   Roosevelt Explains His Policies (1934)

Franklin Delano Roosevelt was one of the most effective political leaders in American history. Himself a patrician from old, pre-Revolutionary stock, he communicated effectively with working-class and middle-class Americans of all origins through the new electronic medium, the radio, and won their support for his policies. In the selection below—one of his famous "fireside chats"—FDR explains his recovery program to a wide audience.

FDR was not a systematic thinker. He was a pragmatist and an improviser. Yet in this radio talk he makes it seem as if the New Deal program for industrial and financial recovery was part of a long-term plan. What is Roosevelt attempting to accomplish in this talk? Whom is he trying to appease? What position on the political spectrum is he seeking to establish for his policies? Why do you suppose he quotes the Republican politician Elihu Root at length?

The Second Fireside Chat of 1934

FRANKLIN DELANO ROOSEVELT

Three months have passed since I talked with you shortly after the adjournment of the Congress. Tonight I continue that report, though, because of the shortness of time, I must defer a number of subjects to a later date.

Recently the most notable public questions that have concerned us all have had to do with industry and labor and with respect to these, certain developments have taken place which I consider of importance. I am happy to report that after years of uncertainty, culminating in the collapse of the spring of 1933, we are bringing order out of the old chaos with a greater certainty of the employment of labor at a reasonable wage and of more business at a fair profit. These governmental and industrial developments hold promise of new achievements for the Nation.

Men may differ as to the particular form of governmental activity with respect to industry and business, but nearly all are agreed that private enterprise in times such as these cannot be left without assistance and without reasonable safeguards lest it destroy not only itself but also our processes of civi-

Franklin D. Roosevelt, *The Public Papers and Addresses of Franklin D. Roosevelt,* ed. Samuel Rosenman (New York: Random House, 1938), vol. 3, pp. 413–417, 420–422.

lization. The underlying necessity for such activity is indeed as strong now as it was years ago when Elihu Root said the following very significant words:

> Instead of the give and take of free individual contract, the tremendous power of organization has combined great aggregations of capital in enormous industrial establishments working through vast agencies of commerce and employing great masses of men in movements of production and transportation and trade, so great in the mass that each individual concerned in them is quite helpless by himself. The relations between the employer and the employed, between the owners of aggregated capital and the units of organized labor, between the small producer, the small trader, the consumer, and the great transporting and manufacturing and distributing agencies, all present new questions for the solution of which the old reliance upon the free action of individual wills appears quite inadequate. And in many directions, the intervention of that organized control which we call government seems necessary to produce the same result of justice and right conduct which obtained through the attrition of individuals before the new conditions arose.

It was in this spirit thus described by Secretary Root that we approached our task of reviving private enterprise in March, 1933. Our first problem was, of course, the banking situation because, as you know, the banks had collapsed. Some banks could not be saved but the great majority of them, either through their own resources or with Government aid, have been restored to complete public confidence. This has given safety to millions of depositors in these banks. Closely following this great constructive effort we have, through various Federal agencies, saved debtors and creditors alike in many other fields of enterprise, such as loans on farm mortgages and home mortgages; loans to the railroads and insurance companies and, finally, help for home owners and industry itself.

In all of these efforts the Government has come to the assistance of business and with the full expectation that the money used to assist these enterprises will eventually be repaid. I believe it will be.

The second step we have taken in the restoration of normal business enterprise has been to clean up thoroughly unwholesome conditions in the field of investment. In this we have had assistance from many bankers and business men, most of whom recognize the past evils in the banking system, in the sale of securities, in the deliberate encouragement of stock gambling, in the sale of unsound mortgages and in many other ways in which the public lost billions of dollars. They saw that without changes in the policies and methods of investment there could be no recovery of public confidence in the security of savings. The country now enjoys the safety of bank savings under the new banking laws, the careful checking of new securities under the Securities Act and the curtailment of rank stock speculation through the Securities Exchange Act. I sincerely hope that as a result people will be discouraged in unhappy efforts to get rich quick by speculating in securities. The average person almost always loses. Only a very small minority of the people of this country believe in gambling as a substitute for the old philosophy of Benjamin Franklin that the way to wealth is through work.

In meeting the problems of industrial recovery the chief agency of the Government has been the National Recovery Administration [N.R.A.]. Under its guidance, trades and industries covering over 90 percent of all industrial employees have adopted codes of fair competition, which have been approved by the President. Under these codes, in the industries covered, child labor has been eliminated. The work day and the work week have been shortened. Minimum wages have been established and other wages adjusted toward a rising standard of living. The emergency purpose of the N.R.A. was to put men to work and since its creation more than four million persons have been reemployed, in great part through the cooperation of American business brought about under the codes.

Benefits of the Industrial Recovery Program have come, not only to labor in the form of new jobs, in relief from overwork and in relief from underpay, but also to the owners and managers of industry because, together with a great increase in the payrolls, there has come a substantial rise in the total of industrial profits—a rise from a deficit figure in the first quarter of 1933 to a level of sustained profits within one year from the inauguration of N.R.A.

Now it should not be expected that even employed labor and capital would be completely satisfied with present conditions. Employed workers have not by any means all enjoyed a return to the earnings of prosperous times, although millions of hitherto underprivileged workers are today far better paid than ever before. Also, billions of dollars of invested capital have today a greater security of present and future earning power than before. This is because of the establishment of fair, competitive standards and because of relief from unfair competition in wage cutting which depresses markets and destroys purchasing power. But it is an undeniable fact that the restoration of other billions of sound investments to a reasonable earning power could not be brought about in one year. There is no magic formula, no economic panacea, which could simply revive overnight the heavy industries and the trades dependent upon them.

Nevertheless the gains of trade and industry, as a whole, have been substantial. In these gains and in the policies of the Administration there are assurances that hearten all forward-looking men and women with the confidence that we are definitely rebuilding our political and economic system on the lines laid down by the New Deal—lines which as I have so often made clear, are in complete accord with the underlying principles of orderly popular government which Americans have demanded since the white man first came to these shores. We count, in the future as in the past, on the driving power of individual initiative and the incentive of fair profit, strengthened with the acceptance of those obligations to the public interest which rest upon us all. We have the right to expect that this driving power will be given patriotically and whole-heartedly to our Nation. . . .

Closely allied to the N.R.A. is the program of public works provided for in the same Act and designed to put more men back to work, both directly on the public works themselves, and indirectly in the industries supplying the materials for these public works. To those who say that our expenditures for public works and other means for recovery are a waste that we cannot afford, I answer that no country, however rich, can afford the waste of its human resources. Demoralization caused by vast unemployment is our greatest extravagance. Morally, it is the greatest menace to our social order. Some people try to tell me that we must make up our minds that for the future we shall permanently have millions of unemployed just as other countries have had them for over a decade. What may be necessary for those countries is not my responsibility to determine. But as for this country, I stand or fall by my refusal to accept as a necessary condition of our future a permanent army of unemployed. On the contrary, we must make it a national principle that we will not tolerate a large army of unemployed and that we will arrange our national economy to end our present unemployment as soon as we can and then to take wise measures against its return. I do not want to think that it is the destiny of any American to remain permanently on relief rolls. . . .

In our efforts for recovery we have avoided, on the one hand, the theory that business should and must be taken over into an all-embracing Government. We have avoided, on the other hand, the equally untenable theory that it is an interference with liberty to offer reasonable help when private enterprise is in need of help. The course we have followed fits the American practice of Government, a practice of taking action step by step, or regulating only to meet concrete needs, a practice of courageous recognition of change. I believe with Abraham Lincoln, that "The legitimate object of Government is to do for a community of people whatever they need to have done but cannot do at all or cannot do so well for themselves in their separate and individual capacities."

I am not for a return to that definition of liberty under which for many years a free people were being gradually regimented into the service of the privileged few. I prefer and I am sure you prefer that broader definition of liberty under which we are moving forward to greater freedom, to greater security for the average man than he has ever known before in the history of America.

8.2: The New Deal and the "Common Man" (1934, 1936)

Roosevelt and the New Deal proved immensely popular with middle- and lower-income Americans. In 1936 FDR won in an extraordinary popular landslide when he ran for reelection.

In the selections below—letters written by working class Americans to New Deal politicians, to FDR's wife, Eleanor, and to the president himself—we learn why the "common man" supported the administration's programs. How would you characterize the sources of this support? What New Deal programs particularly seemed to awaken the gratitude of ordinary Americans?

"Saint Roosevelt"

Cedarburg, Wis.
10:45 A.M. Mar. 5, 1934

Mrs. F. D. Roosevelt
Washington, D.C.

My dear Friend:

Just listened to the address given by your dear husband, our wonderful President. During the presidential campaign of 1932 we had in our home a darling little girl, three years old. My husband & I were great admirers of the Dem. candidate and so Dolores had to listen to much talk about the great man who we hoped and prayed would be our next Pres. We are Lutherans and she is Catholic so you'll get quite a thrill out of what I'm to tell you now. That fall Judge Karel of Mil. sent me a fine picture of our beloved President, which I placed in our Public Library. When I received this fine picture my dear mother (who has since been called Home) said to Dolores "Who is this man?" and Dolores answered without any hesitation "Why who else, but Saint Roosevelt!" The old saying goes fools and children often tell the truth and indeed we all feel if there ever was a Saint. He is one. As long as Pres. Roosevelt will be our leader under Jesus Christ we feel no fear. His speech this morning showed he feels for the "least of these" I am enclosing a snap shot of the dear little girl who acclaimed our President a Saint and rightly so.

I'm sure Pres. Roosevelt had a great day on Feb. 16, the world day of prayer, when many hearts were lifted in prayer for him all over this great land of ours.

We shall continue to ask our heavenly Father to guide and guard him in his great task as leader of the great American people.

With all good wishes for you and your fine family I am your most sincerely

Mrs. L.K.S.

Nov 25, 1934
Arkansas City, Kansas

Mrs. Eleanor Roosevelt
White House
Washington, D.C.

Dear Madam:

I beg to inform you that I have been reading your writings in the Wichita Beacon and I must say that the whole nation should be enthused over them. I especially was carried away with the one on Old Age Pensions. It brought my mind back to the day of the Chicago Convention, when Mr. Roosevelt was nominated for the presidency.

In our little home in Arkansas City, my family and I were sitting around the radio, to hear and we heard you when you flew over from N.Y. and entered the great hall and when he spoke it seems as though some Moses had come to alleviated us of our sufferings. Strange to say when he was speaking to see the moisten eyes and the deep feeling of emotions that gave vent to his every word and when you spoke then we knew that the white house would be filled with a real mother to the nation.

I am . . . glad to say . . . you have not failed us, you have visited the slums, the farms and homes of your people, and formed first handed ideas for their benefits. Oh what a blessing while you have always had a silver spoon in your own mouth you have not failed to try and place one in every mouth in the land and when I read in the Beacon your brilliant ideas of the Old Age Pensions. You said the only thing laking [sic] was the way to do it. So I said the first lady is seeking a way to help us and so let us help her to find it. . . .

Dear Madam, I am afraid to write more to you at this time as this is my first letter to the lady of the land as the others did not seem to be interested in the welfare of the people. Wife and I pray continually to God for your success. Every time the news boy hollers Extra our hearts are filled with fear that something has happened to the president, but as we go marching on to higher hills of prosperity through the new deal we are hoping and working to that point that all will be well. But one thing I was just about to forget I think that the home building program should be furnished means for back taxes included for repairs and etc. As many places are handicapped to get loans from government on account of being back taxes. Our heart in hand is ever with you and the Pres. to carry on.

Respectfuly Yours,
P.F.A. [male]

[Columbus, Ga.
October 24, 1934]

[Dear President Roosevelt:]

I hope you can spare the time for a few words from a cotton mill family, *out of work* and almost out of heart and in just a short while out of a house in which to live. you know of course that the realators are putting the people out when they cannot pay the rent promptly. and how are we to pay the rent so long as the mills refuse us work, merely because we had the nerve to ask or "demand", better working conditions.[1]

I realize *and* appreciate the aid and food which the government is giving to the poor people out of work *Thanks to you.*

[1]This is a reference to the unsuccessful 1934 textile workers' strike—ED.

but is it even partly right for us to be thrown out of our homes, when we have no chance whatever of paying, so long as the big corporations refuse of work. I for one am very disheartened *and* disappointed   guess my notice to move will come next.

what are we to do. wont you try to help us wont you appeal, "for *us* all," to the real estate people and the factories

hoping you'll excuse this, but I've always thought of F.D.R. as my personal friend.

C.L.F. [male]

[Akron, Ohio
February 1936]

My Dear Mrs Roosevelt.[2]

I thought I would write a letter hoping you would find time to read it, and if you thought it was worth while answering it, I would be glad of any advise you would care to give me. A few weeks ago, I heard your talk over the air, on the subject of the Old age pension, and I got to thinking what a blessing it would be to my mother, if it was possible for her to receive that pension, if the bill should pass. My mother has been in this country since April 1914 but she has never made herself a American Citizen, as she was sixty years old when she came here, and now she is eighty.

Mother come out to this country nineteen years ago [from Scotland][3]. . . .

I thought as long as I lived there was no need to worry about her being taken care of, but I never dreamed of a depression like we have had well it has changed the whole course of our lives we have suffered, and no one knowes but our own family, I have two children one nineteen, graduated from high school last June, and the girl graduates this coming June, and we have had the awfullest time trying to get the bare necessary things in life.

I am in no position to do the right thing for mother, I cant give her anything but her living but I thought if it was possible for her to get that pension it would be like a gift from heaven, as in all the years she has been in this country she has never had a dollar of her own.

I wish she could get it her days may not be long on this earth, and if she just had a little money coming once in a while, to make her feel independent of her family, I at least would know that if anything happened to me she could get a living, and not have to go back to the rest of her family, because she says she would rather go to a poor house, than live with any of the others.

Mrs Roosevelt you might think I have lots of nerve writing to you when you have so much to attend to but I could not help admiring you for the

[2]Misspellings are part of the original letter—ED.

[3]Eighteen years ago—ED.

splended way you talked about the old people of this nation I feel sorry for all of them, they seem to be forgotten, and most young people think they have had there day and should be glad to die. but this is not my idea, I think that their last few years should be made as plesent for them as it is possible, I know that if it was in my power to make my mother happy by giving her what she justly deservs, I would gladly do so. Well whither my mother ever gets anything or not, I hope all the other old people that is intilted to it gets it soon, because there is nothing sadder than old people who have struggled hard all there lives to give there family a start in life, then to be forgotten, when they them self need it most.

I will finish now but befor I do I want to thank you Mrs Roosevelt and also Mr Roosevelt for the good both of you are doing for this country you have gave people new hope and every real American has faith in you and may you both be spared to carry on the good work and lead this nation on to victory.

Yours Respectfully,
Mrs J. S.
Akron, Ohio.

8.3:   A New Deal Bureaucrat in Washington (1936 ff.)

During the 1930s hundreds of young professionals found a refuge in New Deal agencies. Faced with the prospect of unemployment and skills going stale, they flocked to Washington to join an exciting political experiment. In the selection below, Joe Marcus, an economist, tells the journalist Studs Terkel what it was like to be at the heart of the New Deal during the stimulating years of the mid-1930s.

Why did Marcus find the Roosevelt administration so vital and interesting? Is he uncritical of the New Deal? Toward the end of his interview, he answers Terkel's question about whether the New Deal "saved this society." Is his answer valid? In what sense did the New Deal save existing American institutions? Was its role, then, conservative or radical?

Joe Marcus Remembers His Years as New Deal Official

I think it was '31 or '32. I was attending the City College of New York. Most were students whose parents were workers or small businessmen hit by the Depression. In the public speaking class, I was called upon to talk about unemployment insurance. I was attacked by most of the students . . . this was

Socialism. I was shocked by their vehemence. If I remember, the American Federation of Labor at its national convention voted it down. The idea of social security was very advanced. Those who were really hungry wanted something. But the intellectuals, the students, the bureaucratic elements— to them it was a horrible thought. It was something subversive. At first.

But they learned quickly. It was a shock to them. When Roosevelt came out with the ideas, it was not a clearly thought-out program. There was much improvisation. What you had was a deep-seated emotional feeling as far as the people were concerned. A willingness to change society, just out of outrage, out of need. I think they would have accepted even more radical ideas.

Roosevelt was reflecting the temper of the time—the emotional more than the intellectual. It wasn't merely a question of the king bestowing favors. The pressure from below was a reality. It was not a concentrated campaign effort. There was no organization with a program that commanded the majority of the people. This was part of the political strangeness of our society. The actions below were very revolutionary. Yet some of the ideas of the people, generally, were very backward.

I graduated college in '35. I went down to Washington and started to work in the spring of '36. The New Deal was a young man's world. Young people, if they showed any ability, got an opportunity. I was a kid, twenty-two or twenty-three. In a few months I was made head of the department. We had a meeting with hot shots: What's to be done? I pointed out some problems: let's define what we're looking for. They immediately had me take over. I had to set up the organization and hire seventy-five people. Given a chance as a youngster to try out ideas, I learned a fantastic amount. The challenge itself was great.

It was the idea of being asked big questions. The technical problems were small. These you had to solve by yourself. But the context was broad: Where was society going? Your statistical questions became questions of full employment. You were not prepared for it in school. If you wanted new answers, you needed a new kind of people. This is what was exciting.

Ordinarily, I might have had a job at the university, marking papers or helping a professor. All of a sudden, I'm doing original research and asking basic questions about how our society works. What makes a Depression? What makes for pulling out of it? Once you start thinking in these terms, you're in a different ball game.

The climate was exciting. You were part of a society that was on the move. You were involved in something that could make a difference. Laws could be changed. So could the conditions of people.

The idea of being involved close to the center of political life was unthinkable, just two or three years before all this happened. Unthinkable for someone like me, of lower middle-class, close to ghetto, Jewish life. Suddenly you were a significant member of society. It was not the kind of closed society you had lived in before.

You weren't in the situation kids are in today, where you're confronted with a consensus of hopelessness . . . unless you just break things up. You were really part of something, changes could be made. Bringing *immediate* results to people who were starving. You could do something about it: that was the most important thing. This you felt.

A feeling that if you had something to say, it would get to the top. As I look back now, memoranda I had written reached the White House, one way or another. The biggest thrill of my life was hearing a speech of Roosevelt's, using a selection from a memorandum I had written.

Everybody was searching for ideas. A lot of guys were opportunists, some were crackpots. But there was a search, a sense of values . . . that would make a difference in the lives of people.

We weren't thinking of remaking society. That wasn't it. I didn't buy this dream stuff. What was happening was a complete change in social attitudes at the central government level. The question was: How can you do it within this system? People working in all the New Deal agencies were dominated by this spirit.

There was the old government bureaucracy that could not administer the new programs. Roosevelt, who was criticized for being a bad administrator, made a great deal of sense out of this. There were weaknesses, but the point is if you wanted to get jobs for people in a hurry, as in WPA,[1] you had to find new people with the spirit, with the drive.

At one stage, Harry Hopkins [2] met with his staff, a lot of people, in a huge auditorium. He explained they'd have to work day and night to get this particular job done. He asked for volunteers, who would start off tonight and work straight through. Practically everybody in the auditorium raised their hands. Youth and fervor.

Normally, administrative people were much older. But even the young of the old bureaucracy were stodgy. They came to work, left their jobs when the day was over, went out for their lunches. . . . Frankly, they didn't work very hard and knocked off whenever they could. What rightwingers say about Government employees was very true in many cases.

The New Dealers were different. I'm not only talking about policy people. I'm talking about the clerks, who felt what they were doing was important. You didn't take time out for lunch because of a job that had to be done. You had a sandwich on the desk. Their job made sense. . . . Of course, I'm romanticizing somewhat, but there was still this difference.

The civil servants were competent people, but they worked within rigid formulas. They worked their hours and when they were through, that was it. The idea of sitting up all night. . . .

The evenings were exciting. Social evenings were spent in discussing policy, in what you were doing. It wasn't bridge playing: It wasn't just idle drinking or gossip. . . .

[1] Works Progress Administration—ED.
[2] A close Roosevelt adviser and head of the WPA in 1935–1940—ED.

His wife, Sue, interjects: "The wives took a very dim view of men getting off in a corner talking about the levels of unemployment. The women were clustered together on the other side, but the husbands were so busy, so involved. . . . We took a dim view, I must say. (Laughs.)

"Every once in a while, we'd say, 'What is it?' We'd be interested. But it was very hard, because they were so terribly involved."

He laughs, then adds: "It would get very technical, I must admit—shop talk."

Sue: "We were interested in what our husbands were doing. We felt as they did, that it was terribly important. Although I remember once, when Joe's boss called about something. They wanted me to look for a piece of paper on the desk. He said, "I hope you don't mind my taking your husband weekends like that.' I said, 'I certainly do.' (Laughs.) When Joe came home, he said, 'Oh, that was a terrible thing you said. After all, it's for the war effort.' This was in the late Thirties. (Laughs.) We understood the philosophical things—that was taken for granted. It's the technical discussions that were so annoying. Other wives, too, felt part of this effort. But on a social level, it sometimes got difficult. They got so immersed in technical questions, the ceiling could have fallen in and they wouldn't have noticed." (Laughs.)

The ambitious young man today takes his work home, too. But it's a question of himself, personal ambition. Not concern with society. Of course, some of our best operators were personally ambitious, but the climate was something else.

There was no difference between leisure time and work time. This doesn't mean we didn't go for a movie or go for a walk in the park. But the people I knew did not build a meaningful life outside of work. And action related to it, in some way.

Sue: "One of the nicest things in Washington, with all the other New Deal people, was that everybody lived on the same level. The notion of keeping up with the Joneses didn't exist. Nobody was pushing for anything, because everybody was involved. . . ."

It was an exciting community, where we lived in Washington. The basic feeling—and I don't think this is just nostalgia—was one of excitement, of achievement, of happiness. Life was important, life was significant.

Were there questions in Washington about the nature of our society?

I don't think revolution as a topic of the day existed. The fact that people acted as they did, in violation of law and order, was itself a revolutionary act. People suddenly heard there was a Communist Party. It was insignificant before then. Suddenly, the more active people, the more concerned people, were in one way or another exposed to it. It never did command any real popular support, though it had influence in key places. This was a new set of ideas, but revolution was never really on the agenda.

F.D.R. was very significant in understanding how best to lead this sort of situation. Not by himself, but he mobilized those elements ready to develop these programs.

There are some who say F.D.R. saved this society. . . .

There's no question about it. The industrialists who had some under-standing recognized this right away. He could not have done what he did without the support of important elements of the wealthy class. They did not sabotage the programs. Just the opposite.

One of the first things the annual report of Morgan & Company dealt with, right after the war, was the question of full employment. This had been considered a Bolshevik idea five years earlier. Business leaders, in the early days of the war, saw the importance of developing more progressive pro-grams. It was a way of rationalizing a corporate society. The New Deal did the same thing.

It was a very unusual Depression in the history of societies. It lasted so long and went so deep. Usually, when you get a depression—even a severe one—you get two, three years of decline and in another two, three years, you're back where you were. But *ten years* . . . . Just think, in 1939, we were back to the industrial production of '29. And you had a ten-year increase in population. If it weren't for the war orders from France and England, there's a question if we would ever have hit that point. The war did end the Depression. That doesn't mean that something else might not have ended it.

8.4:   Attack from the Right (1936)

Wherever it properly belongs on the political spectrum, the New Deal kin-dled opposition both to its right and to its left. Among conservatives no person was so determined an adversary as Herbert Hoover, the ex-presi-dent whom millions of Americans blamed for the Depression. In the selec-tion below, an excerpt from a speech he made during the 1936 election campaign in support of the Republican presidential candidate, Hoover tears into the New Deal. What are the grounds for his attack? What per-sonal factors may have encouraged him in his opposition? What is his evaluation of the New Deal as an agency of recovery? Are Hoover's criti-cisms of the New Deal defensible?

The New Deal Is a Danger to Freedom

HERBERT HOOVER

Through four years of experience this New Deal attack upon free institu-tions has emerged as the transcendent issue in America.

All the men who are seeking for mastery in the world today are using the same weapons. They sing the same songs. They all promise the joys of Elysium without effort.

But their philosophy is founded on the coercion and compulsory organi-zation of men. True liberal government is founded on the emancipation of

New York Times, October 31, 1936.

men. This is the issue upon which men are imprisoned and dying in Europe right now. . . .

Freedom does not die from frontal attack. It dies because men in power no longer believe in a system based upon liberty. . . .

I gave the warning against this philosophy of government four years ago from a heart heavy with anxiety for the future of our country. It was born from many years' experience of the forces moving in the world which would weaken the vitality of American freedom. It grew in four years of battle as President to uphold the banner of free men.

And that warning was based on sure ground from my knowledge of the ideas that Mr. Roosevelt and his bosom colleagues had covertly embraced despite the Democratic platform.

Those ideas were not new. Most of them had been urged upon me.

During my four years powerful groups thundered at the White House with these same ideas. Some were honest, some promising votes, most of them threatening reprisals, and all of them yelling "reactionary" at us.

I rejected the notion of great trade monopolies and price-fixing through codes. That could only stifle the little business man by regimenting him under the big brother. That idea was born of certain American Big Business and grew up to be the NRA.

I rejected the schemes of "economic planning" to regiment and coerce the farmer. That was born of a Roman despot 1,400 years ago and grew up into the AAA.

I refused national plans to put the government into business in competition with its citizens. That was born of Karl Marx.

I vetoed the idea of recovery through stupendous spending to prime the pump. That was born of a British professor.

I threw out attempts to centralize relief in Washington for politics and social experimentation. I defeated other plans to invade States' rights, to centralize power in Washington. Those ideas were born of American radicals.

I stopped attempts at currency inflation and repudiation of government obligation. That was robbery of insurance policy holders, savings bank depositors and wage-earners. That was born of the early Brain Trusters.

I rejected all these things because they would not only delay recovery but because I knew that in the end they would shackle free men.

Rejecting these ideas we Republicans had erected agencies of government which did start our country to prosperity without the loss of a single atom of American freedom. . . .

Our people did not recognize the gravity of the issue when I stated it four years ago. That is no wonder, for the day Mr. Roosevelt was elected recovery was in progress, the Constitution was untrampled, the integrity of the government and the institutions of freedom were intact.

It was not until after the election that the people began to awake. Then the realization of intended tinkering with the currency drove bank depositors into the panic that greeted Mr. Roosevelt's inauguration.

Recovery was set back for two years, and hysteria was used as the bridge to reach the goal of personal government.

I am proud to have carried the banner of free men to the last hour of the term my countrymen entrusted it to me. It matters nothing in the history of a race what happens to those who in their time have carried the banner of free men. What matters is that the battle shall go on.

The people know now the aims of this New Deal philosophy of government.

We propose instead leadership and authority in government within the moral and economic framework of the American System.

We propose to hold to the Constitutional safeguards of free men.

We propose to relieve men from fear, coercion and spite that are inevitable in personal government.

We propose to demobilize and decentralize all this spending upon which vast personal power is being built. We propose to amend the tax laws so as not to defeat free men and free enterprise.

We propose to turn the whole direction of this country toward liberty, not away from it.

The New Dealers say that all this that we propose is a worn-out system; that this machine age requires new measures for which we must sacrifice some part of the freedom of men. Men have lost their way with a confused idea that governments should run machines.

Man-made machines cannot be of more worth than men themselves. Free men made these machines. Only free spirits can master them to their proper use.

The relation of our government with all these questions is complicated and difficult. They rise into the very highest ranges of economics, statesmanship and morals.

And do not mistake. Free government is the most difficult of all government. But it is everlastingly true that the plain people will make fewer mistakes than any group of men no matter how powerful. But free government implies vigilant thinking and courageous living and self-reliance in a people.

Let me say to you that any measure which breaks our dikes of freedom will flood the land with misery.

8.5: Thunder from the Left (1934)

The New Deal not only offended political conservatives; it also angered many radicals. During the opening years of the Roosevelt administration, no organized group was as hostile to it as the Communist Party of the United States. The following selection is from a 1934 Communist Party pamphlet presenting "a program for American labor" that interprets the New Deal as the enemy of the American working class.

Why did the American Communists compare the New Deal with contemporary fascism? What aspects of the New Deal did they have in mind? What did they mean by fascism? *Within a year or two the Communist Party of the United States would do a complete reversal on the Roosevelt administration. Can you guess why? What was the ultimate source of Communist attitudes toward American politics and politicians in these years?*

The Communist Party: The New Deal Means Fascism and War

Mass Starvation and Misery

. . . Sixteen million workers stand idle outside closed factories, mines, suffering from the lack of the very things they could produce in these industries. The total income of the working class is less than 40 per cent of what it was four years ago. The oppressed Negro masses are suffering new economic attacks, and a rising wave of lynch terror. Large sections of poor and middle farmers are being crushed and driven off their land or reduced to the position of tenants and peons for the bankers and monopolists. Great numbers of the middle class intellectuals, professionals, teachers, white collar workers, have likewise been cast into poverty. Especially hard hit as a result of the crisis is the youth of the working class, farmer and middle class. Millions of working class children are suffering from undernourishment and actual starvation, unable to go to school because of lack of food, clothing and even school facilities, which are everywhere reduced.

New Deal—Program of Fascism and War

. . . The "New Deal" of Roosevelt is the aggressive effort of the bankers and trusts to find a way out of the crisis at the expense of the millions of toilers. Under cover of the most shameless demagogy, Roosevelt and the capitalists carry through drastic attacks upon the living standards of the masses, increased terrorism against the Negro masses, increased political oppression and systematic denial of existing civil rights, and are strengthening the control of the big monopolists over the economic and political life of the country. The "New Deal" is a program of fascization and the most intense preparations for imperialist war. Its class character is especially seen in the policy of the subsidies to the railroads, banks, and insurance companies, accompanied by increased parasitism, corruption, and bureaucratism. The devaluation of the dollar has resulted in a rapid rise of prices of commodities, and the lowering of . . . real wages. The N.R.A. machinery, with its labor boards on the one hand, and the most brutal police and military force on the other, has been used for the purpose of breaking up the workers' struggles and

The Way Out: A Program for American Labor (New York: Workers' Library Publishers, 1934), pp. 33–35.

their organizations. Strike struggles, not only those of the independent class unions, against whom the attack has been most vicious, but also the struggles of the workers in the A. F. of L.,[1] have been violently suppressed. Its farm policy has helped to enrich the big farmers and capitalists at the expense of the agricultural workers, the poor and middle farmers.

. . . The right of organization which was so loudly hailed by the social-fascists, which was to be guaranteed by section 7a of the N.R.A., has been used as a new instrument in the hands of the employers for the development of company unions, to block the desire of the workers to organize into real trade unions, independent of the bosses and government. It is an instrument to prop up the boss-controlled A. F. of L. bureaucracy, where the workers cannot be forced into company unions, and a means to divert the fight and organization of the working class away from militant trade unions. The system of codes has been a step in the direction of government control and fascization of the trade unions. The codes fixed minimum wages in the face of inflation and rising prices. The so-called Public Works Program has been used for the building up of the army and navy—an additional important weapon for the whole program of Roosevelt, which is one of preparation for war. All of this proves that the Roosevelt regime is not, as the liberals and Socialist Party leaders claim, a progressive regime, but is a government serving the interests of finance capital and moving toward the fascist suppression of the workers' movement.

Threatening War Danger

. . . The capitalist class is feverishly preparing for war as a way out of the crisis. It has embarked on a naval race with its main imperialist rivals, Great Britain and Japan. The army has been further mechanized, and the world's largest air fleet has been provided for, coast defense has been strengthened, army cantonments throughout the country have been provided; and the C.C.C.[2] has served as a trial mobilization and training ground for a great army, both for imperialist war and for civil war against the workers at home, as openly admitted by Roosevelt's assistant secretary of war, Woodring.

In all the markets of the world, the struggle between Great Britain and the United States grows more acute. The Roosevelt regime, through its inflation, is engaged in a war on British goods and on British currency, in an effort to win world hegemony. The struggle for hegemony in the Pacific between the United States and Japan daily becomes more marked, with both nations building up their naval armaments in anticipation of war. All the chief imperialist powers are clashing for the lion's share in the dismemberment of China. The imperialist aggressiveness of Roosevelt's policies is

---

[1]The American Federation of Labor, a conservative labor group—ED.

[2]The Civilian Conservation Corps, a New Deal program to employ city youths in National Parks and forests under semi-military control—ED.

shown most clearly in Cuba, in Latin America (Bolivia-Paraguay war), and in the Philippines. Roosevelt's policies are interlocked with the policies of world capitalism, characterized everywhere by the desperate attempt to get out of the crisis at the expense of the masses by means of fascism, war and intervention.

. . . The preparations for war are being carried through especially by Roosevelt under the cover of pacifist and "democratic" demagogy. In this trickery of the masses, Roosevelt has the utmost support of the A. F. of L. bureaucrats, Socialists and liberals. The A. F. of L. bureaucrats carry on the most violent attacks against the Socialist fatherland. They support the preparations for an army and navy on the plea that it gives employment. The Socialists have invested the "New Deal" war and fascist program with the halo of Socialism. Now openly and now covertly, they continue their attacks against the Soviet Union. . . .

The Fascization of the American Government

. . . American capitalism is more and more fascizing its rule. This is particularly being performed by the Roosevelt administration under the cover of the "New Deal". Under the mask of saving the "democratic" institutions of the United States, the Roosevelt government and the bourgeoisie are: (a) increasing the violence against the workers, particularly revolutionary workers and Negro masses, against whom they have unleashed a wave of lynch terror; (b) increasing tendencies to suppress and deny the right to strike; (c) establishing labor Arbitration Boards with direct participation of the employers and the bureaucrats, with the object of preventing, suppressing, and disorganizing the struggles of the workers; (d) directly concentrating into the hands of the President almost dictatorial powers, and vesting power, formerly executed by Congress, in direct appointees of the President over matters of most vital concern to millions of toilers; (e) developing a wave of chauvinism and carrying through the whole N.R.A. campaign with the greatest emphasis upon nationalism.

9

Isolation-Intervention

By 1938 the attention of the Roosevelt administration was shifting rapidly from domestic to foreign concerns. Some scholars claim that this change of focus derived from the impasse over the nation's economic problems. Unemployment would simply not go away, and FDR and his colleagues, they say, found foreign affairs more congenial and politically rewarding than the intractable Depression. Other scholars feel there is no need to look beyond the growing menace abroad: the rise of the "dictators," especially the leader of Nazi Germany, Adolf Hitler, which truly threatened the world balance of power and the survival of the liberal democracies, including the United States.

In 1938, as tensions grew in Europe, the administration steeled itself for an eventual confrontation with the "aggressors." But the public's attitudes failed to keep in step. Through the 1920s and well into the 1930s most Americans felt that their country's World War I intervention had been a mistake and rejected any commitment to collective international action to preserve peace. Europe's—and Asia's—concerns were not ours.

The American isolationism of the period between the wars was compounded of many elements: traditional American xenophobia, pacifism, midwestern Progessivism, and an emotional backlash among ethnic groups humiliated during World War I by repressive superpatriotism. It was reinforced by a seductive intellectual construct. During the 1930s a rash of scholarly books and a burst of congressional hearings held by the Nye Committee in 1934–36 blamed American involvement in World War I on the connivance of bankers and munitions manufacturers. The United States, it was argued, had been duped into the war to benefit the "merchants of death." Profits, rather than patriotism, had driven American foreign policy from 1914 to 1917.

Whatever the source of this distancing from foreign concerns, beginning in 1935 Congress enacted a number of Neutrality Acts designed to prevent U.S. entanglement in another great European conflict. These measures prohibited American loans to belligerents, restricted Americans' travel on belligerent ships, and forbade the export of American arms and munitions to belligerents. In effect, Congress sought to keep the United States from becoming enmeshed in Europe's problems, even if it meant surrendering some of its traditional rights.

But Congress had failed to take account of the deteriorating international environment. In 1932 Japan had seized Manchuria from China and five years later began a war to reduce all of the Chinese Republic to colonial status. In Africa the Italian fascist dictator, Benito Mussolini, attacked Ethiopia, virtually the last of Africa's free nations, and in 1936 annexed it as a colony. Most ominous of all was the aggressive posture of Germany under its brutal dictator, Adolf Hitler.

Hitler had risen to power pledged to undo the Versailles Treaty, rearm Germany, and restore it to its former level of influence. In 1936 he remilitarized the Rhineland border with France; in 1938 he annexed Austria to Germany. He was soon demanding Czech surrender of the Sudeten area, a part of the Czechoslovak Republic inhabited mainly by Germans. Meanwhile, in Germany itself he had destroyed the liberal Weimar Republic and imposed a viciously racist totalitarian regime that reversed a century of democratic progress in Europe.

It was against this background of Japanese, Italian, and German militarism and tyranny that Americans debated their country's role in international affairs. Isolationists remained unconvinced of the need for the United States to intrude into these conflicts. Interventionists believed that America's own vital interests, and indeed its very safety, were involved. In the selections below you will encounter samples of both the isolationist and interventionist arguments that shaped the intense debate over peace or war during the 1930s and in the months preceding the Japanese attack on Pearl Harbor in December 1941.

9.1:   Isolationism (1935, 1939)

One of the most prominent of the isolationist spokespersons during the 1930s was the Democratic senator from Missouri, Bennett Champ Clark. A member of the Nye Committee, Clark was an ardent isolationist and opponent of the New Deal. In the following selection, taken from an address he delivered in May 1935, Clark defends the views and policies incorporated into the mid-thirties neutrality legislation.

Clark's attitudes are based on an analysis of how America became involved in World War I. Is the analysis valid? Could the United States have avoided war in 1917 if it had not insisted on its rights as a neu-

tral nation? Had the Neutrality Acts passed in the 1930s been retained, would they have kept the United States out of the great new war emerging on the horizon?

Another prominent isolationist leader was the Republican senator from Ohio, Robert Taft, son of the twenty-seventh president of the United States. By early 1939, when Taft delivered the talk excerpted below, the world was already on the verge of war, and Roosevelt had begun to question the wisdom of the neutrality legislation, which, he believed, helped aggressors and penalized their victims. Roosevelt was particularly concerned that applying the American arms embargo would benefit the rebellion of the far right against the Spanish Loyalists then underway, led by General Francisco Franco and supported by fascist Italy and Nazi Germany.

Taft professes not to oppose collective action to stop aggressors, but he rejects unilateral American action. Is his position sincere, or was it a dodge? Did many isolationists favor American cooperation with other nations to prevent international aggression?

The Experience of the Last War Should Guide Us Today

BENNETT CHAMP CLARK

In the light of experience it is high time that we gave some thought to the hard, practical question of just how we propose to avoid war if it comes again. No one who has made an honest attempt to face the issue will assert that there is any easy answer. No one who has studied the history of our participation in the World War will tell you that there is a simple way out. There is none—no simple panacea, no magic formula. But if we have learned anything at all we know the inevitable and tragic end to a policy of drifting and trusting to luck. We know that however strong is the will of the American people to refrain from mixing in other peoples' quarrels, that will can only be made effective if we have a sound, definite policy from the beginning. No lesson of the last war is more clear than that such a policy cannot be improvised after war breaks out. It must be worked out in advance, before it is too late to apply reason. I say with all possible earnestness that if we want to avoid another war we must begin at once to formulate a policy based upon an understanding of the problem confronting us. . . .

The best way . . . is to examine the forces which are likely to involve us in war. In 1914 we knew very little about those forces. President Wilson issued his proclamation of neutrality and we went on with business as usual, in the happy belief that 3,000 miles of ocean would keep us out of the mess. Our professional diplomats were not much more astute. They assumed that all we had to do to keep out was to observe the rules of international law and insist upon our neutral rights. About 2 weeks after the outbreak of hostilities our

28 May 1935, *Congressional Record*, 74th Cong., 1st sess., 8335–8338.

State Department issued a public circular on the rights and duties of a neutral in war time. They took the position that "the existence of war between foreign governments does not suspend trade or commerce between this country and those at war." They told American merchants that there was nothing in international law to prevent them from trading with the warring nations. They told munitions makers that they were free to sell their war materials to either or both sides. They took no steps to warn American citizens of the dangers of travel on vessels of the warring nations, even after passenger ships had been sunk without warning. This attitude, strange as it may seem today, was in full accord with the rules of international law as generally understood at that time.

We are wiser today. We know more about war and much more about neutrality. And yet it is remarkable how much we seem to have forgotten. In the course of the Senate investigation of the munitions industry this winter Senator Nye and I have had occasion to go rather deeply into the activities of our arms merchants and other traders in war material during the early years of the conflict. We have examined again the tortuous record of our diplomatic correspondence. From this survey four broad conclusions stand out:

1. That a policy based on defense of our so-called "neutral rights" led us into serious diplomatic controversy with both the Allies and the Central Powers, and in the end brought us to a point where we were compelled to choose between surrendering those rights or fighting to defend them. In 1917 we chose to fight.
2. The "national honor" and "prestige" of the nation are inevitably involved when American ships are sunk on the high seas—even though the owners of these ships and their cargoes are private citizens seeking to profit from other nations' wars. Passions are quickly aroused when American lives are lost—even though the citizens who took passage on belligerent ships knew in advance the risks they ran.
3. That the economic forces, set in motion by our huge war trade with the Allies, made it impossible to maintain that "true spirit of neutrality" which President Wilson urged upon his fellow citizens at the outbreak of the conflict.
4. That among these economic forces, those which involved us most deeply were the huge trade in arms and ammunition and other war materials with the Allies.

And just a word about the futility of trying to defend our neutral rights and freedom of the seas. As a neutral we claimed the right to trade in war materials and all other goods with the warring nations. This right—with two main exceptions—had been recognized under the rules of international law which had grown up over more than a hundred years. The exceptions were important: A warring nation, or belligerent, had a right which we recognized, to capture goods called "contraband." Originally "contraband" consisted of guns and explosives and other munitions intended for the use of the armed forces. Great Britain, for example, had a legal right to stop an American ship on the high seas if it could prove that the vessel carried munitions bound for Germany. In 1909 the leading sea powers drew up a list of contraband in a famous statement of maritime law which came to be known as the "Declaration of London."

When the World War broke out, however, this declaration had not been put into force by any of the governments. When our State Department asked the British Government whether it would accept the list of contraband articles in the Declaration of London the British declined. They argued, with some logic, that under modern conditions of war, food and raw materials, and almost everything except ostrich feathers, which were sent to the enemy were just as important as guns and explosives for the army. Modern war is not merely a contest between armies on the field of battle. It involves the entire population of nations and becomes a death struggle in which the warring country tries to overcome the will of the enemy to resist. Anything which helps the enemy to carry on the war is of vital importance. By the end of 1916, therefore, Great Britain had placed almost every article exported by the United States on the lists of contraband. Our State Department protested that the British had no right to change the old rules of international law. We sent a stream of indignant notes to London. But Great Britain was engaged in a death struggle, and we knew that one way to win the war was to starve the enemy. Our notes fell on deaf ears partly through the almost treasonable connivance of our own ambassador.

Our Government protested even more violently to Germany. While British ships were seizing contraband and taking American vessels into port, German submarines were sinking merchant ships on sight. The Imperial German Government argued that their submarine campaign was the only effective means of combatting the allied blockade which was starving the German people. They complained bitterly against the blockade and they protested our huge trade in munitions and war materials with the Allies.

Public opinion in the United States became inflamed at the ruthless destruction of unarmed merchant ships and passenger vessels. When the *Lusitania* was sunk in May, 1915, with the loss of 124 American lives, our patriots began to shout for a strong policy. President Wilson parried with diplomatic notes and for a time Germany offered to compromise. No one, it seems, thought of asking whether private American citizens in pursuit of fat profits had a right to involve us in war. In the end we were led to the point where we had to choose: We could try to defend our neutral rights by force of arms or we could give up those rights and stay out. On April 6, 1917, Congress declared that a state of war existed between the United States and Germany.

The only logical result of attempting to enforce these neutral "rights," as they are described, is to get us into war with both sides or to force us to join hands with one violator of our rights against another. It is logical and it is crazy. . . .

Let us see this logic ahead of time, instead of later, when the only way we can be logical is to be illogical.

Let us foresee that our ships will be seized by England or bombed from the air by Germany.

Let us not claim as a right what is an impossibility.

The only way we can maintain our neutral rights is to fight the whole world.

Failing that, we only pretend to enforce our neutral rights against one side and go to war to defend them against the other side.

But defense of our neutral rights was not the only cause of our being dragged into the World War. There were many factors, including the vast campaign of propaganda which began with the manufactured atrocity stories in the invasion of Belgium. The American people ceased to be neutral almost on the outbreak of hostilities. Our newspapers became violently partisan, and even our best citizens were soon shouting for preservation of the national honor. But among all these forces the economic entanglement of our one-sided but profitable war trade stands out in bold relief.

One point which stands out sharply in this record is that we cannot improvise a policy of neutrality after a war breaks out. . . .

The three resolutions introduced by Senator Nye and me, and the House resolution introduced by Congressman Maverick, embody the major points of a rational, realistic program of neutrality.

In these resolutions we propose that American citizens who want to profit from other people's wars shall not be allowed again to entangle the United States. We learned in our munitions inquiry that some of our American armament firms have been making money by helping Germany rearm with airplanes. We deny that this obliges us to put our own boys on the receiving line when those airplanes start dropping their bombs. We propose to take the American flag off the munitions ships. . . .

This legislation, we frankly admit, cannot safeguard us against poisonous propaganda or the inflaming of people's minds which may follow in the wake of another war. It is not an automatic safeguard of our neutrality. But it does, we believe, lessen some of the most important dangers as revealed by our World War experience.

Let Us Retain the Neutrality Acts

ROBERT TAFT

On January fourth [1939] the President of the United States devoted his annual message to Congress to an appeal for increased armament. He pictured a world about to be enveloped in the flames of war, and he pictured the United States as surrounded by deadly armaments and threats of new aggression. He appealed for increased appropriations for adequate defense. His message was followed several days later by a program calling for approximately $525,000,000, of which only $200,000,000 is to be spent in the fiscal year which ends July 1, 1940.

There can be no difference of opinion among Americans on the principle of providing for this country a completely adequate defense against attack by foreign nations. . . .

Robert Taft, *Vital Speeches*, vol. 5 (February 1, 1939), pp. 254–256. Mt. Pleasant, SC: South Carolina City News Publishing.

But the message of the President suggests that he favors a foreign policy very different from mere defense of the United States, and one which in the end would require much greater armament. A year ago, in Chicago, he declared his belief that we should "quarantine the aggressor nations." Now he says that "The defense of religion, of democracy and of good faith among nations is all the same fight. To save one, we must make up our minds to save all." It is somewhat difficult to see how we can save democracy and good faith among nations by any policy of mere defense of the United States. The President says that we cannot safely be indifferent to international lawlessness anywhere in the world, and cannot let pass, without effective protest, acts of aggression against sister nations. It is true that he assumes that the American people are not willing to go to war in other parts of the world, but he says, "There are many methods short of war, but stronger and more effective than mere words, of bringing home to aggressor government the aggregate sentiments of our own people." He declares against neutrality legislation and implies that he favors the repeal of the neutrality law. All this cannot mean anything except that the President wishes power granted to him by Congress to favor one nation or another in any dispute that arises, and to employ economic sanction or embargoes against a nation that he does not like at the same time that he assists those he does like. . . .

In my opinion, such a policy leads inevitably to foreign war. It is contrary to the traditional policy of the United States from the days of George Washington. The position of this country has always been that it would remain neutral in any foreign war, no matter how much its sympathies might be on one side, as long as its own rights or those of its citizens were not infringed upon. This is a policy which was emphatically reaffirmed by the American people in 1920 when it was proposed that we join the League of Nations.

There is something to be said in favor of a general agreement for collective security by which a number of nations, sufficiently strong to dominate the world, undertake to prevent aggression even though it leads to war. There is a reasonable chance that such a policy must succeed. Our people, however, refused in 1920 to adopt it, and the efforts made under the League of Nations, without our cooperation, have now completely broken down. But the policy of the President . . . is not the policy of a League of Nations; it is completely original. No one has ever suggested before that a single nation should range over the world like a knight-errant, protecting democracy and ideals of good faith, and tilting, like Don Quixote, against the windmills of Fascism. . . .

Of course, such a policy is not only vain, but almost inevitably leads to war. If we enforce an effective embargo against Japan, driving its people to starvation . . . it would be only natural for Japan to attack the Philippines, and our whole standing and prestige would become involved in an Asiatic war. If the Spanish embargo is lifted and an American ship carrying munitions is sunk by an Italian cruiser as it approaches Barcelona, it is hard to see how we could avoid controversy with Italy, which might flame into a general war. We apparently are asked to line up with England and France, and probably Communist Russia, without even knowing what their policies may be or whether they will back up the stand that we may take. . . .

Congress was wise in adopting the neutrality bill, which prohibits the shipment of arms, ammunition, and implements of war to belligerent states, and to states where civil strife exists. I believe the President should long ago have found a state of war to exist between China and Japan, which he had full power to do, so that munitions might not be shipped to Japan. The neutrality bill intends that we shall not manufacture munitions for foreign wars. It provides further that in case of war, nations must come to this country and pay for all articles, other than munitions, to be shipped abroad before they are shipped. Its purpose is to reduce the chances of our becoming involved, and I believe it will assist very much the accomplishment of that purpose. It is in accord in spirit with the whole policy of American neutrality for 150 years.

But now it is suggested that the whole world is different. It is said that distances are so short we cannot possibly avoid being involved in a general war. I don't believe it. I think if we are sufficiently determined not to become involved, we can stay out. We learned our lesson in 1917. We learned that modern war defeats its own purposes. A war to preserve democracy resulted in the destruction of more democracies than it preserved. We may go in on the side of France and England because they are democracies, and find before we are through that they are Communist or Fascist.

Not only that, a war whether to preserve democracy or otherwise would almost certainly destroy democracy in the United States. We have moved far towards totalitarian government already. The additional powers sought by the President in case of war, the nationalization of all industry and all capital and all labor, already proposed in a bill before Congress, would create a socialist dictatorship which it would be impossible to dissolve when the war ended. . . .

There is a general illusion that we see in Germany and Italy forces which threaten to overwhelm England and France, and march on to attack the United States. But this is surely an imaginary fear at the present time. There is no reason to believe that Germany and Italy could defeat England and France in any protracted war. It is hard to see what they would gain even after a successful war by an attack on the United States. Certainly the strength of our position would make any nation hesitate, no matter how strong it might be.

It is natural that the sympathy of the people should be strongly aroused on one side when they see what is going on under the totalitarian governments. Perhaps the President should tell them what we think of them, especially as the day seems to have passed when nations go to war because others call them unpleasant names. But the great majority of the people are determined that those sympathies do not lead us into overt acts of embargo, blockade, or economic sanctions.

Considering the attitude which the President has taken, it seems essential that Congress shall strengthen the neutrality bill rather than repeal it. It seems essential that the President shall not have discretion to take sides in foreign wars, or impose sanctions against those nations which he might find to be aggressor nations. It seems wise not to repeal the Johnson Act, as it is now being suggested, and to maintain a policy of lending as little money as possible abroad. Congress is the body upon whom is conferred by the Constitution power to declare war. It should not permit the executive to go too far towards war, without consulting Congress, that Congress no longer has the power to prevent war.

I do not say that some special situation may not arise in the future, under which it may seem desirable to go to war as the first step in an effective defense. But if such a situation ever arises, it should be undertaken deliberately, after a public discussion by Congress as the representatives chosen by the people.

Many justifiable criticisms can be made of the neutrality act, and of any special type of neutrality. But the horrors of modern war are so great, its futility is so evident, its effect on democracy itself so destructive, that almost any alternative is more to be desired.

9.2:   Interventionists (1935)

Not every American endorsed the prevailing isolationist 'mood of the 1930s. One dissenter was Henry L. Stimson, secretary of state under Herbert Hoover and later, following a long absence from public life, secretary of war under Roosevelt.

Stimson was the quintessential "eastern establishment" figure, a man from an affluent old family with an elite education. As secretary of state he had condemned Japanese aggression against China and, as the 1930s advanced, foresaw increasing danger for America in a chaotic world. Stimson delivered the following radio talk in October 1935, after the Italian attack on Ethiopia.

What is the basis for Stimson's desire that the United States cooperate with the League of Nations to stop Mussolini? Did the United States accept League of Nations sanctions against Italy? Did the sanctions work?

Repeal the Arms Embargo
HENRY L. STIMSON

In discussing the dangers and problems which confront us arising out of the war in Ethiopia, we start from the common ground that we all wish to keep our country out of war. The only differences of opinion between us are as to the methods which will serve to accomplish this common end and will avoid the danger to America of being ultimately embroiled in what is taking place on the other side of the world. The basic difficulty lies in the fact that the modern world has become interconnected and economically interdependent.

A great war anywhere in the world today will seriously affect all the nations, whether they go into that war or not. We have already been given a terrific lesson on this in the great war, but unfortunately in this country we have not all of us learned that lesson. Many of us are accustomed to say that in this great depression we are now suffering from the results of having gone into that war. This is not entirely true. We are really suffering principally from things which happened in that war long before we joined it. For three years we kept out. It was during those three years that the principal economic dislocations took place which have resulted in America's sufferings now.

When in 1914 the European farmers stopped farming and the European manufacturers, traders and laborers left manufacturing and commerce, and all of them concentrated on fighting, the dislocation was begun which has since resulted in the great depression. Our farmers began to plow up new marginal lands in Kansas and other places to take advantage of the high wheat prices which were thus offered; and our manufacturers and traders similarly enlarged their factories and facilities to seek the rich rewards in commerce which were thus thrown at their feet. Out of these dislocations came the foundation for our present trouble. We would have been suffering from them even if we had never entered the war.

From these patent facts we should have learned thoroughly that a war anywhere is dangerous and that a great war will ultimately make us suffer whether we go in or not. We should have learned that the chief problem of the world today is war prevention, not isolation; and that isolation in the modern world is a fantastic impossibility, so far as keeping out of economic trouble is concerned. Most of the other nations of the world have learned this lesson. They have learned that the only method of saving us from war's consequences is for all the nations of the world to cooperate to prevent war from starting. If it starts it must be at once stamped out before it spreads.

The League of Nations is the machinery which these other nations have adopted to secure such cooperation. No one questions the great difficulty of successfully securing cooperative action among the nations of the world, and the work of the League during the last fifteen years has met with much discouragement and opposition. Nevertheless, during those years they have been making progress and have achieved successes which we in this country have never fully appreciated. This autumn the League in its treatment of the war crisis between Italy and Ethiopia has taken more vigorous action and accomplished more signal results than ever before in its history. . . .

These nations of the League are now working upon the steps which shall be taken to stamp out this dangerous conflagration. They have pointed out to Premier [Benito] Mussolini the covenants of the League which he is breaking and have called upon him to stop, and he has thus far defied them and is pushing ahead. Without resorting to arms, they are seeking to hold him back by cutting off their trade with him and thus gradually depriving him of the necessary supplies for his expensive adventure. This is a most delicate undertaking, for it involves the stoppage of normal channels of trade between Italy and many other countries. The process may last a long time and lead to complications which no one can now foresee. Over fifty nations, however, have determined that it must be done. They feel that it is the last recourse left them for preventing a war which may spread to all the rest of the world.

In the face of this situation the conduct of our own government is prescribed by the terms of the joint resolution adopted by our Congress on the 31st of August last [1930], which directs the imposition of an embargo upon the export of "arms, ammunition or implements of war" from this country to either Italy or Ethiopia. Under this law the President on October 5 issued a proclamation containing a list of the commodities which are thus prohibited from export. This list covers only the actually completed articles which constitute arms, ammunition and other engines of warfare. It does not cover the raw materials out of which such arms are manufactured, nor does it cover food and other supplies which are just as necessary as arms to an army in the field. It does not cover copper which goes into shells, or cotton or nitrates which go into powder, or oil which goes into transport.

The evident purpose of our Congress in enacting this resolution was similar to that of the fifty nations who are now taking action against Italy at Geneva—namely, to check the progress of the war by cutting off supplies. But the joint resolution as interpreted in the President's proclamation is likely to do more harm than good. It will have very little deterrent effect upon Italy, who is the aggressor and who is able to manufacture her own arms and ammunition, and it is already threatening to be a serious obstacle to the peace efforts of the other nations. If they take no further action than we have taken, the prospect of stamping out the war by holding back the aggressor, Italy, is much diminished. On the other hand, if they put embargoes on these other supplies which are not on our list, the only effect may be to leave the field entirely open for American traders to rush in and take advantage of the enticing market which is thus presented for selling supplies to Italy. That would produce a very serious danger of ultimate trouble between us and the nations which are doing their best to stamp out this war. . . .

On the same day when [President Roosevelt] proclaimed his embargo on arms, ammunition and implements of war, he took a further step. He uttered a further warning in these words:

"In these specific circumstances I desire to be understood that any of our people who voluntarily engage in transactions *of any character* with either of the belligerents do so at their own risk."

By these words he virtually urged our people to cut off all relations with Italy and Ethiopia and to impose a voluntary boycott upon all transactions with them. If this was rendered necessary on account of the limitations of his Congressional authority, I think it was an act of wise leadership on the part of Mr. Roosevelt, taken to avoid future serious complications, and should be commended.

But in order to make this step effective I think eventually he will have to say more. The American President is the natural leader of the public opinion of his people in all matters of foreign relations, particularly in time of war. They look to him for their information and for their guidance. In this pending crisis not a word has yet been said by our government to indicate to our people the impelling moral reason why they should voluntarily make the sacrifices involved in this warning of the President. Not a word has been said to indicate that there is any moral difference between Italy, which has begun this war, and the other nations which are trying to stop it. Not a word has been uttered to point out that Italy has violated solemn covenants and treaties and that those other nations are endeavoring to uphold these treaties; not a word to recall to our people the promises which Italy made to us in the Pact of Paris in respect to renouncing war, promises which, according to the President's own proclamation of October 5, must have been violated.

In short, nothing has yet been said to rouse in our people any feeling that a moral issue is involved is the present crisis which should impel all patriotic men and women to follow the President's advice and to refrain from embarking on the tempting trade with Italy which the Congressional embargo has left open to them. They have not even been advised of the tremendous moral implications represented by the fact that over fifty nations of the world, with all their national differences and interests have been able to unite in a verdict against the nation which is now seeking our assistance to get supplies for an aggressive war. . . .

The public opinion of America is not indifferent to moral issues. The great masses of our countrymen do not wish to drift into a position of blocking the efforts of other nations to stamp out war. The only person who can effectively rouse and marshal moral opinion is the President of the United States, and when he tries to do so I have no doubt of his eventual success.

9.3:   America First versus Aid to Britain (1940, 1941)

America's sense of security plumetted dramatically in September 1939, when Hitler invaded Germany's neighbor, Poland. Within hours Britain and France, pledged to defend Poland, declared war on Germany.

Poland quickly collapsed under the awesome blows of the Nazi Wehr-macht, and then, in the spring and summer of 1940, the powerful German army attacked Denmark, Norway, Belgium, Holland, and France. In a few weeks of blitzkrieg, the Nazi war machine had smashed all the Western armies arrayed against it.

By the end of 1940 Britain alone of Hitler's enemies held out, protect-ed for the moment by its island position. But few believed Britain could stop the Nazi juggernaut. Meanwhile, in Nazi-occupied Europe a regime of unexampled savagery was being imposed on the helpless conquered people. At the same time, in the Far East militaristic Japan was taking advantage of the European colonial powers' preoccupation with Hitler to expand its empire in China and Southeast Asia.

The startling success of the aggressors, loosely organized as the Rome-Berlin-Tokyo Axis, dismayed most Americans. But public opinion split over how best to confront the international danger. Isolationists believed that the United States should continue to stay aloof from the Old World's wars while arming itself against any possible attack. In September 1940 they organized America First, headed by a prominent group of business-people, politicians, and civic leaders. The interventionists had their own organization, the Committee to Defend America by Aiding the Allies. Led by William Allen White, the Progressive Republican editor from Kansas, the committee sought to rally Americans to support the cause of faltering Britain and the surviving enemies of the Axis powers.

Many of the interventionists were, at heart, convinced that nothing short of full military involvement on Britain's side could protect America's vital interests. But the committee's public focus was on the repeal of the neutrality measures so that the United States could freely supply the anti-Axis forces with the guns, ships, tanks, and planes they needed to survive. The interventionists also sought, even more aggres-sively than their opponents, to build up America's own military power.

In the first selection below interventionist James B. Conant, president of Harvard University, expresses his views in a radio address in late May 1940. Conant's words were delivered just as Belgium surrendered to the Germans and as the defeated British forces in France gathered at the French port of Dunkirk for escape across the English Channel from the advancing Nazi army.

How does Conant seek to arouse American support for Britain? Is he trying to disguise the risk that the United States might be compelled to go to war? Are his arguments about the Nazis' designs on the United States correct? Was Hitler interested in conquering the United States? Could he have done so given the breadth of the Atlantic Ocean? Would a Nazi-dominated Europe have threatened the United States in any way?

The second selection is from a speech made by isolationist Senator Burton K. Wheeler of Montana in 1941. Like a number of other isola- tionists, Wheeler was a liberal from the American heartland who disliked Europe and its age-old quarrels. Here he is speaking in opposition to Roosevelt's recent proposal that Congress enact a measure allowing the president to lease vital arms and supplies to Britain for future repay- ment.

"Lend-lease," as this policy was known, was a late step in the disman- tling of the neutrality legislation of the 1930s. At the end of 1939 Congress had repealed the arms embargo provision of the Neutrality Acts and replaced it with "cash and carry." But that was before the fall of France and the Dunkirk evacuation. Now Britain was running out of cash to pay for vital American supplies, and loans seemed the only way to guarantee it could fight on. In mid-December 1940 the president pro- posed that the United States "lend" or "lease" military equipment to Hitler's only remaining enemy with payment for the portion not returned after use to be postponed until after the war.[1]

Wheeler attacks the president's proposal on several grounds. What are these? To what American emotions and views is Wheeler playing?

We Must Aid the Allies

JAMES B. CONANT

There is no need for me to dwell on the agonizing news of the last few days. Tonight the Germans stand on the shores of the English Channel and along the Somme. Tomorrow looms before us like a menacing question-mark. A total victory for German arms is now well within the range of possibility. . . .

Let me ask you to visualize our future as a democratic free people in a world dominated by ruthless totalitarian states. There are those who argue that Hitler's war machine, when its task is done in Europe, will be converted to an instrument of peaceful industrial activity. I do not think so. There are those who imagine that a government which has broken promise after promise, which has scorned the democratic countries and all they stand for, which mocks and laughs at free institutions as a basis for civilization,—that such a government can live in a peaceful relationship with the United States. I do not think so.

To my mind a complete Nazi victory over France and England would be, by necessity, but a prelude to Hitler's attempt to dominate the world. If

---

[1] The proposal was specious: the United States could not conceivably be interested in any used guns, tanks, and airplanes that might be returned after the war. Roosevelt was actually propos- ing nothing less than that the United States supply Britain with arms for free.

Congressional Record, 76th Cong., 3rd sess., Appendix, 3669–3670.

Germany were triumphant, as best there would result an armed truce. This country would be feverishly endeavoring to put itself into an impregnable position based on a highly militarized society. Our way of life would be endangered for years to come. If this be so, what should we do in these desperate, tragic hours?

We must rearm at once, that much is clear. The vision rises before us of the United States suddenly left alone and unprotected in a totalitarian and destructive world. It is obvious we are unprepared to meet an emergency of this nature. It is also obvious that our first aim must be to prepare with all rapidity. England's failure to listen to Winston Churchill, warning of approaching danger, is responsible for her plight. We must not make the same mistake. We are all agreed on that. . . .

My purpose tonight is to urge another course of action equally important. I am advocating immediate aid to the Allies. I shall mince no words. *I believe the United States should take every action possible to insure the defeat of Hitler.* And let us face honestly the possible implications of such a policy. The actions we propose might eventuate in war. But fear of war is no basis for a national policy. In a free state public opinion must guide the Government, and a wise public opinion on matters of foreign policy can result only if there is a continuous, clear-headed, realistic discussion of all eventualities, including war.

At this moment, the entry of the United States into the war certainly does not seem necessary or wise. . . .

What are then the actions that can be taken at once?

Let us state a few of them: first, the release to France and England of army and navy airplanes and other implements of war, without impairing our own security; second, repeal of the laws which prevent United States citizens from volunteering to serve in foreign armies; third, control of exports with the purpose of aiding the Allies by avoiding leaks to Germany and giving priority to France and England; four, the cooperation of our Maritime Commission with the Allies in every way possible under our present laws to expedite the sending of supplies and munitions. These steps, if promptly taken by our Government, would render effective aid which some experts believe might tip the scales in favor of an Allied victory. Furthermore, they would be of infinite value in strengthening the morale of the Allied nations and would serve notice to the world that our resources were now enlisted in the democratic cause.

I have purposely avoided the use of the words "moral issues." The younger generation in particular is highly suspicious of this phrase. Their feeling is chiefly due to a widespread misinterpretation of the reasons for America's participation in the war in 1914–1918. I have avoided this issue, not because I sympathize with those who proclaim that there is no fundamental difference between the actions and aims of the democracies on the one hand and the totalitarian powers on the other. Far from it. There is to my mind all the difference between piracy and peaceful trade, all the difference between ruthless tyranny and enlightened intercourse among free men.

But I am endeavoring to confine my argument this evening to a realistic appraisal of our foreign policy. Let me make this clear. I advocate no moral crusade to distant lands. If crusading were a proper policy, we should have had more than one provocation for war in the last dozen years. I am arguing that the changed military situation in Europe actually threatens our way of life.

At this moment, today, the war is in effect veering towards our shores. The issue before the United States is, I repeat, can we live as a free, peaceful, relatively unarmed people in a world dominated by the totalitarian states? Specifically, can we look with indifference as a nation (as a nation, mind you, not as individuals) on the possible subjugation of England by a Nazi State? If your answer is yes, then my words are in vain. If your answer is no, I urge you as a citizen to act.

Write or telegraph to the President of the United States, to your Congressman and your Senators, stating your belief that this nation must give immediate, effective aid to the Allies. Let your elected agents of Government have your thoughts. Urge that Congress stay in session to consider emergency legislation as may be necessary, and speed the process of rearmament.

Above all else, let us consider the situation boldly. This is no time for defeatism or despair. The Allies may be expected to hold out if they have help from us and the promise of further help to come. The wrath of moral indignation is impotent in days like these. A struggle to the death is once again in progress on the fields of western Europe. The British Isles are making ready to stand a siege. . . . It is not too late but it is long past time to act. I urge you, let your voice be heard!

Lend-Lease Will Lead to War

BURTON K. WHEELER

The lend-lease policy, translated into legislative form, stunned a Congress and a nation wholly sympathetic to the cause of Great Britain. The Kaiser's blank check to Austria-Hungary in the first World War[1] was a piker compared to the Roosevelt blank check of World War II. It warranted my worst fears for the future of America, and it definitely stamps the President as warminded.

The lend-lease-give program is the New Deal's triple A foreign policy; it will plow under every fourth American boy.[2]

Never before have the American people been asked or compelled to give so bounteously and so completely of their tax dollars to any foreign nation. Never before has the Congress of the United States been asked by any

---

Congressional Record, 77th Cong., 1st sess., Appendix, 178–179.

[1] Supposedly the German kaiser had promised to aid Austria-Hungary if war ensued from its 1914 ultimatum to Serbia—ED.

[2] A reference to the policy set by the Agricultural Adjustment Administration (AAA) in 1933 of destroying crops to raise farm prices—ED.

President to violate international law. Never before has this Nation resorted to duplicity in the conduct of its foreign affairs. Never before has the United States given to one man the power to strip this Nation of its defenses. Never before has a Congress coldly and flatly been asked to abdicate.

If the American people want a dictatorship—if they want a totalitarian form of government and if they want war—this bill should be steam-rollered through Congress, as is the wont of President Roosevelt.

Approval of this legislation means war, open and complete warfare. I, therefore, ask the American people before they supinely accept it, Was the last World War worth while?

If it were, then we should lend and lease war materials. If it were, then we should lend and lease American boys. President Roosevelt has said we would be repaid by England. We will be. We will be repaid, just as England repaid her war debts of the first World War—repaid those dollars wrung from the sweat of labor and the toil of farmers with cries of "Uncle Shylock." Our boys will be returned—returned in caskets, maybe; returned with bodies maimed; returned with minds warped and twisted by sights of horrors and the scream and shriek of high-powered shells.

Considered on its merits and stripped of its emotional appeal to our sympathies, the lend-lease-give bill is both ruinous and ridiculous. Why should we Americans pay for war materials for Great Britain who still has $7,000,000,000 in credit or collateral in the United States? Thus far England has fully maintained rather than depleted her credits in the United States. The cost of the lend-lease-give program is high in terms of American tax dollars, but it is even higher in terms of our national defense. Now it gives to the President the unlimited power to completely strip our air forces of its every bomber, of its every fighting plane.

It gives to one man—responsible to no one—the power to denude our shores of every warship. It gives to one individual the dictatorial power to strip the American Army of our every tank, cannon, rifle, or antiaircraft gun. No one would deny that the lend-lease-give bill contains provisions that would enable one man to render the United States defenseless, but they will tell you, "The President would never do it." To this I say, "Why does he ask the power if he does not intend to use it?" Why not, I say, place some check on American donations to a foreign nation?

Is it possible that the farmers of America are willing to sell their birthright for a mess of pottage?

Is it possible that American labor is to be sold down the river in return for a place upon the Defense Commission, or because your labor leaders are entertained at pink teas?

Is it possible that the American people are so gullible that they will permit their representatives in Congress to sit supinely by while an American President demands totalitarian powers—in the name of saving democracy?

I say in the kind of language used by the President—shame on those who ask the powers—and shame on those who would grant them.

You people who oppose war and dictatorship, do not be dismayed because the war-mongers and interventionists control most of the avenues of propaganda, including the motion-picture industry.

Do not be dismayed because Mr. Willkie,[3] of the Commonwealth & Southern, agrees with Mr. Roosevelt. This merely puts all the economic and foreign "royalists" on the side of war.

Remember, the interventionists control the money bags, but you control the votes.

9.4:   Undeclared War (1941)

By mid-1941 Roosevelt was convinced that the United States could not avoid intervening militarily to stop the Axis powers. By defeating the German attempt to destroy the Royal Air Force, Britain had thwarted a cross-Channel Nazi invasion from occupied France, but it was losing the battle of supply against Axis U-boats on the Atlantic and was incapable of striking back effectively against the Germans on the continent. Meanwhile, by this time Japan was reeling in much of Southeast Asia like a large fish. Then, in June, Hitler attacked the Soviet Union, and in a few weeks Nazi columns had plunged deep into the Russian heartland, in the process destroying much of the Soviet army and air force.

In the fall of 1941, with the submarine menace growing more serious by the day, Roosevelt ordered the American navy to help escort lend-lease supplies to Britain and the Soviet Union. American navy ships and Nazi submarines were soon exchanging fire on the North Atlantic.

In the selection below from a speech of late October 1941, FDR reveals a new tone. Some historians believe that he was preparing the American public for an actual shooting war on the Atlantic as a back door to full American military participation in the anti-Axis struggle. Does Roosevelt seem to be setting things up for war? (It has been said that he also goaded the Japanese into attacking Pearl Harbor by freezing their financial assets in the United States and embargoing scrap iron and petroleum, both vital to Japan.) How convincing are Roosevelt's remarks about a secret map showing Nazi plans for conquest in the Western Hemisphere and his statement about Hitler's scheme to abolish all religion? Are they demagogic claims, playing on the ill-informed fears of the American people? Given the gravity of the Nazi menace, can the President be forgiven some exaggeration? Did the ends justify the means in this instance?

---

[3] Wendell Willkie, the Republican presidential nominee in 1940. He had been president of the Commonwealth and Southern Utility Company—ED.

The German Menace

FRANKLIN DELANO ROOSEVELT

Five months ago tonight I proclaimed to the American people the existence of a state of unlimited emergency. Since then much has happened. Our Army and Navy are temporarily in Iceland in the defense of the Western Hemisphere.

Hitler has attacked shipping in areas close to the Americas in the North and South Atlantic.

Many American-owned ships have been sunk on the high seas. One American destroyer was attacked on September 4. Another destroyer was attacked and hit on October 17. Eleven brave and loyal men of our Navy were killed by the Nazis.

We have wished to avoid shooting. But the shooting has started. And history has recorded who fired the first shot. In the long run, however, all that will matter is who fired the last shot.

America has been attacked. . . .

The purpose of Hitler's attacks was to frighten, frighten the American people off the high seas—to force us to make a trembling retreat. This is not the first time that he has misjudged the American spirit. And today that spirit is . . . aroused.

If our national policy were to be dominated by the fear of shooting, then all of our ships and those of our sister republics would have to be tied up in home harbors. Our Navy would have to remain respectfully, abjectly, behind any line which Hitler might decree on any ocean as his own dictated version of his own war zone.

Naturally we reject that absurd and insulting suggestion. We reject it because of our own self-interest, because of our own self-respect and because, most of all, of our own good faith. Freedom of the seas is now, as it always has been, the fundamental policy of your government and mine.

Hitler has often protested that his plans for conquest do not extend across the Atlantic Ocean. But his submarines and raiders prove otherwise. And so does the entire design of his new world order.

For example, I have in my possession a secret map made in Germany by Hitler's government, by the planners of the new world order. It is a map of South America and a part of Central America, as Hitler proposes to reorganize it. Today in this area there are fourteen separate countries. But the geographical experts of Berlin have ruthlessly obliterated all existing boundary lines. They have divided South America into five vassal States, bringing the whole continent under their domination. And they have also so arranged it that the territory of one of these new puppet States includes the Republic of Panama and our great life line, the Panama Canal.

New York Times, October 28, 1941.

That is his plan. It will never go into effect.

And that map, my friends, makes clear the Nazi design, not only against South America but against the United States as well.

And your government has in its possession another document, a document made in Germany by Hitler's government. It is a detailed plan, which, for obvious reasons, the Nazis do not wish to publicize just yet, but which they are ready to impose a little later on a dominated world, if Hitler wins.

It is a plan to abolish all existing religions, Catholic, Protestant, Mohammedan, Hindu, Buddhist and Jewish alike. The property of all churches will be seized by the Reich and its puppets. The cross and all other symbols of religion are to be forbidden. The clergy are to be ever liquidated, silenced under penalty of the concentration camps, where even now so many fearless men are being tortured because they have placed God above Hitler.

In the place of the churches of our civilization there is to be set up an international Nazi church, a church which will be served by orators sent out by the Nazi government. And in the place of the Bible, the words of "Mein Kampf"[1] will be imposed and enforced as Holy Writ. And in the place of the cross of Christ will be put two symbols, the swastika and the naked sword.

A god, the god of blood and iron, will take the place of the God of love and mercy. Let us well ponder that statement which I have made tonight.

These grim truths which I have told you of the present and future plans of Hitlerism will of course be hotly denied tonight and tomorrow in the controlled press and radio of the Axis powers. And some Americans, not many, will continue to insist that Hitler's plans need not worry us—that we should not concern ourselves with anything that goes on beyond rifle shot of our own shores.

The protestations of these few American citizens will, as usual, be paraded with applause through the Axis press and radio during the next few days in an effort to convince the world that the majority of Americans are opposed to their duly chosen government, and in reality are only waiting to jump on Hitler's band wagon when it comes this way.

The motive of such Americans is not the point at issue. The fact is that Nazi propaganda continues in desperation to seize upon such isolated statements as proof of American disunity.

The Nazis have made up their own list of modern American heroes. It is, fortunately, a short list and I am glad that it does not contain my name.

And so all of us Americans, of all opinions, in the last analysis are faced with the choice between the kind of world we want to live in and the kind of world which Hitler and his hordes would impose upon us.

None of us wants to burrow under the ground and live in total darkness like a comfortable mole.

The forward march of Hitler and of Hitlerism can be stopped, and it will be stopped.

---

[1] *Mein Kampf* was the title of Hitler's memoirs, an account of his life and ideology and a blueprint for his future career as Germany's ruler—ED.

Very simply and very bluntly—we are pledged to pull our own oar in the destruction of Hitlerism.

And when we have helped to end the curse of Hitlerism, we shall help to establish a new peace which will give to decent people everywhere a better chance to live and prosper in security and in freedom and in faith.

Every day that passes we are producing and providing more and more arms for the men who are fighting on actual battlefronts. That is our primary task.

And it is the nation's will that these vital arms and supplies of all kinds shall neither be locked up in American harbors nor sent to the bottom of the sea. It is the nation's will that America shall deliver the goods. In open defiance of that will, our ships have been sunk and our sailors have been killed.

And I say that we do not propose to take this lying down.

That determination of ours not to take it lying down has been expressed in the orders to the American Navy to shoot on sight. And those orders stand.

Furthermore, the House of Representatives has already voted to amend a part of the Neutrality Act of 1937, today outmoded by force of violent circumstances. And the Senate Committee on Foreign Relations has also recommended the elimination of other hamstringing provisions in that act. That is the course of honesty and of realism.

Our American merchant ships must be armed to defend themselves against the rattlesnakes of the sea.

Our American merchant ships must be free to carry our American goods into the harbors of our friends.

And our American merchant ships must be protected by our American Navy.

In the light of a good many years of personal experience I think that it can be said that it can never be doubted that the goods will be delivered by this nation, whose Navy believes in the tradition of "damn the torpedoes; full steam ahead!"

Yes, our nation will and must speak from every assembly line—yes, from every coal mine, the all-inclusive whole of our vast industrial machine. Our factories and our shipyards are constantly expanding. Our output must be multiplied. . . .

The lines of our essential defense now cover all the seas; and to meet the extraordinary demands of today and tomorrow our Navy grows to unprecedented size. Our Navy is ready for action. . . . Its officers and men need no praise from me.

Our new Army is steadily developing the strength needed to withstand the aggressors. Our soldiers of today are worthy of the proudest traditions of the United States Army. But tradition cannot shoot down dive-bombers or destroy tanks. That is why we must and shall provide for every one of our soldiers equipment and weapons, not merely as good but better than that of any other army on earth. And we are doing that right now.

For this, and all of this, is what we mean by total national defense.

The first objective of that defense is to stop Hitler. He can be stopped and can be compelled to dig in. And that will be the beginning of the end of his downfall, because dictatorship of the Hitler type can live only through continuing victories and increasing conquests.

The facts of 1918 are proof that a mighty German Army and a tired German people can crumble rapidly and go to pieces when they are faced with successful resistance.

Nobody who admires qualities of courage and endurance can fail to be stirred by the full-fledged resistance of the Russian people. The Russians are fighting for their own soil and their own homes. Russia needs all kinds of help—planes and tanks, guns and medical supplies and other aids—toward the successful defense against the invaders. From the United States and from Britain she is getting great quantities of these essential supplies. But the needs of her huge army will continue, and our help and British help will also continue.

The other day the Secretary of State of the United States was asked by a Senator to justify our giving aid to Russia. His reply was:

"The answer to that, Senator, depends on how anxious a person is to stop, to destroy the march of Hitler in his conquest of the world. If he were anxious enough to defeat Hitler, he would not worry about who was helping to defeat him."

Upon our American production falls the colossal task of equipping our own armed forces, and helping to supply the British and the Russians and the Chinese. In the performance of that task we dare not fail. And we will not fail.

10

The Fifties

The decade and a half following World War II was a period of mending and a time for Americans to get back to normal life. It was also an era of prosperity. Spurred by pent-up consumer demand and government programs to ease veterans' return to civilian life, the economy boomed. The new affluence produced a wave of optimism and self-congratulation that was startling for anyone who remembered the anxious, insecure, and painful days of the Depression and World War II.

The chief beneficiaries of the boom were the American middle-class and skilled workers. With steadily rising incomes they achieved the security that had escaped them since the 1920s. As if to make up for lost time they went on a buying spree, snapping up new cars, appliances, and, after 1950, television sets, by the millions.

No aspect of the postwar material culture was as consequential as the housing boom, however. After a period of difficult reconversion the construction industry churned out thousands of new homes, primarily for young families and predominantly in the suburbs. Suburban living ushered in a new way of life for millions of Americans marked by large families, house pride, and enhanced domesticity.

In reality the fifties were far from perfect. Minorities felt excluded from the postwar economic surge. Blacks continued to face legal inequality, job discrimination, and limited educational opportunity. To intellectuals the era seemed unpleasantly self-congratulatory, materialistic, conformist, and timid. And then there was the fear and intellectual intolerance triggered by the Cold War confrontation of the United States and the Soviet Union. Indeed, during the fifties all Americans felt oppressed in some degree by that superpower rivalry, since it threatened nuclear confrontation and possible world obliteration.

In the selections below you will encounter diverse views of three issues that stirred controversy during the fifties: the extent and significance of the new prosperity, the virtues of the new suburban life style, and the validity of the anti-Communist panic.

10.1:   The Effects of Affluence (1959, 1957)

The economic surge of the 1950s narrowed the income gap between the middle class and the working class. In 1960 the United States would be a less unequal society than in 1930.

Significant cultural consequences seemed to flow from the equalizing force of postwar economic growth. Prosperity had seeped down to blue-collar wage earners and, said some observers, inoculated them with middle-class values and styles. But not all agreed on the narrowing of class differences. Industrial workers, some critics insisted, had not ceased to have hard lives. Privilege and exploitation were alive and well in post–World War II America, and working people did not all buy the middle-class vision.

The first reading below is from a 1959 article by Daniel Seligman for Fortune *magazine, a monthly publication devoted to business and economic affairs. Seligman's focus is on the tastes and buying habits of suburban blue-collar residents, but he also describes how fifties prosperity had changed social structure in America. He writes, for example, about class convergence as a result of relative affluence. Was there less inequality in the fifties than in other recent eras? Seligman also describes the loss of ethnic individuality during the fifties. Did this take place? Why might it have taken place? Might Seligman's overall views regarding fifties change have been influenced by the business orientation of a publication like* Fortune*?*

The second selection is by Harvey Swados, a novelist and journalist with socialist views. In what ways, according to Swados, were industrial workers still disadvantaged in the 1950s? Does he completely reject the notion that the postwar period was a prosperous one? Why might a socialist discount views such as Seligman's? Who was right, Seligman or Swados, about the survival of a working-class ethos into the 1950s—and beyond?

The New Masses

DANIEL SELIGMAN

Only ten years ago, the following description of an American family's style of life would have enabled one to form some fairly firm impressions about the father's occupation and the general social "rank" of the family:

> *The parents, who are about forty, live with their two boys in a comfortable six-room suburban house outfitted with a full line of appliances, a television set that is in more or*

Daniel Seligman, "The New Masses," *Fortune*, May 1959, pp. 106–11, 257–58. © 1959 Time Inc. All rights reserved.

less constant use, and a car in which the father drives to work. The car is also used for camping trips during the summer. The mother shops at a local supermarket and at several local department stores; the boys attend the good local public schools; and on weekends the family often goes swimming at a local beach, although recently the father and mother and their older son have begun to take an interest in golf.

Given these facts in 1949, one might have inferred quite reasonably, that the head of the house was a lower or middle-echelon executive, or salesman, or the proprietor or part owner of some small business, or a professional man, and that the family's position in society was solidly middle class.

Given these facts in 1959, one could deduce practically nothing about the family's social rank or the father's occupation. For the fact is that in the past few years the broad style of life described above has become available, not only to an identifiable "middle class," but to a great mass of Americans, perhaps even a majority. The family head today might be a truck driver earning $5,500, a college professor earning $7,000, a life-insurance salesman earning $8,000, a skilled production worker earning $9,000, an airline pilot earning $15,000, or an executive earning $18,000. In the new American society, it is increasingly difficult to tell the players apart without subpoenaing their tax returns. . . .

Many otherwise alert Americans continue to think and talk of their countrymen as though all of them could be sorted out into three clear-cut classes. The biggest of these, of course, would be low-income *working class,* or simply *workers* ("lower class" has never come easily to American lips), symbolized most aptly by the "blue collars" in manufacturing but also including farmers. Then there would be the middle-income *middle class,* whose prototype is the small proprietor, or the professional or white collar employee. And at the top there would be a small layer of important businessmen, prominent professionals, government officials, etc. Europeans would forthrightly call this the American *upper class;* Americans are more likely to speak of *rich people, society people, big shots,* etc., and of course nobody is more reluctant to say "upper class" than a qualified member.

These traditional class concepts still have a shorthand utility in connoting various styles of life, but when they are used to denote a neatly layered social pyramid they are today simply a source of confusion. For one thing, the shape is all wrong: by income standards, at least, what we have in the U.S. today more nearly resembles a diamond than a pyramid—i.e., there are more people in the middle than there are at the top or bottom. . . .

The most conspicuous breakdown of class lines is the one that has taken place just in the past five years as the ex-"proletarians" who are now at the heart of the middle-income class began finally to adopt a middle-class style of life. This phenomenon, portentous in its implications for the markets of the 1960's, is hard to express statistically, but there can no longer be any doubt about the broad facts of the case. Nelson Foote, a distinguished sociologist who recently left academic life to work for General Electric, says that he has observed the change even in Detroit, a city where class consciousness dies hard. "During the war [World War II]," Foote says, "you could sit in a street-car and tell at a glance who were the defense workers and who were the white collars. Then, while the war was still on, the companies did something which has had a profound effect on our society: they installed cafeterias and lockers in the plants. After a while you stopped seeing lunch boxes and work clothes on the street-cars and today you just can't tell who's who. The city is full of auto workers whose wives shop at Hudson's[1]—who wouldn't be caught dead buying a pair of shoes at Sears." . . .

How many blue-collar families have arrived in the suburbs? Even if no sociologists had observed the phenomenon, it can be inferred from available government data that a sizable number of blue collars *have to be* in suburban, or in semi-suburban, areas. Families headed by blue collars comprise about 60 per cent of nonfarm families today. It is manifest that they cannot all be in the metropolitan areas' inner cities (which have about 25 per cent of the nonfarm population) and in the smaller cities and towns (which have about 30 per cent). . . .

The young white collar usually regards his first suburban home as a temporary lodgement on the way to a better one. The blue collar sees it as security for his old age, and for this reason, perhaps, is much more concerned with getting a durable physical property than the white collar is.

But the significant fact is that, while these differences persist, the living habits of the blue and white collars have been converging in many respects; indeed, one might regard the suburbs today as the new American melting pot. A community leader in Royal Oak, a Detroit suburb, notes that the auto workers who followed the plants out of town were "swallowed up" when they lived in Detroit. "When they came out here, they seemed hungry for community affairs." Indeed, the fact that they regard their first suburban homes as permanent living places often gives the blue collars a stake in local government that the more transient white collars do not feel they have. . . .

The increased bunching of Americans around the middle-income levels, the increased blurring of occupational distinctions, and the increased adoption of middle-class living styles by families of diverse occupational background, have all tended to make the U.S. a much more homogeneous society. At this point it may be interesting to observe that we have been "homogenized" in several other respects as well:

- National backgrounds have less meaning than they used to. About 95 per cent of all Americans today are native-born (vs. 87 per cent in 1920), and about 80 per cent of them are at least "third generation" Americans (vs. 65 per cent in 1920)— i.e., both their parents were also native-born. With immigration averaging only about 250,000 a year, about 85 per cent of the U.S. population will be at least third generation by 1970. And though the point cannot be verified statistically, it is nonetheless clear that Americans are less prone than they once were to think of

[1] The major Detroit department store, which closed in the 1980s—ED.

other Americans as "Swedes," or "Irishmen," or "Italians"—in part because the old-country ways and languages are largely unknown to the third and fourth generations, and in part because these generations so often have hopelessly *mixed* national backgrounds.

- Religious differences are also less meaningful. A number of theologians have remarked, with some bitterness, that while Americans are more interested than they used to be in having a religion, they are much less interested in the *content* of religion, or in religious differences. Americans are increasingly being admonished, on television, for example, to "attend your place of worship this weekend"—and the inference is plain that it doesn't matter which one you attend. . . . Where religion once divided Americans on strongly felt sectarian lines, the new good fellowship and good works tend to emphasize non-sectarian activities (e.g., running nursery schools open to children of all religious backgrounds).

- Political differences are also becoming blurred. American political debate is increasingly conducted in a bland, even-tempered atmosphere, and extremists of every kind are becoming rarer. The political expression of the new society, in which more and more families are bunched around the middle-income levels, and adapting to middle-class ways, is a Congress in which more and more politicians are bunched around the middle road, in which both parties are increasingly dominated by "reasonable" liberals who were called in a recent article in *Commentary* by Karl E. Meyer, the "Smooth Dealers." . . .

The net of these "homogenizing" trends is that we all seem to be alike—or, at least, a great many of us live and think and dress more nearly alike than we used to. Many Americans appear to be disturbed by this trend, and to detect in it a threat to their own sense of individuality; they are endlessly complaining about all the "conformity" and "togetherness" in American life.

But the complaints seem to miss a crucial point about the new society—a point that most marketing men have *not* missed. The point is that while our society is more homogeneous, the individual's own opportunities to live in diverse fashions have been expanded considerably. The man in the Ivy League suit may be a millionaire or a skilled machinist, and so may the man at the wheel of the sports car and the man at the beach in Miami. To the spectator this may look like the new uniformity; to the machinist, it involves a new diversity—a diversity that, it may safely be presumed, he is enjoying immensely.

The Myth of the Happy Worker

HARVEY SWADOS

"From where we sit in the company," says one of the best personnel men in the country, "we have to look at only the aspects of work that cut across all sorts of jobs—administration and human relations. Now these are aspects of work, abstractions, but it's easy for personnel people to get so hipped on their importance that they look on the specific tasks of making things and selling them as secondary . . ."

The Organization Man by William H. Whyte Jr.

Harvey Swados, "The Myth of the Happy Worker," *Nation*, August 17, 1957, pp. 65–68. This article is reprinted from *The Nation* Magazine. © The Nation Company, Inc.

The personnel man who made this remark to Mr. Whyte differed from his brothers only in that he had a moment of insight. Actually, "the specific tasks of making things" are now not only regarded by his white-collar fellows as "secondary," but as irrelevant to the vaguer but more "challenging" tasks of the man at the desk. This is true not just of the personnel man, who places workers, replaces them, displaces them—in brief, manipulates them. The union leader also, who represents workers and sometimes manipulates them, seems increasingly to regard what his workers do as merely subsidiary to the job he himself is doing in the larger community. This job may be building the Red Cross or the Community Chest, or it may sometimes be—as the Senate hearings suggest—participating in such communal endeavors as gambling, prostitution, and improving the breed. In any case, the impression is left that the problems of the workers in the background (or underground) have been stabilized, if not permanently solved.

With the personnel man and the union leader, both of whom presumably see the worker from day to day, growing so far away from him, it is hardly to be wondered at that the middle class in general, and articulate middle-class intellectuals in particular, see the worker vaguely, as through a cloud. One gets the impression that when they do consider him, they operate from one of two unspoken assumptions: (1) The worker has died out like the passenger pigeon, or is dying out, or becoming acculturated, like the Navajo; (2) If he is still around, he is just like the rest of us—fat, satisfied, smug, a little restless, but hardly distinguishable from his fellow TV viewers of the middle class.

Lest it be thought that (1) is somewhat exaggerated, I hasten to quote from a recently published article apparently dedicated to the laudable task of urging slothful middle-class intellectuals to wake up and live: "The old-style sweat-shop crippled mainly the working people. Now there are no workers left in America; we are almost all middle class as to income and expectations." I do not believe the writer meant to state—although he comes perilously close to it—that nobody works any more. If I understand him correctly, he is referring to the fact that the worker's rise in real income over the last decade, plus the diffusion of middle-class tastes and values throughout a large part of the underlying population, have made it increasingly difficult to tell blue-collar from white-collar worker without a program. In short, if the worker earns like the middle class, votes like the middle class, dresses like the middle class, dreams like the middle class, then he ceases to exist as a worker.

But there is one thing that the worker doesn't do like the middle class: he works like a worker. The steel mill puddler does not yet sort memos, the coal miner does not yet sit in conferences, the cotton mill hand does not yet sip martinis from his lunchbox. The worker's attitude toward his work is generally compounded of hatred, shame, and resignation.

Before I spell out what I think this means, I should like first to examine some of the implications of the widely held belief that "we are almost all middle class as to income and expectations." I am neither economist, sociologist, nor politician, and I hold in my hand no doctored statistics to be haggled over. I am by profession a writer who has had occasion to work in factories at various times during the Thirties, Forties, and Fifties. The following observations are simply impressions based on my last period of factory servitude, in 1956.

The average automobile worker gets a little better than two dollars an hour. As such he is one of the best-paid factory workers in the country. After twenty years of militant struggle led by the union that I believe to be still the finest and most democratic labor organization in the United States, he is earning less than the starting salaries offered to inexperienced and often semiliterate college graduates without dependents. After compulsory deductions for taxes, social security, old-age insurance and union dues, and optional deductions for hospitalization and assorted charities, his pay check for forty hours of work is going to be closer to seventy than to eighty dollars a week. Does this make him middle class as to income? Does it rate with the weekly take of a dentist, an accountant, a salesman, a draftsman, a journalist? Surely it would be more to the point to ask how a family man can get by in the Fifties on that kind of income. I know how he does it, and I should think the answers would be a little disconcerting to those who wax glib on the satisfactory status of the "formerly" underprivileged.

For one thing, he works a lot longer than forty hours a week—when he can. Since no automobile company is as yet in a position to guarantee its workers anything like fifty weeks of steady forty-hour paychecks, the auto worker knows he has to make it while he can. During peak production periods he therefore puts in nine, ten, eleven and often twelve hours a day on the assembly line for weeks on end. And that's not all. If he has dependents, as like as not, he also holds down a "spare time" job. I have worked on the line with men who doubled as mechanics, repairmen, salesmen, contractors, builders, farmers, cab drivers, lumberyard workers, countermen. I would guess that there are many more of these than show up in the official statistics: often a man will work for less if he can be paid under the counter with tax-free dollars.

Nor is that all. The factory worker with dependents cannot carry the debt load he now shoulders—the middle-class debt load, if you like, of nagging payments on car, washer, dryer, TV, clothing, house itself—without family help. Even if he puts in fifty, sixty or seventy hours a week at one or two jobs, he has to count on his wife's paycheck, or his son's, his daughter's, his brother-in-law's; or on his mother's social security, or his father's veteran's pension. The working-class family today is not typically held together by the male wage earner, but by multiple wage earners often of several generations who club together to get the things they want and need—or are pressured into believing they must have. It is at best a precarious arrangement; as for its toll on the physical organism and the psyche, that is a question perhaps worthy of further investigation by those who currently pronounce themselves bored with Utopia Unlimited in the Fat Fifties.

But what of the worker's middle-class expectations? I had been under the impression that this was the rock on which Socialist agitation had foundered for generations: it proved useless to tell the proletarian that he had a world to win when he was reasonably certain that with a few breaks he could have his own gas station. If these expectations have changed at all in recent years, they would seem to have narrowed rather than expanded, leaving a psychological increment of resignation rather than of unbounded optimism (except among the very young—and even among them the optimism focuses more often on better-paying opportunities elsewhere in the labor market than on illusory hopes of swift status advancement). The worker's expectations are for better pay, more humane working conditions, more job security. As long as he feels that he is going to achieve them through an extension of existing conditions, for that long he is going to continue to be a middle-class conservative in temper. But only for that long.

I suspect that what middle-class writers mean by the worker's middle-class expectations are his cravings for commodities—his determination to have not only fin-tailed cars and single-unit washer-dryers, but butterfly chairs in the rumpus room, African masks on the wall and power boats in the garage. Before the middle-class intellectuals condemn these expectations too harshly, let them consider, first, who has been utilizing every known technique of suasion and propaganda to convert luxuries into necessities, and second, at what cost these new necessities are acquired by the American working-class family.

Now I should like to return to the second image of the American worker: satisfied, doped by TV, essentially middle-class in outlook. This is an image bred not of communication with workers (except as mediated by fired interviewers sent "into the field" like anthropologists or entomologists), but of contempt for people, based perhaps on self-contempt and on a feeling among intellectuals that the worker has let them down. In order to see this clearly, we have to place it against the intellectual's changing attitudes toward the worker since the Thirties.

At the time of the organization of the C.I.O. [Congress of Industrial Organizations], the middle-class intellectual saw the proletarian as society's figure of virtue—heroic, magnanimous, bearing in his loins the seeds of a better future; he would have found ludicrous the suggestion that a sit-down striker might harbor anti-Semitic feelings. After Pearl Harbor, the glamorization of the worker was taken over as a function of government. Then, however, he was no longer the builder of the future good society; instead he was second only to the fighting man as the vital winner of the war. Many intellectuals, as government employees, found themselves helping to create this new portrait of the worker as patriot.

But in the decade following the war intellectuals have discovered that workers are no longer either building socialism or forging the tools of victory. All they are doing is making the things that other people buy. That, and participating in the great commodity scramble. The disillusionment, it would seem, is almost too terrible to bear. Word has gotten around among the highbrows that the worker is not heroic or idealistic; public opinion polls prove that he wants barbecue pits more than foreign aid and air conditioning more than desegregation, that he doesn't particularly want to go on strike, that he is reluctant to form a Labor Party, that he votes for Stevenson and often even for Eisenhower and Nixon—that he is, in short, animated by the same aspirations as drive the middle class onward and upward in suburbia.

There is of course a certain admixture of self-delusion in the middle-class attitude that workers are now the same as everybody else. For me it was expressed most precisely last year in the dismay and sympathy with which middle-class friends greeted the news that I had gone back to work in a factory. If workers are now full-fledged members of the middle class, why the dismay? What difference whether one sits in an office or stands in a shop? The answer is so obvious that one feels shame at laboring the point. But I have news for my friends among the intellectuals. The answer is obvious to workers, too.

They know that there is a difference between working with your back and working with your behind (I do not make the distinction between handwork and brainwork, since we are all learning that white-collar work is becoming less and less brainwork). They know that they work harder than the middle class for less money. Nor is it simply a question of status, that magic word so dear to the hearts of the sociologues, the new anatomizers of the American corpus. It is not simply status hunger that makes a man hate work which pays *less* than other work he knows about, if *more* than any other work he has been trained for (the only reason my fellow workers stayed in the assembly line, they told me again and again). It is not simply status hunger that makes a man hate work that is mindless, endless, stupefying, sweaty, filthy, noisy, exhausting, insecure in its prospects and practically without hope of advancement.

The plain truth is that factory work is degrading. It is degrading to any man who ever dreams of doing something worthwhile with his life; and it is about time we faced the fact. The more a man is exposed to middle-class values, the more sophisticated he becomes and the more production-line work is degrading to him. The immigrant who slaved in the poorly lighted, foul, vermin-ridden sweatshop found his work less degrading than the native-born high school graduate who reads Judge Parker, Rex Morgan, M.D., and Judd Saxon, Business Executive, in the funnies, and works in a fluorescent factory with ticker-tape production-control machines. For the immigrant laborer, even the one who did not dream of socialism, his long hours were going to buy him freedom. For the factory worker of the Fifties, his long hours are going to buy him commodities . . . and maybe reduce a few of his debts.

Almost without exception, the men with whom I worked on the assembly line last year felt like trapped animals. Depending on their age and personal circumstances, they were either resigned to their fate, furiously angry at *themselves* for what they were doing, or desperately hunting other work that would pay as well and in addition offer some variety, some prospect of change and betterment. They were sick of being pushed around by harried foremen (themselves more pitied than hated), sick of working like blinkered donkeys, sick of being dependent for their livelihood on a maniacal production-merchandising setup, sick of working in a place where there was no spot to relax during the twelve-minute rest period. (Some day—let us hope—we will marvel that production was still so worshipped in the Fifties that new factories could be built with every splendid facility for the storage and movement of essential parts, but with no place for a resting worker to sit down for a moment but on a fire plug, the edge of a packing case, or the sputum- and oil-stained stairway of a toilet.)

The older men stay put and wait for their vacations. But since the assembly line demands young blood (you will have a hard time getting hired if you are over thirty-five), the factory in which I worked was aswarm with new faces every day; labor turnover was so fantastic and absenteeism so rampant, with the young men knocking off a day or two every week to hunt up other jobs, that the company was forced to overhire in order to have sufficient workers on hand at the starting siren.

To those who will object—fortified by their readings in C. Wright Mills and A. C. Spectorsky—that the white-collar commuter, too, dislikes his work, accepts it only because it buys his family commodities, and is constantly on the prowl for other work, I can only reply that for me at any rate this is proof not of the disappearance of the working class but of the proletarianization of the middle class. Perhaps it is not taking place quite in the way that Marx envisaged it, but alienation of the white-collar man (like that of the laborer) from both his tools and whatever he produces, the slavery that chains the exurbanite to the commuting timetable (as the worker is still chained to the timeclock), the anxiety that sends the white-collar man home with his briefcase for an evening's work (as it degrades the workingman into pleading for long hours of overtime), the displacement of the white-collar slum from the wrong side of the tracks to the suburbs (just as the working-class slum is moved from old-law tenements to skyscraper barracks)—all these mean to me that the white-collar man is entering (though his arms may be loaded with commodities) the gray world of the working man.

Three quotations from men with whom I worked may help to bring my view into focus:

Before starting work: "Come on, suckers, they say the Foundation wants to give away *more* than half a billion this year. Let's do and die for the old Foundation."

During rest period: "Ever stop to think how we crawl here bumper to bumper, and crawl home bumper to bumper, and we've got to turn out more every minute to keep our jobs, when there isn't even any room for them on the highways?"

At quitting time (this from older foremen, whose job is not only to keep things moving, but by extension to serve as company spokesmen): "You're smart to get out of here. . . . I curse the day I ever started, now I'm stuck: any man with brains that stays here ought to have his head examined. This is no place for an intelligent human being."

Such is the attitude toward the work. And toward the product? On the one hand it is admired and desired as a symbol of freedom, almost a substitute for freedom, not because the worker participated in making it, but because our whole culture is dedicated to the proposition that the automobile is both necessary and beautiful. On the other hand it is hated and despised—so much that if your new car smells bad it may be due to a banana peel crammed down its gullet and sealed up thereafter, so much so that if your dealer can't locate the rattle in your new car you might ask him to open the welds on one of those tail fins and vacuum out the nuts and bolts thrown in by workers sabotaging their own product.

Sooner or later, if we want a decent society—by which I do not mean a society glutted with commodities or one maintained in precarious equilibrium by overbuying and forced premature obsolescence—we are going to have to come face to face with the problem of work. Apparently the Russians have committed themselves to the replenishment of their labor force through automatic recruitment of those intellectually incapable of keeping up with severe scholastic requirements in the public educational system. Apparently we, too, are heading in the same direction: although our economy is not directed, and although college education is as yet far from free, we seem to be operating in this capitalist economy on the totalitarian assumption that we can funnel the underprivileged, undereducated, or just plain underequipped, into the factory, where we can proceed to forget about them once we have posted the minimum fair labor standards on the factory wall.

If this is what we want, let's be honest enough to say so. If we conclude that there is nothing noble about repetitive work, but that it is nevertheless good enough for the lower orders, let's say that, too, so we will at least know where we stand. But if we cling to the belief that other men are our brothers, not just Egyptians, or Israelis, or Hungarians, but *all* men, including millions of Americans who grind their lives away on an insane treadmill, then we will have to start thinking about how their work and their lives can be made meaningful. That is what I assume the Hungarians, both workers and intellectuals, have been thinking about. Since no one has been ordering us what to think, since no one has been forbidding our intellectuals to fraternize with our workers, shouldn't it be a little easier for us to admit, first, that our problems exist, then to state them, and then to see if we can resolve them?

10.2:   Suburbia (1954, 1957)

Suburbia became a center of controversy during the fifties. Millions of Americans chose it as a place, and a way, to live. The detached private house, the automobile, domestic concerns, family and child rearing—all represented altered personal emphases for millions of young married couples.

Clearly a large number of Americans voted for suburbia "with their feet." Much of the suburban population were transplanted urbanities. And some of the nation's social observers approved heartily of their choice. In the first selection below, the editors of McCall's *magazine, a publication targeted at middle-class women, describe with undisguised delight one key aspect of the suburban surge—"togetherness." The second selection is by John Keats, a journalist and sociology popularizer, who expresses intense hostility toward suburbia.*

What special aspect of the suburban phenomenon was McCall's *referring to? What were the implications for women of the changes the magazine was highlighting and commending? Why might a magazine with a predominantly women's readership feature an article such as "A Man's Place Is in the Home"? Can you see any drawbacks to "togetherness"?*

What are Keats's objections to the suburban experience? How valid are his criticisms? What might have been the social or cultural sources of his opinions?

Live the Life of *McCall's*

Togetherness

If we'd made this suggestion in 1870, when *McCall's* was first published as the *Queen of Fashion* magazine, we would have been referring to a life of ease and elegance. For in the years before the turn of the century every woman aspired to be a lady and every lady envied Mrs. Astor. The world of women as reflected in their magazines was a rosy realm of fashion and folderol.

By 1902, when the *Queen of Fashion* broadened into *McCall's*, the ladies' magazines were mirroring the nature of life with Father. Those were the days when Papa ruled the roost, children were seen and not heard and women were delineated as mysterious and unpredictable creatures given to vagaries and vaporings.

Then came the battle of the sexes, followed by the First World War. You fought and won the fight for political equality. And *McCall's*, together with

"Live the Life of *McCall's*," and "A Man's Place Is in the Home," *McCall's*, May 1954, pp. 27, 28–35.

the other women's magazines, helped you to carve out large areas of living formerly forbidden to your sex.

Throughout the bright days of the Twenties and the twilight of the Thirties—the long years of the War, the bitter peace and the Korean conflict—in fact, right up to this moment, *McCall's* has been sensitive to [your] needs *as women first.*

In common with all other women's service magazines *McCall's* has been striving to widen your horizons, inspire you to lead lives of greater satisfaction, help you in your daily tasks. There's evidence that we're winning that victory.

Today women are not a sheltered sex. Men and women in ever increasing numbers are marrying at an earlier age, having children at an earlier age and rearing larger families. For the first time in our history the majority of men and women own their own homes and millions of these people gain their deepest satisfaction from making them their very own.

We travel more. We earn more, spend more, save more. We listen to finer music, read more and better books. We worship more. And in ever greater numbers we enjoy the advantages of higher education.

Thanks to our heritage of freedom, our national culture and our creative ingenuity, this wider range of living is an expression of the private conscience and the common hopes of the greatest number of people in this land of ours.

But the most impressive and the most heartening feature of this change is that men, women and children are achieving it *together.* They are creating this new and warmer way of life not as women *alone* or men *alone,* isolated from one another, but as a *family* sharing a common experience.

From this day forward *McCall's* will be edited to meet the needs and excite the interests of all who are or wish to be partners in this way of life—the life of *McCall's.* And through exploring, interpreting and reporting that life we shall do our very best to help you—*as a family*—to live it well.

Otis Wiese
Editor and Publisher

A Man's Place Is in the Home

Meet a Modern American Husband and Father . . .

Here's Ed Richtscheidt of Pine Lake, New Jersey, his wife Carol and their three children. They live in a gray shingle split-level house with three bedrooms, one bath and an unfinished basement room that will one day be a game room. On the north side of their lot, where they plan to build a barbecue, Ed has made a play yard for the children.

We're introducing Ed and his family because, like millions of other married couples today, they're living the life of *McCall's,* a more casual but a richer life than that of even the fairly recent past.

Ed's place in this new way of living is something he takes for granted. He doesn't stop to think about the changes that have taken place since he was a boy. Had Ed been a father twenty-five years ago he would have had little time to think to play and work along with his children. The running of the household would have been left entirely in the hands of his wife. Husbands and fathers were loved and respected then, but they weren't friends and companions to their families. Household chores were beneath them.

Today the chores as well as the companionship make Ed part of his family. He and Carol have centered their lives almost completely around their children and their home. Every inch of their house and yard is lived in and enjoyed. And it's a very happy place. . . .

Ed and His Family Live Together and Love It

Caring for three lively children—Ricky, 6, Chris, 4, and Susie, 2—makes tremendous demands on Carol Richtscheidt. But Ed is a cheerful working partner to her, helps with the children and housework whenever he can, gives everything he has to make his family happy. In return they give him all the love and affection a husband and father could hope for.

Ed likes to	*Ed doesn't like to*
putter around the house, make things, paint	dust or vacuum, or to finish jobs he's started
select furniture, rugs and draperies	repair furniture, fix electrical connections and plumbing, hang draperies
dry dishes	wash pots and pans and dishes
read to the children and put them to bed	pick up after the children
work in the garden	shovel snow or mow the lawn
feed and dress the children and bathe them	change diapers
pick up the baby-sitter	take the baby-sitter home
attend P.T.A. meetings	visit school
cook	do the laundry, iron
buy clothes for his wife	buy clothes for the children
buy groceries	go back for groceries Carol forgot to list

Down with Suburbia

JOHN KEATS

Welcome to the Inquest

For literally nothing down—other than a simple two per cent and a promise to pay, and pay, and pay until the end of your life—you too, like a man I'm going to call John Drone, can find a box of your own in one of the fresh-air slums we're building around the edges of America's cities. There's room for all in any price range, for even while you read this, whole square miles of identical boxes are spreading like gangrene throughout New England, across the Denver prairie, around Los Angeles, Chicago, Washington, New York, Miami—everywhere. In any one of these new neighborhoods, be it in Hartford or Philadelphia, you can be certain all other houses will be precisely like yours, inhabited by people whose age, income, number of children, problems, habits, conversation, dress, possessions and perhaps even blood type are also precisely like yours. In any one of these neighborhoods it is possible to make enemies of the folks next door with unbelievable speed. If you buy a small house, you are assured your children will leave you perhaps even sooner than they should, for at once they will learn never to associate home with pleasure. In short, ladies and gentlemen, we offer here for your inspection facts relative to today's housing developments—developments conceived in error, nurtured by greed, corroding everything they touch. They destroy established cities and trade patterns, pose dangerous problems for the areas they invade, and actually drive mad myriads of housewives shut up in them.

These facts are well known to responsible economists, sociologists, psychiatrists, city managers and bankers, and certainly must be suspected by the people who live in the suburban developments, yet there's no end in sight to the construction. Indeed, Washington's planners exult whenever a contractor vomits up five thousand new houses on a rural tract that might better have remained in hay, for they see in this little besides thousands of new sales of labor, goods and services. Jobs open for an army of bulldozer operators, carpenters, plasterers, plumbers, electricians, well-diggers, bricklayers, truck drivers, foremen and day laborers. Then come the new householders, followed by their needs. A shopping center and supermarket are hurriedly built, and into this pours another army of clerical and sales personnel, butchers, bakers, janitors, auto dealers, restaurateurs, waitresses, door-to-door salesmen, mail carriers, rookie cops, firemen, schoolteachers, medicine men of various degrees—the whole ruck and stew of civilization's auxiliaries. Thus, with every new development, jobs are born, money is earned, money is spent, and pretty soon everyone can afford a new television set, and Washington calls this prosperity.

That such prosperity is entirely material, possibly temporary and perhaps even illusory, causes little concern at present. It's money, isn't it? Well, maybe it is and maybe it isn't. A later chapter [in the book to which this is an introduction] will show whether any development householder really owns the house he thinks he's bought—whether he owns the things he uses. It's sufficient at this point to suggest the rooftrees of the nation's Levittowns[1] are held up by levitation.

---

[1] Levittown became the generic name of large, mass-produced suburban developments after a Long Island builder William J. Levitt constructed his immensely successful community of small houses in the 1950s—ED.

Meanwhile, let's step back in time to consider the history of today's housing developments.

The first good intentions which pave our modern Via Dolorosa were laid at war's end. Conscious of the fact that some 13,000,000 young men risked disfigurement, dismemberment and death in circumstances not of their choosing, a grateful nation decided to show its appreciation to the survivors. The GI Bill of Rights was enacted, and one of the articles provided an incentive for bankers to assume low-interest mortgages on houses purchased by veterans. The deal was, the bankers could recover a certain guaranteed sum from the government in event of the veteran's default. The real-estate boys read the Bill, looked at one another in happy amazement, and the dry, rasping noise they made rubbing their hands together could have been heard as far away as Tawi Tawi. Immediately, thanks to modern advertising, movable type, radio, television and other marvels, the absurdity was spread—and is still spread—that the veteran should own his home.

There was never the slightest justification for this nonsense. Never in the last 180 years of United States history was there an indication that a young man entering civil life from childhood or war should thereupon buy a house.

It is and has always been the nature of young people to be mobile. Rare indeed is the man whose life is a straight arrow's-flight from the classroom to the job he'll hold until he dies. Many a retiring corporate officer put in his early years driving a bread truck, then had a fling at a little unsuccessful business of his own, then wandered into the door-to-door sale of cemetery lots before catching on at the buttonworks he was one day to direct. Owning property implies a certain permanence—precisely that quality a bright young man should, and does, lack. A young man should be mobile until he finds his proper path. A man with a house is nailed to its floor.

The housing article in the GI Bill, however, opened vast vistas. Not only was there a government guarantee to be had, but there was also land to be sold, and since the veteran had been led both by private and government propaganda to believe he should own his home, the remaining consideration in the hard, practical minds of the real-estate men was how much house could be offered for how little money. Or, to put it in the more usual way, how little house could be offered for how much money. Cost became the sole criterion of the first postwar house, and the first economy was in space.

The typical postwar development operator was a man who figured how many houses he could possibly cram onto a piece of land and have the local zoning board hold still for it. Then he whistled up the bulldozers to knock down all the trees, bat the lumps off the terrain, and level the ensuing desolation. Then up went the houses, one after another, all alike, and none of those built immediately after the war had any more floor space than a moderately-priced, two-bedroom apartment. The dining room, the porch, the basement, and in many cases the attic, were dispensed with and disappeared from the American scene. The result was a little box on a cold concrete slab containing two bedrooms, bath, and an eating space the size of a broom closet tucked between the living room and the tiny kitchen. A nine-by-twelve rug spread across the largest room wall to wall, and there was a sheet of plate glass in the living-room wall. That, the builder said, was the picture window. The picture it framed was of the box across the treeless street. The young Americans who moved into these cubicles were not, and are not, to know the gracious dignity of living that their parents knew in the big two- and three-story family houses set well back on the grassy lawns off the shady streets of, say, Watertown, New York. For them and their children, there would be only the box on its slab. The Cape Cod Rambler had arrived.

It was inevitable that the development house was looked upon as an expedient by the young purchasers. It was most certainly not the house of their dreams, nor was the ready-made neighborhood a thing to make the soul sing. It was, simply, the only thing available. They had no choice—they couldn't afford to build their house, nor were they given a choice of architecture. Instead, they were offered a choice between a house they didn't much want and the fantastic rents that bobbed to the surface as soon as the real-estate lobby torpedoed rent control. The development house was the only living space on the market priced just within the means of the young veterans.

It is still a maxim with responsible land agents that you should never purchase a home in which you do not intend to dwell for at least ten years. Moreover, they'll say, a house in which you have no equity cannot be considered an investment. Despite these truths, houses were bought on the assumption they would serve only as brief campsites on life's wilderness trail, and incredibly enough, the government in the past two years has given encouragement to this singular point of view. With government blessing, purchasers are now being advised that buying a new house is like buying a new car. Old one too small for the growing family? Trade your old home in and buy a new one, the government suggests, meanwhile helping the developers to continue their dirty work in order that prosperity's bubble doesn't burst.

The first veterans' developments set a pattern for the builders. They sold the first houses like hotcakes, so they've been making hotcakes ever since. Today's new houses differ from those of 1947 only insofar as the materials are better and the workmen have now mastered their jobs. The basic living problems are unchanged—they're built right in. These problems will remain unchanged unless the whole construction pattern changes; until a housing development becomes something more than just a lot of houses.

First of all, a housing development cannot be called a community, for that word implies a balanced society of men, women and children wherein work and pleasure are found and the needs of all the society's members are served. Housing developments offer no employment and as a general rule lack recreational areas, churches, schools, or other cohesive influences.

A second present and future national danger lies in the fact that developments are creating stratified societies of singular monotony in a nation whose triumph to date has depended on its lack of a stratified society, on the diversity of its individuals. Yet today it is possible to drive through the various developments that surround one of our cities and tell at a glance the differing social strata.

Here is the $10,000 development—two bedrooms, low-priced cars, average income $75 a week after taxes, three children, average food budget $25 weekly; jobs vary from bus driver to house painter. Here is the $13,950 house—three bedrooms, available to foremen and successful newspapermen, medium-priced cars, two and a half children per average home; men's shoes cost $12 to $20 at this level. Next is the $17,450 split level, especially designed for split personalities, upper-medium cars; liquor bill is $25 weekly; inmates take fly-now-pay-later air rides to Europe.

The appearance of several square miles of new housing units in a once rural area adjacent to a city normally brings about a violent clash of interests. The young new householders, conscious only of their unmet needs, are intolerant of the political milieu they've invaded. Indeed, if there was any cohesive force acting on typical development householders, it would be that of hatred. Well might they form a sort of mutual loathing society where the first target of their wrath is the builder, the second, the community around them.

For its part, the invaded community eyes the newcomers with something less than wild enthusiasm. The administrative problems handed a county government by the sudden appearance of several thousand new families are enough to make a strong man blanch. And, when the guts of a city are deserted by a middle class that flocks to the suburbs, the tax problems created for the city fathers are even more frightening.

In any discussion of housing developments, however, we must first and last consider that poor devil, the householder. John Drone did not know it when he signed the deed, but appalling human tensions were a condition of the sale. Now these tensions are a tightening, knotted cord about his temples as he stands there on tiptoes, his hands tied, struggling for balance on the sharp roof of the house he may not own, nostril-deep in swirling debt.

10.3:   The Red Scare (1950)

One serious blot on the comfort and complacency of the fifties was the era's anxiety over "disloyalty" and the "Communist menace." Whether the danger of subversion was real or a case of hysteria, the issue of domestic Communism roiled the placid surface of the decade as did few other issues.

At the center of the storm, although not its instigator, was the junior senator from Wisconsin, Joseph R. McCarthy. McCarthy came to the

Senate in 1946, a banner year for conservative Republicans, and served much of his first term as an undistinguished backbench partisan. By 1950, without the record of achievement that an incumbent could normally show the voters, he faced the prospect of a hazardous reelection campaign two years down the road.

But there was an issue at hand that might bail him out—anti-Communism. This was a time of the emerging Cold War, when Americans perceived a remorseless spread of Communist influence over ever larger portions of the globe. This advance, many felt, did not derive solely from Communist aggression abroad; it must also stem from subversion within.

Out of this suspicion McCarthy would forge a potent political weapon. Day after day his charges of hidden Communists in the government, the media, the clergy, and other influential portions of American society made headlines and cast the Wisconsin senator in the role of champion of true Americanism. McCarthy won reelection in 1952 and, in tandem with other obsessive anti-Communists, helped make the remainder of the fifties a decade of fear and repression.

The following selections represent opening shots in the battles that would swirl around McCarthyism. The first is a speech by McCarthy himself before a women's Republican group in Wheeling, West Virginia, on Lincoln's Birthday in 1950.[1] Is McCarthy's indictment of Communism valid? Was his claim that Communism had made great gains since the end of World War II correct? What is McCarthy's explanation for these gains? Does his explanation hold up to examination? Are there qualities of his attack that might be disturbing to a prudent thinker and policy-maker?

The second selection is from a report by a Senate subcommittee, headed by Senator Millard Tydings of Maryland, that was empowered to investigate McCarthy's charges against the State Department. The subcommittee, clearly critical of the Wisconsin senator, held hearings and examined official files. It called the Wisconsin senator to testify in defense of his charges. McCarthy and his supporters fought back with angry attacks on Tydings and the investigating committee.

It is difficult for students to tell, without more information than it is possible to provide here, whether the charges of Communists in the State Department were correct. But you can evaluate Tydings's claims regarding the effects of charges like McCarthy's on public attitudes, the morale of government employees, and the climate of tolerance in the country.

---

[1] Actually, this text is a later reconstruction of the speech. The original seems lost forever.

In evaluating the McCarthy controversy, you should consider matters like the differences between subversion and espionage, the valid limits of political and ideological dissent in a democracy, and the connection between the Cold War and demands for internal intellectual and ideological conformity. You also should consider whether there was a political motive at work in the anti-Communist campaign. McCarthy was a Republican; Tydings a Democrat. Was the party difference significant?

Why Communism Is Gaining

JOSEPH R. McCARTHY

Ladies and gentlemen, tonight as we celebrate the one hundred and forty-first birthday of one of the greatest men in American history, I would like to be able to talk about what a glorious day today is in the history of the world. As we celebrate the birth of this man who with his whole heart and soul hated war, I would like to be able to speak of peace in our time, of war being outlawed, and of worldwide disarmament. These would be truly appropriate things to be able to mention as we celebrate the birthday of Abraham Lincoln.

Five years after a world war has been won, men's hearts should anticipate a long peace, and men's minds should be free from the heavy weight that comes with war. But this is not such a period—for this is not a period of peace. This is a time of the "cold war." This is a time when all the world is split into two vast, increasingly hostile armed camps—a time of a great armaments race.

Today we can almost physically hear the mutterings and rumblings of an invigorated god of war. You can see it, feel it, and hear it all the way from the hills of Indochina, from the shores of Formosa, right over into the very heart of Europe itself.

The one encouraging thing is that the "mad moment" has not yet arrived for the firing of the gun or the exploding of the bomb which will set civilization about the final task of destroying itself. There is still a hope for peace if we finally decide that no longer can we safely blind our eyes and close our ears to those facts which are shaping up more and more clearly. And that is that we are now engaged in a show-down fight—not the usual war between nations for land areas or other material gains, but a war between two diametrically opposed ideologies.

The great difference between our western Christian world and the atheistic Communist world is not political, ladies and gentlemen, it is moral. There are other differences, of course, but those could be reconciled. For instance, the Marxian idea of confiscating the land and factories and running the entire economy as a single enterprise is momentous. Likewise,

Congressional Record, 81st Cong., 2d sess., 96, 1950, 1954, 1946, 1957.

Lenin's invention of the one-party police state as a way to make Marx's idea work is hardly less momentous.

Stalin's resolute putting across of these two ideas, of course, did much to divide the world. With only those differences, however, the East and the West could most certainly still live in peace.

The real, basic difference, however, lies in the religion of immoralism—invented by Marx, preached feverishly by Lenin, and carried to unimaginable extremes by Stalin. This religion of immoralism, if the Red half of the world wins—and well it may—this religion of immoralism will more deeply wound and damage mankind than any conceivable economic or political system.

Karl Marx dismissed God as a hoax, and Lenin and Stalin have added in clear-cut, unmistakable language their resolve that no nation, no people who believe in a God, can exist side by side with their communistic state.

Karl Marx, for example, expelled people from his Communist Party for mentioning such things as justice, humanity, or morality. He called this soulful ravings and sloppy sentimentality.

While Lincoln was a relatively young man in his late thirties, Karl Marx boasted that the Communist specter was haunting Europe. Since that time, hundreds of millions of people and vast areas of the world have fallen under Communist domination. Today, less than 100 years after Lincoln's death, Stalin brags that this Communist specter is not only haunting the world, but is about to completely subjugate it.

Today we are engaged in a final, all-out battle between communistic atheism and Christianity. The modern champions of communism have selected this as the time. And, ladies and gentlemen, the chips are down—they are truly down.

Lest there be any doubt that the time has been chosen, let us go directly to the leader of communism today—Joseph Stalin. Here is what he said—not back in 1928, not before the war, not during the war—but 2 years after the last war was ended: "To think that the Communist revolution can be carried out peacefully, within the framework of a Christian democracy, means one has either gone out of one's mind and lost all normal understanding, or has grossly and openly repudiated the Communist revolution."

And this is what was said by Lenin in 1919, which was also quoted with approval by Stalin in 1947:

"We are living," said Lenin, "not merely in a state, but in a system of states, and the existence of the Soviet Republic side by side with Christian states for a long time is unthinkable. One or the other must triumph in the end. And before that end supervenes, a series of frightful collisions between the Soviet Republic and the Bourgeois states will be inevitable."

Ladies and gentlemen, can there be anyone here tonight who is so blind as to say that the war is not on? Can there be anyone who fails to realize that the Communist world has said, "The time is now"—that this is the time for the show-down between the democratic Christian world and the Communist atheistic world?

Unless we face this fact, we shall pay the price that must be paid by those who wait too long.

Six years ago, at the time of the first conference to map out the peace— Dumbarton Oaks[1]—there was within the Soviet orbit 180,000,000 people. Lined up on the antitotalitarian side there were in the world at that time roughly 1,625,000,000 people. Today, only 6 years later, there are 800,000,000 people under the absolute domination of Soviet Russia—an increase of over 400 percent. On our side, the figure has shrunk to around 500,000,000. In other words, in less than 6 years the odds have changed from 9 to 1 in our favor to 8 to 5 against us. This indicates the swiftness of the tempo of Communist victories and American defeats in the cold war. As one of our outstanding historical figures once said, "When a great democracy is destroyed, it will not be because of enemies from without, but rather because of enemies from within."

The truth of this statement is becoming terrifyingly clear as we see this country each day losing on every front.

At war's end we were physically the strongest nation on earth and, at least potentially, the most powerful intellectually and morally. Ours could have been the honor of being a beacon in the desert of destruction, a shining living proof that civilization was not yet ready to destroy itself. Unfortunately, we have failed miserably and tragically to arise to the opportunity.

The reason why we find ourselves in a position of impotency is not because our only powerful potential enemy has sent men to invade our shores, but rather because of the traitorous actions of those who have been treated so well by this Nation. It has not been the less fortunate or members of minority groups who have been selling this Nation out, but rather those who have had all the benefits that the wealthiest nation on earth has had to offer—the finest homes, the finest college education, and the finest jobs in Government we can give.

This is glaringly true in the State Department. There the bright young men who are born with silver spoons in their mouths are the ones who have been worst.

Now I know it is very easy for anyone to condemn a particular bureau or department in general terms. Therefore, I would like to cite one rather unusual case—the case of a man who has done much to shape our foreign policy.

When Chiang Kai-shek was fighting our war, the State Department had in China a young man named John S. Service. His task, obviously, was not to work for the communization of China. Strangely, however, he sent official

---

[1] Dumbarton Oaks near Washington, D.C., was the site of a conference of the anti-Axis powers in 1944 where plans were made for a United Nations organization after victory—ED.

reports back to the State Department urging that we torpedo our ally Chiang Kai-shek and stating, in effect, that communism was the best hope of China.

Later, this man—John Service—was picked up by the Federal Bureau of Investigation for turning over to the Communists secret State Department information. Strangely, however, he was never prosecuted. However, Joseph Grew, the Under Secretary of State, who insisted on his prosecution, was forced to resign. Two days after Grew's successor, Dean Acheson, took over as Under Secretary of State, this man—John Service—who had been picked up by the FBI and who had previously urged that communism was the best hope of China, was not only reinstated in the State Department but promoted. And finally, under Acheson, placed in charge of all placements and promotions.

Today, ladies and gentlemen, this man Service is on his way to represent the State Department and Acheson in Calcutta—by far and away the most important listening post in the Far East.

Now, let's see what happens when individuals with Communist connections are forced out of the State Department. Gustave Duran, who was labeled as (I quote) "a notorious international Communist," was made assistant to the Assistant Secretary of State in charge of Latin American affairs. He was taken into the State Department from his job as a lieutenant colonel in the Communist International Brigade. Finally, after intense congressional pressure and criticism, he resigned in 1946 from the State Department—and, ladies and gentlemen, where do you think he is now? He took over a high-salaried job as Chief of Cultural Activities Section in the office of the Assistant Secretary General of the United Nations.

Then there was a Mrs. Mary Jane Kenny, from the Board of Economic Warfare in the State Department, who was named in an FBI report and in a House committee report as a courier for the Communist Party while working for the Government. And where do you think Mrs. Kenny is —she is now an editor in the United Nations Document Bureau.

Another interesting case was that of Julian H. Wadleigh, economist in the Trade Agreements Section of the State Department for 11 years and [*sic*] was sent to Turkey and Italy and other countries as United States representative. After the statute of limitations had run [out] so he could not be prosecuted for treason, he openly and brazenly not only admitted but proclaimed that he had been a member of the Communist Party . . . that while working for the State Department he stole a vast number of secret documents . . . and furnished these documents to the Russian spy ring of which he was a part.

You will recall last spring there was held in New York what was known as the World Peace Conference—a conference which was labeled by the State Department and Mr. Truman as the sounding board for Communist propaganda and a front for Russia. Dr. Harlow Shapley was the chairman of that conference. Interestingly enough, according to the news release put out by the Department in July, the Secretary of State appointed Shapley on a commission which acts as liaison between UNESCO [United Nations Economic and Social Council] and the State Department.

This, ladies and gentlemen, gives you somewhat of a picture of the type of individuals who have been helping to shape our foreign policy. In my opinion the State Department, which is one of the most important government departments, is thoroughly infested with Communists.

I have in my hand 57 cases of individuals who would appear to be either card carrying members or certainly loyal to the Communist Party, but who nevertheless are still helping to shape our foreign policy.

One thing to remember in discussing the Communists in our Government is that we are not dealing with spies who get 30 pieces of silver to steal the blueprints of a new weapon. We are dealing with a far more sinister type of activity because it permits the enemy to guide and shape our policy. . . .

This brings us down to the case of one Alger Hiss[2] who is important not as an individual any more, but rather because he is so representative of a group in the State Department. It is unnecessary to go over the sordid events showing how he sold out the Nation which had given him so much. Those are rather fresh in all of our minds.

However, it should be remembered that the facts in regard to his connection with this international Communist spy ring were made known to the then Under Secretary of State [Adolf] Berle 3 days after Hitler and Stalin signed the Russo-German alliance pact. At that time one Whittaker Chambers—who was also part of the spy ring—apparently decided that with Russia on Hitler's side, he could no longer betray our Nation to Russia. He gave Under Secretary of State Berle—and this is all a matter of record—practically all, if not more, of the facts upon which Hiss' conviction was based.

Under Secretary Berle promptly contacted Dean Acheson and received word in return that Acheson (and I quote) "could vouch for Hiss absolutely"—at which time the matter was dropped. And this, you understand, was at a time when Russia was an ally of Germany. This condition existed while Russia and Germany were invading and dismembering Poland, and while the Communist groups here were screaming "warmonger" at the United States for their support of the allied nations.

Again in 1943, the FBI had occasion to investigate the facts surrounding Hiss' contacts with the Russian spy ring. But even after that FBI report was submitted, nothing was done.

Then late in 1948—on August 5—when the Un-American Activities Committee called Alger Hiss to give an accounting, President Truman at once issued a Presidential directive ordering all Government agencies to refuse to turn over any information whatsoever in regard to the Communist

---

[2] Alger Hiss was a former New Deal official accused by Whittaker Chambers, a former editor of *Time,* of being a Soviet spy. Hiss' guilt or innocence became a major political issue between liberals and the left on the one hand, and conservatives on the other—ED.

activities of any Government employee to a congressional committee.

Incidentally, even after Hiss was convicted—it is interesting to note that the President still labeled the exposé of Hiss as a "red herring."

If time permitted, it might be well to go into detail about the fact that Hiss was Roosevelt's chief adviser at Yalta when Roosevelt was admittedly in ill health and tired physically and mentally . . . and when, according to the Secretary of State, Hiss and Gromyko drafted the report on the conference.

According to the then Secretary of State Edward Stettinius, here are some of the things that Hiss helped to decide at Yalta. (1) The establishment of a European High Commission; (2) the treatment of Germany—this you will recall was the conference at which it was decided that we would occupy Berlin with Russia occupying an area completely circling the city, which, as you know, resulted in the Berlin airlift which cost 31 American lives; (3) the Polish question; (4) the relationship between UNRRA [United Nations Relief and Rehabilitation Administration] and the Soviet Union; (5) the rights of Americans on control commissions of Rumania, Bulgaria, and Hungary; (6) Iran; (7) China—here's where we gave away Manchuria; (8) Turkish Straits question; (9) international trusteeships; (10) Korea.

Of the results of this conference, Arthur Bliss Lane of the State Department had this to say: "As I glanced over the document, I could not believe my eyes. To me, almost every line spoke of a surrender to Stalin."

As you hear this story of high treason, I know that you are saying to yourself, "Well, why doesn't the Congress do something about it?" Actually, ladies and gentlemen, one of the important reasons for the graft, the corruption, the dishonesty, the disloyalty, the treason in high Government positions— one of the most important reasons why this continues is a lack of moral uprising on the part of the 140,000,000 American people. In the light of history, however, this is not hard to explain.

It is the result of an emotional hang-over and a temporary moral lapse which follows every war. It is the apathy to evil which people who have been subjected to the tremendous evils of war feel. As the people of the world see mass murder, the destruction of defenseless and innocent people, and all of the crime and lack of morals which go with war, they become numb and apathetic. It has always been thus after war.

However, the morals of our people have not been destroyed. They still exist. This cloak of numbness and apathy has only needed a spark to rekindle them. Happily, this spark has finally been supplied.

As you know, very recently the Secretary of State[3] proclaimed his loyalty to a man guilty of what has always been considered as the most abominable of all crimes—of being a traitor to the people who gave him a position of great trust.[4] The Secretary of State in attempting to justify his continued devotion to the man who sold out the Christian world to the atheistic world, referred

---

[3] Dean Acheson—ED.

[4] Acheson, without condoning any crime that Hiss might have committed, had stated publicly that he would not "turn his back" on his former colleague.

to Christ's Sermon on the Mount as a justification and reason therefor, and the reaction of the American people to this would have made the heart of Abraham Lincoln happy.

When this pompous diplomat in striped pants, with a phony British accent, proclaimed to the American people that Christ on the Mount endorsed communism, high treason, and betrayal of a sacred trust, the blasphemy was so great that it awakened the dormant   indignation of the American people.

He has lighted the spark which is resulting in a moral uprising and will end only when the whole sorry mess of twisted, warped thinkers are swept from the national scene so that we may have a new birth of national honesty and decency in Government.

McCarthy's Charges Are False

MILLARD TYDINGS COMMITTEE

Of the 81 alleged State Department employees,[1] only 40 were found to be employed by the State Department at the time of the review. Seven of the so-called 81 were never employed by the State Department and the remaining 33 are no longer in the Department, having been separated either through resignation, termination, or reduction in force. Specifically, of the 33 former employees, 3 were separated in 1949; 16, in 1948; 12, in 1947; and 2, in 1946. . . .

. . . We have carefully and conscientiously reviewed each and every one of the loyalty files relative to the individuals charged by Senator McCarthy. In no instance was any one of them now employed in the State Department found to be a "card-carrying Communist," a member of the Communist Party, or "loyal to the Communist Party." Furthermore, in no instance have we found in our considered judgment that the decision to grant loyalty and security clearance has been erroneously or improperly made in the light of existing loyalty standards. Otherwise stated, we do not find basis in any instance for reversing the judgment of the State Department officials charged with responsibility for employee loyalty; or concluding that they have not conscientiously discharged their duties. . . .

What the State Department knows concerning an employee's loyalty is to be found in its loyalty and security files. These files contain all information bearing on loyalty, obtained from any and all sources, including, of course, the reports of full field investigations by the FBI. Interestingly, in this regard, no sooner had the President indicated that the files would be available for review by the subcommittee than Senator McCarthy charged they were being "raped," altered, or otherwise subjected to a "housecleaning." This charge was found to be utterly without foundation in fact. The files were reviewed

---

[1] McCarthy had charged that 81 State Department employees were "loyalty risks"—ED.

Senate Committee on Foreign Relations, *State Department Loyalty Investigation*, 81st Cong., 2d sess., 20 July 1950, S. Rept. 2108, pt. 1, 9–11, 149–152, 167.

by representatives of the Department of Justice, and the Department has certified that all information bearing on the employee's loyalty as developed by the FBI appears in the files which were reviewed by the subcommittee. . . .

The Facts behind the Charge of "Whitewash"

Seldom, if ever, in the history of congressional investigations has a committee been subjected to an organized campaign of vilification and abuse comparable to that with which we have been confronted throughout this inquiry. This campaign has been so acute and so obviously designed to confuse and confound the American people that an analysis of the factors responsible therefor is indicated.

The first of these factors was the necessity of creating the impression that our inquiry was not thorough and sincere in order to camouflage the fact that the charges made by Senator McCarthy were groundless and that the Senate and the American people had been deceived. No sooner were hearings started than the cry of "whitewash" was raised along with the chant "investigate the charges and not McCarthy." This chant we have heard morning, noon, and night for almost 4 months from certain quarters for readily perceptible motives. Interestingly, had we elected to investigate Senator McCarthy, there would have been ample basis therefor, since we have been reliably informed that at the time he made the charges initially he had no information whatever to support them, and, furthermore, it early appeared that in securing Senate Resolution 231[2] a fraud had been perpetrated upon the Senate of the United States.

From the very outset of our inquiry, Senator McCarthy has sought to leave the impression that the subcommittee has been investigating him and not "disloyalty in the State Department." The reason for the Senator's concern is now apparent. He had no facts to support his wild and baseless charges, and lived in mortal fear that this situation would be exposed.

Few people, cognizant of the truth in even an elementary way, have, in the absence of political partisanship, placed any credence in the hit-and-run tactics of Senator McCarthy. He has stooped to a new low in his cavalier disregard of the facts.

The simple truth is that in making his speech at Wheeling, Senator McCarthy was talking of a subject and circumstances about which he knew nothing. His extreme and irresponsible statements called for emergency measures. As Senator Wherry[3] told Emmanuel S. Larsen, "Oh, Mac has gone out on a limb and kind of made a fool of himself and we have to back him up now." Starting with nothing, Senator McCarthy plunged headlong forward, desperately seeking to develop some information, which colored with distortion and fanned by a blaze of bias, would forestall a day of reckoning.

---

[2] A resolution authorizing an investigation of disloyalty in the State Department—ED.

[3] Conservative Republican Senator Kenneth Wherry of Nebraska—ED.

Certain elements rallied to his support, particularly those who ostensibly fight communism by adopting the vile methods of the Communists themselves and in so doing actually hinder the fight of all right-minded people who detest and abhor communism in all its manifestations. We cannot, however, destroy one evil by the adoption of another. Senator McCarthy and McCarthyism have been exposed for what they are—and the sight is not a pretty one. . . .

General Observations

In concluding our report, we are constrained to make observations which we regard as fundamental.

It is, of course, clearly apparent that the charges of Communist infiltration of and influence upon the State Department are false. This knowledge is reassuring to all Americans whose faith has been temporarily shaken in the security of their Government by perhaps the most nefarious campaign of untruth in the history of our Republic.

We believe, however, that this knowledge and assurance, while important, will prove ultimately of secondary significance in contemplating the salutory aspects of our investigation. For, we believe that, inherent in the charges that have been made and the sinister campaign to give them ostensible verity, are lessons from which the American people will find inspiration for a rededication to the principles and ideals that have made this Nation great.

We have seen the technique of the "Big Lie," elsewhere employed by the totalitarian dictator with devastating success, utilized here for the first time on a sustained basis in our history. We have seen how, through repetition and shifting untruths, it is possible to delude great numbers of people.

We have seen the character of private citizens and of Government employees virtually destroyed by public condemnation on the basis of gossip, distortion, hearsay, and deliberate untruths. By the mere fact of their associations with a few persons of alleged questionable proclivities an effort has been made to place the stigma of disloyalty upon individuals, some of whom are little people whose only asset is their character and devotion to duty and country. This has been done without the slightest vestige of respect for even the most elementary rules of evidence or fair play or, indeed, common decency. Indeed, we have seen an effort not merely to establish guilt by association but guilt by accusation alone. The spectacle is one we would expect in a totalitarian nation where the rights of the individual are crushed beneath the juggernaut of statism and oppression; it has no place in America where government exists to serve our people, not to destroy them.

We have seen an effort to inflame the American people with a wave of hysteria and fear on an unbelievable scale in this free Nation. Were this campaign founded in truth it would be questionable enough; where it is fraught with falsehood from beginning to end, its reprehensible and contemptible character defies adequate condemnation.

We sincerely believe that charges of the character which have been made in this case seriously impair the efforts of our agencies of Government to combat the problem of subversion. Furthermore, extravagant allegations, which cannot be proved and are not subject to proof, have the inevitable effect of dulling the awareness of all Americans to the true menace of communism. . . .

At a time when American blood is again being shed to preserve our dream of freedom, we are constrained fearlessly and frankly to call the charges, and the methods employed to give them ostensible validity, what they truly are: A fraud and a hoax perpetrated on the Senate of the United States and the American people. They represent perhaps the most nefarious campaign of half-truths and untruth in the history of this Republic. For the first time in our history, we have seen the totalitarian technique of the "big lie" employed on a sustained basis. The result has been to confuse and divide the American people, at a time when they should be strong in their unity, to a degree far beyond the hopes of the Communists themselves whose stock in trade is confusion and division. In such a disillusioning setting, we appreciate as never before our Bill of Rights, a free press, and the heritage of freedom that has made this Nation great.

11

The Cold War

The international rivalry of the United States and the Soviet Union was, of course, the ultimate source of McCarthyism. Wartime allies against the Axis powers, America and the USSR became global antagonists after 1945 and remained so for almost half a century. During this period of Cold War, they battled ferociously for ideological, diplomatic, technological, and economic supremacy. Meanwhile, both the superpowers and their allies and satellites engaged in an immense, draining arms race that piled up mountains of weapons of mass destruction. At several points of crisis the world would cower under the threat of nuclear holocaust and the possible extinction of the human race. This disaster never happened, of course, but a number of times, through allies and stand-ins, superpower differences boiled over into costly conventional military confrontations.

Americans have disagreed over the origins of the Cold War. A majority have undoubtedly blamed it on Soviet aggression and the need to check it. A smaller group has seen the United States as primarily at fault: to protect capitalism, they say, America pursued unnecessarily provocative policies. And some have assigned responsibility more evenly than either of these two positions.

Below are documents that focus on early American moves to contain what most Washington policy-makers perceived as dangerous and illegitimate Soviet expansionism. These actions set the stage, on the American side, for the long and menacing struggle that has finally subsided only since the end of the 1980s.

11.1: "Mr. X" and the Soviet Menace (1947, 1952)

Wartime British and American suspicions of the Soviet Union did not surface officially until the postwar peace-making process began. Then, after Germany's defeat, the Soviet Union imposed its will and system on the nations along its western borders and began to fish for political advantage in the waters of a troubled and impoverished Western Europe. Whether propelled by legitimate concern for its national security, Stalinist paranoia, or inherent Marxist imperatives, the USSR's actions set off alarm bells in Western capitals.

One man who detected aggressive Soviet designs early on was George Kennan, a scholarly American career diplomat familiar with the USSR from his service at the American embassy in Moscow and from his long study of Russian history. In late 1945 Kennan sent a riveting telegraphic dispatch to the U.S. State Department from Moscow predicting serious difficulties with the Soviet Union in the emerging postwar period.

In July 1947, back in Washington, Kennan published an article in the prestigious journal Foreign Affairs, *which he signed "X" to disguise his official position on the State Department's Policy Planning Staff. In it he clearly outlined the sources of Soviet foreign policy and recommended an approach—known as containment—for checking Soviet expansion. Containment soon became the guiding principle of American foreign policy and continued to govern America's relations with the Soviet Union until the 1990s.*

Not every American was impressed by the analysis of Mr. "X" and the policies that flowed from it. In 1948 a million voters would support former Vice President Henry Wallace in his demands for a more generous interpretation of Soviet motives and new American policies to restore the Soviet-American amity and cooperation of the World War II era. One such dissenter was William Appleman Williams, a foreign policy scholar who became an influential figure in the revisionist school of Cold War historiography.

The selections below mirror this division of opinion. The first is Kennan's Mr. "X" article. According to Kennan, what impelled Soviet leaders in their relations to the outside world? Does he say anything about the sources of American *policy? What would be required, in his view, to contain Soviet expansionism. How would containment achieve its goals? How long would it be necessary for the United States to continue its policies? In light of events since 1989, was Kennan a good prophet? Did containment work?*

The second selection is a 1952 article by Williams in the left-wing periodical Monthly Review *that is critical of containment. What are his objections to Kennan's analyses of the behavior of the Soviet leadership? How does he differ from Kennan on the role of the United States in instigating the Cold War? What does he say about the probable response of the Soviet Union to containment? Does he believe containment is likely to encourage or to under mine peace? Williams's observation that Kennan later retreated from his original views is correct. In fact Kennan became still more of a "dove" in the 1980s. Does this defection by containment's author call into question his initial analysis?*

The Sources of Soviet Conduct

"X" [GEORGE KENNAN]

The political personality of Soviet power as we know it today is the product of ideology and circumstances: Ideology inherited by the present Soviet leaders from the movement in which they had their political origin, and circumstances of the power which they have now exercised for nearly three decades in Russia. . . .

It is difficult to summarize the set of ideological concepts with which the Soviet leaders came into power. Marxian ideology . . . has always been in process of subtle evolution. . . . But the outstanding features of Communist thought as it existed in 1916 may perhaps be summarized as follows: (a) that the central factor in the life of man, the fact which determines the character of public life and the "physiognomy of society," is the system by which material goods are produced and exchanged; (b) that the capitalist system of production is a nefarious one which inevitably leads to the exploitation of the working class by the capital-owning class and is incapable of developing adequately the economic resources of society or of distributing fairly the material goods produced by human labor; (c) that capitalism contains the seeds of its own destruction and must, in view of the inability of the capital-owning class to adjust itself to economic change, result eventually and inescapably in a revolutionary transfer of power to the working class; and (d) that imperialism, the final phase of capitalism, leads directly to war and revolution. . . .

The circumstances of the immediate post-Revolution period [after the Bolshevik takeover in November 1917]—the existence in Russia of civil war and foreign intervention,[1] together with the obvious fact that the Communists represented only a tiny minority of the Russian people—made the establishment of dictatorial power a necessity. . . . [Joseph] Stalin, and those whom he led in the struggle for succession to Lenin's position of leadership, were not the men to tolerate rival political forces in the sphere of power which they coveted. Their sense of insecurity was too great. Their particular brand of fanaticism, unmodified by any of the Anglo-Saxon traditions of compromise, was too fierce and too jealous to envisage any permanent sharing of power. From the Russian-Asiatic world out of which they had emerged they carried with them a skepticism as to the possibilities of perma-

"X" [George Kennan], "The Sources of Soviet Conduct," *Foreign Affairs,* July 1947, pp. 566–582.
[1] A combination of anger at the new Soviet regime for making peace with the Germans in 1918 while the Western Allies were still fighting the Central Powers and disdain for the radical Marxist government led to intervention by British, French, American, and Japanese forces in Russian affairs for a time.—ED.

nent and peaceful coexistence of rival forces. Easily persuaded of their own doctrinaire "rightness," they insisted on the submission or destruction of all competing power. Outside of the Communist Party, Russian society was to have no rigidity. There were to be no forms of collective human activity or association which would not be dominated by the Party. No other force in Russian society was to be permitted to achieve vitality or integrity. Only the Party was to have structure. All else was to be an amorphous mass.

And within the Party the same principle was to apply. The mass of Party members might go through the motions of election, deliberation, decision and action, but in these motions they were to be animated not by their own individual wills but by the awesome breath of the Party leadership. . . .

Now the outstanding circumstance concerning the Soviet regime is that down to the present day this process of political consolidation has never been completed and the men in the Kremlin have continued to be predominantly absorbed with the struggle to secure and make absolute the power which they seized in November 1917. They have endeavored to secure it primarily against forces at home, within Soviet society itself. But they have also endeavored to secure it against the outside world. For ideology . . . taught them that the outside world was hostile and that it was their duty eventually to overthrow the political forces beyond their borders. . . .

Now it lies in the nature of the mental world of the Soviet leaders, as well as in the character of their ideology, that no opposition to them can be officially recognized as having any merit or justification whatsoever. Such opposition can flow . . . only from the hostile and incorrigible forces of dying capitalism. . . . [S]ince capitalism no longer existed in Russia and since it could not be admitted that there could be serious or widespread opposition to the Kremlin springing spontaneously from the . . . masses under its authority, it became necessary to justify the retention of the dictatorship by stressing the menace of capitalism abroad. . . .

By the same token, tremendous emphasis has been placed on the original Communist thesis of a basic antagonism between the capitalist and Socialist worlds. It is clear . . . that this emphasis is not founded in reality. . . . But there is ample evidence that the stress laid in Moscow on the menace confronting Soviet society from the world outside its borders is founded not on the realities of foreign antagonism but the necessity of explaining away the maintenance of dictatorial authority at home. . . .

So much for the historical background. What does it spell in terms of the political personality of Soviet power as we know it today?

Of the original ideology, nothing has been officially junked. Belief is maintained in the basic badness of capitalism, in the inevitability of its destruction, in the obligation of the proletariat to assist in that destruction and to take power into its own hands. But stress has come to be laid primarily on those concepts which relate most specifically to the Soviet regime itself: to its position as the sole truly Socialist regime in a dark and misguided world, and the relationships of power within it.

The first of these concepts is that of the innate antagonism between capitalism and Socialism. . . . It has profound implications for Russia's conduct as a member of international society. It means that there can never be on Moscow's side any sincere assumption of a community of aims between the Soviet Union and powers which are regarded as capitalist. It must invariably be assumed in Moscow that the aims of the capitalist world are antagonistic to the Soviet regime and, therefore, to the interests of the peoples it controls. If the Soviet government occasionally sets its signature to documents which would indicate the contrary, this is to be regarded as a tactical maneuver permissible in dealing with the enemy . . . and should be taken in the spirit of *caveat emptor.*[2] Basically, the antagonism remains. . . . And from it flow many of the phenomena which we find disturbing in the Kremlin conduct of foreign policy: the secretiveness, the lack of frankness, the duplicity, the . . . suspiciousness, and the basic unfriendliness of purpose. . . . [W]e should not be misled by tactical maneuvers. These characteristics of Soviet policy . . . are basic to the internal nature of Soviet power, and will be with us . . . until the internal nature of Soviet policy is changed.

This means that we are going to continue for a long time to find the Russians difficult to deal with. It does not mean that they should be considered as embarked upon a do-or-die program to overthrow our society by a given date. . . . The forces of progress can take their time in preparing the final *coup de grâce*. Meanwhile, what is vital is that the "Socialist fatherland"— that oasis of power which has already been won for Socialism in the person of the Soviet Union—should be cherished and defended by all good Communists at home and abroad, its fortunes promoted, its enemies badgered and confronted. The promotion of premature, "adventuristic" revolutionary projects abroad which might embarrass Soviet power in any way would be inexcusable. . . . The cause of Socialism is the support and promotion of Soviet power as defined in Moscow. . . .

But we have seen the Kremlin is under no ideological compulsion to accomplish its purposes in a hurry. Like the Church, it is dealing in ideological concepts which are of long-term validity, and it can afford to be patient. . . .The main thing is that there should always be pressure, increasing constant pressure, toward the desired goal. . . .

These considerations make Soviet diplomacy at once easier and more difficult to deal with than the diplomacy of individual aggressive leaders like Napoleon and Hitler. On the one hand it is more sensitive to contrary force. . . . On the other hand it cannot be easily defeated or discouraged by a single victory on the part of its opponents. And the patient persistence by which it is animated means that it can be effectively countered not by sporadic acts which represent the momentary whims of democratic opinion but only by intelligent long-range policies on the part of Russia's adversaries—

---

[2] Literally, "let the buyer beware," or, more or less, "you do so at your own risk"—ED.

policies no less steady in their purpose, and no less variegated and resourceful in their application, than those of the Soviet Union itself.

In these circumstances it is clear that the main element of any United States policy toward the Soviet Union must be that of a long-term, patient but firm and vigilant containment of Russian expansive tendencies. It is important to note, however, that such a policy has nothing to do with outward histrionics: with threats or blustering or superfluous gestures of outward "toughness." While the Kremlin is basically flexible in its reaction to political realities, it is by no means unamenable to considerations of prestige. Like almost any other government, it can be placed by tactless and threatening gestures in a position where it cannot afford to yield even though this might be dictated by its sense of realism. The Russian leaders are keen judges of human psychology, and as such they are highly conscious that loss of temper and of self-control is never a source of strength in political affairs. They are quick to exploit such evidences of weakness. . . .

In the light of the above, it will be clearly seen that the Soviet pressure against the free institutions of the Western world is something that can be contained by the adroit and vigilant application of counter-force at a series of constantly shifting geographical and political points, corresponding to the shifts and maneuvers of Soviet policy, but which cannot be charmed or talked out of existence. The Russians look forward to a duel of infinite duration, and they see that already they have scored great successes. . . .

It is clear that the United States cannot expect in the foreseeable future to enjoy political intimacy with the Soviet regime. It must continue to regard the Soviet Union as a rival, not a partner, in the political arena. It must continue to expect that Soviet policies will reflect no abstract love of peace and stability, no real faith in the possibility of a permanent happy coexistence of the Socialist and capitalist worlds, but rather a cautious, persistent pressure toward the disruption and weakening of all rival influence and rival power.

Balanced against this are the facts that Russia, as opposed to the Western world in general, is still by far the weaker party, that Soviet policy is highly flexible, and that Soviet society may well contain deficiencies which will eventually weaken its own total potential. This would of itself warrant the United States entering with reasonable confidence upon a policy of firm containment, designed to confront the Russians with unalterable counter-force at every point where they show signs of encroaching on the interests of a peaceful and stable world. . . .

It would be an exaggeration to say that American behavior unassisted and alone could exercise a power of life and death over the Communist movement and bring about the early fall of Soviet power in Russia. But the United States has it in its power to increase enormously the strains under which Soviet policy must operate, to force upon the Kremlin a far greater degree of moderation and circumspection than it has had to observe in recent years, and in this way promote tendencies which must eventually find their outlet in either the breakup or the gradual mellowing of Soviet power. . . .

Thus the decision will really fall in large measure on this country itself. The issue of Soviet-American relations is in essence a test of the over-all worth of the United States as a nation among nations. To avoid destruction the United States need only measure up to its own best traditions and prove itself worthy of preservation as a great nation.

A Second Look at Mr. X

WILLIAM APPLEMAN WILLIAMS

George Frost Kennan's appointment as United States Ambassador to the Soviet Union was a move of vital significance in the Cold War. For the choice of Kennan, self-acknowledged author of the policy of containment and publicly proclaimed "inside strategist" of the Cold War, reemphasized Washington's determination to press the original policy of containment— even though Kennan himself has hinted at the grave fallacy of his master plan. And while the Truman administration has yet to take note of its own expert's apparently changed views, the Republicans, under the guidance of John Foster Dulles,[1] bid fair to push containment to its logical conclusion— preventive or provoked war. Clearly, these aspects of current American policy toward Russia point up the need to take a second look at Kennan.

The errors of fact, violations of logic, and cases of judgment by double standard that may be found in Kennan's published writings comprise a total far beyond the scope of a single paper. But the fundamental character of his work is apparent in the famous "X" article, first printed in *Foreign Affairs* in July, 1947, and later republished in Kennan's volume on *American Diplomacy, 1900–1950*. Ostensibly an article on the Soviet political structure, Kennan's "X" article was originally written as a policy document for Secretary of Defense James Forrestal—and actually was but a condensation of the views Kennan had expressed as early as the first part of 1946. This background is important, for it reveals that Kennan's policy of containment was the product of long-term reflection on American-Russian relations; and Kennan was the leader of that small coterie of State Department personnel specifically trained in that field.

Despite the care that went into its preparation, the "X" article contains two signal weaknesses: Kennan's failure to probe the relationship between economic forces and foreign policy; and his attempt to analyze the history of the world since 1917 (and make recommendations for the present) without acknowledging, or addressing himself to, the fundamental challenge that the Bolshevik Revolution presented to the western world in general, and to the United States in particular. For the challenge of contemporary Russia is far more than that of a giant military machine: the Soviet Union is equally

William Appleman Williams, "A Second Look at Mr. X," *Monthly Review*, vol. 4, no. 4, (August 1952), pp. 123–128, and back cover. Copyright © 1952 by Monthly Review Inc. Reprinted by permission of Monthly Review Foundation.

[1] Secretary of state under Dwight Eisenhower, 1953–59—ED.

potent as the symbol of a fundamental critique of capitalist society that is currently the basis of action in many non-Russian areas of the world.

To evade or ignore this aspect of American-Russian relations is to explain the past inadequately and to formulate current policy without comprehending the basic forces that condition day-to-day actions and decisions. It would require one to account for the non-Russian centers of Communism, for example, *solely* on the basis of pre-1917 concepts of political treason or a quite inexplicable index of psychiatric maladjustment. And that pattern of causation (while apparently accepted by many in the western world) has little relevance to the rise of Russian influence in China.

Even within his own frame of reference, however, Kennan's review of American-Soviet relations is open to serious question. There was "little" that the United States "could have done," he observes in *American Diplomacy*, "to moderate" the Soviet's "burning hostility" toward the West. Begging the question of what foundation in fact that antagonism might have had (both during and after the Bolshevik Revolution), Kennan concludes that "it was hardly to be altered by anything" the United States could have done directly, and observes that the "best reaction to it on our part would have been at all times an attitude of great reserve, consistency, and dignity." (P. 81.)

That is certainly not a unique view of American-Soviet relations, but since Kennan is an expert on the question, his omission of several key aspects of history is difficult to understand. Surely Kennan is aware that Secretary of State Robert Lansing was avowedly and militantly opposed to the Bolshevik Revolution because of its economic and social goals; that the Wilson administration ignored several specific overtures from Lenin for collaboration against Germany and Japan; and that President Wilson openly "cast in his lot with the rest" and actively supported counter-revolutionary forces in an attempt to overthrow the Soviets.

Hard to comprehend, in short, is Kennan's decision to ignore the fact that from the early days of the November Revolution to the failure of the 1937 Brussels Conference on Japanese aggression in China, the Soviet Union persistently wooed the United States in search of an understanding that would serve to decrease the probability of a conflict that Kennan describes as "at best a war of defense" for the West. Since Kennan is apparently unaware that Tsarist Russia made three overtures of a similar nature to the United States between 1905 and 1912, his failure to place these Soviet advances in a broad framework is perhaps understandable; but even considered as purely post-1917 moves, they can hardly be explained as examples of "burning hostility." Indeed, they document a remarkable Marxist heresy by the very torchbearers of the faith. For economic and political collaboration with the United States designed to preserve Moscow would also preserve Washington—a fact that could not have been missed by the men in the Kremlin. Far from being forced to alter unmitigated antagonism, as Kennan implies, the United States had a standing opportunity to respond to positive advances.

Nor does Kennan deal candidly with American foreign policy as a whole during the interwar years. Far from isolationism, Washington's policy is perhaps best described as an attempt to exercise dominant power within a framework of "freedom without responsibility." Political and economic (and in some cases military) intervention in Latin America, Europe, and China is not isolationism. And the Roosevelt administration's disinterest in the terms of appeasement offered to Mussolini and Hitler as long as they did not touch American interests is striking evidence of the refusal to accept responsibility. These are but the most glaring examples of Kennan's failure to grapple with basic problems in their entirety. The result is clear: Kennan's recommendations lack validity. That these conclusions can be accepted as a basis for action is a matter of record, but to expect them to promote the "national interest" (a well-worn generality that Kennan declines to define) is neither logical, necessary, nor possible.

Kennan's statement of the policy of containment is major evidence in support of this judgment. For when he came to apply his "theoretical foundation" to the specific problem of policy-making, the result was a recommendation for action designed to effect either a definitive change in, or the actual destruction of, the Soviet Union. To be sure, his point of departure is an admission that the sincerity of Soviet leaders cannot be questioned—that they do desire the betterment of life in Russia—but he immediately concludes that they have explained what Kennan takes to be lack of progress in that direction by the prior necessity to establish the security of the government.

Kennan's first problem, therefore, is to establish the validity of this thesis. For a review of the facts, however, he substitutes a statement that enables him to label the security argument as no more than a rationale by which the Soviet leaders maintain themselves in power—no more, in short, than a technique of control. "Tremendous emphasis," Kennan writes, "has been placed on the original Communist thesis of a basic antagonism between the capitalist and Socialist worlds." But, he continues, "it is clear, from many indications that this emphasis is not founded in reality. The real facts concerning it have been confused by the existence abroad of a genuine resentment provoked by Soviet philosophy and tactics and occasionally by the existence of great centers of military power, notably the Nazi regime in Germany and the Japanese Government of the late 1930's, which did indeed have aggressive designs against the Soviet Union." There is, Kennan then concludes, "ample evidence that the stress laid in Moscow on the menace confronting Soviet society . . . is founded not in the realities of foreign antagonism but in the necessity of explaining away the maintenance of dictatorial authority at home." (P. 113.)

These comments and interpretations require further examination. Two notable omissions are Kennan's failure to point out that capitalist leaders militantly opposed socialism (both verbally and more actively) long years before the existence of the Soviet state, and his like failure to note Soviet overtures to the United States from 1917 to 1937. He also neglects to mention the fact and character of allied intervention in Russia. Nor does the reader find any reference to the avowed policy aims of Herbert Hoover (the "abandonment of their present economic system" on the part of the Bolsheviks) and Charles Evan Hughes[1] (who conditioned recognition on "fundamental changes" in the Soviet economic system). Likewise peculiar is the use of the word "occasionally" and the chronology "in the late 1930's" to characterize the threat to Russia from Germany and Japan.

"Occasionally" can hardly be applied to an armed challenge that concerned the world for the majority of the interwar years. And the phrase "in the late 1930's" does not take account of Japan's activities in the intervals from 1917 to 1922 and from 1931 to 1941—or Hitler's from 1934 forward. Kennan's argument that neither Japan's occupation of eastern Siberia and subsequent attacks along the border between Manchuria and Russia nor Hitler's expansion in Central Europe was a threat to Soviet security contrasts strangely with his claim that Moscow was a dire threat to America at a time when the United States had the only stockpile of atom bombs. Yet upon this questionable foundation Kennan proceeds to build his entire argument.

Kennan goes on to deal with two other factors that are central to an analysis of his policy recommendation. "The theory of the inevitability of the eventual fall of capitalism," he writes, "has the fortunate connotation that there is no hurry about it." (P. 116.) And again, "the Kremlin is under no ideological compulsion to accomplish its purposes in a hurry." (P. 118.) He points out, however, that the Soviet Government, "like almost any other government . . . can be placed in a position where it cannot afford to yield even though this might be dictated by its sense of realism." (P. 119.)

For this reason, Kennan emphasizes, "it is a *sine qua non* of successful dealing with Russia that the foreign government in question should remain at all times cool and collected and that demands on Russian policy should be put forward in such a manner as to leave the way open for a compliance not too detrimental to Russian prestige." (P. 119.) This statement would appear to indicate that Kennan (despite his inaccurate and misleading presentation of past policies toward Soviet Russia) envisaged some careful effort to establish a basic security accommodation with Moscow. His actual conclusion, however, can hardly be described in that manner.

Rather does Kennan prescribe the use of "unanswerable force," a coupling of words that has no meaning save in a military sense. Nor is his formulation vague. The United States, he concludes, "has it in its power to increase enormously the strains under which Soviet policy must operate, to force upon the Kremlin a far greater degree of moderation and circumspection than it has had to observe in recent years, and in this way promote tendencies which must eventually find their outlet in either the break-up or the

[1] Hughes, later Chief Justice of the Supreme Court, was Secretary of State in the early 1920s—ED.

gradual mellowing of Soviet power." . . . And Kennan's choice of words further emphasizes his resort to force: had he meant "a result to be expected," he would have used the phrase *will eventually*. Instead he wrote *must eventually*, an expression of obligation under "physical or logical necessity." But men do not surrender nations or social systems to the dictates of logic, as Kennan himself admits.

Thus Kennan disregards both his own warning about "tactless and threatening gestures" and his concern "to leave the way open for a compliance not too detrimental to Russian prestige." For his policy calls for the application of a steadily rising military pressure to challenge existing Soviet leadership. (Pp. 119, 120.) To this the Soviet leaders can hardly be expected to reply other than by preparations for a short-range showdown. This will hardly bring a "mellowing" of internal controls in Russia. By the same token, Kennan's proposals destroy the "fortunate connotation" in Soviet theory that there is "no hurry." A more classic non-sequitur could hardly be conceived— even as an exercise in mental gymnastics. But the responsibility for the future of American-Russian relations cannot be classed as intellectual amusement, for upon their character depends the immediate future of the world. And freedom is not nurtured by nations preparing for war.

There is considerable evidence that Kennan later came to realize the fallacy of his 1946 policy recommendations. In 1951, while on leave of absence from the Department of State, he was a bit less disingenuous—and considerably more moderate—in his statements. First, he cautioned that no war (a more candid substitute for his earlier phrase "unanswerable force") with Russia "could be more than relatively successful" (pp. 129–30); took care to point out that even a defeated Russia would not emerge in the image of America (p. 131); sharply redefined the character of the role that the United States could play—from "has it in its power to increase enormously the strains" to "our role can be at best a marginal one"; and finally warned that any attempt "at direct talking by one nation to another about the latter's political affairs is a questionable procedure." (Pp. 130, 53, 152.)

Later still, on the eve of his departure for Moscow, Kennan more openly indicated doubts about his earlier analysis. "I want to assume that everything I've thought up to now is wrong," he is reported to have observed, "and see whether I come out at the same place this time." He remarked, however, that any change in his earlier conclusions was "improbable"—an admission that raised serious questions as to Kennan's ability to free himself from the thought patterns of the "X" article. Kennan left no doubt, though, that he was worried by the consequences of containment, for he expressed a fear that it was "a lesson that Americans have learned rather too well." (*The New Yorker*, May 17, 1952, pp. 111, 112.) His concern is well founded, but nothing can alter the fact that it was Kennan himself who served as their tutor.

Central to Kennan's shift was his belated realization that the United States will never have enough power to force Russia to "unquestionably yield to it." Once he awoke to this basic error of his "X" article, Kennan quickly saw that his policy in action could well "increase [the Russians'] fear of being warred upon." (*New Yorker*, pp. 112, 116.) Small wonder that he seemed to be giving expression to a fear that his policy of containment is one for which he does not relish ultimate responsibility.

But Kennan cannot escape that responsibility. If he has in fact abandoned containment, he owes the world a formal statement of his decision—for his was the conception and the early implementation of the policy. To date, it has not been abandoned by the United States. If its author now finds it lacking in validity and dangerous in its consequences, then his is the responsibility to throw his weight on the side of revision.

Yet Kennan's greatest failure lies in his inability to define that "something which goes deeper and looks further ahead"—without which containment, by his own admission, "can only remain sterile and negative," (*American Diplomacy*, p. 153.) That "something" is no less than the courage to acknowledge the broad challenge of the Bolshevik Revolution. One must conclude that so far, at any rate, Kennan is unaware of the challenge, and until he faces that issue candidly he cannot be expected to formulate an effective response to the challenge of Soviet power.

11.2: The Truman Doctrine and the Marshall Plan (1947, 1949)

Intellectual formulations such as George Kennan's were important in shaping American Cold War policy, but actual events were even more compelling. In 1946–47 the Soviet Union provoked a Western response by a series of moves in the Middle East and the Mediterranean designed to extend Soviet power. It refused at first to remove occupation troops that had been stationed in Iran during World War II. It next put pressure on Turkey to surrender control of the strategic Dardenelles Straits and to allow the USSR to base troops and ships on Turkish soil. It fed arms and money to a Communist-led guerrilla war in Greece against the existing pro-Western government.

Concerned with preserving its communications with India, Britain had been the traditional guarantor of autonomy for Greece and Turkey, but in January 1947 the war-exhausted British told the Americans that they could no longer afford to help them. The signal to the United States was clear: either the Americans stepped in or the eastern Mediterranean would fall under Soviet domination.

Meanwhile, a more diffuse crisis was developing in Western Europe. There, following Axis defeat, chaos threatened. On the continent war devastation, social disruption, and moral exhaustion, aggravated by the severe winter of 1946–47, played into the hands of radical political forces that looked to the Soviet Union for leadership. During this grim period millions of Western Europeans lost their faith in capitalism and liberal democratic institutions and joined pro-Soviet Communist parties. If something were not done soon, said democratic leaders in Europe and America, the Communists might achieve power through legal parliamentary processes. They would then destroy democracy and impose pro-Soviet authoritarian regimes.

The American response to these crises took the form of the Truman Doctrine and the Marshall Plan. The first was announced on March 12, 1947, when President Harry Truman appeared before a joint session of Congress to request American aid to Greece and Turkey. The heart of his speech is excerpted in the first document below.

What were the bases for Truman's request for U.S. money for the Greek and Turkish governments? His reasons are couched in idealistic terms. Was it idealism alone that moved Truman? Many scholars consider the speech one of the most important ever made by a president. Why was it so important? What long-established precedents in American foreign policy might Truman be brushing aside?

The Marshall Plan, first announced by Secretary of State George Marshall at the Harvard University commencement in June 1947, sought to check Communist advance by restoring the prosperity of the whole European continent, East as well as West.[1] Eventually Congress appropriated billions of dollars to implement the plan, and, before long, food, equipment, coal, and steel were flowing to Europe in enormous volume.

What are Marshall's avowed motives for American aid? Why does he say that "our policy is directed not against any country or doctrine"? Was the Soviet Union excluded from Marshall Plan aid? Do you know what the results of the Marshall Plan were?

The final item is a critique of the Marshall Plan by a Marxist economist, Paul M. Sweezy, published in 1949, when the program was still new. Was Sweezy right about the failure of the Marshall Plan to restore European prosperity? Why might someone with Sweezy's political orientation have been skeptical of the plan? Is his claim that the authors of the Marshall Plan wished to save capitalism correct? What does he see as the only alternative to Marshall Plan aid as a way to prevent war?

---

[1] In the end the Soviet Union and its satellites refused to accept Marshall Plan aid, considering it an American plot—ED.

Aid to Greece and Turkey

HARRY S TRUMAN

Mr. President, Mr. Speaker, Members of the Congress of the United States:

The gravity of the situation which confronts the world today necessitates my appearance before a joint session of the Congress.

The foreign policy and the national security of this country are involved.

One aspect of the present situation, which I wish to present to you at this time for your consideration and decision, concerns Greece and Turkey.

The United States has received from the Greek Government an urgent appeal for financial and economic assistance. Preliminary reports from the American Economic Mission now in Greece and reports from the American Ambassador in Greece corroborate the statement of the Greek Government that assistance is imperative if Greece is to survive as a free nation.

I do not believe that the American people and the Congress wish to turn a deaf ear to the appeal of the Greek Government.

Greece is not a rich country. Lack of sufficient natural resources has always forced the Greek people to work hard to make both ends meet. Since 1940 this industrious and peace-loving country has suffered invasion, four years of cruel enemy occupation, and bitter internal strife. . . .

The very existence of the Greek state is today threatened by the terrorist activities of several thousand armed men, led by Communists, who defy the Government's authority at a number of points, particularly along the northern boundaries. A commission appointed by the United Nations Security Council is at present investigating disturbed conditions in northern Greece and alleged border violations along the frontier between Greece on the one hand and Albania, Bulgaria, and Yugoslavia on the other.

Meanwhile, the Greek Government is unable to cope with the situation. The Greek Army is small and poorly equipped. It needs supplies and equipment if it is to restore authority to the Government throughout Greek territory.

Greece must have assistance if it is to become a self-supporting and self-respecting democracy.

The United States must supply that assistance. We have already extended to Greece certain types of relief and economic aid, but these are inadequate.

There is no other country to which democratic Greece can turn.

No other nation is willing and able to provide the necessary support for a democratic Greek Government.

The British Government, which has been helping Greece, can give no further financial or economic aid after March 31. Great Britain finds itself

The Public Papers of the Presidents . . . Harry S Truman . . . 1947 (Washington, DC: Government Printing Office, 1963), pp. 176–180.

under the necessity of reducing or liquidating its commitments in several parts of the world, including Greece.

We have considered how the United Nations might assist in this crisis. But the situation is an urgent one requiring immediate action, and the United Nations and its related organizations are not in a position to extend help of the kind that is required.

It is important to note that the Greek Government has asked for our aid in utilizing effectively the financial and other assistance we may give to Greece, and in improving its public administration. It is of the utmost importance that we supervise the use of any funds made available to Greece, in such a manner that each dollar spent will count toward making Greece self-supporting, and will help to build an economy in which a healthy democracy can flourish.

No government is perfect. One of the chief virtues of a democracy, however, is that its defects are always visible and under democratic processes can be pointed out and corrected. The Government of Greece is not perfect. Nevertheless it represents 85 percent of the members of the Greek Parliament who were chosen in an election last year. Foreign observers, including 692 Americans, considered this election to be a fair expression of the views of the Greek people.

The Greek Government has been operating in an atmosphere of chaos and extremism. It has made mistakes. The extension of aid by this country does not mean that the United States condones everything that the Greek Government has done or will do. We have condemned in the past, and we condemn now, extremist measures of the right or the left. We have in the past advised tolerance, and we advise tolerance now.

Greece's neighbor, Turkey, also deserves our attention.

The future of Turkey as an independent and economically sound state is clearly no less important to the freedom-loving peoples of the world than the future of Greece. The circumstances in which Turkey finds itself today are considerably different from those of Greece. Turkey has been spared the disasters that have beset Greece. And during the war the United States and Great Britain furnished Turkey with material aid.

Nevertheless, Turkey now needs our support.

Since the war Turkey has sought additional financial assistance from Great Britain and the United States for the purpose of effecting that modernization necessary for the maintenance of its national integrity.

That integrity is essential to the preservation of order in the Middle East.

The British Government has informed us that, owing to its own difficulties, it can no longer extend financial or economic aid to Turkey.

As in the case of Greece, if Turkey is to have the assistance it needs, the United States must supply it. We are the only country able to provide that help.

I am fully aware of the broad implications involved if the United States is the creation of conditions in which we and other nations will be able to work out a way of life free from coercion. This was a fundamental issue in the war with Germany and Japan. Our victory was won over countries which sought to impose their will, and their way of life upon other nations.

To insure the peaceful development of nations, free from coercion, the United States has taken a leading part in establishing the United Nations. The United Nations is designed to make possible lasting freedom and independence for all its members. We shall not realize our objectives, however, unless we are willing to help free peoples to maintain their free institutions and their national integrity against aggressive movements that seek to impose upon them totalitarian regimes. This is no more than a frank recognition that totalitarian regimes imposed upon free peoples, by direct or indirect aggression, undermine the foundations of international peace and hence the security of the United States.

The peoples of a number of countries of the world have recently had totalitarian regimes forced upon them against their will. The Government of the United States has made frequent protests against coercion and intimidation, in violation of the Yalta agreement, in Poland, Rumania, and Bulgaria. I must also state that in a number of other countries there have been similar developments.

At the present moment in world history nearly every nation must choose between alternative ways of life. The choice is too often not a free one.

One way of life is based upon the will of the majority, and is distinguished by free institutions, representative government, free elections, guaranties of individual liberty, freedom of speech and religion, and freedom from political oppression.

The second way of life is based upon the will of a minority forcibly imposed upon the majority. It relies upon terror and oppression, a controlled press and radio, fixed elections, and the suppression of personal freedoms.

I believe that it must be the policy of the United States to support free peoples who are resisting attempted subjugation by armed minorities or by outside pressures.

I believe that we must assist free peoples to work out their own destinies in their own way.

I believe that our help should be primarily through economic and financial aid which is essential to economic stability and orderly political processes.

The world is not static, and the *status quo* is not sacred. But we cannot allow changes in the *status quo* in violation of the Charter of the United Nations by such methods as coercion, or by such subterfuges as political infiltration. In helping free and independent nations to maintain their freedom, the United States will be giving effect to the principles of the Charter of the United Nations.

It is necessary only to glance at a map to realize that the survival and integrity of the Greek nation are of grave importance in a much wider situation. If Greece should fall under the control of an armed minority, the effect upon its neighbor, Turkey, would be immediate and serious. Confusion and disorder might well spread throughout the entire Middle East.

Moreover, the disappearance of Greece as an independent state would have a profound effect upon those countries in Europe whose peoples are struggling against great difficulties to maintain their freedoms and their independence while they repair the damages of war.

It would be an unspeakable tragedy if these countries, which have struggled so long against overwhelming odds, should lose that victory for which they sacrificed so much. Collapse of free institutions and loss of independence would be disastrous not only for them but for the world. Discouragement and possibly failure would quickly be the lot of neighboring peoples striving to maintain their freedom and independence.

Should we fail to aid Greece and Turkey in this fateful hour, the effect will be far-reaching to the West as well as to the East.

We must take immediate and resolute action.

I therefore ask the Congress to provide authority for assistance to Greece and Turkey in the amount of $400,000,000 for the period ending June 30, 1948. In requesting these funds, I have taken into consideration the maximum amount of relief assistance which would be furnished to Greece out of the $350,000,000 which I recently requested that the Congress authorize for the prevention of starvation and suffering in countries devastated by the war.

In addition to funds, I ask the Congress to authorize the detail of American civilian and military personnel to Greece and Turkey, at the request of those countries, to assist in the tasks of reconstruction, and for the purpose of supervising the use of such financial and material assistance as may be furnished. I recommend that authority also be provided for the instruction and training of selected Greek and Turkish personnel.

Finally, I ask that the Congress provide authority which will permit the speediest and most effective use, in terms of needed commodities, supplies, and equipment, of such funds as may be authorized.

If further funds, or further authority, should be needed for purposes indicated in this message, I shall not hesitate to bring the situation before the Congress. On this subject the Executive and Legislative branches of the Government must work together.

This is a serious course upon which we embark.

I would not recommend it except that the alternative is much more serious.

The United States contributed $341,000,000,000 toward winning World War II. This is an investment in world freedom and world peace.

The assistance that I am recommending for Greece and Turkey amounts to little more than one-tenth of one percent of this investment. It is only common sense that we should safeguard this investment and make sure that it was not in vain.

The seeds of totalitarian regimes are nurtured by misery and want. They spread and grow in the evil soil of poverty and strife. They reach their full growth when the hope of a people for a better life has died.

We must keep that hope alive.

The free peoples of the world look to us for support in maintaining their freedoms.

If we falter in our leadership, we may endanger the peace of the world—and we shall surely endanger the welfare of our own Nation.

Great responsibilities have been placed upon us by the swift movement of events.

I am confident that the Congress will face these responsibilities squarely.

We Must Help Europe Recover

GEORGE MARSHALL

I need not tell you gentlemen that the world situation is very serious. That must be apparent to all intelligent people. I think one difficulty is that the problem is one of such enormous complexity that the very mass of facts presented to the public by press and radio make it exceedingly difficult for the man in the street to reach a clear appraisement of the situation. Furthermore, the people of this country are distant from the troubled areas of the earth and it is hard for them to comprehend the plight and consequent reactions of the longsuffering peoples, and the effect of those reactions on their governments in connection with our efforts to promote peace in the world.

In considering the requirements for the rehabilitation of Europe, the physical loss of life, the visible destruction of cities, factories, mines, and railroads was correctly estimated, but it has become obvious during recent months that this visible destruction was probably less serious than the dislocation of the entire fabric of European economy. For the past ten years conditions have been highly abnormal. The feverish preparation for war and the more feverish maintenance of the war effort engulfed all aspects of national economies. Machinery has fallen into disrepair or is entirely obsolete. Under the arbitrary and destructive Nazi rule, virtually every possible enterprise was geared into the German war machine. Long-standing commercial ties, private institutions, banks, insurance companies, and shipping companies disappeared, through loss of capital, absorption through nationalization, or by simple destruction. In many countries, confidence in the local currency has been severely shaken. The breakdown of the business structure of Europe

The Department of State Bulletin, vol. 16 (June 15, 1947), pp. 1159–60.

during the war was complete. Recovery has been seriously retarded by the fact that two years after the close of hostilities a peace settlement with Germany and Austria has not been agreed upon. But even given a more prompt solution of these difficult problems, the rehabilitation of the economic structure of Europe quite evidently will require a much longer time and greater effort than had been foreseen.

There is a phase of this matter which is both interesting and serious. The farmer has always produced the foodstuffs to exchange with the city dweller for the other necessities of life. This division of labor is the basis of modern civilization. At the present time it is threatened with breakdown. The town and city industries are not producing adequate goods to exchange with the food-producing farmer. Raw materials and fuel are in short supply. Machinery is lacking or worn out. The farmer or the peasant cannot find the goods for sale which he desires to purchase. So the sale of his farm produce for money which he cannot use seems to him an unprofitable transaction. He, therefore, has withdrawn many fields from crop cultivation and is using them for grazing. He feeds more grain to stock and finds for himself and his family an ample supply of food, however short he may be on clothing and the other ordinary gadgets of civilization. Meanwhile people in the cities are short of food and fuel. So the governments are forced to use their foreign money and credits to procure these necessities abroad. This process exhausts funds which are urgently needed for reconstruction. Thus a very serious situation is rapidly developing which bodes no good for the world. The modern system of the division of labor upon which the exchange of products is based is in danger of breaking down.

The truth of the matter is that Europe's requirements for the next three or four years of foreign food and other essential products—principally from America—are so much greater than her present ability to pay that she must have substantial additional help or face economic, social, and political deterioration of a very grave character.

The remedy lies in breaking the vicious circle and restoring the confidence of the European people in the economic future of their own countries and of Europe as a whole. The manufacturer and the farmer throughout wide areas must be able and willing to exchange their products for currencies the continuing value of which is not open to question.

Aside from the demoralizing effect on the world at large and the possibilities of disturbances arising as a result of the desperation of the people concerned, the consequences to the economy of the United States should be apparent to all. It is logical that the United States should do whatever it is able to do to assist in the return of normal economic health in the world, without which there can be no political stability and no assured peace. Our policy is directed not against any country or doctrine but against hunger, poverty, desperation, and chaos. Its purpose should be the revival of a working economy in the world so as to permit the emergence of political and social conditions in which the free institutions can exist. Such assistance, I am convinced, must not be on a piecemeal basis as various crises develop. Any assistance that this Government may render in the future should provide a cure rather than a mere palliative. Any government that is willing to assist in the task of recovery will find full cooperation, I am sure, on the part of the United States Government. Any government which maneuvers to block the recovery of other countries cannot expect help from us. Furthermore, governments, political parties, or groups which seek to perpetuate human misery in order to profit therefrom politically or otherwise will encounter the opposition of the United States.

It is already evident that, before the United States Government can proceed much further in its efforts to alleviate the situation and help start the European world on its way to recovery, there must be some agreement among the countries of Europe as to the requirements of the situation and the part of those countries themselves will take in order to give proper effect to whatever action might be undertaken by this Government. It would be neither fitting nor efficacious for this Government to undertake to draw up unilaterally a program designed to place Europe on its feet economically. This is the business of the Europeans. The initiative, I think, must come from Europe. The role of this country should consist of friendly aid in the drafting of a European program and of later support of such a program so far as it may be practical for us to do so. The program should be a joint one, agreed to by a number, if not all, European nations.

An essential part of any successful action on the part of the United States is an understanding on the part of the people of America of the character of the problem and the remedies to be applied. Political passion and prejudice should have no part. With foresight, and a willingness on the part of our people to face up to the vast responsibility which history has clearly placed upon our country, the difficulties I have outlined can and will be overcome.

. . . This program will cost our country billions of dollars. It will impose a burden on the American taxpayer. It will require sacrifices today in order that we may enjoy security and peace tomorrow. Should the Congress approve the program for European recovery, as I urgently recommend, we Americans will have made an historic decision of our peacetime history.

A nation in which the voice of its people directs the conduct of its affairs cannot embark on an undertaking of such magnitude and significance for light or purely sentimental reasons. Decisions of this importance are dictated by the highest considerations of national interest. There are none higher, I am sure, than the establishment of enduring peace and the maintenance of true freedom for the individual. In the deliberations of the coming weeks I ask that the European Recovery Program be judged in these terms and on this basis. . . .

The program is *not* one of a series of piecemeal relief measures. I ask that you note this difference, and keep it in mind throughout our explanations. The difference is absolutely vital.

The Marshall Plan, An Instrument of Peace

PAUL M. SWEEZY

The annual question of how much money should be appropriated to carry out the purposes of the Marshall Plan is again before the Congress. It is a good time to recall what those purposes were supposed to be and to examine the extent to which they are being realized in practice.

The Marshall Plan was sold to the American people as a program of aid to the countries of western Europe which would enable them to achieve, within the space of about five years, full economic independence. That is certainly a praiseworthy aim. Economically independent countries can also afford to be politically independent. A politically independent western Europe, tied to no blocs and defending its own interests in the arena of international politics, would be a powerful force for peace. If the Marshall Plan were really calculated to create an independent Western Europe, it should receive support.

It is for precisely this reason that by far the most important fact about the Marshall Plan is that it is not creating an economically independent western Europe. There is not the slightest prospect that it will create an economically independent western Europe.

Official analyses of the Marshall Plan reveal this fact even though they dare not admit it. Honest evaluations of the Marshall Plan say it frankly and unequivocally.

Here, for example, is what Walter Lippman[1] had to say in his column in the *Herald-Tribune* of June 13:

> There is current a good deal of pretense and propaganda about how well in hand everything is. Yet ever since the report of the Marshall Plan countries which was made available at the end of 1948 it has been known to the relatively few who studied it that the goal of European recovery, in the official and popular sense of the words, was unattainable by 1952—during the period set by Congress and agreed to by the Marshall Plan countries. It was certain that even with almost unlimited wishful thinking the leading industrial countries of Europe could not become self-supporting and still achieve and maintain a tolerable standard of life by 1952, or in fact at any foreseeable date.

I believe this is a sober statement of the truth—the bedrock from which any rational evaluation of the Marshall Plan must start.

Why is the Marshall Plan failing to achieve its announced goals? Many theories are currently being put forward to explain this. Some say that it is because the United States is perverting the Marshall Plan into an instrument of American imperialism. Some say that it is because the British are selfishly looking out for their own recovery and neglecting the interests of western

Paul M. Sweezy, "The Marshall Plan, An Instrument of Peace?" *Monthly Review*, vol. 1, no. 3 (July 1949), pp. 80–84. Copyright © 1949 by Monthly Review Inc. Reprinted by permission of Monthly Review Foundation.

[1] Lippman was a famous columnist and political pundit—ED.

Europe as a whole. Some say that it is because of the maze of regulations and restrictions which are choking trade among the Marshall Plan countries themselves.

There is, of course, something to each one of these theories. But they are all essentially superficial, and even if the conditions to which they call attention were remedied the situation as a whole would not be decisively altered. The Marshall Plan might be administered without a thought for the interests of American business. The British might be as altruistic as they are alleged to be selfish. Trade restrictions among the Marshall Plan countries might be completely eliminated. There would still be no economically independent western Europe by the end of 1952.

The truth is that the Marshall Plan does not touch the real problem of western Europe. The Marshall Plan is based on the tacit assumption that western Europe was temporarily knocked out by the war and that what it needs is help in getting back on its feet again. This is a totally inadequate diagnosis. In fact the war was merely the climax of a long-term trend. The *status quo ante* in western Europe is dead; no amount of outside assistance can bring it to life again. To quote Thomas Balogh, an eminent Oxford economist: "Western Europe's crisis is not a temporary or short lived departure from an 'equilibrium position' to which it is easy to return. It is a historically unique, harsh break with all that has gone before, a fundamental crisis."

In broad outline the nature of this crisis is clear and simple. Western Europe was the original home of capitalism. During the 18th and 19th centuries it was economically by far the most advanced region in the world. It used its wealth and power to establish relations with the rest of the world which were enormously advantageous to western Europe. On the strength of these advantageous relations with the rest of the world, western Europe developed a very numerous population and provided it with a relatively high standard of living.

It is easy to see now, looking back, that the foundation of western Europe's extraordinary prosperity was temporary. The rest of the world was bound to catch up and to demand a redefinition of its relations with western Europe. When that happened western Europe could no longer go on living in the old way. It would have to face up to the problem of reconstructing and reorienting its economy to meet the requirements of a changed world.

The two world wars greatly accelerated this inevitable historical development. Already in the inter-war period, the day of reckoning was clearly approaching. By the end of World War II it was obvious that it had at last arrived.

What were the practical alternatives?

First, outside aid which would permit western Europe to evade the real problem but would in no sense contribute to its solution.

Or, second, a thorough-going economic revolution which would cut through centuries-old vested interests, drastically redirect and reorganize the utilization of human and material resources, and open the way for a planned coordination of the western European economy with the economies of other regions which would be both willing and able to enter into firm long-term commitments of a mutually beneficial nature. The watchword of such a revolution would have to be planning and still more planning—vigorous, disciplined, comprehensive.

Only a political imbecile could believe that the traditional ruling classes of western Europe would or could carry through such a revolution. It would have to be done by the working class which has few privileges to lose and is capable of toil and sacrifice for a communal goal. And in the very process of carrying out this great revolution, the workers of western Europe would inevitably be forced to scrap the old capitalist system of production for profit and to substitute a new socialist system of production for use.

In the actual circumstances which prevailed after World War II such a revolution was a very real possibility. On the continent the Resistance movements, under the leadership of Socialists and Communists, were everywhere spearheading the drive for radical economic reform. In England the Labor Party was swept into power on a wave of popular enthusiasm for its stated socialist aims. A firm Socialist-Communist front could have led the way forward despite all obstacles.

But the leaders of the United States, and especially those who have their offices in the skyscrapers of New York rather than in the government buildings of Washington, feared nothing so much as a real revolution in western Europe. They had one, and only one, weapon with which to fight it—economic subsidies which would give the old order a new lease on life and permit western Europe, for the time being at any rate, to evade rather than tackle the basic problem which confronted it. They used their weapon skillfully and ruthlessly; and they found valuable allies among the social democratic leaders of western Europe.

At first the subsidies took the form of a variety of loans and grants. Later they were systematized in the more effective form of the Marshall Plan with its centralized administrative apparatus, its network of bilateral treaties, and its agents in each of the countries affected.

Thus we see that while the Marshall Plan was sold to the American people as a *solution* to the crisis of western Europe, in reality it is just the opposite. It is the means by which American capitalism seeks to prevent western Europe from solving its own crisis in the only possible way it can solve the crisis, by the adoption of socialism.

It is only against this background that we can properly evaluate the relation of the Marshall Plan to peace and war. The relation is not a simple one and nothing is gained by pretending that it is.

If the ruling elements in the United States were prepared to continue the Marshall Plan indefinitely, if the support of the American people for such a policy could be secured, and if the economy of the United States could be stabilized by a continuing export surplus of this magnitude, then the

Marshall Plan would have a tendency to reduce international tensions, at least for a considerable period. Western Europe would become the passive dumping ground for an economic system which is always in danger of choking on its own surplus product.

But none of these conditions is likely to be fulfilled. Subsidizing western Europe is not a directly profitable form of investment for American capitalists; the people of the United States are not sufficiently initiated into the mysteries of capitalist economics to understand the need for giving away 5 or 6 billion dollars a year forever; and in any case 5 or 6 billion dollars is not enough to keep American capitalism from choking.

Hence the Marshall Plan must be looked upon as a stopgap expedient which solves neither the problems of western Europe nor the problems of the United States. Being essentially temporary and inadequate by any standards, it cannot but play a disturbing role in international relations.

And yet it is hardly accurate to say that the Marshall Plan as such is a threat to peace.

The real threat to peace comes from the utter and complete inability of the rulers of the United States to devise a non-warlike program for dealing with the overwhelming problems which are pressing in on them from all sides.

When the Marshall Plan runs out, the crisis of western Europe will be no nearer solution than it was two years ago—and it may be added that the obvious and continued success of socialist planning in eastern Europe will by that time have shown the western Europeans how they can solve their crisis if they but have the will and the resolve. American capitalism is already giving signs of sliding into the inevitable depression which all the world expects and which our rulers know will deal a bodyblow to their prestige and authority. Worst of all from their point of view, if something isn't done, even the American people may wake up from their propaganda-created nightmare of Soviet aggression and Communist plots to discover that the real world is one in which those nations and peoples who manage their affairs in their own interests go forward in spite of all obstacles, while those who put their trust in the gods of free enterprise find themselves hopelessly stuck in the mire of economic insecurity and political reaction.

These are the problems which stare the rulers of America in the face. They do not know how to overcome them. In truth there is no way to overcome them within the framework of the self-contradictory system to which they are wedded. In the long run the replacement of capitalism by a rational socialist order is as certain in the United States as elsewhere. But in the meantime, the greatest danger to world peace, and indeed to much that is best in human civilization itself, is that the rulers of America will seek to put off the day of reckoning by embarking on a career of unlimited militarism and imperialism.

They are already moving in this direction—whether consciously or not is beside the point. If they continue, war may not come soon; but it is hard to see how it can be avoided indefinitely. Militarism and imperialism have their own logic, and its final term is war.

Is it too late to call a halt? That will depend on how quickly the people everywhere, but especially the people of western Europe and America, can be brought to understand that the only possible guarantee of lasting peace is a new social order which puts the interests of producers and consumers above the interests of private capital.

12

The Civil Rights Revolution

Black Americans have struggled for respect and equal rights for generations, but except for the brief Reconstruction period, made little headway until after World War II. Well into the 1950s, black citizens virtually everywhere were victims of racial discrimination that denied them equal access to jobs, housing, training, education, and private amenities. In the South, state and local laws imposed a system of segregation (Jim Crow) that confined them to separate, and almost invariably inferior, public services and facilities, while legal sleight of hand, intimidation, and subterfuge also denied them the right to vote.

A victory over a malevolent racist ideology, World War II changed the racial climate. Many white Americans came to recognize the pernicious effects of racism; black soldiers returned from the fighting fronts with new determination to resist bigotry at home. Partially suspended during the war, the movement for racial justice vigorously revived after 1945.

During the late forties and early fifties the civil rights drive was led by the National Association for the Advancement of Colored People (NAACP), a coalition of white liberals and black activists that had as its ultimate goal an integrated society where race and color would cease to matter. The NAACP's chief weapon was suits in the federal courts to compel enforcement of the equal treatment principles enjoined by the Constitution but long ignored. Its strategy culminated in the 1954 Supreme Court decision *Brown* v. *Board of Education of Topeka*, declaring segregated schools in violation of the equal protection clause of the Fourteenth Amendment.

By the end of the 1950s nonviolent civil disobedience, as employed by the Southern Christian Leadership Conference (SCLC) headed by the Baptist minister Martin Luther King, Jr., had began to eclipse the NAACP's legal action approach. Yet even in this new period the civil rights movement remained committed to a color-blind, integrated society of "black and white together." King inspired millions of both races through his writings and through his highly visible protest tactics of boycotts and marches. The eloquence and bravery of King and his followers deeply moved the liberal public and helped undermine a tottering system of legal discrimination and disfranchisement.

By the mid-sixties, however, the civil rights movement had become more separatist and militant. Although Jim Crow was now virtually dead, blacks still remained poor and relatively powerless. These realities, amplified by the confrontational mood of the decade in general, encouraged black separatism and the willingness to consider aggressive means to force the larger society to confer greater political and economic equality.

In the selections below you will find a small sampling of the extensive literature of the civil rights movement. The writings include several competing varieties of civil rights thought as well as prosegregation, anti–civil rights documents. Carefully consider them for insight into the minds of participants in the momentous civil rights revolution.

12.1:   School Desegregation (1954, 1965)

After years of slow progress, the breakthrough in the legal attack on Jim Crow came in 1954 with the Supreme Court decision Brown v. Board of Education of Topeka. *The conclusion of a suit brought by the NAACP Legal Defense Fund headed by Thurgood Marshall, the* Brown *decision overthrew the precedent established by* Plessy v. Ferguson *(1896) allowing segregated public facilities for blacks, notwithstanding the Fourteenth Amendment, so long as they were* equal *to those provided for whites.* Separate, *by its very nature, said Chief Justice Earl Warren in the* Brown *decision, must be considered* unequal.

The Court would soon enjoin "all deliberate speed" for the implementation of its school desegregation order. In a few places in the Upper South school districts quickly complied. But in many southern communities the Brown *decision was met by massive resistance. The Ku Klux Klan revived and soon marshaled its weapons of violence and intimidation against school desegregation. More effective were the White Citizens' Councils, composed of "respectable" middle-class conservatives who deplored the crude methods of the Klan but used moral and economic pressure and legal maneuvering to preserve the Jim Crow system. In several southern states conservative administrations countered NAACP legal action with court suits of their own to delay application of the* Brown *decision.*

The two documents below represent the poles of opinion on the school desegregation issue. The first is an excerpt from the Brown decision itself, written by Chief Justice Warren. Consider the basis for Warren's rejection of "separate but equal." Is his reasoning convincing? Why did the justices who originally announced the Plessy v. Ferguson doctrine in the 1890s see matters differently from Warren in 1954?

The second selection is part of an article from The Citizen, the official publication of the White Citizens' Councils. It was written for members of the Councils on the occasion of a leadership conference held in Chattanooga, Tennessee, in late 1965. Is the piece militantly racist? How convincing are the author's arguments for segregated schools? Consider the principle of segregation by ability, which is rejected. Is the argument against it convincing? Does the author find any gaps in the integrationists' armor? There is much in this article on the need to preserve religion in the schools. Was there a cultural link between segregationism and some kinds of traditional Christian faith? What seems to be the Citizens' Councils practical solution to the desegregation dilemma?

Brown v. Board of Education of Topeka

WARREN, C. J. (Chief Justice). These cases come to us from the States of Kansas, South Carolina, Virginia, and Delaware. They are premised on different facts and different local conditions, but a common legal question justifies their consideration together in this consolidated opinion.

In each of these cases, minors of the Negro race, through their legal representatives, seek the aid of the courts in obtaining admission to the public schools of their community on a nonsegregated basis. In each instance, they have been denied admission to schools attended by white children under laws requiring or permitting segregation according to race. This segregation was alleged to deprive the plaintiffs of the equal protection of the laws under the Fourteenth Amendment. In each of the cases, other than the Delaware case, a three-judge federal district court denied relief to the plaintiffs on the so-called "separate but equal" doctrine announced by this Court in Plessy v. Ferguson. . . . Under that doctrine, equality of treatment is accorded when the races are provided substantially equal facilities, even though these facilities be separate. . . .

The plaintiffs contend that segregated public schools are not "equal": and cannot be made "equal," and hence they are deprived of the equal protection of the laws. Because of the obvious importance of the question presented, the Court took jurisdiction. Argument was heard in the 1952 Term, and reargument was heard this Term on certain questions propounded by the Court.

[*Brown* v. *Board of Education of Topeka*], 347 U.S. 483

Reargument was largely devoted to the circumstances surrounding the adoption of the Fourteenth Amendment in 1868. It covered exhaustively consideration of the Amendment in Congress, ratification by the states, then existing practices in racial segregation, and the views of proponents and opponents of the Amendment. This discussion and our own investigation convince us that, although these sources cast some light, it is not enough to resolve the problem with which we are faced. At best they are inconclusive. . . .

In the first cases in the Court construing the Fourteenth Amendment, decided shortly after its adoption, the Court interpreted it as proscribing all state-imposed discrimination against the Negro race. The doctrine of "separate but equal" did not make its appearance in this Court until 1896 in the case of Plessy v. Ferguson . . . , involving not education but transportation. American courts have since labored with the doctrine for over half a century. In this Court, there have been six cases involving the "separate but equal" doctrine in the field of public education. . . . In none of these cases was it necessary to grant relief to the Negro plaintiff. And in Sweatt v. Painter . . . , the Court expressly reserved decision on the question whether Plessy v. Ferguson should be held inapplicable to public education.

In the instant case, that question is directly presented. Here . . . there are findings below that the Negro and white schools involved have been equalized, or are being equalized, with respect to buildings, curricula, qualifications and salaries of teachers, and other "tangible" factors. Our decision, therefore, cannot turn on merely a comparison of these tangible factors in the Negro and white schools involved in each of the cases. We must look instead to the effect of segregation itself on public education.

In approaching this problem, we cannot turn the clock back to 1868 when the Amendment was adopted, or even to 1896 when Plessy v. Ferguson was written. We must consider public education in the light of its full development and its present place in American life throughout the Nation. Only in this way can it be determined if segregation in public schools deprives these plaintiffs of the equal protection of the laws.

Today, education is perhaps the most important function of state and local governments. Compulsory school attendance and the great expenditures for education both demonstrate our recognition of the importance of education to our democratic society. It is required in the performance of our most basic responsibilities, even service in the armed forces. It is the very foundation of good citizenship. Today it is a principal instrument in awakening the child to cultural values, in preparing him for later professional training, and in helping him to adjust normally to his environment. In these days, it is doubtful that any child may reasonably be expected to succeed in life if he is denied the opportunity of an education. Such an opportunity, where the state has undertaken to provide it, is a right which must be made available to all on equal terms.

We come then to the question presented: Does segregation of children in public schools solely on the basis of race, even though the physical facilities and other "tangible" factors may be equal, deprive the children of the minority group of equal educational opportunities? We believe that it does.

In Sweatt v. Painter, . . . in finding that a segregated law school for Negroes could not provide them equal educational opportunities, this Court relied in large part on "those qualities which are incapable of objective measurement but which make for greatness in a law school." In McLaurin v. Oklahoma State Regents, . . . the Court, in requiring that a Negro admitted to a white graduate school be treated like all other students, again resorted to intangible considerations: ". . . his ability to study, to engage in discussion and exchange views with other students and, in general, to learn his profession." Such considerations apply with added force to children in grade and high schools. To separate them from others of similar age and qualifications solely because of their race generates a feeling of inferiority as to their status in the community that may affect their hearts and minds in a way unlikely ever to be undone. . . .

Whatever may have been the extent of psychological knowledge at the time of Plessy v. Ferguson, this finding is amply supported by modern authority. Any language contrary to this finding is rejected.

We conclude that in the field of public education the doctrine of "separate but equal" has no place. Separate educational facilities are inherently unequal. Therefore, we hold that the plaintiffs and others similarly situated for whom the actions have been brought are, by reason of the segregation complained of, deprived of the equal protection of the laws guaranteed by the Fourteenth Amendment. This disposition makes unnecessary any discussion whether such segregation also violates the Due Process Clause of the Fourteenth Amendment.

How Can We Educate Our Children?

WHITE CITIZENS' COUNCILS

Schools are not merely the mark of a civilization. They are the means of maintaining civilization.

Our American school system is at once an inheritance from Europe and an original contribution to the modern world. Ultimately, our system derives from the medieval universities such as Oxford and Cambridge, and from the "grammar" and other schools established to prepare for those universities. . . .

All the universities of the Middle Ages and the earliest universities or colleges in America were established by groups of Christians, whose basic concern was perpetuation of the gospel.

American state universities were frankly imitative of these educational institutions of the Christian church. Early American schools, like their European predecessors, aimed at beginning for children a course of study leading toward college. In this country, however, a new element came to be emphasized—the training of every child, whether he would or would not go

Citizens Councils, "How Can We Educate Our Children?" *The Citizen*, November 1965, pp. 4–7.

to college. This vital feature of our society has now reached the point of undertaking to see that every child goes to college.

It is this widening of the doors of opportunity which has been the special contribution of America to the world, for to some degree the rest of the world is following us in it.

What needs to be remembered is that there is no point in widening the doors if the treasure within be lost in the process. Our schools and colleges became valuable because they led their student to skill in the arts and knowledge in the sciences, very specifically including the Holy Scripture and the Christian life.

Too often in our time the curriculum has been broadened at the expense of becoming shallower and recently all religious content has been dictatorially excluded from state operated schools. Of course some positive attitude toward religion is inseparable from an educational enterprise. . . .

In the world revolution now being everywhere attempted, the conscious overthrow of the traditional American school system, with its roots in the Christian culture of Western Europe, is a priority item. Many revolutionary techniques have been employed, many massive assaults have been made on the ramparts of the "three R's" and especially of the fourth "R," religion. . . .

No other blow against our educational structure has been quite so violent or damaging as the hysterical attack of the racial integrationists. The results in the District of Columbia are notorious. The school system of the nation's capital was once among the finest in the country. Today it is an educational desert—with one oasis in the far Northwest thanks to a process of *de facto* resegregation.

Central High School in Little Rock was found by a survey in the mid-1950's to be one of the 25 best secondary schools in the United States. Today, even though integration there is hardly more than a token, it is scarcely thought of in terms of overall excellence.

Dr. Henry Garrett and other experts have shown that a sound program of schooling is intrinsically impossible where significant numbers of white and black children are herded together in one classroom. The essential disparity, mentally and temperamentally, is just too great. The mania for homogenization has not yet reached the point where high school boys and girls are integrated in the same gym classes. Yet it would be hardly more absurd than the forced congregation of Negro with white children above the preschool level.

(In the Old South, white children played with Negro children regularly before reaching school age, and even later—outside the school. This fact sometimes caused painful personal readjustments later, which integrationists attribute to the eventual segregation, but which could just as well be attributed to the early integration. More reasonably, one could simply recognize that a full life involves many readjustments.)

Some object to segregationist arguments based on IQ differences by saying: "Well then, group them in class by IQ, or other ability test, without reference to race!" The rejoinder to this is twofold: (1) it is not at all what the militant integrationists want, since it would leave a racially unbalanced situation; and (2) it would create new psychological problems, possibly much more serious than any we now have, and would result in an ever widening gap between the predominantly white group, with its adopted superior Negroes, and the predominantly Negro group with its adopted subnormal whites.

Intelligence is not everything—not enough to justify breaking up groups with other sources of internal cohesion. But a group's average intelligence is important enough to justify separate education for groups with significantly different averages, even if there is some "overlap." By way of analogy, the existence of Amazonian women and effeminate men does not justify drafting women for combat military service (though the Russians have used women for such service).

Not to pursue further the speculative reasons for segregation, a recent analysis of practical school problems which gives the strongest kind of objective support to the segregationist position appeared in, of all places, the *New York Times Magazine* (May 2, 1965) by one Martin Mayer—subjectively, it would appear, an integrationist, but an intelligent observer and skillful writer. Following are excerpts from this revealing article:

> "Public confidence in the [New York City] school system is fearfully low and dropping: White children are leaving the city public schools at a rate of 40,000 a year. . . . Of the leaders of the school system itself—the nine-member Board of Education and the 20-odd deputy and associate superintendents—only a handful have children who attend or ever did attend a New York Public school. . . . Of the Negro leaders of the integration drive, . . . not one has or has had a child in a New York public school. . . . "

Integration is the main, but not the only threat to the American school system. Indeed, integration itself would not be promoted so fanatically if too many educators had not adopted a philosophy which says that the spirit of man is the result of material processes, and that there is no spirit beyond.

Materialism begins by exalting the schools, for it holds that through them society and the nature of man himself may undergo a revolutionary transformation. Yet materialism ends by destroying the schools, for it reduces them to budgets, buildings, and bureaucracy, where blossom at best the beatniks of Berkeley,[1] and from which finer spirits escape altogether. . . .

Because of the integration-at-any-cost policy of both the Federal government and the majority of the nation's educational bureaucrats, the public is daily losing faith in the "serviceability of public education." This is not a condition which the Citizens' Councils have created, but it is one which we recognize. The purpose of the Chattanooga Leadership Conference is to pro-

---

[1]Nineteen fifties social-cultural nonconformists whose dress, attitudes, and life styles offended many conventional middleclass people—ED.

mote the rapidly expanding private school movement as a means of protecting both racial integrity and American education.

12.2:   Christian Love versus Racial Anger (1964, 1967)

The Brown *decision of 1954 unleashed forces that soon dismantled the entire system of legal discrimination. Each step of the way was marked by further court decisions and new federal legislation to enforce job equality and voting rights. But government agencies, whether the courts, Congress, or the Justice Department, would not have moved so fast without the bold challenges to southern practices by brave civil rights workers willing to face intimidation and physical attack. Inevitably, these challenges created martyrs, but they dramatized the plight of southern black people and revealed the continuing defiance of the law of the land by conservative whites. The process stirred waves of sympathy among white Americans that impressed Congress and the White House, accelerating the process of federal intervention.*

By the mid-sixties even these more militant tactics seemed too feeble to some civil rights activists. Driven by an emerging black nationalism and by frustration at the slow pace of economic progress for blacks, the militants lashed out angrily and defiantly at white America, including white liberal sympathizers. In place of the color-blind society, the ideal until this point, they proposed one where distinctive black institutions would function separately from those of the larger society. Infused with such "black power" views, the Student Non-Violent Coordinating Committee[1] (SNCC), along with the Congress of Racial Equality (CORE), expelled their white members and declared themselves separatist organizations. Meanwhile, organizations like the Black Panthers, a menacing paramilitary group from California, adopted Marxist or anticolonialist Third World revolutionary theories to guide their struggles against white America.

By this time outright violence had begun to sweep the inner-city black ghettos. Beginning in Watts in Los Angeles in 1965 and continuing for three years, riots erupted in the ghettos each summer. Often triggered by anger at police brutality, the uprisings expressed the frustrated expectations of the black urban poor. They culminated in April 1968, following

---

[1]This group was originally a biracial offshoot of the 1960 student lunch counter sit-in movement of 1960 that helped desegregate restaurants and cafeterias in the South. Composed primarily of students and young men and women, it was affiliated with SCLC, although from the first it often refused to accept SCLC's direction.

the assassination of Martin Luther King, Jr., by a white supremacist, in a spasm of ghetto rage that raised visions of racial apocalypse.

White liberals urged compassion and understanding, but many white Americans resented and feared the new militancy. It soon triggered a surge of antiblack resentment labeled "white backlash." Backlash, King's tragic death, and the discouraging pace of African-American economic progress stopped the civil rights movement in its tracks. Advance would eventually resume, but it would be once more primarily through the slow and quiet processes of legislation, legal challenge, bureaucratic ruling, and court review.

The first selection below is an SCLC statement of its approach and goals probably composed in 1964. It summarizes the philosophy that guided King and his supporters. What are the intellectual sources of SCLC's philosophy? Do SCLC's tactics place great psychological burdens on its practitioners? What were the SCLC's goals for the American society of the future? Were these goals realistic?

The second document is a statement made by SNCC after it had been taken over by the black power militants and repudiated SCLC and its tactics. How would you characterize the tone of this document? Was this late-period SNCC approach practical? Could its plan have been implemented? What do you think of the specific tactics to undermine the system suggested here? One element of this new mood was pan-Africanism. What forces or events help explain this identification of black Americans with Africa in the late 1960s? Have you encountered this view before in this volume? How would you expect most whites to respond to a manifesto such as this one?

This Is SCLC
SOUTHERN CHRISTIAN LEADERSHIP CONFERENCE

Aims and Purposes of SCLC

The Southern Christian Leadership Conference has the basic aim of achieving full citizenship rights, equality, and the integration of the Negro in all aspects of American life. SCLC is a service agency to facilitate coordinated action of local community groups within the frame of their indigenous organizations and natural leadership. SCLC activity revolves around two main focal points: the use of nonviolent philosophy as a means of creative protest; and securing the right of the ballot for every citizen.

Philosophy of SCLC

The basic tenets of Hebraic-Christian tradition coupled with the Gandhian concept of *satyagraha*—truth force—is at the heart of SCLC's philosophy.

Southern Christian Leadership Conference, *This Is SCLC*, rev. ed., 1964.

Christian nonviolence actively resists evil in any form. It never seeks to humiliate the opponent, only to win him. Suffering is accepted without retaliation. Internal violence of the spirit is as much to be rejected as external physical violence. At the center of nonviolence is redemptive love. Creatively used, the philosophy of nonviolence can restore the broken community in America. SCLC is convinced that nonviolence is the most potent force available to an oppressed people in their struggle for freedom and dignity.

SCLC and Nonviolent Mass Direct Action

SCLC believes that the American dilemma in race relations can best and most quickly be resolved through the action of thousands of people, committed to the philosophy of nonviolence, who will physically identify themselves in a just and moral struggle. It is not enough to be intellectually dissatisfied with an evil system. The true nonviolent resister presents his physical body as an instrument to defeat the system. Through nonviolent mass direct action, the evil system is creatively dramatized in order that the conscience of the community may grapple with the rightness or wrongness of the issue at hand. . . .

SCLC and Voter-Registration

The right of the ballot is basic to the exercise of full citizenship rights. All across the South, subtle and flagrant obstacles confront the Negro when he seeks to register and vote. Poll taxes, long form questionnaires, harassment, economic reprisal, and sometimes death, meet those who dare to seek this exercise of the ballot. In areas where there is little or no attempt to block the voting attempts of the Negro, apathy generally is deeply etched upon the habits of the community. SCLC, with its specialized staff, works on both fronts: aiding local communities through every means available to secure the right to vote (e.g. filing complaints with the Civil Rights Commission) and arousing interest through voter-registration workshops to point up the importance of the ballot. Periodically, SCLC, upon invitation, conducts a voter-registration drive to enhance a community's opportunity to free itself from economic and political servitude. SCLC believes that the most important step the Negro can take is that short walk to the voting booth.

SCLC and Civil Disobedience

SCLC sees civil disobedience as a natural consequence of nonviolence when the resister is confronted by unjust and immoral laws. This does not imply that SCLC advocates either anarchy or lawlessness. The Conference firmly believes that all people have a moral responsibility to obey laws that are just. It recognizes, however, that there also are unjust laws. From a purely moral point of view, an unjust law is one that is out of harmony with the moral law of the universe, or, as the religionist would say, out of harmony with the Law of God. More concretely, an unjust law is one in which the minority is compelled to observe a code which is not binding on the majority. An unjust law is one in which people are required to obey a code that they had no part in making because they were denied the right to vote. In the face of such obvious inequality, where difference is made legal, the nonviolent resister has no alternative but to disobey the unjust law. In disobeying such a law, he does so peacefully, openly and nonviolently. Most important, he *willingly* accepts the penalty for breaking the law. This distinguishes SCLC's position on civil disobedience from the "uncivil disobedience" of the racist opposition in the South. In the face of laws they consider unjust, they seek to defy, evade, and circumvent the law, BUT they are *un-willing* to accept the penalty for breaking the law. The end result of their defiance is anarchy and disrespect for the law. SCLC, on the other hand, believes that civil disobedience involves the highest respect for the law. He who openly disobeys a law that conscience tells him is unjust and willingly accepts the penalty is giving evidence that he so respects the law that he belongs in jail until it is changed. . . .

SCLC and Segregation

SCLC is firmly opposed to segregation in any form that it takes and pledges itself to work unrelentingly to rid every vestige of its scars from our nation through nonviolent means. Segregation is an evil and its presence in our nation has blighted our larger destiny as a leader in world affairs. Segregation does as much harm to the *segregator* as it does to the *segregated*. The *segregated* develops a false sense of inferiority and the *segregator* develops a false sense of superiority, both contrary to the American ideal of democracy. America must rid herself of segregation not alone because it is politically expedient, but because it is morally right!

SCLC and Constructive Program

SCLC's basic program fosters nonviolent resistance to all forms of racial injustice, including state and local laws and practices, even when this means going to jail; and imaginative, bold constructive action to end the demoralization caused by the legacy of slavery and segregation—inferior schools, slums, and second-class citizenship. Thus, the Conference works on two fronts. On the one hand, it resists continuously the system of segregation which is the basic cause of lagging standards; on the other hand, it works constructively to improve the standards themselves. There MUST be a balance between attacking the causes and healing the effects of segregation.

SCLC and the Beloved Community

The ultimate aim of SCLC is to foster and create the "beloved community" in America where brotherhood is a reality. It rejects any doctrine of black supremacy for this merely substitutes one kind of tyranny for another. The Conference does not foster moving the Negro from a position of disadvantage to one of advantage for this would thereby subvert justice. SCLC works for integration. Our ultimate goal is genuine intergroup and interpersonal living—*integration*. Only through nonviolence can reconciliation and the creation of the beloved community be effected. The international focus on America and her internal problems against the dread prospect of a hot war, demand our seeking this end.

We Want Black Power

STUDENT NON-VIOLENT COORDINATING COMMITTEE

Black Men of America Are a Captive People

The black man in America is in a perpetual state of slavery no matter what the white man's propaganda tells us.

The black man in America is exploited and oppressed the same as his black brothers are all over the face of the earth by the same white man. We will never be free until we are all free and that means all black oppressed people all over the earth.

We are not alone in this fight, we are a part of the struggle for self-determination of all black men everywhere. We here in America must unite ourselves to be ready to help our brothers elsewhere.

We must first gain BLACK POWER here in America. Living inside the camp of the leaders of the enemy forces, it is our duty to our Brothers to revolt against the system and create our own system so that we can live as MEN.

We must take over the political and economic systems where we are in the majority in the heart of every major city in this country as well as in the rural areas. We must create our own black culture to erase the lies the white man has fed our minds from the day we were born.

The Black Man in the Ghetto Will Lead the Black Power Movement

The black Brother in the ghetto will lead the Black Power Movement and make the changes that are necessary for its success.

The black man in the ghetto has one big advantage that the bourgeois Negro does not have despite his 'superior' education. He is already living outside the value system white society imposes on all black Americans.

He has to look at things from another direction in order to survive. He is ready. He received his training in the streets, in the jails, from the ADC[1]

Student Non-Violent Coordinating Committee, Chicago Office, *We Want Black Power*, 1967.
[1] Aid to Dependent Children, a major feature of the federal welfare system—ED.

check his mother did not receive in time and the head-beatings he got from the cop on the corner.

Once he makes that first important discovery about the great pride you feel inside as a BLACK MAN and the great heritage of the mother country, Africa, there is no stopping him from dedicating himself to fight the white man's system.

This is why the Black Power Movement is a true revolutionary movement with the power to change men's minds and unmask the tricks the white man has used to keep black men enslaved in modern society.

The Bourgeois Negro Cannot Be a Part of the Black Power Movement

The bourgeois Negro has been force-fed the white man's propaganda and has lived too long in the half-world between white and phony black bourgeois society. He cannot think for himself because he is a shell of a man full of contradictions he cannot resolve. He is not to be trusted under any circumstances until he has proved himself to be 'cured.' There are a minute handful of these 'cured' bourgeois Negroes in the Black Power Movement and they are most valuable but they must not be allowed to take control. They are aware intellectually but under stress will react emotionally to the pressures of white society in the same way a white 'liberal' will expose an unconscious prejudice that he did not even realize he possessed.

What Brother Malcolm X Taught Us about Ourselves

Malcolm X[2] was the first black man from the ghetto in America to make a real attempt to get the white man's fist off the black man. He recognized the true dignity of man—without the white society prejudices about status, education and background that we all must purge from our minds.

Even today, in the Black Power Movement itself we find Brothers who look down on another Brother because of the conditions that life has imposed upon him. The most beautiful thing that Malcolm X taught us is that once a black man discovers for himself a pride of his blackness, he can throw off the shackles of mental slavery and become a MAN in the truest sense of the word. We must move on from the point our Great Black Prince had reached.

We Must Become Leaders for Ourselves

We must not get hung-up in the bag of having one great leader who we depend upon to make decisions. This makes the Movement too vulnerable

---

[2] The former Malcolm Little, a convert to the Nation of Islam, a black separatist group. He was eventually assassinated, apparently by a rival black group—ED.

to those forces the white man uses to keep us enslaved, such as the draft, murder, prison or character assassination.

We have to all learn to become leaders for ourselves and remove all white values from our minds. When we see a Brother using a white value through error it is our duty to the Movement to point it out to him. We must thank our Brothers who show us our own errors. We must discipline ourselves so that if necessary we can leave family and friends at a moment's notice, maybe forever, and know our Brothers have pledged themselves to protect the family we have left behind.

As a part of our education, we must travel to other cities and make contracts with the Brothers in all the ghettos in America so that when the time is right we can unite as one under the banner of BLACK POWER.

Learning to Think Black and Remove White Things from Our Minds

We have got to begin to say and understand with complete assuredness what black is. Black is an inner pride that the white man's language hampers us from expressing. Black is being a complete fanatic, who white society considers insane.

We have to learn that black is so much better than belonging to the white race with the blood of millions dripping from their hands that it goes far beyond any prejudice or resentment. We must fill ourselves with hate for all white things. This is not vengeance or trying to take the white oppressors' place to become new black oppressors but is a oneness with a worldwide black brotherhood.

We must regain respect for the lost religion of our fathers, the spirits of the black earth of Africa. The white man has so poisoned our minds that if a Brother told you he practiced Voodoo you would roll around on the floor laughing at how stupid and superstitious he was.

We have to learn to roll around on the floor laughing at the black man who says he worships the white Jesus. He is truly sick.

We must create our own language for these things that the white man will not understand because a Black Culture exists and it is not the woodcarvings or native dancing it is the black strength inside of true men.

Ideas on Planning for the Future of Black Power

We must infiltrate all government agencies. This will not be hard because black clerks work in all agencies in poor paying jobs and have a natural resentment of the white men who run these jobs.

People must be assigned to seek out these dissatisfied black men and women and put pressure on them to give us the information we need. Any man in overalls, carrying a tool box, can enter a building if he looks like he knows what he is doing.

Modern America depends on many complex systems such as electricity, water, gas, sewerage and transportation and all are vulnerable. Much of the government is run by computers that must operate in air conditioning. Cut off the air conditioning and they cannot function.

We must begin to investigate and learn all of these things so that we can use them if it becomes necessary. We cannot train an army in the local park but we can be ready for the final confrontation with the white man's system.

Remember your Brothers in South Africa and do not delude yourselves that it could not happen here. We must copy the white man's biggest trick, diversion, (Hitler taught them that) and infiltrate all civil rights groups, keep them in confusion so they will be neutralized and cannot be used as a tool of the white power structure.

The civil rights, integrationist movement says to the white man, "If you please, Sir, let us, the 10 percent minority of American have our rights. See how nice and nonviolent we are?"

This is why SNCC calls itself a Human Rights Organization. We belive that we belong to the 90 percent majority of the people on earth that the white man oppresses and that we should not beg the white man for anything. We want what belongs to us as human beings and we intend to get it through BLACK POWER.

How to Deal with Black Traitors

Uncle Tom is too kind of a word. What we have are black traitors, quisslings [sic], collaborators, sell-outs, white Negroes.

We have to expose these people for once and for all for what they are and place them on the side of the oppressor where they belong. Their black skin is a lie and their guilt the shame of all black men. We must ostracize them and if necessary exterminate them.

We must stop fighting a "fair game." We must do whatever is necessary to win BLACK POWER. We have to hate and disrupt and destroy and blackmail and lie and steal and become blood-brothers like the Mau-Mau.

We must eliminate or render ineffective all traitors. We must make them fear to stand up like puppets for the white men, and we must make the world understand that these so-called men do not represent us or even belong to the same black race because they sold out their birthright for a mess of white society pottage. Let them choke on it.

Pitfalls to Avoid on the Path to Black Power

We must learn how close America and Russia are politically. The biggest lie in the world is the cold-war. Money runs the world and it is controlled completely by the white man.

Russia and America run the two biggest money systems in the world and they intend to keep it under their control under any circumstances. Thus, we cannot except any help from Communism or any other "ism."

We must seek out poor peoples movements in South America, Africa and Asia and make our alliances with them. We must not be fooled into thinking that there is a ready-made doctrine that will solve all our problems.

There are only white man's doctrines and they will never work for us. We have to work out our own systems and doctrines and culture.

Why Propaganda Is Our Most Important Tool

The one thing that the white man's system cannot stand is the TRUTH because his system is all based on lies.

There is no such thing as "justice" for a black man in America. The white man controls everything that is said in every book, newspaper, magazine, TV and radio broadcast.

Even the textbooks used in the schools and the bible that is read in the churches are designed to maintain the system for the white man. Each and every one of us is forced to listen to the white man's progaganda every day of our lives.

The political system, economic system, military system, educational system, religious system and anything else you name is used to preserve the status quo of white America getting fatter and fatter while the black man gets more and more hungry.

We must spend our time telling our Brothers the truth.

We must tell them that any black woman who wears a diamond on her finger is wearing the blood of her Brothers and Sisters in slavery in South Africa where one out of every three black babies die before the age of one, from starvation, to make the white man rich.

We must stop wearing the symbols of slavery on our fingers.

We must stop going to other countries to exterminate our Brothers and Sisters for the white man's greed.

We must ask our Brothers which side they are on.

Once you know the truth for yourself it is your duty to dedicate your life to recruiting your Brothers and to counteract the white man's propaganda.

We must disrupt the white man's system to create our own. We must publish newspapers and get radio stations. Black Unity is strength—let's use it now to get BLACK POWER.

13

The Great Society

The nation's political climate was transformed by the election of John F. Kennedy as president in 1960. JFK was not a flaming liberal, but he was young and bold, and his victory, after eight years of the grandfatherly old soldier, Dwight Eisenhower, in the White House, created a sense of new political possibilities.

In fact, the Kennedy administration's domestic achievements were rather modest. The president aroused the idealism of youth with his Peace Corps program and fed American pride by his program to land a human being on the moon during the decade. But virtually all of his liberal New Frontier legislation stalled in Congress. By the time of his tragic assassination in November 1963 little of it had been enacted into law.

Most of the bold legislative advances of the decade started with Kennedy's successor. Lyndon B. Johnson was a very different person from the young man he succeeded. A physically massive Texan, LBJ lacked the polish, glamour, and personal magnetism of his predecessor, but he made up for them by his extraordinary political skills honed by twenty years in Congress and a decade of Democratic party leadership in the Senate. Johnson was able to break the legislative logjam through persuasion, cajolery, deal-making, and arm-twisting. Between early 1964 and 1968 Congress enacted most of his Great Society program, the most sweeping reform agenda since the New Deal a generation before.

These programs established new systems of health-care benefits for retirees (Medicare) and for the needy (Medicaid). They provided massive aid to public education and scholarships for college students. Clean air, clean water, and highway beautification measures supplemented the environmental legislation of the New Deal era. There were also new federal subsidies for the arts and for academic scholarship.

Most innovative and dramatic of all was the War on Poverty, a federal campaign to eliminate want in America through Headstart, the JOB Corps, subsidized legal services, a Community Action Program, and many more initiatives, all under an Office of Economic Opportunity.

The Great Society clearly benefited from initial public support. Running in 1964 for president in his own right against conservative Barry Goldwater, Johnson achieved one of the most sweeping electoral victories in this century, carrying every state but Arizona and a few in the South, and leading his party to unprecedented majorities in both houses of Congress.

LBJ interpreted this success as a liberal mandate, and it was. With prices stable and economic growth high, the nation felt flush—and generous, and Congress was quick to approve the costly new social programs.

In the selections below you will find responses to the Great Society by three groups: defenders, detractors on the right, and detractors on the left. Try to analyze the reasons and reasoning behind each position. Also consider the validity of each viewpoint.

13.1: Defenders (1964)

No one was as eloquent on the goals of the Great Society as Lyndon Johnson himself. The following extract is from the president's speech at the University of Michigan graduation ceremonies in May 1964, where he laid out his ambitious Great Society plan.

Was Johnson's vision utopian, or was it realistic? Can you detect in it antecedents in the form of similar views held by previous reformers? Although a one-time protégé of Franklin Roosevelt, in his previous career as a representative and senator, Johnson was not considered a liberal. At most he seemed a centrist who reflected the racial views and economic interests of his native Texas. How do you explain the apparent shift, as exemplified by the Great Society, when he became president? Can you think of other political leaders whose perspectives changed when they changed office?

The Great Society[1]

LYNDON B. JOHNSON

I have come today from the turmoil of your capital to the tranquility of your campus to speak about the future of your country.

Public Papers of the Presidents of the United States: Lyndon B. Johnson, 1963–64, vol. 1, (Washington, DC: U.S. Government Printing Office, 1965), pp. 704–707.
[1]Footnotes deleted.

The purpose of protecting the life of our nation and preserving the liberty of our citizens is to pursue the happiness of our people. Our success in that pursuit is the test of our success as a nation.

For a century we labored to settle and to subdue a continent. For half a century we called upon unbounded invention and untiring industry to create an order of plenty for all of our people.

The challenge of the next half century is whether we have the wisdom to use that wealth to enrich and elevate our national life, and to advance the quality of our American civilization.

Your imagination, your initiative, and your indignation will determine whether we build a society where progress is the servant of our needs, or a society where old values and new visions are buried under unbridled growth. For in your time we have the opportunity to move not only toward the rich society and the powerful society, but upward to the Great Society.

The Great Society rests on abundance and liberty for all. It demands an end to poverty and racial injustice, to which we are totally committed in our time. But that is just the beginning.

The Great Society is a place where every child can find knowledge to enrich his mind and to enlarge his talents. It is a place where leisure is a welcome chance to build and reflect, not a feared cause of boredom and restlessness. It is a place where the city of man serves not only the needs of the body and the demands of commerce but the desire for beauty and the hunger for community.

It is a place where man can renew contact with nature. It is a place which honors creation for its own sake and for what it adds to the understanding of the race. It is a place where men are more concerned with the quality of their goals than the quantity of their goods.

But most of all, the Great Society is not a safe harbor, a resting place, a final objective, a finished work. It is a challenge constantly renewed, beckoning us toward a destiny where the meaning of our lives matches the marvelous products of our labor.

So I want to talk to you today about three places where we begin to build the Great Society—in our cities, in our countryside, and in our classrooms.

Many of you will live to see the day, perhaps fifty years from now, when there will be 400 million Americans—four-fifths of them in urban areas. In the remainder of this century urban population will double, city land will double, and we will have to build homes, highways, and facilities equal to all those built since this country was first settled. So in the next forty years we must rebuild the entire urban United States.

Aristotle said: "Men come together in cities in order to live, but they remain together in order to live the good life." It is harder and harder to live the good life in American cities today.

The catalogue of ills is long: there is the decay of the centers and the despoiling of the suburbs. There is not enough housing for our people or transportation for our traffic. Open land is vanishing and old landmarks are violated.

Worst of all expansion is eroding the precious and time-honored values of community with neighbors and communion with nature. The loss of these values breeds loneliness and boredom and indifference.

Our society will never be great until our cities are great. Today the frontier of imagination and innovation is inside those cities and not beyond their borders. . . .

A second place where we begin to build the Great Society is in our countryside. We have always prided ourselves on being not only America the strong and America the free, but America the beautiful. Today that beauty is in danger. The water we drink, the food we eat, the very air that we breathe, are threatened with pollution. Our parks are overcrowded, our seashores overburdened. Green fields and dense forests are disappearing.

A few years ago we were greatly concerned about the "Ugly American." Today we must act to prevent an ugly America.

For once the battle is lost, once our natural splendor is destroyed, it can never be recaptured. And once man can no longer walk with beauty or wonder at nature his spirit will wither and his sustenance be wasted.

A third place to build the Great Society is in the classrooms of America. There your children's lives will be shaped. Our society will not be great until every young mind is set free to scan the farthest reaches of thought and imagination. We are still far from that goal. . . .

Each year more than 100,000 high school graduates, with proved ability, do not enter college because they cannot afford it. And if we cannot educate today's youth, what will we do in 1970 when elementary school enrollment will be 5 million greater than 1960? And high school enrollment will rise by 5 million. College enrollment will increase by more than 3 million.

In many places, classrooms are overcrowded and curricula are outdated. Most of our qualified teachers are underpaid, and many of our paid teachers are unqualified. So we must give every child a place to sit and a teacher to learn from. Poverty must not be a bar to learning, and learning must offer an escape from poverty.

But more classrooms and more teachers are not enough. We must seek an educational system which grows in excellence as it grows in size. This means better training for our teachers. It means preparing youth to enjoy their hours of leisure as well as their hours of labor. It means exploring new techniques of teaching, to find new ways to stimulate the love of learning and the capacity for creation.

These are three of the central issues of the Great Society. While our government has many programs directed at those issues, I do not pretend that we have the full answer to those problems. . . .

But I do promise this: We are going to assemble the best thought and the broadest knowledge from all over the world to find those answers for America. I intend to establish working groups to prepare a series of White House conferences and meetings—on the cities, on natural beauty, on the quality of education, and on other emerging challenges. And from these meetings and from this inspiration and from these studies we will begin to set our course toward the Great Society.

The solution to these problems does not rest on a massive program in Washington, nor can it rely solely on the strained resources of local authority. They require us to create new concepts of cooperation, a creative federalism, between the national capital and the leaders of local communities.

Within your lifetime powerful forces, already loosed, will take us toward a way of life beyond the realm of our experience, almost beyond the bounds of our imagination.

For better or for worse, your generation has been appointed by history to deal with those problems and to lead America toward a new age. You have the chance never before afforded to any people in any age. You can help build a society where the demands of morality, and the needs of the spirit, can be realized in the life of the nation.

So, will you join in the battle to give every citizen the full equality which God enjoins and the law requires, whatever his belief, or race, or the color of his skin?

Will you join in the battle to give every citizen an escape from the crushing weight of poverty?

Will you join in the battle to make it possible for all nations to live in enduring peace—as neighbors and not as mortal enemies?

Will you join in the battle to build the Great Society, to prove that our material progress is only the foundation on which we will build a richer life of mind and spirit?

There are those timid souls who say this battle cannot be won; that we are condemned to a soulless wealth. I do not agree. We have the power to shape the civilization that we want. But we need your will, your labor, your hearts, if we are to build that kind of society.

Those who came to this land sought to build more than just a new country. They sought a new world. So I have come here today to your campus to say that you can make their vision our reality. So let us from this moment begin our work so that in the future men will look back and say: It was then, after a long and weary way, that man turned the exploits of his genius to the full enrichment of his life.

13.2: The Attack from the Right (1965)

Predictably, the political right considered the Great Society misdirected and wasteful, another example of good intentions gone berserk. The following brief article by M. Stanton Evans, an associate editor of The National Review, *is representative of the conservative response to the Johnson programs. The* National Review, *published by William F. Buckley, the talented young right-winger who helped keep the conservative banner aloft during the drought years of the 1960s, was, and is, a major voice of the political right in America.*

What are the values and attitudes implicit in Stanton's attack? How do they fit into the evolving conservative agenda? Do they foreshadow the conservatism of a later period? How valid were Stanton's fears and concerns?

The Great Society Condemned

M. STANTON EVANS

Lyndon Johnson's outline of "the Great Society" in his first 1965 address to Congress puts this department in mind of the old saying: If we had some ham, we could have ham and eggs—if we had some eggs.

It begins to appear that in Johnson's patchwork Utopia, the same thought will apply: If we had some free enterprise, we could have free enterprise and economy in government—if we had some economy in government. For despite his obeisances to liberty and to reduction of "waste," it becomes clear that Johnson means to conduct us with all deliberate speed into a society which is at once compulsory and insolvent.

The President's "State of the Union" address [of January 1965] made it clear that, whatever the legislative specifics, he intends to thrust the authority of the Federal Government into every conceivable sector of national life. To elevate "the quality of our people," a dubious task for government, Johnson proposed new or enlarged federal intrusion into health, education, job training, unemployment compensation, area redevelopment, transportation, housing, dentistry, mental illness, municipal life, landscaping, training of law enforcement officers, air pollution, "natural beauty," and, of course, poverty.

Added to this program for a society directed by the compulsions of government was Johnson's bid for augmented compulsory unionism through repeal of section 14(b) of the Taft-Hartley law (which allows passage of state right-to-work statutes), described with a bland Orwellian twist as a measure "to reduce conflicts" that "divide" our citizens. The characterization, on second thought, is true enough. Freedom tends to divide people.

All of this was rounded off with some sonorous prose about fighting "waste" and seeking "economies" in government, words which look as curious alongside the bulk of Johnson's address as do the remarks about American freedom with which he began his speech. In point of fact, the schedule of spending suggested by his program of intervention would send federal outlays to new heights—outlays which have already reached the record level of $125 billion annually.

As an example of his opposition to "waste," Johnson said he had managed to save $3.5 billion in the past year. He did not make clear just what this sta-

M. Stanton Evans, "At Home," *The National Review,* February 2, 1965, p. 6. © 1965 by National Review, Inc., 150 East 35th Street, New York, NY 10016. Reprinted by permission.

tistic was based on, but it has the logical resonance of the housewife's argument that purchase of a coat for $50 when it originally cost $75 is a "saving" of $25. The discernible truth of the matter is that, under Johnson, spending has exceeded the stratospheric levels it achieved under Kennedy. This fact has been concealed by a number of devices, including spending authorized by LBJ which was tagged to the last Kennedy budget, and a request for nearly $10 billion in "new obligational authority" which was not reflected in the cash budget for Fiscal '65.

Should all the things Johnson mentioned be realized in legislation, America will have virtually completed its transition from free enterprise to the planned economy. This new overlay of paternalism would create a web of federal authority so far-reaching and powerful that it is doubtful the United States could recover the vigor of its once-free institutions. Even without Johnson's proposals, the reach of federal power is immense, much more so than is generally realized. What Johnson is proposing is to fill in the lacunae, to complete the edifice of power which has been a-building for 30 years.

The Federal Government already wields with considerable effect the power inherent in heavy taxation, inflation, and control of the banking system. It exerts pressure on all those who receive subsidies from it—and who thereby accept controls from it as well. It tells subsidized farmers how much they can plant, and punishes non-subsidized businessmen for a wide assortment of federally-designated misdemeanors. It sets prices of commodities from steel to milk, regulates the sale of stocks and bonds, hectors the management of the drug industry, polices advertising, seeks to dictate terms for packaging and lending, and sets the conditions for selling a pack of cigarettes.

Federal authority also decides how much money people will be paid for working (through minimum wage legislation), and for not working (through unemployment legislation). It decides whom a businessman shall hire and fire, and to whom barbecue stands and hot dog emporiums will purvey their services. It forbids employers to give truthful information to employees concerning unions, and even forbids an entrepreneur from going out of business if he so chooses. It regulates railroads, airlines, truckers, power companies, radio and TV stations. And more.

To these already staggering powers, Johnson would add still others, completing and tightening the web of regulation. In his so-called "Consumer's Package" last year, he advocated federal superintendence of butchers, cosmetic producers, commercial advertising, lenders, etc. Through a program of subsidies, he would extend the hand of federal authority into the administration of the country's elementary and secondary schools. Through his "medicare" proposal, he and his supporters would put federal power amidships of the delicate relationship between patient and doctor. Through the U.S. Employment Service, his regime would have federal authority involved in the ordinary hiring practices of American businessmen.

Just where, we may well wonder, is federal power *not* to be exerted? If Johnson's agenda for intervention is enacted into law, America will have become a society of drones without liberty or responsibility, reminiscent of Tocqueville's all-powerful state, which "provides for their security, foresees and supplies their necessities, facilitates their pleasures, manages their principal concerns, directs their industry, regulates the descent of property, and subdivides their inheritances."

13.3:   The Attack from the Left (1966)

The years of the Great Society also witnessed a powerful revival of left-wing political activism in the United States. During this period university students, civil rights militants, and cultural dissenters all came to view white, middle-class, liberal America as repressive, exploitative, and stultifying. To most of the new radicals the Great Society was at best a feeble response to the country's real problems, and at worst an effort to evade those problems and deflect any fundamental attempt to solve them.

In the selections below two left-wing activists, Jack Minnis of the Student Non-Violent Coordinating Committee, and Tom Hayden, a founder of the key student New Left[1] organization, Students for a Democratic Society, attack aspects of the Great Society programs.

Minnis, a white radical, was director of SNCC's research department, and worked in SNCC's Atlanta headquarters. He describes a small corner of the Great Society as it operated in the south. But he obviously intends his criticism to apply more widely. What in essence is Minnis saying about the Great Society at the grass-roots level? Is he being fair to the Job Development Program?

Hayden's attack is broader. He is deeply skeptical of the so-called welfare state and of liberal reform generally. Why might a radical hold such views? Are his charges that the Great Society programs were underfunded correct? What does he mean when he says the poverty program acted like a "parent"? What sort of social change do you suppose Hayden would have preferred to the Great Society programs?

How the Great Society Solves the Servant Problem

JACK MINNIS

On February 1 [1966] Lyndon announced that he was launching yet another battle in the war on poverty. He said he had instructed his Secretary of Labor to use existing funds and laws for what he called his Job Development

---

[1]The New Left was a political movement of the 1960s that recruited young people particularly. It emphasized "participatory democracy" as the cure for social injustice and bitterly opposed American Cold War foreign policy.

Jack Minnis, *Life with Lyndon in the Great Society*, vol. 1, no. 6.

Program. Lyndon said that there is a labor shortage in employment areas such as domestic service, and he wanted Secretary Wirtz to do something to provide more trained servants for families which don't like to do their dirty work for themselves.

The *Washington Post* calls the new program "dignifying the service jobs that are necessary to running a modern home and meeting the needs of family life today." The *Post* did not explain just how you could inject dignity of any kind into a relationship which requires that one person, in order to live, binds himself to the personal service of another. Nor did the *Post* explain what's to become of those families that can't afford to hire someone to run "a modern home" for them. But the *Post* did describe one of Lyndon's Job Development Programs which is underway in LaGrange, Georgia.

Lyndon's Office of Manpower and Training (OMAT) got together with a retired schoolteacher, Emmy Murray, in LaGrange. OMAT put up the money to redecorate an old roadhouse, and to equip it with various household appliances. Emmy is now teaching prospective household servants "cleanliness and work discipline," which is to say she's teaching Negro women how to address Miss Anne and Mr. Charlie with the proper degree of deference, teaching them how to shuffle their feet and tug their forelocks and convince the white folks of their profound satisfaction with a life of servitude.

The top wage available to the best-trained household servants in LaGrange—that is, the top graduates of Emmy's careful instruction—is $4 per day. If the servant works every day of the year (and this is usually the case) she makes $1,460 per year. This is just half of what Lyndon says (out of the other side of his mouth) is necessary for a minimum subsistence, and about one-fourth of what is really necessary for a decent standard of living. And this is being done with federal tax money from Lyndon, the Second Great Emancipator of Black America.

There are two kinds of people in LaGrange who will be employing Emmy's graduates. The first kind is represented by the Callaway family. They own Callaway Mills, a textile manufacturer which is LaGrange's largest employer, employing more than 3,000 persons in a town of 23,000. The Callaway family owns the mills in a peculiar way. They don't own the stock of the corporation personally. Rather they control tax-exempt foundations, which, in turn, own the stock. In this way dividends paid by the mills to the foundations are free of federal income tax.

Callaway Mills received more than $600,000 of federal money last year as part of Lyndon's program of subsidizing the textile manufacturers. If they used all this to employ household servants for the various branches of the family, they'd be able to hire about 410 servants as the going wage. Thus the Callaways could use the money Lyndon gave them, which is tax free, to employ more servants than an Oriental Potentate, the servants having been trained to the peak of servile perfection with money supplied by Lyndon from the federal taxes from which the Callaway's are exempt.

   The second kind of prospective employers for Emmy's graduates are the workers in the Callaway Mills. Diane McKaig, who works in the Atlanta office of Lyndon's Labor Department, explains that these Callaway employees don't make much money (she doesn't explain why, nor does she compare the amount they make with the amount the Callaways make), so the servants—she calls them "homemaking aides," a bit of double-talk worthy of Lyndon himself—have to be "taught to make low-cost dishes, including surplus foods." She doesn't say whether the servants will be preparing surplus foods for themselves, or for the Callaway employees—perhaps both, considering the general level of wages.

   The white female Callaway employees, of course, can't work in the mills unless they can find Negroes to care for their children and homes while they're at the mills. Since the Callaways don't pay their workers much, the workers can't pay their Negro servants much. So the upshot of Lyndon's new job program, is to provide cheap and well-trained servants for the Callaway employees, at a price the employees can afford to pay without requiring a raise from the Callaways.

   The Callaways exploit their white workers at low wages, and the white workers exploit their Negro servants at even lower wages. Lyndon lavishes hundreds of thousands a year on the Callaways, in the form of textile subsidies, and provides federal money with which to train Negro servants for the Callaways and their white mill employees.

   It takes the guts of a burglar to call a sewer like this the Great Society. But, whatever he's short of, Lyndon's always been long on guts.

Welfare Liberalism and Social Change

TOM HAYDEN

Americans find it unthinkable that their country can be corrupt at the center, guilty as a society of inhuman behavior. This is true even among American reformers, most of whom hold that discrimination, poverty, and foreign intervention are simply flaws in a generally humanitarian record. While the massacre of the Vietnamese grinds on, while Negro uprisings spread to every city, while the public looks back on August 6 as Luci's wedding[1] and Hiroshima is forgotten, the progressive American—he may be a liberal businessman, university president, technical assistance expert, or trade unionist—is perhaps uneasy but remains basically complacent, secure in the justness of our objectives at home and abroad.

   Since early in the century, the task of American leaders has been to make "peace," "self-determination" and the promise of a better life the language that explains American purposes. Probably none of them has ever willfully

Tom Hayden, "Welfare Liberalism and Social Change." From *The Great Society Reader*, edited by Marvin Gettleman and David Mermelstein. Copyright © 1967 by Random House, Inc. Reprinted by permission of Random House, Inc.

[1]Luci Baines Johnson, LBJ's younger daughter, who was married in 1965—ED.

deprived a man of food or killed another in cold blood; they order political and economic suppression and murder—by gas, napalm, or nuclear weapons—only as a means of realizing peace and preserving democracy.

Until the day their language changes to that of naked power, it is easy to assume they are not fiends but honorable men. This is the assumption that makes reformers hope for their country. But it is sheer indulgence not to confront the consequences of our leaders' actions. We need to stop giving weight to protestations of good intentions, and to examine instead the worth of American words in the light of American deeds.

The general contradiction most worth examining is between the philosophy and the practice of the liberal-welfare state that has been constructed at home and is now being forcibly exported to other parts of the world. It is the belief in our commitment to welfare that, more than anything else, allows our honorable men to sleep at night while other men are murdered, jailed or hungry.

The legitimacy gained by the industrial unions, the welfare legislation passed in the thirties and forties, and now the civil rights and antipoverty reforms of the sixties—these are seen as part of a long sweep toward a society of economic and social justice. But there is, in fact, little evidence to justify the view that the social reforms of the past thirty years actually improved the quality of American life in a lasting way, and there is much evidence which suggests that many of the reforms gained were illusory or token, serving chiefly to sharpen the capacity of the system for manipulation and oppression. . . .

Look closely at the social legislation upon which the notion of domestic improvement is based. The Wagner Act was supposed to effect unionization of workers; but today the unionized labor force is shrinking. . . . The Social Security laws were supposed to support people in distress, but today many are still not covered, and those who are solely dependent on Social Security payments cannot make ends meet. Unemployment compensation policies were supposed to aid men in need of jobs, but today many are still without coverage, while benefits represent a smaller and smaller share of the cost of living. . . . The difficult struggle to enact even a token policy of public medical care, the hollow support for public education, the stagnation and starvation of broader programs for health, recreation, and simple city services—all this suggests that the welfare state is more machinery than substance. . . .

Seen in this context, the 1965 antipoverty program should evoke little optimism. The amount of money allotted is a pittance, and most of it is going to local politicians, school boards, welfare agencies, housing authorities, professional personnel and even the police; its main thrust is to shore up sagging organizational machinery, not to offer the poor a more equitable share of income and influence. Meaningful involvement of the poor is frustrated by the poverty planners' allegiance to existing local power centers. In reality, the poor only flavor the program. A few are co-opted into it, but only as atomized individuals. They do not have independent organizational strength, as do the machines and social agencies.

Some of the more sophisticated poverty planners believe that the involvement of the poor is essential to effective programs; thus the heavy emphasis on, and debate about, the need for "maximum feasible participation" of the poor. This policy concept rests upon the conviction that the modern poor cannot be socialized upward and into the mainstream of American life in the tradition of the earlier immigrants.

The slavery period has left the Negro poor, according to this view, without the tight-knit culture, the economic skills, and the expanding market opportunities that were so common in the life of the immigrants. The result is the breakdown of the family, at least in its function of preparing the young to take their places in the slots offered by the established industrial machine.

Though it is not officially put this way, the poverty program thus seeks to be a substitute parent more than a meal ticket, an agency of socialization more than of welfare. Not only is this the conception that underlies the Job Corps camps and the new batteries of "psychological service" counsellors; it underlies the Community Action Program as well.

Self-organization, the development of skills, helping oneself through social action, are supposedly the means by which the ghetto residents ("the target population") will be rehabilitated. The amount and kind of conscious stress on this process vary from city to city. One view is evident in testimony given to a congressional subcommittee by Denton Brooks, director of the Chicago antipoverty program. Asked whether the tactics of conflict, such as rent strikes, might be necessary for progress, his answer was negative for this reason:

> Once you get the interaction of all groups, once you have a policy that something should be done for the poor, once this becomes a national policy, then you work on a problem and find a positive solution. Then the need for protest is eliminated.

The practical impact of such policies was explained by Father Theodore R. Gibson, assigned as federal trouble-shooter for Newark in the summer of 1965. Gibson was

> convinced that the antipoverty program was the key to racial peace in Newark this summer. . . . "All the things I saw that would make for trouble got their answer in the antipoverty program," asserted the Community Relations Service representative. "What saved the community more than anything else was the involvement of so many people in so many things. Even members of the most militant groups," he said, "were so busy working on antipoverty projects that they had little time to stir up dissension."

Many of the poverty planners concede that progress will involve some element of conflict and that the poor cannot be painlessly assimilated into the greater society. The feeling is that change can be accomplished through a "dialogue" between the poor and the powerful, in which the poor assert their needs as clearly as necessary. But while dialogue is promoted, final decisions remain in traditional hands. Sargent Shriver[2] encourages "representative neighborhood advisory organizations" to give "advice on programs," which can then be "channeled" to the community action agency. This is all Shiver sees as necessary to give neighborhood people "an effective voice in the conduct and administration of neighborhood-based programs."

The poverty program, in short, assumes the poor are groups of damaged individuals who need charity, relief, technical aid, or retraining. What the program cannot accept is the possibility that the poor are "natives" pitted against "colonial" structures at home that exclude and exploit them. . . .

Welfare liberalism has brought new insecurities to the American exploited. The poor are without the effective ability to control any economic resources in the welfare state. Antipoverty funds are controlled "from above" by city or federal officials. There is no unionization of tenants or welfare clients to provide financing and protection. Unable to gather independent capital from the public sector, the poor are considered unqualified for credit by banks and lending institutions. This lack of meaningful economic power divides the contemporary poor from earlier immigrant generations, who entered an expanding economy and formed unions and co-ops to advance their interests. Lacking any security or power, the "left out" whites and the poor Negroes are more likely to vote for their "masters"—those who control the public housing, welfare, and unemployment checks—or not vote at all, rather than risk an independent political initiative.

The "colonial power" maintains control of the ghetto from the outside, through the police, social agencies, and a cultivated group of colonized natives ("Uncle Toms"). The idea is conveyed, by every means, that only the governors are qualified to govern, that the only chance for self-gain, even survival, lies in trying to be like the governors, that protest is a sign of maladjustment and furthermore can never succeed. This colonialism is as real as the more traditional colonialism of Britain and France, despite our official national ideology of equality. . . .

Defenders of the welfare state—professional or activist—say that its critics overlook (1) the political and material gains that have been made for the poor under its auspices, and (2) the relative freedom to continue organizing protest that it guarantees. The point, however, is not to deny the gains. No economic improvement or civil liberty, however small, should be underestimated. But it is something else to point to those gains in defense of an entire system. In the first place, the gains are minute in relation to what the American productive system could make available to its people. Second, the very security of those gains is not guaranteed without continuous militant pressure. Third, the struggle for those gains left most white workers with more security but at the price of remaining racist in outlook, while still work-

---

[2]Shriver, a brother-in-law of John Kennedy, was Johnson's appointee as head of the Office of Economic Opportunity, the agency that administered the War on Poverty—ED.

ing under alienating conditions. Fourth, the process of reform seemed to undermine the spirit of insurgency itself by institutionalizing and limiting it.

Consider the caseworker who tells the client she should have died in slavery, and the civic action worker who calls the peasant an uncivilized pig; the policeman beating the Negro even after he collapses unconscious; the administrator ordering shock treatment for the mental patient screaming about his rights; the executive looking for a black prostitute during lunch; the professor interviewing an Asian official while a beaten prisoner lies on the floor; the worker reading about the machine that will replace him; the judge at juvenile court deciding to put away the young delinquent until she is 21; the landlord come with the constable to evict the tenants on rent strike. These are the everyday realities of a society that preaches liberal intentions.

We see, then, that welfare liberalism is more than a system of co-optation, more than an air-conditioned nightmare. It is also a system that punishes, with whatever violence is necessary, those who balk at its embrace. In this sense its liberalism is a facade over a more coercive conservative core.

The need is not to expand the welfare state, not to incorporate the "backward" parts into it, but to replace it altogether with a political economy that serves, rather than denies, the needs of the poor and millions of other people in this country and abroad. But replacing the political economy is not a negotiable issue arrived at through institutional reform. It is a revolutionary issue, resolved by building new institutions to replace the old. . . .

A Summary Word

It would be foolish to make of these speculations predictions-to-live-by. Revolutionaries are often among the last to know whether they are succeeding. In the 1930s radicals were surprised by the staying power of a capitalism that they had thought doomed. In the 1960s radicals may yet be surprised by the collapse of a welfare-capitalism that now seems flexible but invulnerable.

At any rate, humane opposition to the American welfare empire must be constructed not in speculative theory, but in action. Ideas, after all, are welcome commodities, easily absorbed in the new system. Only through combined action will ordinary men create the beginning of a different society. The experience and practice of solidarity is a deeper form of opposition to the welfare empire than any radical critique. Only a community contributing its own movements and institutions can fill the vacuum of local political life that the authoritarian society creates. Only men who know themselves to be capable decision-makers can consider fighting for a thoroughly democratic society. Only men able to improvise and invent vocations of their own will be prepared to demand, and live in, a decentralized, automated society of the future. Only men with experience in a universe of mixed races and cultures will be able to shed national chauvinism and ethnocentrism. Furthermore, masses of men will only be persuaded of change when some of them create a compelling, if very imperfect, example of what the future might be.

The real alternative to bureaucratic welfarism is to be found budding in the experience of men who form communities—whether a freedom school, a community union, a teach-in, or a wildcat strike—to struggle as equals for their own self-determination. Such communities come and go, existing at their best during intense periods of solidarity. But even where they fail to achieve institutional reality, these communities become a permanent part of this generation's consciousness of the possible. The new society still takes shape in the womb of the old.

14

The New Feminism

The social insurgency of the 1960s extended beyond the civil rights movement. Other Americans besides blacks, feeling themselves denied respect, excluded from power, or kept from economic advancement, also mobilized for collective action against the social and economic status quo. During the sixties and seventies Hispanic Americans, gay Americans, Native Americans, and others formed defense or liberation organizations, often closely modeled on the black civil rights groups.

None of these liberation movements had such pervasive consequences as the New Feminism. Like the others, it owed much to the civil rights crusade, but it had distinctive roots of its own. The new movement was in part a rebound from the 1950s, when most women had acquiesced in the domestic suburban life style and feminism as an ideology virtually disappeared. It also drew sustenance from the frustration of well-educated postwar American women with bright, well-furnished minds and no interesting and rewarding place to go. It differed from the feminism of the past, which emphasized political and civil rights, by its focus on social and economic equality and its sharper challenge to traditional gender roles.

The New Feminism can probably be dated from 1961 with the creation by John F. Kennedy of the President's Commission on the Status of Women. Although it accomplished little directly, the commission helped create a network of activists dedicated to expanding women's rights and improving women's lot. Two years later a Long Island housewife and magazine writer, Betty Friedan, jolted the New Feminism into full life with a three hundred-page manifesto, *The Feminine Mystique*, that denounced the gilded cage of postwar suburbia and called for a revitalized woman's movement.

In 1966 the activists organized NOW, the National Organization for Women, with Friedan as president. Dedicated to bringing "women into full participation in the mainstream of American society . . . [and] exercising all the privileges and responsibilities thereof in truly equal partnership with men," NOW was middle class in membership and hierarchical in structure. It accepted male members. It lobbied for its goals in Congress and the state legislatures and supported politicians who favored its programs. By the 1970s one of NOW's chief goals was to secure adoption of the Equal Rights Amendment to the Constitution forbidding both the states and the federal government to deny "equality of rights under the law . . . on account of sex."

Toward the end of the sixties still newer groups of feminists who favored more militant tactics and supported more radical goals challenged NOW's positions and leadership. Many of these activists were recruits from the student New Left that had appeared in the early sixties and caught the public's attention for its attacks on university administrations, racism, and the Vietnam War.

The militants favored more than reforming of "sexist" society by laws expanding and protecting women's rights. Rather, they sought to overthrow the "patriarchal" system they considered fundamental to all oppressive societies and to replace it with one where gender was socially and politically irrelevant. Many demanded the radical transformation of existing male-female relationships and the total reordering of the family. Such militants generally had little faith in electoral politics or legislative lobbying. Some favored inciting socialist revolution to destroy patriarchy. Others believed change would come through the transformation of social sensibility by propaganda, civil disobedience, militant demonstrations, and "consciousness-raising." Most radical feminist groups sought to avoid top-down, hierarchical control of their organizations and often grouped themselves into egalitarian "collectives."

The selections below provide an opportunity to discuss and evaluate the New Feminism, both the middle-of-the-road sort and the more radical kind. You will also find antifeminist viewpoints. Feminism is still a controversial issue today, and it may not be easy to be objective about some of the opinions expressed below. But once again try to use your critical judgment in considering the competing positions.

14.1:   The National Organization for Women's Bill of Rights (1967)

At its first annual conference in 1967 NOW adopted the following Bill of Rights. The document of course was intended to parallel the first ten amendments to the federal Constitution, which are the original Bill of Rights. Does the NOW manifesto put forth a program that was bold for its time? Does it still seem bold today? Are any parts of the NOW Bill of Rights still controversial? Which one(s)? Why?

Bill of Rights

NOW (NATIONAL ORGANIZATION FOR WOMEN)

Adopted at NOW's first national conference, Washington, D.C., 1967

I. Equal Rights Constitutional Amendment
II. Enforce Law Banning Sex Discrimination in Employment
III. Maternity Leave Rights in Employment and in Social Security Benefits
IV. Tax Deduction for Home and Child Care Expenses for Working Parents
V. Child Day Care Centers
VI. Equal and Unsegregated Education
VII. Equal Job Training Opportunities and Allowances for Women in Poverty
VIII. The Right of Women to Control Their Reproductive Lives

WE DEMAND:

I.   That the U.S. Congress immediately pass the Equal Rights Amendment to the Constitution to provide that "Equality of rights under the law shall not be denied or abridged by the United States or by any State on account of sex," and that such then be immediately ratified by the several States.

II.   That equal employment opportunity be guaranteed to all women, as well as men, by insisting that the Equal Employment Opportunity Com-mission enforces the prohibitions against racial discrimination.

III.   That women be protected by law to ensure their rights to return to their jobs within a reasonable time after childbirth without loss of seniority or other accrued benefits, and be paid maternity leave as a form of social security and/or employee benefit.

IV.   Immediate revision of tax laws to permit the deduction of home and child-care expenses for working parents.

V.   That child-care facilities be established by law on the same basis as parks, libraries, and public schools, adequate to the needs of children from the pre-school years through adolescence, as a community resource to be used by all citizens from all income levels.

VI.   That the right of women to be educated to their full potential equally with men be secured by Federal and State legislation, eliminating all discrimination and segregation by sex, written and unwritten, at all levels of education, including colleges, graduate and professional schools, loans and fellowships, and Federal and State training programs such as the Job Corps.

VII.   The right of women in poverty to secure job training, housing, and family allowances on equal terms with men, but without prejudice to a parent's right to remain at home to care for his or her children; revision of welfare legislation and poverty programs which deny women dignity, privacy, and self-respect.

VIII. The right of women to control their own reproductive lives by removing from the penal code laws limiting access to contraceptive information and devices, and by repealing penal laws governing abortion.

14.2: Radical Feminism (1969, 1968)

Radical feminism came in several varieties. Some radical feminists emphasized the economic roots of women's oppression. Others saw sexism as independent of economic systems. In some ways the second version was more radical than the first, since its partisans often attacked the nuclear family itself as inherently oppressive to women—and children.

Below are two examples of radical feminist views dating from the late 1960s. The first item is a statement adopted by the New York Radical Feminists to express their overall philosophy at their founding meeting in 1969. The second is a manifesto issued by the Radical Feminists' precursors, Radical women, shortly before the group held a widely publicized protest demonstration at the 1968 Miss America Beauty Pageant in Atlantic City.

Is the Radical Feminists' statement antimale, as critics have charged? What forces does it emphasize as crucial for molding women's attitudes and characteristics? Is its grim picture of women as totally oppressed valid?

The Miss America Pageant protest created a sensation and undoubtedly made a broad public aware of radical feminist views. But it probably did not endear the group or their positions to a majority of Americans. Although none of the protesters at Atlantic City actually burned their brassieres, the media dismissively labeled them "bra-burners," and the tag stuck.

Why would the demonstration at the Miss America Pageant have offended conventional Americans? How might you defend the radical feminist positions and tactics? Was the pageant a valid target for feminists? What feminist attitudes lay behind their attack on such a public ritual?

Politics of the Ego: A Manifesto for New York Radical Feminists[1]

ANNE KOEDT

Radical feminism recognizes the oppression of women as a fundamental political oppression wherein women are categorized as an inferior class based upon their sex. It is the aim of radical feminism to organize politically to destroy this sex class system.

[Anne Koedt], "Politics of the Ego: A Manifesto for New York Radical Feminists," in *Notes from the Second Year* (n.p., n.d.).
[1]Footnotes deleted.

As radical feminists we recognize that we are engaged in a power struggle with men, and that the agent of our oppression is man insofar as he identifies with and carries out the supremacy privileges of the male role. For while we realize that the liberation of women will ultimately mean the liberation of men from their destructive role as oppressor, we have no illusion that men will welcome this liberation without a struggle.

Radical feminism is political because it recognizes that a group of individuals (men) have organized together for power over women, and that they have set up institutions throughout society to maintain this power.

A political power institution is set up for a purpose. We believe that the purpose of male chauvinism is primarily to obtain psychological ego satisfaction, and that only secondarily does this manifest itself in economic relationships. For this reason we do not believe that capitalism, or any other economic system, is the cause of female oppression, nor do we believe that female oppression will disappear as a result of a purely economic revolution. The political oppression of women has its own class dynamic; and that dynamic must be understood in terms previously called "non-political"—namely the politics of the ego.[2]

Thus the purpose of the male power group is to fulfill a need. That need is psychological, and derives from the supremacist assumptions of the male identity—namely that the male identity be sustained through its ability to have power over the female ego. Man establishes his "manhood" in direct proportion to his ability to have his ego override woman's, and derives his strength and self-esteem through this process. This male need, though destructive, is in that sense impersonal. It is not out of a desire to hurt the woman that man dominates and destroys her; it is out of a need for a sense of power that he necessarily must destroy her ego and make it subservient to his. Hostility to women is a secondary effect, to the degree that a man is not fulfilling his own assumptions of male power he hates women. Similarly, a man's failure to establish himself supreme among other males (as for example a poor white male) may make him channel his hostility into his relationship with women, since they are one of the few political groups over which he can still exercise power.

As women we are living in a male power structure, and our roles become necessarily a function of men. The services we supply are services to the male ego. We are rewarded according to how well we perform these services. Our skill—our profession—is our ability to be feminine—that is, dainty, sweet, passive, helpless, ever-giving and sexy. In other words, everything to help reassure man that he is primary. If we perform successfully, our skills are rewarded. We "marry well"; we are treated with benevolent paternalism; we are deemed successful women, and may even make the "women's pages."

If we do not choose to perform these ego services, but instead assert ourselves as primary to ourselves, we are denied the necessary access to alterna-

---

[2]Ego: We are using the classical definition rather than the Freudian: that is, the sense of individual self as distinct from others.

tives to express our self-assertion. Decision-making positions in the various job fields are closed to us; politics (left, right or liberal) are barred in other than auxiliary roles; our creative efforts are *a priori* judged not serious because we are females; our day-to-day lives are judged failures because we have not become "real women."

Rejection is economic in that women's work is underpaid. It is emotional in that we are cut off from human relationships because we choose to reject the submissive female role. We are trapped in an alien system, just as the worker under capitalism is forced to sell his economic services in a system which is set up against his self-interest.

Sexual Institutions

The oppression of women is manifested in particular institutions, constructed and maintained to keep women in their place. Among these are the institutions of marriage, motherhood, love, and sexual intercourse (the family unit is incorporated by the above). Through these institutions the woman is taught to confuse her biological sexual differences with her total human potential. Biology is destiny, she is told. Because she has childbearing capacity, she is told that motherhood and child rearing is her function, not her option. Because she has childbearing capacity she is told that it is her function to marry and have the man economically maintain her and "make the decisions." Because she has the physical capacity for sexual intercourse, she is told that sexual intercourse too is her function, rather than just a voluntary act which she may engage in as an expression of her general humanity.

In each case *her* sexual difference is rationalized to trap her within it, while the male sexual difference is rationalized to imply an access to all areas of human activity.

Love, in the context of an oppressive male-female relationship, becomes an emotional cement to justify the dominant-submissive relationship. The man "loves" the woman who fulfills her submissive ego-boosting role. The woman "loves" the man she is submitting to—that is, after all, why she "lives for him." LOVE, magical and systematically unanalyzed, becomes the emotional rationale for the submission of one ego to the other. And it is deemed every woman's natural function to love.

Radical feminism believes that the popularized version of love has thus been politically to cloud and justify an oppressive relationship between men and women, and that in reality there can be no genuine love until the need to *control* the growth of another is replaced by love *for* the growth of another.

Learning to Become Feminine

The process of training women for their female role begins as far back as birth, when a boy child is preferred over a girl child. In her early years, when the basic patterns of her identity are being established, it is reinforced in her that her female role is not a choice but a fact. Her future will be spent performing the same basic functions as her mother and women before her. Her life is already determined. She is not given the choice of exploring activity toys. Her brothers play astronaut, doctor, scientist, race-car driver. She plays little homemaker, future mother (dolls), and nurse (doctor's helper). Her brothers are given activity toys; the world is their future. She is given service toys. She is already learning that her future will be in the maintenance of others. Her ego is repressed at all times to prepare her for this future submissiveness. She must dress prettily and be clean; speak politely; seek approval; please. Her brothers are allowed to fight, get dirty, be aggressive and be self-assertive.

As she goes through school she learns that subjects which teach mastery and control over the world, such as science and math, are male subjects; while subjects which teach appearance, maintenance, or sentiment, such as home economics or literature, are female subjects. School counselors will recommend nursing for girls, while they will encourage boys to be doctors. Most of the best colleges will accept only a token sprinkling of women (quota system), regardless of academic abilities.

By the time she is of marrying age she has been prepared on two levels. One, she will realize that alternatives to the traditional female role are both prohibitive and prohibited; two, she will herself have accepted on some levels the assumptions about her female role.

Internalization

It is not only through denying women human alternatives that men are able to maintain their positions of power. It is politically necessary for any oppressive group to convince the oppressed that they are in fact inferior, and therefore deserve their situation. For it is precisely through the destruction of women's egos that they are robbed of their ability to resist.

For the sake of our own liberation, we must learn to overcome this damage to ourselves through internalization. We must begin to destroy the notion that we are indeed only servants to the male ego, and must begin to reverse the systematic crushing of women's egos by constructing alternate selves that are healthy, independent and self-assertive. We must, in short, help each other to transfer the ultimate power of judgment about the value of our lives from men to ourselves.

It remains for us as women to fully develop a new dialectic of sex class—an analysis of the way in which sexual identity and institutions reinforce one another.

No More Miss America![1]

RADICAL WOMEN (ORGANIZATION)

August 1968

On September 7th in Atlantic City, the Annual Miss America Pageant will again crown "your ideal." But this year, reality will liberate the contest auc-

"NOW (National Organization for Women) Bill of Rights" and "No More Miss America" from *Sisterhood Is Powerful: An Anthology of Writings from the Women's Liberation Movement,* edited by Robin Morgan. (New York: Vintage Books, 1970), pp. 521–524. Copyright © 1970 by Robin Morgan. Reprinted by permission of Edite Kroll Literary Agency.
[1]Footnotes deleted.

tion-block in the guise of "genyooine" de-plasticized, breathing women. Women's Liberation Groups, black women, high-school and college women, women's peace groups, women's welfare and social-work groups, women's job-equality groups, pro-birth control and pro-abortion groups—women of every political persuasion—all are invited to join us in a day-long boardwalk-theater event, starting at 1:00 p.m. on the Boardwalk in front of Atlantic City's Convention Hall. We will protest the image of Miss America, an image that oppresses women in every area in which it purports to represent us. There will be: Picket Lines; Guerrilla Theater; Leafleting; Lobbying Visits to the contestants urging our sisters to reject the Pageant Farce and join us; a huge Freedom Trash Can (into which we will throw bras, girdles, curlers, false eyelashes, wigs, and representative issues of *Cosmopolitan, Ladies' Home Journal, Family Circle,* etc.—bring any such woman-garbage you have around the house); we will also announce a Boycott of all those commercial products related to the Pageant, and the day will end with a Women's Liberation rally at midnight when Miss America is crowned on live television. Lots of other surprises are being planned (come and add your own!) but we do not plan heavy disruptive tactics and so do not expect a bad police scene. It should be a groovy day on the Boardwalk in the sun with our sisters. In case of arrests, however, we plan to reject all male authority and demand to be busted by policewomen only. (In Atlantic City, women cops are not permitted to make arrests—dig that!)

Male chauvinist-reactionaries on this issue had best stay away, nor are male liberals welcome in the demonstrations. But sympathetic men can donate money as well as cars and drivers.

Male reporters will be refused interviews. We reject patronizing reportage. *Only newswomen will be recognized.*

The Ten Points

We Protest:

1. *The Degrading Mindless-Boob-Girlie Symbol.* The Pageant contestants epitomize the roles we are all forced to play as women. The parade down the runway blares the metaphor of the 4-H Club county fair, where the nervous animals are judged for teeth, fleece, etc., and where the best "specimen" gets the blue ribbon. So are women in our society forced daily to compete for male approval, enslaved by ludicrous "beauty" standards we ourselves are conditioned to take seriously.
2. *Racism with Roses.* Since its inception in 1921, the Pageant has not had one Black finalist, and this has not been for a lack of test-case contestants. There has never been a Puerto Rican, Alaskan, Hawaiian, or Mexican-American winner. Nor has there ever been a *true* Miss America—an American Indian.
3. *Miss America as Military Death Mascot.* The highlight of her reign each year is a cheerleader-tour of American troops abroad—last year she went to Vietnam to pep-talk our husbands, fathers, sons and boyfriends into dying and killing with a better spirit. She personifies the "unstained patriotic American womanhood our boys are fighting for." The Living Bra and the Dead Soldier. We refuse to be used as Mascots for Murder.

4. *The Consumer Con-Game.* Miss America is a walking commercial for the Pageant's sponsors. Wind her up and she plugs your product on promotion tours and TV—all in an "honest, objective" endorsement. What a shill.

5. *Competition Rigged and Unrigged.* We deplore the encouragement of an American myth that oppresses men as well as women: the win-or-you're-worthless competitive disease. The "beauty contest" creates only one winner to be "used" and forty-nine losers who are "useless."

6. *The Woman as Pop Culture Obsolescent Theme.* Spindle, mutilate, and then discard tomorrow. What is so ignored as last year's Miss America? This only reflects the gospel of our society, according to Saint Male: women must be young, juicy, malleable—hence age discrimination and the cult of youth. And we women are brainwashed into believing this ourselves!

7. *The Unbeatable Madonna-Whore Combination.* Miss America and Playboy's centerfold are sisters over the skin. To win approval, we must be both sexy and wholesome, delicate but able to cope, demure yet titillatingly bitchy. Deviation of any sort brings, we are told, disaster: "You won't get a man!!"

8. *The Irrelevant Crown on the Throne of Mediocrity.* Miss America represents what women are supposed to be: unoffensive, bland, apolitical. If you are tall, short, over or under what weight The Man prescribes you should be, forget it. Personality, articulateness, intelligence, commitment—unwise. Conformity is the key to the crown—and, by extension, to success in our society.

9. *Miss America as Dream Equivalent To—?* In this reputedly democratic society, where every little boy supposedly can grow up to be President, what can every little girl hope to grow to be? Miss America. That's where it's at. Real power to control our own lives is restricted to men, while women get patronizing pseudo-power, an ermine cloak and a bunch of flowers; men are judged by their actions, women by their appearance.

10. *Miss America as Big Sister Watching You.* The Pageant exercises Thought Control, attempts to sear the Image onto our minds, to further make women oppressed and men oppressors; to enslave us all the more in high-heeled, low-status roles; to inculcate false values in young girls; to use women as beasts of buying; to seduce us to prostitute ourselves before our own oppression.

NO MORE MISS AMERICA

14.3:   The Counterattack (1977)

The opposition of many men to the feminist campaign, especially to its more militant versions, was predictable. But the feminist movement also made enemies among women. One of the most ardent of these was Phyllis Schlafly, a successful Illinois lawyer and mother of six. In the 1970s Schlafly would become a leading opponent of the Equal Rights Amendment to the Constitution, and her conservative Eagle Forum would take credit for preventing its final adoption.

The document below is Schlafly's indictment of the New Feminism in all its versions, moderate and radical alike, and her defense of traditional views of women and feminity. Do you find her position convincing in whole or in part? Schlafly emphasizes the biological bases for male–female differences. Does biology profoundly influence the roles and achieve-

ments of the two sexes? What group of women, defined socially or cultur-
ally, might consider her views congenial? Why? Schlafly was herself a well-
educated professional woman. Was her appeal largely to women
like herself?

Understanding the Difference

PHYLLIS SCHLAFLY

The first requirement for the acquisition of power by the Positive Woman[1] is
to understand the differences between men and women. Your outlook on
life, your faith, your behavior, your potential for fulfillment, all are determined by the parameters of your original premise. The Positive Woman
starts with the assumption that the world is her oyster. She rejoices in the
creative capability within her body and the power potential of her mind and
spirit. She understands that men and women are different, and that those
very differences provide the key to her success as a person and fulfillment as
a woman.

The women's liberationist, on the other hand, is imprisoned by her own
negative view of herself and of her place in the world around her. This view
of women was most succinctly expressed in an advertisement designed by the
principal women's liberationist organization, the National Organization for
Women (NOW), and run in many magazines and newspapers and as spot
announcements on many television stations. The advertisement showed a
darling curlyheaded girl with the caption: "This healthy, normal baby has a
handicap. She was born female."

This is the self-articulated dog-in-the-manger, chip-on-the-shoulder, fundamental dogma of the women's liberation movement. Someone—it is not
clear who, perhaps God, perhaps the "Establishment," perhaps a conspiracy
of male chauvinist pigs — dealt women a foul blow by making them female.
It becomes necessary, therefore, for women to agitate and demonstrate and
hurl demands on society in order to wrest from an oppressive male-dominated social structure the status that has been wrongfully denied to women
through the centuries.

By its very nature, therefore, the women's liberation movement precipi-
tates a series of conflict situations—in the legislatures, in the courts, in the
schools, in industry—with man targeted as the enemy. Confrontation
replaces cooperation as the watchword of all relationships. Women and men
become adversaries instead of partners.

The second dogma of the women's liberationists is that, of all the injustices perpetrated upon women through the centuries, the most oppressive is

[1]This is Schlafly's version of the fulfilled modern woman, someone, one assumes, like herself—
ED.

the cruel fact that women have babies and men do not. Within the confines of the women's liberationist ideology, therefore, the abolition of this over-riding inequality of women becomes the primary goal. This goal must be achieved at any and all costs—to the woman herself, to the baby, to the family, and to society. Women must be made equal to men in their ability *not* to become pregnant and *not* to be expected to care for babies they may bring into the world.

This is why women's liberationists are compulsively involved in the drive to make abortion and child-care centers for all women, regardless of religion or income, both socially acceptable and government-financed. Former Congresswoman Bella Abzug has defined the goal: "to enforce the constitutional right of females to terminate pregnancies that they do not wish to continue."

If man is targeted as the enemy, and the ultimate goal of women's liberation is independence from men and the avoidance of pregnancy and its consequences, then lesbianism is logically the highest form in the ritual of women's liberation. Many, such as Kate Millett, come to this conclusion, although many others do not.

The Positive Woman will never travel that dead-end road. It is self-evident to the Positive Woman that the female body with its baby-producing organs was not designed by a conspiracy of men but by the Divine Architect of the human race. Those who think it is unfair that women have babies, whereas men cannot, will have to take up their complaint with God because no other power is capable of changing that fundamental fact. On some college campuses, I have been assured that other methods of reproduction will be developed. But most of us must deal with the real world rather than with the imagination of dreamers.

Another feature of the woman's natural role is the obvious fact that women can breast-feed babies and men cannot. This functional role was not imposed by conspiratorial males seeking to burden women with confining chores, but must be recognized as part of the plan of the Divine Architect for the survival of the human race through the centuries and in the countries that know no pasteurization of milk or sterilization of bottles.

The Positive Woman looks upon her femaleness and her fertility as part of her purpose, her potential, and her power. She rejoices that she has a capability for creativity that men can never have.

The third basic dogma of the women's liberation movement is that there is no difference between male and female except the sex organs, and that all those physical, cognitive, and emotional differences you *think* are there, are merely the result of centuries of restraints imposed by a male-dominated society and sex-stereotyped schooling. The role imposed on women is, by definition, inferior, according to the women's liberationists.

The Positive Woman knows that, while there are some physical competitions in which women are better (and can command more money) than men, including those that put a premium on grace and beauty, such as figure skating, the superior physical strength of males over females in competitions of strength, speed, and short-term endurance is beyond rational dispute. . . .

The Positive Woman remembers the essential validity of the old prayer: "Lord, give me the strength to change what I can change, the serenity to accept what I cannot change, and the wisdom to discern the difference." The women's liberationists are expending their time and energies erecting a make-believe world in which they hypothesize that *if* schooling were gender-free, and *if* the same money were spent on male and female sports programs, and *if* women were permitted to compete on equal terms, *then* they would prove themselves to be physically equal. Meanwhile, the Positive Woman has put the ineradicable physical differences into her mental computer, programmed her plan of action, and is already on the way to personal achievement. . . .

Despite the claims of the women's liberation movement, there are countless physical differences between men and women. The female body is 50 to 60 percent water, the male 60 to 70 percent water, which explains why males can dilute alcohol better than women and delay its effect. The average woman is about 25 percent fatty tissue, while the male is 15 percent, making women more buoyant in water and able to swim with less effort. Males have a tendency to color blindness. Only 5 percent of persons who get gout are female. Boys are born bigger. Women live longer in most countries of the world, not only in the United States where we have a hard-driving competitive pace. Women excel in manual dexterity, verbal skills, and memory recall. . . .

Does the physical advantage of men doom women to a life of servility and subservience? The Positive Woman knows that she has a complementary advantage which is at least as great—and, in the hands of a skillful woman, far greater. The Divine Architect who gave men a superior strength to lift weights also gave women a different kind of superior strength.

The women's liberationists and their dupes who try to tell each other that the sexual drive of men and women is really the same, and that it is only societal restraints that inhibit women from an equal desire, an equal enjoyment, and an equal freedom from the consequences, are doomed to frustration forever. It just isn't so, and pretending cannot make it so. The differences are not a woman's weakness but her strength. . . .

The new generation can brag all it wants about the new liberation of the new morality, but it is still the woman who is hurt the most. The new morality isn't just a "fad"—it is a cheat and a thief. It robs the woman of her virtue, her youth, her beauty, and her love—for nothing, just nothing. It has produced a generation of young women searching for their identity, bored with sexual freedom, and despondent from the loneliness of living a life without commitment. They have abandoned the old commandments, but they can't find any new rules that work.

The Positive Woman recognizes the fact that, when it comes to sex, women are simply not the equal of men. The sexual drive of men is much stronger than that of women. That is how the human race was designed in order that it might perpetuate itself. The other side of the coin is that it is easier for women to control their sexual appetites. A Positive Woman cannot defeat a man in a wrestling or boxing match, but she can motivate him, inspire him, encourage him, teach him, restrain him, reward him, and have power over him that he can never achieve over her with all his muscle. How or whether a Positive Woman uses her power is determined solely by the way she alone defines her goals and develops her skills.

The differences between men and women are also emotional and psychological. Without woman's innate maternal instinct, the human race would have died out centuries ago. There is nothing so helpless in all earthly life as the newborn infant. It will die within hours if not cared for. Even in the most primitive, uneducated societies, women have always cared for their newborn babies. They didn't need any schooling to teach them how. They didn't need any welfare workers to tell them it is their social obligation. Even in societies to whom such concepts as "ought," "social responsibility", and "compassion for the helpless," were unknown, mothers cared for their new babies.

Why? Because caring for a baby serves the natural maternal need of a woman. Although not nearly so total as the baby's need, the woman's need is nonetheless real. . . .

This is not to say that every woman must have a baby in order to be fulfilled. But it is to say that fulfillment for most women involves expressing their natural maternal urge by loving and caring for someone.

The women's liberation movement complains that traditional stereotyped roles assume that women are "passive" and that men are "aggressive." The anomaly is that a woman's most fundamental emotional need is not passive at all, but active. A woman naturally seeks to love affirmatively and to show that love in an active way by caring for the object of her affections.

The Positive Woman finds somebody on whom she can lavish her maternal love so that it doesn't well up inside her and cause psychological frustrations. Surely no woman is so isolated by geography or insulated by spirit that she cannot find someone worthy of her maternal love. All persons, men and women, gain by sharing something of themselves with their fellow humans, but women profit most of all because it is part of their very nature.

15

The Vietnam War

The Vietnam War has been described as America's longest war. It was also America's most demoralizing, divisive, and ultimately most despised war.

The Vietnam conflict was an extension into Southeast Asia of the Cold War between the superpowers and their clients. As viewed by American policy-makers in the 1960s, the United States, as prime defender of the free world, had to prevent the conquest of pro-Western South Vietnam by a pro-Soviet regime in North Vietnam led by the Communist leader Ho Chi Minh. If we failed in our mission, it would consign much of the region to ultimate Communist domination.

Whatever the rationale, the United States drifted, almost absentmindedly, into a military and political commitment in the region. Vietnam had been part of French Indochina, a dependency of France since the nineteenth century. The Japanese occupied the country during World War II, and when they left in 1945 the French sought to reestablish political control. They were opposed by Indochinese groups determined to oust France and establish independent nations in the former colony.

The most effective of these insurgent forces was the Viet Minh, concentrated around Hanoi in northern Vietnam and led by the Moscow-trained Ho Chi Minh. Ho and his supporters were determined to unite all of Vietnam as a Marxist state under their leadership.

Despite a flood of American money and military supplies, the French failed to subdue the Viet Minh, and after their defeat in battle at Dien Bien Phu in 1954, they agreed to leave their former colony. Their departure left Indochina divided into four small countries: Communist-dominated North Vietnam with its capital at Hanoi; a pro-Western South Vietnam governed from Saigon; and two small states, Laos and Cambodia, which tried to maintain a neutral position.

The Geneva Accords of 1954, confirming French defeat, mandated national elections in two years to decide on the unification of the two Vietnams. But the vote was never held. In the south the pro-Western regime led by Ngo Dinh Diem, fearing defeat, ignored the election provision of the Geneva agreement. Frustrated by this check to reunification of both Vietnams under its control, Ho's regime in the north supported a guerrilla war by the Communist Vietcong (the National Liberation Front) against the Saigon government.

The American government tried to prop up the Diem regime in South Vietnam with arms, food, and money. In 1961 President Kennedy dispatched the first American military personnel to South Vietnam, although they were advisers to the South Vietnamese armed forces, not combat troops. This aid was not enough. The Diem regime was corrupt, arbitrary, and bigoted, and, while failing to win over South Vietnam's peasants, offended the influential Buddhists.

In late 1963 the United States encouraged the overthrow of the Diem regime by pro-American generals. For the next few years confusion reigned in Saigon as various factions and individuals fought for power. By now Lyndon Johnson was president, and the American commitment to preserving the status quo in Vietnam was about to get a major boost.

Soon after LBJ's election in 1964 he escalated the American military investment in Vietnam. In March 1965 he ordered a major bombing campaign ("Rolling Thunder") against North Vietnam to discourage further aid to the Vietcong. Soon after the first American combat troops arrived in South Vietnam. By the end of the year there would be almost 200,000 U.S. fighting men in the country. Each month thereafter the number grew. At the peak of the Vietnam War in late 1968, some 536,000 American troops would be engaged in a struggle to stop Hanoi from reuniting the two Vietnams under its sole authority.

At home the war proved to be the most divisive in American history. Constrained by fears of Chinese or Soviet intervention, the administration refused to employ nuclear weapons. It also failed to make an effective case to the American people for an all-out war and in fact sought to hide the costs of the American commitment lest they arouse too much domestic opposition. To make matters worse, the American client regime in Saigon never seemed to care as much about saving itself as the United States did; its generals and troops seldom engaged the enemy aggressively.

Significant domestic opposition to the war erupted in early 1965, and thereafter the antiwar movement grew with each new increment of U.S. military investment. Antiwar feelings were amplified by the nightly TV news, which showed the bombings, the firefights, and the daily "body counts" in Vietnam to an appalled American viewership. The president and his advisers kept reassuring the public that there was "light at the end of the tunnel," and that with a few thousand more men and a little more effort, the enemy would collapse. Americans soon greeted each new claim with derision. In late January 1968, after months of optimistic predictions, the prowar "hawks" suffered a devastating setback when a coordinated, multicity Vietcong attack on South Vietnamese and American posts and installations during the Vietnamese Tet new year festival caught the Americans by surprise. The Vietcong captured the provincial capital of Hue and penetrated the American embassy compound in Saigon.

In the end Vietcong losses were appalling, but the Tet Offensive demolished the administration's claim of imminent victory. To the very end a bloc of "hawk" loyalists continued to support the war. But by this time many Americans had lost faith in their government, a mood that fed the political and cultural left and propelled a stream of recruits into such organizations as Students for a Democratic Society, the Resistance, and the Yippies.

In 1968 antiwar Democrats, led by Senators Eugene McCarthy of Minnesota and Robert Kennedy of New York, forced Johnson to drop his reelection bid. The Democratic presidential candidate that year, Hubert Humphrey, was hobbled by his loyalty to Johnson and lost narrowly to Richard Nixon in November. Once in office Nixon began to reduce American combat troops and turn the fighting over to the South Vietnamese, a process he called "Vietnamization." Meanwhile American and North Vietnamese officials conducted frustrating peace negotiations in Paris, out of the public's sight. Yet the fighting continued, and the antiwar activists accused Nixon of hypocrisy.

In January 1973 the United States, North Vietnam, South Vietnam, and the Vietcong finally concluded an agreement to stop the fighting, exchange prisoners, and form a National Council of Reconciliation to determine future relations between Hanoi and Saigon. In March 1973 the last American troops left South Vietnam.

The Nixon administration claimed that the South Vietnamese could protect themselves if the United States continued to provide money and equipment. It was untrue, however, and in any event Congress was unwilling to provide the resources. In April 1975, under powerful attack by North Vietnamese forces, the South Vietnamese government collapsed. As the Communist tanks rumbled into Saigon, the United States hurriedly evacuated the remaining Americans and hundreds of South Vietnamese supporters from the U.S. embassy grounds by helicopter. Over the next few years, as the North Vietnamese imposed a totalitarian regime in the South, hundreds of thousands of South Vietnamese "boat people" fled the Communists, many eventually finding haven in the United States.

America's longest war had ended on a bitter note, leaving behind a legacy of neo-isolationism, internal domestic division, dismay at excessive presidential power, and skepticism of American goals and purposes. It would take years before the wounds healed.

The selections below represent the positions of various groups on the American role in Vietnam. Included are defenders of the administration policies, American peace advocates, and even the Communist North Vietnamese. Needless to say, the disagreements among the parties are striking.

15.1:   The Hawk Position (1954, 1965)

As far back as the 1950s American leaders saw a victory for the Vietnamese Communists as a grave danger to the other non-Communist regimes in East Asia. Influenced by the containment policy in Europe and the experience of the Korean War, they warned that if the North Vietnamese were not stopped, the Communist virus would soon spread to neutral or pro-Western East Asian nations. This in turn would expand the power of the Soviet Union and the Communist People's Republic of China at the free world's expense.

The most famous expression of this pessimistic view came at a 1954 press conference, reported below, at which President Dwight Eisenhower likened the non-Communist nations of the region to a row of dominoes that would tip over one by one if the Hanoi regime were successful in reuniting Vietnam under its aegis. Yet despite his convictions, Eisenhower proved unwilling to commit American combat forces to Vietnam. Students will want to ask if there were plausible reasons to believe in the "domino effect"? Did events prove Eisenhower to be correct?

It took more than a decade before the sort of thinking behind Eisenhower's statement produced a full-scale American military commitment to the defense of South Vietnam. The second item below is a February 1965 memo from National Security Adviser McGeorge Bundy to President Lyndon Johnson expressing what came to be called the hawk position. Bundy was writing from Vietnam, where he had gone on a scouting trip for the president. At the time of his visit Vietcong guerrillas were engaged in a major offensive against the forces of the South Vietnamese government and had recently inflicted severe casualties on them. American military "advisers," moreover, were already stationed in Vietnam, and just the day before the Bundy memo the Vietcong had attacked U.S. military installations at Pleiku, killing nine Americans.

What is Bundy's estimate of the situation in South Vietnam? What are his recommendations to meet that situation? What seems to be his estimate of the will and capacity of the South Vietnamese to defend themselves? Did events ultimately confirm or refute Bundy's estimate? What sort of reprisals actually followed soon after his recommendations?

The Domino Theory

DWIGHT D. EISENHOWER

Q: Robert Richards, Copley Press: Mr. President, would you mind commenting on the strategic importance of Indochina to the free world? I think there has been, across the country, some lack of understanding on just what it means to us.

The President: You have, of course, both the specific and the general when you talk about such things.

First of all, you have the specific value of a locality in its production of materials that the world needs.

Then you have the possibility that many human beings pass under a dictatorship that is inimical to the free world.

Finally, you have broader considerations that might follow what you would call the "falling domino" principle. You have a row of dominoes set up, you knock over the first one, and what will happen to the last one is the certainty that it will go over very quickly. So you could have a beginning of a disintegration that would have the most profound influences.

Now, with respect to the first one, two of the items from this particular area that the world uses are tin and tungsten. They are very important. There are others, of course, the rubber plantations and so on.

Then with respect to more people passing under this domination, Asia, after all, has already lost some 450 million of its people to the Communist dictatorship, and we simply can't afford greater losses.

But when we come to the possible sequence of events, the loss of Indochina, of Burma, of Thailand, of the Peninsula, and Indonesia following, now you begin to talk about areas that not only multiply the disadvantages that you would suffer through loss of materials, sources of materials, but now you are talking really about millions and millions and millions of people.

Finally, the geographical position achieved thereby does many things. It turns the so-called island defensive chain of Japan, Formosa, of the Philippines and to the southward; it moves in to threaten Australia and New Zealand.

It takes away, in its economic aspects, that region that Japan must have as a trading area or Japan, in turn, will have only one place in the world to go—that is, toward the Communist areas in order to live.

So, the possible consequences of the loss are just incalculable to the free world.

Public Papers of the Presidents of the United States: Dwight D. Eisenhower, 1954 (Washington, DC: Government Printing Office, 1958), pp. 381–390.

The Situation in Vietnam

McGEORGE BUNDY

Re: The Situation in Vietnam

This memorandum attempts to describe the situation, the stakes and the measures which I think should now . . . [be] taken.

I. Summary Conclusions

The situation in Vietnam is deteriorating, and without new U.S. action defeat appears inevitable—probably not in a matter of weeks or perhaps even months, but within the next year or so. There is still time to turn it around, but not much.

The stakes in Vietnam are extremely high. The American investment is very large, and American responsibility is a fact of life which is palpable in the atmosphere of Asia, and even elsewhere. The international prestige of the United States, and a substantial part of our influence, are directly at risk in Vietnam. There is no way of unloading the burden on the Vietnamese themselves, and there is no way of negotiating ourselves out of Vietnam which offers any serious promise at present. It is possible that at some future time a neutral non-Communist force may emerge, perhaps under Buddhist leadership, but no such force currently exists, and any negotiated U.S. withdrawal today would mean surrender on the installment plan.

The policy of graduated and continuing reprisal . . . is the most promising course available, in my judgment. The judgment is shared by all who accompanied me from Washington, and I think by all members of the country team.

The events of the last twenty-four hours have produced a practicable point of departure for this policy of reprisal, and for the removal of U.S. dependents. They may also have catalyzed the formation of a new Vietnamese government. If so, the situation may be at a turning point. There is much that can and should be done to support and to supplement our present effort, while adding sustained reprisals. But I want to stress one important general conclusion which again is shared by all members of my party: the U.S. mission is composed of outstanding men, and U.S. policy within Vietnam is mainly right and well directed. None of the special solutions or criticisms put forward with zeal by individual reformers in government or in the press is of major importance, and many of them are flatly wrong. No man is perfect, and not every tactical step of recent months has been perfectly chosen, but when you described the Americans in Vietnam as your first team, you were right.

Gareth Porter, ed., *Vietnam: The Definitive Documentation of Human Decisions* (Stanfordville, NY: Earl M. Coleman Enterprises, Inc., Publishers, 1979), vol. 2, pp. 349–354.

II. The General Situation

For the last year—and perhaps for longer—the overall situation in Vietnam has been deteriorating. The Communists have been gaining and the anti-Communist forces have been losing. As a result there is now great uncertainty among Vietnamese as well as Americans as to whether Communist victory can be prevented. There is nervousness about the determination of the U.S. Government. There is recrimination and fear among Vietnamese political leaders. There is an appearance of wariness among some military leaders. There is a worrisome lassitude among the Vietnamese generally. There is a distressing absence of positive commitment to any serious social or political purpose. Outside observers are ready to write the patient off. All of this tends to bring latent anti-Americanism dangerously near to the surface.

To be an American in Saigon today is to have a gnawing feeling that time is against us. Junior officers in all services are able, zealous and effective within the limits of their means. Their morale is sustained by the fact that they know that they are doing their jobs well and that they will not have to accept the responsibility for defeat. But near the top, where responsibility is heavy and accountability real, one can sense the inner doubts of men whose outward behavior remains determined.

The situation is not all black. The overall military effectiveness of the Vietnamese armed forces in open combat continues to grow. The month of January was one of outstanding and genuine success in offensive military action, showing the highest gross count of Viet Cong dead of any month of the war, and a very high ratio also of enemy to friendly losses. We believe that General William Westmoreland is right (and General Alsop wrong) when he says that the Viet Cong do not now plan to expose themselves to large-scale military engagements in which their losses on the average would be high and their gains low. (The operation of Binh Gia is analyzed as a special case, representing the taking of a friendly Catholic village as bait rather than a decision to force pitched battle—more such cases are expected and the particular military problem posed is difficult.)

Moreover the Vietnamese people, although war weary, are also remarkably tough and resilient, and they do not find the prospect of Communist domination attractive. Their readiness to quit is much lower than the discouraging events of recent months might lead one to expect. It is probable that most Vietnamese think American withdrawal is more likely than an early switch to neutralism or surrender by major elements within Vietnam.

Nevertheless the social and political fabric is stretched thin, and extremely unpleasant surprises are increasingly possible—both political and military.

And it remains a stubborn fact that the percentage of the countryside which is dominated or threatened by the Viet Cong continues to grow. Even in areas which are "cleared," the follow-on pacification is stalled because of widespread belief that the Viet Cong are going to win in the long run. The areas which can be regarded as truly cleared and pacified and safe are few and shrinking. . . .

III. The Political Situation

Next only to the overall state of the struggle against the Viet Cong, the shape and structure of the government is [sic] the most important element of the Saigon situation. We made it our particular business to examine the question whether and to what degree a stable government is a necessity for the successful prosecution of our policy in Vietnam. We reached a mixed conclusion.

For immediate purposes—and especially for the initiation of reprisal policy, we believe that the government need be no stronger than it is today with General Khanh[1] as the focus of raw power while a weak caretaker government goes through the motions. Such a government can execute military decisions and it can give formal political support to joint US/GVN[2] policy. That is about all it can do.

In the longer run, it is necessary that a government be established which will in one way or another be able to maintain its political authority against all challenges over a longer time than the governments of the last year and a half.

The composition and direction of such a government is [sic]a most difficult problem, and we do not wholly agree with the mission in our estimate of its nature.

The mood of the mission with respect to the prospect of obtaining such a government is one of pessimism and frustration. This is only natural in terms of the events of the past many weeks. Two dominant themes predominate: a government headed by Khanh will be difficult if not impossible to deal with and, in any case, would be short lived; the Buddhists (or, more specifically, the few politically activist Bonzes[3]) must be confronted and faced down (by military means if necessary) lest they maintain their power to unseat any government that does not bow to their every demand. We tend to differ with the mission on both counts.

Specifically, we believe that General Khanh, with all his faults, is by long odds the outstanding military man currently in sight—and the most impressive personality generally. We do not share the conclusion of Ambassador [Maxwell] Taylor that he must somehow be removed from the military and political scene.

There are strong reasons for the Ambassador's total lack of confidence in

---

[1]Nguyen Khanh, leader of a group of South Vietnamese junior officers who overthrew the junta that had, in November 1963, overthrown Ngo Dinh Diem, the former tyrannical client of the United States—ED.

[2]The GVN means government of Vietnam, the regime in Saigon—ED.

[3]Buddhist monks—ED.

Khanh. At least twice Khanh has acted in ways that directly spelled Ambassador Taylor's high hopes for December. When he abolished the High National Council he undercut the prospect of the stable government needed for Phase II action against the North. In January he overthrew Huong just when the latter, in the Embassy's view, was about to succeed in putting the bonzes in their place.

Khanh is not an easy man to deal with. It is clear that he takes a highly tactical view of truth, although General Westmoreland asserts that Khanh has never deceived him. He is intensely ambitious and intent above all else on maintaining and advancing his own power. He gravely lacks the confidence of many of his colleagues—military and civilian—and he seems not to be personally popular with the public. He is correctly assessed as tricky. He remains able, energetic, perceptive and resilient, and in our judgment he will pursue the fight against the Communists as long as he can count on U.S. help. (If he should conclude that the U.S. was violently against him personally, he might well seek a way to power by some anti-American path, a path which would lead to disaster for both Vietnam and the United States.)

But our principal reason for opposing any sharp break with Khanh is that we see no one else in sight with anything like his ability to combine military authority with some sense of politics.

We also differ from the Embassy in our estimate of the Buddhist leaders. The dominant Embassy view is that "the Buddhists" are really just a handful of irresponsible and designing clerics and that they must be curbed by firmness. We agree that they may well have to be limited at some point, especially in their use of mobs, but we also think they must be offered some accommodation.

We feel that the operative concept should be *incorporation* into the affairs of government rather than confrontation. This is easier said than done, because the Buddhists have many of the bad habits of men who have prospered by irresponsible opposition. Still there are signs that both Buddhist laymen and bonzes are now taking a more positive stance. We feel that the mission might do more in attempting to direct or channel the Buddhists into a more useful and positive role—and active rather than a passive approach. The Buddhists now play a key role in the balance of political forces, so that something more than "confrontation" must be achieved if there is to be any active government at all.

Having registered these two immediate and important differences of emphasis, we should add that in our judgment the mission has acted at about the right level of general involvement in the problem of Vietnamese government-making. American advice is sought by all elements, and all try to bond it to their own ends. The mission attempts to keep before all elements the importance of stable government, and it quietly presses the value of those who are known to be good, solid, able ministerial timber.

In a situation in which confidence is low and uncertainty great, strongly ambitious forces like Khanh and the Buddhists might react very vigorously against an overt American attempt to form or actively support a government against their liking. Anti-Americanism is a theme that is potentially explosive, and therefore tempting to those who feel that we are blocking their ambitions. This is one lesson, to us, of the outburst in Hue last month.

On the other hand, no power whose stake is as great and whose presence as clear as those of the United States in Vietnam can afford to stand aside entirely, and such a passive posture would not be understood or approved by the Vietnamese themselves.

It is important, therefore, that the mission maintain a constant and active concern with the politics of government-making. This it is doing. While it is very difficult to second-guess this effort, we do recommend a telegram of guidance which might take into account the marginal differences from mission thinking which are suggested above. In the light of further discussion, a message of this sort will be drafted for consideration.

IV. Strengthening the Pacification Program

If we suppose that new hopes are raised—at least temporarily—by a reprisal program, and if we suppose further that a government somewhat better than the bare minimum is established, the most urgent order of business will then be the improvement and broadening of the pacification program, especially in its non-military elements.

The mission fully concurs in the importance of this effort. We believe, however, that consideration should be given to important modifications in its organization for this purpose. In particular we believe that there should be intensive effort to strengthen our program at the margin between military advice and economic development—in the area which implies civil government for the soldiers and police action for the aid mission. These efforts, important as they are understood to be, are somehow at the edge of vision for both parties. General Westmoreland and his people inevitably think first of military programs, though they have been imaginative and understanding about the importance of other aspects. Mr. Killen and the USOM people are centrally concerned with problems of aid and of economic improvement, although they talk with conviction and energy about their increasing police effort. It remains a fact that its own organization for helping to provide real security for an area which has been "cleared" in crude military terms is unfinished business for the U.S. mission. What is true of our side is doubly true of the Vietnamese.

We do not offer a definite solution to this problem. We are inclined to suggest, however, that one important and unemployed asset is the Special Forces of the Defense Department. Because of the predominant role of the U.S. military, and because of the generous spirit and broad mind of General Westmoreland himself, we are inclined to believe that the easiest growing edge for this work may be through the use of some of these versatile and flexible units.

We would think it important, however, that an effort of this kind be coordinated at a high level between the Defense Department and AID, and we believe that a joint mission which would include either Director Bell or Mr. Gaud from AID is urgently needed for the purpose of building this missing link into our program.

V. A Sense of Positive Hope

Vietnamese talk is full of the need for "revolution." Vietnamese practice is empty of action to match the talk—so much so that the word "revolution" sometimes seems to have no real meaning. Yet in fact there is plainly a deep and strong yearning among the young and the unprivileged for a new and better social order. This is what the Buddhist leaders are groping toward; this is what the students and young Turk generals are seeking. This yearning does not find an adequate response in American policy as Vietnamese see it. This is one cause of latent anti-American feeling. We only perceived this problem toward the end of our visit. We think it needs urgent further attention. We make no present recommendations. We do believe that over the long pull our military and political firmness must be matched by our political and economic support for the hopes that are embodied to Vietnamese in the word "revolution."

VI. The Basic U.S. Commitment

The prospect in Vietnam is grim. The energy and persistence of the Viet Cong are astonishing. They can appear anywhere—and at almost any time. They have accepted extraordinary losses and they come back for more. They show skill in their sneak attacks and ferocity when cornered. Yet the weary country does not want them to win.

There are a host of things the Vietnamese need to do better and areas in which we need to help them. The place where we can help most is in the clarity and firmness of our own commitment to what is in fact as well as in rhetoric a common cause. There is one grave weakness in our posture in Vietnam which is within our own power to fix—and that is a widespread belief that we do not have the will and force and patience and determination to take the necessary action and stay the course.

This is the overriding reason for our present recommendation of a policy of sustained reprisal. Once such a policy is put in force, we shall be able to speak in Vietnam on many topics and in many ways, with growing force and effectiveness.

One final word. At its very best the struggle in Vietnam will be long. It seems to us important that this fundamental fact be made clear and our understanding of it be made clear to our people and to the people of Vietnam. Too often in the past we have conveyed the impression that we expect an early solution when those who live with this war know that no early solution is possible. It is our own belief that the people of the United States have the necessary will to accept and to execute a policy that rests upon the reality that there is no short cut to success in South Vietnam.

15.2:   The North Vietnamese Analyze American Intervention (1965)

During their decade of conflict with the United States, the North Vietnamese often displayed a more realistic capacity for analysis than the Americans. The selection below is from a July 1965 talk by Le Duan, a high-ranking official in the North Vietnamese Communist Party. His remarks, which were a "pep talk" to a group of Communist leaders, also represent a careful dissection of American options. What factors, according to Le Duan, would influence American choices in Vietnam? Does he emphasize American military weakness or political vulnerability? Was his assessment shrewd or wide of the mark?

The North Vietnamese Analyze American Intervention

LE DUAN

We know that the U.S. sabotaged the Geneva Agreement and encroached on South Vietnam in order to achieve three objectives:

1. To turn the South into a colony of a new type.
2. To turn the South into a military base, in order to prepare to attack the North and the Socialist bloc.
3. To establish a South Vietnam-Cambodia-Laos defensive line in order to prevent the socialist revolution from spreading through Southeast Asia.

At present, we fight the U.S. in order to defeat their first two objectives to prevent them from turning the South into a new-type colony and military base.

We do not yet aim at their third objective, essentially to divide the ranks of the imperialist and to make other imperialists disagree with the U.S. in broadening the war in Vietnam and also to attract the support of other democratic and independent countries for our struggle in the South. Our revolutionary struggle in the South has the character of a conflict between the two camps in fact, but we advocate not making that conflict grow but limiting it in order to concentrate our forces to resolve the contradiction between the people and U.S. imperialism and its lackeys, to complete the national democratic revolution in the whole country. It is for this reason that we put forward the slogan "peace and neutrality" for the South, a flexible slogan to win victory step by step. We are not only determined to defeat the U.S. but must know how to defeat the U.S. in the manner most appropriate to the relation of forces between the enemy and us during each historical

Gareth Porter, ed., *Vietnam: The Definitive Documentation of Human Decisions* (Stanfordville, NY: Earl M. Coleman Enterprises, Inc., Publishers, 1979), vol. 2, pp. 383–385.

phase. Putting forward the slogan peace and neutrality for the South as well as the five points of the National Liberation Front of South Vietnam and the four points in our government's declaration read before the National Assembly as bases for the revolution of the Vietnamese problem, means that we know how to fight and defeat the Americans most advantageously.

. . .[T]he U.S. is still strong enough to enter into a limited war in Vietnam, by sending not only 200,000–250,000 but 300,000–400,000 troops to South Vietnam. But if it switches to limited war, the U.S. still will have weaknesses which it cannot overcome. The U.S. rear area is very far away, and American soldiers are "soldiers in chains", who cannot fight like the French, cannot stand the weather conditions, and don't know the battlefield but on the contrary have many weaknesses in their opposition to people's war. If the U.S. puts 300–400,000 [sic] troops into the South, it will have stripped away the face of its neocolonial policy and revealed the face of an old style colonial invader, contrary to the whole new-style annexation policy of the U.S. in the world at present. Thus, the U.S. will not be able to maintain its power with regard to influential sectors of the United States. If the U.S. itself directly enters the war in the South it will have to fight for a prolonged period with the people's army of the South[1], with the full assistance of the North and of the Socialist bloc.[2] To fight for a prolonged period is a weakness of U.S. imperialism. The Southern revolution can fight a protracted war, while the U.S. can't, because American military, economic and political resources must be distributed throughout the world. If it is bogged down in one place and can't withdraw, the whole effort will be violently shaken. The U.S. would lose its preeminence in influential sectors at home and create openings for other competing imperialists, and lose the American market. Therefore at present, although the U.S. can immediately send 300,000 to 400,000 troops at once, why must the U.S. do it step by step? Because even if it does send many troops like that, the U.S. would still be hesitant; because that would be a passive policy full of contradictions; because of fear of protracted war, and the even stronger opposition of the American people and the world's people, and even of their allies who would also not support widening the war.

With regard to the North, the U.S. still carries out its war of destruction, primarily by its air force: Besides bombing military targets, bridges and roads to obstruct transport and communications, the U.S. could also indiscriminately bomb economic targets, markets, villages, schools, hospitals, dikes, etc., in order to create confusion and agitation among the people. But the North is determined to fight back at the U.S. invaders in a suitable manner, determined to punish the criminals, day or night, and determined to make them pay the blood debts which they have incurred to our people in both

[1] The Vietcong—ED.
[2] That is, the other Communist nations of the world, especially China and the Soviet Union—ED.

zones. The North will not flinch for a moment before the destructive acts of the U.S., which could grow increasingly made with every passing day. The North will not count the cost but will use all of its strength to produce and fight, and endeavor to help the South. For a long time, the Americans have boasted of the strength of their air force and navy but during five to six months of directly engaging in combat with the U.S. in the North, we see clearly that the U.S. cannot develop that strength in relation to the South as well as in relation to the North, but revealed more clearly every day its weak-points. We have shot down more than 400 of their airplanes, primarily with rifles, anti-aircraft guns; [but] the high level of their hatred of the aggressors, and the spirit of determination to defeat the U.S. invaders [are strong]. Therefore, if the U.S. sends 300,000–400,000 troops into the South, and turns special war into direct war in the South, escalating the war of destruction in the North, they still can't hope to avert defeat, and the people of both North and South will still be determined to fight and determined to win.

If the U.S. is still more adventurous and brings U.S. and puppet troops of all their vassal states to attack the North, broadening it into a direct war in the entire country, the situation will then be different. Then it will not be we alone who still fight the U.S. but our entire camp. First the U.S. will not only be doing battle with 17 million people in the North but will also have to battle with hundreds of millions of Chinese people. Attacking the North would mean that the U.S. intends to attack China, because the North and China are two socialist countries linked extremely closely with each other, and the imperialists cannot attack this socialist country without also intending to attack the other. Therefore the two countries would resist together. Could the American imperialists suppress hundreds of millions of people? Certainly they could not. If they reach a stage of desperation, would the U.S. use the atomic bomb? Our camp also has the atomic bomb. The Soviet Union has sufficient atomic strength to oppose any imperialists who wish to use the atomic bomb in order to attack a socialist country, and threaten mankind. If U.S. imperialism uses the atomic bomb in those circumstances they would be committing suicide. The American people themselves would be the ones to stand up and smash the U.S. government when that government used atomic bombs. Would the U.S. dare to provoke war between the two blocks, because of the Vietnam problem; would it provoke a third world war in order to put an early end to the history of U.S. imperialism and of the entire imperialist system in general? Would other imperialist countries, factions in the U.S., and particularly the American people, agree to the U.S. warmongers throwing them into suicide? Certainly, the U.S. could not carry out their intention, because U.S. imperialism is in a weak position and not in a position of strength.

But the possibility of the broadening [of] the direct war to the North is a possibility which we must pay utmost attention, because U.S. imperialism could be adventurous. We must be vigilant and prepared to cope with each worst possibility. The best way to cope, and not to let the U.S. broaden the direct warfare in the South or in the North is to fight even more strongly and more accurately in the South, and make the puppet military units—the primary mainstay of the U.S.—rapidly fall apart, push military and political struggle forward, and quickly create the opportune moment to advance to complete defeat of U.S. imperialism and its lackeys in the South.

15.3:   The Antiwar Movement Strikes Back (1965, 1966)

As the dreary and painful months and years passed with no resolution of the Vietnam conflict, more and more Americans began to question the wisdom of their country's commitment and demand that it extricate itself from the East Asian morass.

The opposition to the war took many forms. Some Americans opposed it primarily on pragmatic grounds: the United States had no vital interest in Vietnam and no reason to pay a high price for a dispute not ours. Others considered the war wicked: America was acting as a brutal imperialist nation determined to impose its will on a weaker people.

A majority of the war's opponents confined themselves to petitions, marches, rallies, and protests. For young men of draft age, these measures often did not suffice. Many sought to avoid military service through fraudulent medical exemptions, conscientious objector status, or flight from the country. Organized opposition to Vietnam began with campus "teach-ins" in response to Lyndon Johnson's bombing campaign in the spring of 1965. Thereafter, numerous peace groups—moderates demanding early negotiations, radicals demanding immediate withdrawal—held rallies and demonstrations in major American cities around the country. Professional bodies, religious associations, and circles of intellectuals and artists denounced the war in resolutions and paid advertisements that often depicted Johnson as a coarse and brutal murderer of innocents. Militant black civil rights groups demanded that America get out of Vietnam.

The first reading below is from a pamphlet distributed by the Vietnam Day Committee (VDC) to army inductees and enlisted men at military bases in northern California. The VDC had been the organizing agency for the Berkeley teach-in in May 1965 following Johnson's "Rolling Thunder" attack. Afterward it became a semipermanent antiwar organization that drew support largely from the student radicals who, some months before, had led the Berkeley Free Speech Movement, the first of the major campus uprisings of the 1960s.

What seems to be the basis for the VDC case against American involvement in Vietnam? Is it ideological? Is it pragmatic? Does it seem to be anti-American? Why do the authors draw an analogy between the American cause in Vietnam and the Nazi rampage in Europe during World War II? Is the analogy valid? Why might the authorities have been particularly dismayed by the circulation of this pamphlet?

The second selection is a statement by the Student Nonviolent Coordinating Committee, the militant civil rights group that emerged from the 1960 student lunch-counter sit-ins in the South. By 1966, when SNCC launched this attack, its members were thoroughly disenchanted with American policy in Vietnam. Other groups were also hostile, but SNCC felt that blacks had special reasons to deplore the nation's involvement in Southeast Asia.

What were these reasons? Consider the costs of the war. Were blacks paying a disproportionate price? In what ways? What other attitudes common in the civil rights movement after 1965 might have influenced SNCC's views? Do you know if Martin Luther King, Jr., a centrist civil rights leader, ever broke with the Johnson administration over Vietnam?

Attention All Military Personnel

VIETNAM DAY COMMITTEE

You may soon be sent to Vietnam. You have heard about the war in the news; your officers will give you pep talks about it. But you probably feel as confused and uncertain as most Americans do. Many people will tell you to just follow orders and leave the thinking to others. But you have the right to know as much about this war as anyone. After all, it's you—not your Congressman—who might get killed.

Why Are We Fighting in Vietnam?

We are supposed to be fighting to protect democracy in Vietnam, and yet your own government admits that South Vietnam is run by a dictatorship. General Ky,[1] the latest military dictator, is as bad as they come. In a recent interview he said: "People ask me who my heroes are. I have only one— Hitler. I admire Hitler because he pulled his country together when it was in a terrible state" (*London Sunday Mirror*, July 4, 1965).

General Ky doesn't mean much to us; we're not even sure how to pronounce his name, but the South Vietnamese have lived under men like him for years. As far as the Vietnamese are concerned, we are fighting on the side of Hitlerism: and they hope we lose.

Vietnam Day Committee, "Attention All Military Personnel" (pamphlet, May 1965).

[1]Nguyen Cao Ky, a South Vietnamese air force general who, along with Nguyen Van Thieu, emerged as successor to Ngo Dinh Diem as ruler in Saigon—ED.

Who Is the Enemy?

U.S. military spokesmen have often said that their greatest problem is finding the enemy. The enemy, they say, is everywhere. The old woman feeding her chickens may have a stock of hand grenades in her hut. The little boy who trails after the American soldiers during the day slips out to give information to the guerrillas at night. The washerwoman at the American air base brings a bomb to work one day. It is impossible, say the military, to tell which are the Viet Cong and which are the civilians.

And so, because the whole Vietnamese people seem to be the enemy, the military is taking no chances. They use tear gas—a weapon designed for use against civilians. They order American troops to fire at women and children—because women and children, after all, are firing at American troops. American fighter planes destroy civilian villages with napalm; American B-52s are flattening whole regions. That is why the war in Vietnam is so often called a "dirty war."

When the South Vietnamese people see you in your foreign uniform, they will think of you as *their* enemy. You are the ones bombing their towns. They don't know whether you're a draftee or a volunteer, whether you're for the war or against it; but they're not taking any chances either.

Free Elections

The Vietnamese would like to *vote* the foreigners out of their country, but they have been denied the chance. According to the Geneva Agreement of 1954, there were supposed to be elections throughout Vietnam in 1956. But the U.S. government was certain that our man in Vietnam, Premier Diem, would lose. So we decided not to allow any election until we were sure we could win. Diem set up a political police force and put all political opposition—Communist and anti-Communist—in jail. By 1959, it was clear there weren't going to be any elections, and the guerrillas known as the Viet Cong began to fight back. By 1963 our government was fed up with Diem, but still wasn't willing to risk elections. Our CIA helped a group of Vietnamese generals to overthrow Diem and kill him. Since then there have been a series of "better" military dictators. General Ky—the man who admires Hitler—is the latest one.

Fighting for Democracy

Your job as a soldier is supposed to be "to win the people of South Vietnam." Win them to what—democracy? No, we keep military dictators in power. What then? The American way of life? But why should they care any more about our way of life than we care about theirs? We can't speak their language or even pronounce their names. We don't know anything about their religion or even what it is. We never even heard of Vietnam until Washington decided to run it.

You are supposed to be fighting "to save the Vietnamese people from

Communism." Certainly Communist influence is very strong in the National Liberation Front [NLF], the rebel government. Yet most of the people support the NLF. Why? Many of the same people who now lead the NLF led the Vietnamese independence movement against the Japanese during World War II, and then went on to fight against French colonial rule. Most Vietnamese think of the NLF leaders as their country's outstanding patriots. In fact, many anti-Communists have joined the guerrilla forces in the belief that the most important thing is to get rid of foreign domination and military dictators. On the other hand, very few Vietnamese support the official government of General Ky. His army has low morale and a high desertion rate.

The Guerrillas

The newspapers and television have told us again and again what a tough fighter the Vietnamese guerrilla is. Short of ammunition and without any air cover, he can beat forces that outnumber him five or ten to one. Why do they have such high morale? They are not draftees; no draftees ever fight like that. They are not high-paid, professional soldiers. Most of them are peasants who work their fields; they can't even spare the ammunition for target practice.

Their secret is that they know why they are fighting. They didn't hear about Vietnam in the newspapers; they've lived there all their lives. While we were in high school, they were living under the Diem regime and hating it. Now American planes are bombing their towns and strafing their fields; American troops have occupied their country; and if they complain out loud, an American-supported dictator sentences them to jail or the firing squad. Is it any wonder that they fight so fiercely?

Crushing the Resistance

The war in Vietnam is not being fought according to the rules. Prisoners are tortured. Our planes drop incendiary bombs on civilian villages. Our soldiers shoot at women and children. Your officers will tell you that it is all necessary, that we couldn't win the war any other way. *And they are right.* Americans are no more cruel than any other people; American soldiers don't enjoy this kind of war. But if you are going to wage war against an entire people, you have to become cruel.

The ordinary German soldier in occupied Europe wasn't especially cruel, either. But as the resistance movements grew, he *became* cruel. He shot at women and children because they were shooting at him; he never asked himself *why* they were shooting at him. When a certain town became a center of resistance activity, he followed his orders and destroyed the whole town. He knew that SS men were torturing captured resistance fighters, but it wasn't his business to interfere.

Following Orders

As a soldier you have been trained to obey orders, but as a human being you must take responsibility for your own acts. International and American law recognize that an individual soldier, even if acting under orders, must bear final legal and moral responsibility for what he does. This principle became a part of law after World War II, when the Allied nations, meeting in London, decided that German war criminals must be punished even if they committed war crimes under orders. This principle was the basis of the Nuremberg trials. We believe that the entire war in Vietnam is criminal and immoral. We believe that the atrocities which are necessary to wage this war against the people of Vietnam are inexcusable.

Oppose the War

We hope that you too find yourself, as a human being, unable to tolerate this nightmare war, and we hope that you will oppose it. We don't know what kind of risks we are taking in giving you this leaflet; you won't know what risk you will be taking in opposing the war. A growing number of GIs have already refused to fight in Vietnam and have been court-martialed. They have shown great courage. We believe that they, together with other courageous men who will join them, will have influence far out of proportion to their numbers.

There may be many other things you can do; since you are in the service, you know better than civilians what sorts of opposition are possible. But whatever you do, keep your eyes open. Draw your own conclusions from the things you see, read, and hear. At orientation sessions, don't be afraid to ask questions, and if you're not satisfied with the answers, keep asking. Take every chance you get to talk to your fellow soldiers about the war.

You may feel the war is wrong, and still decide not to face a court-martial. You may then find yourself in Vietnam under orders. You might be forced to do some fighting—but don't do any more than you have to. Good luck.

The U.S. Government Has Deceived Us

STUDENT NON-VIOLENT COORDINATING COMMITTEE

The Student Nonviolent [sic] Coordinating Committee has a right and a responsibility to dissent with United States foreign policy on any issue when it sees fit. The Student Nonviolent Coordinating Committee now states its opposition to United States' involvement in Vietnam on these grounds:

Student Non-Violent Coordinating Committee, "The U.S. Government Has Deceived Us" (broadside, 1966).

We believe the United States government has been deceptive in its claims of concern for the freedom of the Vietnamese people, just as the government has been deceptive in claiming concern for the freedom of colored people in such other countries as the Dominican Republic, the Congo, South Africa, Rhodesia, and in the United States itself.

We, the Student Nonviolent Coordinating Committee, have been involved in the black people's struggle for liberation and self-determination in this country for the past five years. Our work, particularly in the South, has taught us that the United States government has never guaranteed the freedom of oppressed citizens, and is not yet truly determined to end the rule of terror and oppression within its own borders.

We ourselves have often been victims of violence and confinement executed by United States governmental officials. We recall the numerous persons who have been murdered in the South because of their efforts to secure their civil and human rights, and whose murderers have been allowed to escape penalty for their crimes.

The murder of Samuel Young [a young black man] in Tuskegee, Alabama, is no different than the murder of peasants in Vietnam, for both Young and the Vietnamese sought, and are seeking, to secure the rights guaranteed them by law. In each case, the United States government bears a great part of the responsibility for these deaths.

Samuel Young was murdered because United States law is not being enforced. Vietnamese are murdered because the United States is pursuing an aggressive policy in violation of international law. The United States is no respecter of persons or law when such persons or laws run counter to its needs or desires.

We recall the indifference, suspicion, and outright hostility with which our reports of violence have been met in the past by government officials.

We know that for the most part, elections in this country, in the North as well as the South, are not free. We have seen that the 1965 Voting Rights Act and the 1964 Civil Rights Act have not yet been implemented with full federal power and sincerity.

We question, then, the ability and even the desire of the United States government to guarantee free elections abroad. We maintain that our country's cry of "preserve freedom in the world" is a hypocritical mask behind which it squashes liberation movements which are not bound, and refuse to be bound, by the expediencies of United States Cold War policies.

We are in sympathy with, and support, the men in this country who are unwilling to respond to a military draft which would compel them to contribute their lives to United States aggression in Vietnam in the name of "freedom" we find so false in this country.

We recoil with horror at the inconsistency of a supposedly "free" society where responsibility to freedom is equated with the responsibility to lend oneself to military aggression. We take note of the fact that 16 per cent of the draftees from this country are Negroes called on to stifle the liberation of Vietnam, to preserve a "democracy" which does not exist for them at home.

We ask, where is the draft for the freedom fight in the United States?

We therefore encourage those Americans who prefer to use their energy in building democratic forms within this country. We believe that work in the civil rights movement and with other human relations organizations is a valid alternative to the draft. We urge all Americans to seek this alternative, knowing full well that it may cost them their lives—as painfully as in Vietnam.

16

Watergate

Watergate is the name of a luxury apartment complex on the Potomac River in Washington, D.C. It is also the name given to a political scandal that reached the highest levels of the American government and ultimately forced a president to resign. The president was Richard Nixon.

Nixon fought ferociously for every political success he achieved. As Dwight Eisenhower's vice-presidential running-mate in 1952, he was almost pushed off the ticket by a scandal over political contributions. In 1960 he lost the presidential race by the narrowest of margins to John Kennedy and, when he ran for governor of California in 1962, he lost again. Six years later he defeated Hubert Humphrey for the presidency but the result was a squeaker. Running for reelection in 1972, he would leave nothing to chance. This time he intended to win big to make up for all the disappointments and close races of the past.

The collection of crimes and deceptions called Watergate grew out of this win-at-all-costs attitude. Running Nixon's 1972 reelection campaign was former attorney general John Mitchell, head of the Committee for the Re-Election of the President (CRP). Under him was a collection of political operators and tricksters. The CRP (called "CREEP" by the Democrats) had large amounts of money, much of it extracted from corporations by promises of government favors or threats of disfavor, and laundered to disguise its origins.

If the CRP had stopped at drowning the Democrats in cash, disaster could have been avoided. But Mitchell and other Nixon cronies insisted on using every trick in the book to confuse, distract, unbalance, and obstruct their opponents. One of these "dirty trick" operations was a break-in on June 18, 1972, at the Democratic National Committee headquarters in the Watergate complex by a group nicknamed the "plumbers," apparently to rifle files for incriminating information on the Democrats and to bug their telephones. The break-in was discovered by the police while underway, and the Watergate burglars were arrested and indicted.

Nixon apparently did not order the break-in, nor, it seems, did he know about it until his aides told him a week later that the men caught at the Watergate worked for either the White House or the CRP. His accusers would claim, however, that he approved the efforts of aides H. R. Haldeman, John Dean, and John D. Ehrlichman to hide the connection between the Watergate "plumbers" and the administration and, still more serious, to offer the arrested men executive clemency and money in exchange for their silence. In the end, it was this cover-up attempt that brought the president down.

During the summer and fall of 1972, George McGovern, the Democratic presidential candidate, sought to make the mysterious Watergate break-in a campaign issue, but the administration was able to hide it until after the Republican election sweep in November. Then the cover-up began to come apart. In January 1973 the "plumbers" were tried before Judge John Sirica, and one of them confessed that he and his fellow defendants had committed perjury in denying their connection to the White House. In February the Senate established a select committee to investigate Watergate, headed by Sam Ervin of North Carolina, and in May the committee began televised hearings that revealed that the break-in had originated with the CRP and that the president may have condoned an attempt to obstruct justice. On July 16, 1973, one of the witnesses before the Ervin committee revealed that since 1971 all confidential discussions in the Oval Office and the Executive Office Building had been taped, which meant that everything that Nixon and his colleagues had said and done about Watergate could be checked. Meanwhile, two *Washington Post* reporters, Carl Bernstein and Robert Woodward, intrigued by the mysterious events at the Watergate, began to follow a trail of proliferating leads. Their sensational revelations soon ignited a race among the media to ferret out details of the complex operations of the CRP and other administration agents. The public watched transfixed as almost daily new details emerged of misdeeds by the White House.

Nixon resisted every effort to make him surrender the tapes to a special prosecutor he had agreed, under pressure, to appoint. When the prosecutor, Archibald Cox, became too aggressive, Nixon fired him in what came to be called the "Saturday Night Massacre." The storm of public outrage that followed forced Nixon to appoint another prosecutor, Leon Jaworski, a conservative Texas lawyer who refused to be intimidated. In late April 1974, under the prodding of Jaworski and Congress, Nixon released 1,200 pages of edited tape transcript that revealed the president as a mean-spirited, bigoted, win-at-any-price man, but contained no "smoking gun" directly linking him to an illegal attempt to obstruct justice.

On May 1 the House Judiciary Committee denied that the transcripts submitted represented full compliance with their demands; Nixon had held back crucial sections. In July, with support for the president fast dropping away, the Judiciary Committee began public debate on impeachment, and on the twenty seventh voted three articles of impeachment against Nixon for attempting to "delay, impede, and obstruct the investigation" of the Watergate incident and to "cover-up, conceal, and protect those responsible" for the break-in.

The next step in the constitutional procedure would have been trial by the Senate under the House articles for "high crimes and misde-meanors," with conviction bringing removal from office. This would have been the first impeachment trial of a president since Andrew Johnson's in 1868. It was not to be. On August 5, under order by the Supreme Court, Nixon surrendered the last of the tapes, which included the long-sought "smoking gun": on June 23, 1972, the president had discussed the break-in with Haldeman, and had told him that the FBI and CIA must be ordered to desist from any further investigation of the incident on national security grounds.

This second batch of tapes ended the charade. On August 7, 1974, Senators Barry Goldwater of Arizona and Hugh Scott of Pennsylvania, representing both wings of the Republican Party, advised Nixon to resign to spare the country the long agony of an impeachment trial. Goldwater told reporters that he had counted only fifteen senators who would vote against conviction. The next evening Nixon appeared on national television to tell the American people that he had decided to resign the presidency. Shortly after noon the following day, as Nixon and his family flew to California, Gerald Ford took the oath of office as thirty-eighth president of the United States.

Watergate was a devastating blow to American pride and self-confi-dence. Coming so soon after defeat in Vietnam, it further eroded the legitimacy of the American political process. But did it deserve the response it evoked? In June 1972 White House press secretary Ronald Ziegler had called the break-in a "third-rate burglary," and to this day some people accept this conclusion. To many Nixon loyalists, not to speak of Nixon himself, the president had done nothing seriously wrong, and they see the destruction of his administration as a politically partisan act by liberal enemies. As you read the selections that follow, see if you can objectively evaluate the significance of the acts and the decisions that destroyed the Nixon presidency and shook Americans' faith in "the system."

16.1:   The Tapes (1972)

The Watergate transcripts doomed the Nixon presidency. The House Judiciary Committee, the media, and the American people all concluded from their contents that the president was guilty of obstructing justice and deserved to be impeached. Most Americans were also appalled by the glimpse they afforded of the president's personality and of the slipshod way a great nation was being governed.

The excerpt from the Watergate tapes below is the "smoking-gun" segment of June 23, 1972. Does it prove that Nixon sought to obstruct justice? What does it tell us about his view of the American political process and his opponents? Does it provide any insight into Nixon's personality? What, if anything, does it tell us about the American presidency in these years?

Everyone was appalled by the vulgarity of the president's remarks ("expletive deleted") and his weak syntax and unfocused quality. But remember, this conversation was an unguarded private one between close associates. How many private conversations of people under stress would sound better if reported verbatim? Would your own?

The Smoking Gun

RICHARD NIXON

June 23, 1972

[H. R.] Haldeman: Now, on the investigation, you know the Democratic break-in thing, we're back in the problem area because the FBI is not under control, because [Director Patrick] Gray doesn't exactly know how to control it and they have—their investigation is now leading into some productive area. . . . They've been able to trace the money—not through the money itself—but through the bank sources—the banker. And it goes in some directions we don't want it to go. Ah, also there have been some [other] things—like an informant came in off the street to the FBI in Miami who was a photographer or has a friend who is a photographer who developed some films through this guy [Bernard] Barker and the films had pictures of Democratic National Committee letterhead documents and things. So it's things like that that are filtering in. . . . [John] Mitchell came up with yesterday, and John Dean analyzed very carefully last night and concludes, concurs now with Mitchell's recommendation that the only way to solve this . . . is for us to have [CIA Assistant Director Vernon] Walters call Pat Gray and just say, "Stay to hell out of this—this is ah, [our] business here. We don't want you to go any further on it." That's not an unusual development, and ah, that would take care of it.

President: What about Pat Gray—you mean Pat Gray doesn't want to?

Hearings before the Committee on the Judiciary, House of Representatives, 93rd Congress, 2d Session (Washington, DC: Government Printing Office, 1974), pp. 512–514.

Haldeman: Pat does want to. He doesn't know how to, and he doesn't have any basis for doing it. Given this, he will then have the basis. He'll call [FBI Assistant Director] Mark Felt in, and the two of them—and Mark Felt wants to cooperate because he's ambitious—

President: Yeah.

Haldeman: He'll call him in and say, "We've got the signal from across the river [1] to put the hold on this." And that will fit rather well because the FBI agents who are working the case, at this point, feel that's what it is.

President: This is CIA? They've traced the money? Who'd they trace it to?

Haldeman: Well, they've traced it to a name, but they haven't gotten to the guy yet.

President: Would it be somebody here?

Haldeman: Ken Dahlberg.

President: Who the hell is Ken Dahlberg?

Haldeman: He gave $25,000 in Minnesota and, ah, the check went directly to this guy Barker.

President: It isn't from the Committee though, from [Maurice] Stans?

Haldeman: Yeah. It is. It's directly traceable and there's some more through some Texas people that went to the Mexican bank which can also be traced to the Mexican bank—they'll get their names today.

President: Well, I mean, there's no way—I'm just thinking if they don't cooperate, what do they say? That they were approached by the Cubans? That's what Dahlberg has to say, the Texans too.

Haldeman: Well, if they will. But then we're relying on more and more people all the time. That's the problem and they'll [the FBI] . . . stop if we could take this other route.

President: All right.

Haldeman: [Mitchell and Dean] say the only way to do that is from White House instructions. And it's got to be to [CIA Director Richard] Helms and to—ah, what's his name? . . . Walters.

President: Walters.

Haldeman: And the proposal would be that . . . [John] Ehrlichman and I call them in, and say, ah—

President: All right, fine. How do you call him in—I mean you just—well, we protected Helms from one hell of a lot of things.

Haldeman: That's what [John] Ehrlichman says.

---

[1]The CIA headquarters were located in Virginia, across the Potomac from the White House—ED.

President: Of course; this [Howard] Hunt [business.] That will uncover a lot of things. You open that scab there's a hell of a lot of things and we just feel that it would be very detrimental to have this thing go any further. This involves these Cubans, Hunt, and a lot of hanky-panky that we have nothing to do with ourselves. Well, what the hell, did Mitchell know about this?

Haldeman: I think so. I don't think he knew the details, but I think he knew.

President: He didn't know how it was going to be handled though—with Dahlberg and the Texans and so forth? Well who was the asshole that did? Is it [G. Gordon] Liddy? Is that the fellow? He must be a little nuts!

Haldeman: He is.

President: I mean he just isn't well screwed on, is he? Is that the problem?

Haldeman: No, but he was under pressure, apparently, to get more information, and as he got more pressure, he pushed the people harder.

President: Pressure from Mitchell?

Haldeman: Apparently. . . .

President: All right, fine, I understand it all. We won't second-guess Mitchell and the rest. Thank God it wasn't [Special White House Counsel Charles] Colson.

Haldeman: The FBI interviewed Colson yesterday. They determined that would be a good thing to do. To have him take an interrogation, which he did, and the FBI guys working the case concluded that there were one or two possibilities—one, that this was a White House (they don't think that there is anything at the Election Committee) they think it was either a White House operation and they have some obscure reasons for it—non-political, or it was a—Cuban [operation] and [involved] the CIA. And after their interrogation of Colson yesterday, they concluded it was not the White House, but are now convinced it is a CIA thing, so the CIA turnoff would—

President: Well, not sure of their analysis, I'm not going to get that involved. I'm (unintelligible).

Haldeman: No, sir, we don't want you to.

President: You call them in.

Haldeman: Good deal.

President: Play it tough. That's the way they play it and that's the way we are going to play it. . . .

President: O.K. . . . Just say (unintelligible) very bad to have this fellow Hunt, ah, he knows too damned much. . . . If it gets out that this is all involved, the Cuba thing, it would be a fiasco. It would make the CIA look bad, it's going to make Hunt look bad, and it is likely to blow the whole Bay of Pigs thing which we think would be very unfortunate—both for CIA, and for the country, at this time, and for American foreign policy. Just tell him to lay off. Don't you [think] so?

Haldeman: Yep. That's the basis to do it on. Just leave it at that. . . .

16.2:   Nixon Defends Himself (1973)

As the details of Watergate unfolded, the president sought to staunch the political hemorrhage by appealing to the voters. On April 30, 1973, he went on television to defend himself and to announce the "resignations" of three of his top aides who, he said, had failed to inform him of the "plumbers" operation. The selection that follows is an excerpt from that speech.

What is Nixon's strategy in delivering this speech? Is he throwing Erhlichman, Haldeman, and Dean to the wolves to save his neck, as critics charged? Does he deal with the question of obstruction of justice? Or does he focus purely on the illegality of the break-in and the failure of his aides to admit its authorization by the CRP? Compare Nixon's words here with his private remarks made in the Oval Office on June 23 of the previous year.

I Did Not Know about Watergate

RICHARD M. NIXON

Good evening:

I want to talk to you tonight from my heart on a subject of deep concern to every American.

In recent months, members of my Administration and officials of the Committee for the Re-election of the President—including some of my closest friends and most trusted aides—have been charged with involvement in what has come to be known as the Watergate affair. These include charges of illegal activity during and preceding the 1972 Presidential election and charges that responsible officials participated in efforts to cover up that illegal activity.

The inevitable result of these charges has been to raise serious questions about the integrity of the White House itself. Tonight I wish to address those questions.

Last June 17, while I was in Florida trying to get a few days rest after my visit to Moscow, I first learned from news reports of the Watergate break-in. I was appalled at this senseless, illegal action, and I was shocked to learn that employees of the Re-election Committee were apparently among those

Congressional Quarterly, *Historic Documents, 1973* (Washington, DC: Congressional Quarterly, Inc., 1974), pp. 502–506.

guilty. I immediately ordered an investigation by appropriate Government authorities. On September 15, as you will recall, indictments were brought against seven defendants in the case.

As the investigations went forward, I repeatedly asked those conducting the investigation whether there was any reason to believe that members of my Administration were in any way involved. I received repeated assurances that there were not. Because of these continuing reassurances, because I believed the reports I was getting, because I had faith in the persons from whom I was getting them, I discounted the stories in the press that appeared to implicate members of my Administration or other officials of the campaign committee.

Until March of this year, I remained convinced that the denials were true and that the charges of involvement by members of the White House Staff were false. The comments I made during this period, and the comments made by my Press Secretary in my behalf, were based on the information provided to us at the time we made those comments. However, new information then came to me which persuaded me that there was a real possibility that some of these charges were true, and suggesting further that there had been an effort to conceal the facts both from the public, from you, and from me.

As a result, on March 21, I personally assumed the responsibility for coordinating intensive new inquiries into the matter, and I personally ordered those conducting the investigations to get all the facts and to report them directly to me, right here in this office.

I again ordered that all persons in the Government or at the Re-election Committee should cooperate fully with the FBI, the prosecutors, and the grand jury. I also ordered that anyone who refused to cooperate in telling the truth would be asked to resign from government service. And, with ground rules adopted that would preserve the basic constitutional separation of powers between the Congress and the Presidency, I directed that members of the White House Staff should appear and testify voluntarily under oath before the Senate committee which was investigating Watergate.

I was determined that we should get to the bottom of the matter, and that the truth should be fully brought out—no matter who was involved.

At the same time, I was determined not to take precipitate action, and to avoid, if at all possible, any action that would appear to reflect on innocent people. I wanted to be fair. But I knew that in the final analysis, the integrity of this office—public faith in the integrity of this office—would have to take priority over all personal considerations.

Announcement of Resignations

Today, in one of the most difficult decisions of my Presidency, I accepted the resignations of two of my closest associates in the White House—Bob Haldeman, John Ehrlichman—two of the finest public servants it has been my privilege to know.

I want to stress that in accepting these resignations, I mean to leave no implication whatever of personal wrongdoing on their part, and I leave no implication tonight of implication on the part of others who have been charged in this matter. But in matters as sensitive as guarding the integrity of our democratic process, it is essential not only that rigorous legal and ethical standards be observed, but also that the public, you, have total confidence that they are both being observed and enforced by those in authority and particularly by the President of the United States. They agreed with me that this move was necessary in order to restore that confidence.

Because Attorney General [Richard] Kleindienst—though a distinguished public servant, my personal friend for 20 years, with no personal involvement whatever in this matter—has been a close personal and professional associate of some of those who are involved in this case, he and I both felt that it was also necessary to name a new Attorney General.

The Counsel to the President, John Dean, has also resigned.

As the new Attorney General, I have today named Elliot Richardson, a man of unimpeachable integrity and rigorously high principle. I have directed him to do everything necessary to ensure that the Department of Justice has the confidence and the trust of every law abiding person in this country.

I have given him absolute authority to make all decisions bearing upon the prosecution of the Watergate case and related matters. I have instructed him that if he should consider it appropriate, he has the authority to name a special supervising prosecutor for matters arising out of the case.

Whatever may appear to have been the case before, whatever improper activities may yet be discovered in connection with this whole sordid affair, I want the American people, I want you to know beyond the shadow of a doubt that during my term as President, justice will be pursued fairly, fully, and impartially, no matter who is involved. This office is a sacred trust and I am determined to be worthy of that trust.

Looking back at the history of this case, two questions arise:

How could it have happened?
Who is to blame?

Political commentators have correctly observed that during my 27 years in politics I have always previously insisted on running my own campaigns for office.

But 1972 presented a very different situation. In both domestic and foreign policy, 1972 was a year of crucially important decisions, of intense negotiations, of vital new directions, particularly in working toward the goal which has been my overriding concern throughout my political career—the goal of bringing peace to America, peace to the world.

That is why I decided, as the 1972 campaign approached, that the Presidency should come first and politics second. To the maximum extent possible, therefore, I sought to delegate campaign operations, to remove the day-to-day campaign decisions from the President's office and from the White House. I also, as you recall, severely limited the number of my own campaign appearances.

Who Is to Blame?

Who, then, is to blame for what happened in this case?

For specific criminal actions by specific individuals, those who committed those actions must, of course, bear the liability and pay the penalty.

For the fact that alleged improper actions took place within the White House or within my campaign organization, the easiest course would be for me to blame those to whom I delegated the responsibility to run the campaign. But that would be a cowardly thing to do.

I will not place the blame on subordinates—on people whose zeal exceeded their judgment, and who may have done wrong in a cause they deeply believed to be right.

In any organization, the man at the top must bear the responsibility. That responsibility, therefore, belongs here, in this office. I accept it. And I pledge to you tonight, from this office, that I will do everything in my power to ensure that the guilty are brought to justice, and that such abuses are purged from our political processes in the years to come, long after I have left this office.

Some people, quite properly appalled at the abuses that occurred, will say that Watergate demonstrates the bankruptcy of the American political system. I believe precisely the opposite is true. Watergate represented a series of illegal acts and bad judgments by a number of individuals. It was the system that has brought the facts to light and that will bring those guilty to justice—a system that in this case has included a determined grand jury, honest prosecutors, a courageous judge, John Sirica, and a vigorous free press.

It is essential now that we place our faith in that system—and especially in the judicial system. It is essential that we let the judicial process go forward, respecting those safeguards that are established to protect the innocent as well as to convict the guilty. It is essential that in reacting to the excesses of others, we not fall into excesses ourselves.

It is also essential that we not be so distracted by events such as this that we neglect the vital work before us, before this Nation, before America, at a time of critical importance to America and the world.

Since March, when I first learned that the Watergate affair might, in fact, be far more serious than I had been led to believe, it has claimed far too much of my time and my attention.

Whatever may now transpire in the case, whatever the actions of the grand jury, whatever the outcome of any eventual trials, I must now turn my full attention—and I shall do so—once again to the larger duties of this office. I owe it to this great office that I hold, and I owe it to you—to my country.

I know that as Attorney General, Elliot Richardson will be both fair and he will be fearless in pursuing this case wherever it leads. I am confident that with him in charge, justice will be done.

There is vital work to be done toward our goal of a lasting structure of peace in the world—work that cannot wait, work that I must do.

Tomorrow, for example, Chancellor Brandt of West Germany will visit the

White House for talks that are a vital element of "The Year of Europe," as 1973 has been called. We are already preparing for the next Soviet-American summit meeting later this year.

This is also a year in which we are seeking to negotiate a mutual and balanced reduction of armed forces in Europe, which will reduce our defense budget and allow us to have funds for other purposes at home so desperately needed. It is the year when the United States and Soviet negotiators will seek to work out the second and even more important round of our talks on limiting nuclear arms, and of reducing the danger of a nuclear war that would destroy civilization as we know it. It is a year in which we confront the difficult tasks of maintaining peace in Southeast Asia and in the potentially explosive Middle East.

There is also vital work to be done right here in America: to ensure prosperity, and that means a good job for everyone who wants to work; to control inflation, that I know worries every housewife, everyone who tries to balance a family budget in America; to set in motion new and better ways of ensuring progress toward a better life for all Americans.

When I think of this office—of what it means—I think of all the things that I want to accomplish for this Nation, of all the things I want to accomplish for you.

16.3:   *Time* Asks Nixon to Resign (1973)

Time was a conservative weekly news magazine at the time of Watergate and was naturally inclined to give the besieged president the benefit of the doubt. But after the "Saturday Night Massacre" even Time deserted him. The magazine had always concentrated on news and had never before carried an editorial. But on November 12, 1973, it broke with this fifty-year precedent and printed the following editorial demanding that Nixon resign.

Why is Time so outraged? What does the editorial say about allowing the president leeway? And what about the argument it poses at the end only to reject: that considering what responsibilities rest on the president, Watergate was a minor infraction of the rules?

An Editorial: The President Should Resign

TIME MAGAZINE

Richard Nixon and the nation have passed a tragic point of no return. It now seems likely that the President will have to give up his office: he has irredeemably lost his moral authority, the confidence of most of the country, and therefore his ability to govern effectively.

The most important decision of Richard Nixon's remarkable career is before him, whether he will give up the presidency rather than do further damage to his country. If he decides to fight to the end, he faces impeachment by the House, for he has indeed failed his obligation under the Constitution to uphold the law. Whether two-thirds of the Senate would vote to convict him can not be certain. But even if he were to be acquitted, the process would leave him and the country devastated. Events have achieved an alarming momentum; additional facts that would be brought out under subpoena power at an impeachment trial could strike in many unforeseen and dangerous directions.

Moreover, a trial would take at least several months, during which the country would be virtually leaderless. The White House would be paralyzed while the U.S. and the world awaited the outcome. The Republic would doubtless survive. But the wise and patriotic course is for Richard Nixon to resign, sparing the country and himself this agony.

Nixon should of course be succeeded by a Republican. The Republicans did win the presidency last November (not because of Watergate or dirty tricks), and fortunately there seems no disposition among congressional Democrats to try to rewrite the election returns. We assume and hope that Congress will speedily confirm Gerald Ford's nomination as Vice President. If Nixon did leave office before this confirmation and Speaker Carl Albert became President, there is good reason to think that Albert would resign as long as Ford was confirmed.

Gerald Ford would be an unmistakable improvement over the grievously wounded Nixon. Barring some unforeseen revelations, Ford has the immense asset of a corruption-free reputation. He has a solid if unimaginative record in domestic policy, stands somewhere near the American center, and is greatly liked and respected on Capitol Hill. In foreign affairs, he is obviously inexperienced, but other Presidents have risen above such limitations, as the example of Harry Truman demonstrates. With Henry Kissinger's help, Ford should be able to carry on the basically sound Nixon policies. He would have one overriding advantage in dealing with foreign powers: their certainty that Ford would be in the White House for at least three more years. Nixon's great skills in foreign affairs are now alarmingly offset by the uncertainties about his future and his patent loss of power at home.

It was just one year ago this week that Richard Nixon was celebrating his fabulous electoral sweep and seemed to stand at the very summit of power and opportunity. Hard-core Nixon haters may gloat over his fall from those heights; for most Americans it is a matter of profound disappointment. The editors of TIME Inc. speaking on the editorial page of TIME's sister publication LIFE, have endorsed Nixon for President three times, in 1960, 1968 and 1972. We did so with acknowledgments that aspects of the Nixon record and temperament were troubling, but we believed that his strengths of intellect and experience and his instinct for political leadership equipped him well for the office. In endorsing Nixon in 1972, following on his first-term achievements in foreign policy, we expressed a hope that by the end of his second term we could "salute him as a great President." Thus we come with deep reluctance to our conclusion that he must leave office. We consider the situation so unprecedented, the issue so crucial to the country, that we publish this first editorial in TIME's 50-year history.

In the almost daily rush of revelations, it is not easy for the numbed citizen to keep in mind the full enormity of "Watergate." Despite ample instances of past Government corruption, nothing can be found in U.S. history even remotely approaching the skein of events that the word Watergate no longer defines or contains. A Vice President, twice personally chosen by Nixon, forced to resign to escape jail. A former Attorney General and intimate adviser to Nixon under indictment. Another former Cabinet member under indictment. One of the two most powerful presidential aides under indictment. Six other White House aides or Administration officials indicted, convicted or having pleaded guilty; seven more fired or resigned. Most of them shown to have been either in charge of, or aware of, illegal operations. The whole White House pervaded by an atmosphere of aggressive amorality—amorality almost raised to a creed. A ruthless determination to hide as much of this as possible from the public and investigators.

The question that once seemed so important—Did the President know about the cover-up?—was always somewhat beside the point. Whatever he knew or did not know he must be held accountable for the actions of his top aides and the standards he established. To the extent that the question had meaning, it was almost impossible from the start to answer it in the President's favor: the men involved were too close to him to make his ignorance plausible; after initial indignant denials, each of his later explanations gradually admitted more knowledge, thereby conceding each previous explanation to have been at least partly false. One cannot think of any organization, public or private—including some dictatorships—where a Chief Executive could survive in office after such a performance.

The catalogue of the President's involvement in illegal or grossly improper acts has become all too familiar. He approved the so-called Huston plan, which permitted illegal means (including burglary) to combat radicals. He established the "plumbers" unit, ostensibly to plug leaks, and it used illegal methods (wiretaps, forgery) to embarrass or spy on political foes. He impeded an investigation of the plumbers on specious national-security grounds while his aides tried to use the CIA and FBI to help the cover-up. He had a job offer (chief of the FBI) dangled before the judge presiding over the trial of Daniel Ellsberg. He withheld knowledge of the Ellsberg-psychiatrist burglary from that judge for at least a month. His aides offered Executive clemency to some of the Watergate defendants; others, including his personal lawyer, used campaign contributions for payments to Watergate defendants.

President Nixon's most recent actions come as a staggering climax to all that went before. We devoutly hope that it *is* the climax. When he originally refused to hand over the White House tapes either to the Senate Watergate committee or to Special Prosecutor Archibald Cox, his argument for the confidentiality of the President's deliberations certainly deserved consideration. Then the court narrowed the issue in such a way that confidentiality could be largely safeguarded; only the judge was to hear the tapes, and only for the purpose of deciding whether any parts were potential evidence in the cases arising from Watergate. If the President had wanted to contest this ruling, he had a clear opportunity to have the matter settled in the Supreme Court, by whose decision he had earlier said that he would abide.

Instead, the President and his lawyer worked out the "compromise" under which summaries would be provided (they would not hold up as evidence in court), and Special Prosecutor Archibald Cox was to be forbidden any further recourse to the courts in seeking presidential papers. Cox sensibly refused, and was promptly fired in flagrant violation of the President's pledge to the Senate, through then–Attorney General-designate Richardson, that Cox would be independent and could be dismissed only for gross improprieties. That brought on the resignation of Richardson and the dismissal of his principal assistant, honorable men who both refused to carry out the President's order to fire Cox. After an outpouring of indignation from Congress and country, which saw Nixon as defying the courts and setting himself above the law, came the President's abrupt reversal and his decision to hand the tapes to the court after all. And only a few days ago, there was the sudden claim that two crucial tapes do not exist.

Now the President has found a new Attorney General and a new special prosecutor, equipped with not quite convincing promises of independence. Both are reputable men, but it seems to us that these appointments, or even the possible appointment of a prosecutor by the court, can no longer clear away the hopeless miasma of deceit and suspicion.

The right of free men to choose their leaders is precious and rare in a world mainly ruled by authoritarian governments. It is the genius of the American Constitution that it combines stability with liberty; it does so in part by fixing a term for the Chief Executive and largely protecting him from the caprices of parliamentary governments. An American President must be given the widest freedom of action, the utmost tolerance, the most generous benefit of every doubt. It is a system that has served us well.

A President's Gallup rating can fluctuate as much as the Dow Jones. He may push unpopular programs or oppose popular ones. Being a political as well as a national leader, he may dissemble within more or less accepted political limits. His Administration may be touched by corruption, provided that he does not condone it. He may make mistakes, many of them. He may fight the other branches of Government, for this is sometimes necessary to get things done. None of these matters—especially since they are always subject to partisan interpretation—are sufficient in themselves to justify the removal of a President.

Yet there is a limit beyond which even such "permissible" offenses, even such instances of "mere" misgovernment, become intolerable. And the situation changes fundamentally when the effect of the President's actions and the actions of his appointees is to subvert the constitutional system itself. He then betrays his formal oath of office and his informal compact with the people.

There are legitimate fears about the precedent that would be set by the President's resignation or impeachment. In two centuries, no American President has been removed from office other than by death or the voters' will. Once the spell is broken, would it become too easy for political opponents of any future President to oust him? We think not. Watergate is unique. In fact, the really dangerous precedent would be the opposite: to allow a President with Nixon's record to continue in office. This would be a terrible circumstance to lodge in our history, a terrible thing to explain to our children and their children.

In recent decades, the American presidency has assumed an almost sacrosanct aura. It is time to remember that quite literally, and not as a flourish of speech, the sovereign in America is not the President but the people. It is true that the people elect him, which gives him his unique mandate, but to conclude from this that a President must be preserved in all circumstances, at any cost, is the first unwitting step toward dictatorship.

As Watergate and related events emerged in congressional hearings and in the press, many patriotic Americans were nagged by a sense of disproportion. Crookedness and corner cutting? Yes. Crimes? No doubt—but after all, as the phrase went, "No one was killed." How could these acts, however shady or offensive, be weighed against the life-and-death responsibilities of the President? This rationalization will not stand; a President's "big decisions" cannot be put into a compartment separate from his other actions, his total behavior. His integrity and trustworthiness are perhaps the most important facts about him to his country and to the world. And these Nixon has destroyed.

The nightmare of uncertainty must be ended. A fresh start must be made. Some at home and abroad might see in the President's resignation a sign of American weakness and failure. It would be a sign of the very opposite. It would show strength and health. It would show the ability of a badly infected political system to cleanse itself. It would show the true power of popular government under law in America.

16.4:   The Vote for Impeachment (1974)

In July 1974, for the first time in over a century, the Judiciary Committee of the House of Representatives voted articles of impeachment against a president. The selection below is a transcription of these articles. They would have become the basis for Nixon's trial by the Senate had he not resigned first.

Based on the evidence you have seen, were the articles valid? Note that none of the articles were adopted unanimously. Most of the negative votes came from Republicans. Does this support a political interpretation of Watergate? Keep in mind that Nixon himself was a highly partisan politician. He seldom sought or expected consensus, and his partisanship aroused similar responses in his Democratic and liberal opponents. Would a less partisan president have avoided the searching investigation of Watergate that destroyed him? Do you know if other presidents have employed political espionage or "dirty tricks" against their enemies?

Impeachment Articles

House Judiciary Committee

Article I

In his conduct of the office of President of the United States, Richard M. Nixon, in violation of his constitutional oath faithfully to execute the office of President of the United States and, to the best of his ability, preserve, protect, and defend the Constitution of the United States, and in violation of his constitutional duty to take care that the laws be faithfully executed, has prevented, obstructed, and impeded the administration of justice, in that:

On June 17, 1972, and prior thereto, agents of the Committee for the Re-election of the President committed unlawful entry of the headquarters of the Democratic National Committee in Washington, District of Columbia, for the purpose of securing political intelligence. Subsequent thereto, Richard M. Nixon, using the powers of his high office, engaged personally and through his close subordinates and agents, in a course of conduct or plan designed to delay, impede, and obstruct the investigation of such unlawful entry; to cover up, conceal and protect those responsible; and to conceal the existence and scope of other unlawful covert activities.

The means used to implement this course of conduct or plan included one or more of the following:

1. making false or misleading statements to lawfully authorized investigative officers and employees of the United States;
2. withholding relevant and material evidence or information from lawfully authorized investigative officers and employees of the United States;
3. approving, condoning, acquiescing in, and counseling witnesses with respect to the giving of false or misleading statements to lawfully authorized investigative officers and employees of the United States and false or misleading testimony in duly instituted judicial and congressional proceedings;
4. interfering or endeavoring to interfere with the conduct of investigations by the Department of Justice of the United States, the Federal Bureau of Investigation, the Office of Watergate Special Prosecution Force, and Congressional Committees;

Congressional Quarterly, *Historic Documents, 1974* (Washington, DC: Congressional Quarterly Inc., 1975), pp. 656–660.

5. approving, condoning, and acquiescing in, the surreptitious payment of substantial sums of money for the purpose of obtaining the silence or influencing the testimony of witnesses, potential witnesses or individuals who participated in such unlawful entry and other illegal activities;
6. endeavoring to misuse the Central Intelligence Agency, an agency of the United States;
7. disseminating information received from officers of the Department of Justice of the United States to subjects of investigations conducted by lawfully authorized investigative officers and employees of the United States, for the purpose of aiding and assisting such subjects in their attempts to avoid criminal liability.
8. making or causing to be made false or misleading public statements for the purpose of deceiving the people of the United States into believing that a thorough and complete investigation had been conducted with respect to allegations of misconduct on the part of personnel of the executive branch of the United States and personnel of the Committee for the Re-election of the President, and that there was no involvement of such personnel in such misconduct; or
9. endeavoring to cause prospective defendants, and individuals duly tried and convicted, to expect favored treatment and consideration in return for their silence or false testimony, or rewarding individuals for their silence or false testimony.

In all of this, Richard M. Nixon has acted in a manner contrary to his trust as President and subversive of constitutional government, to the great prejudice of the cause of law and justice and to the manifest injury of the people of the United States.

Wherefore Richard M. Nixon, by such conduct, warrants impeachment and trial, and removal from office.

—Adopted July 27 by a 27–11 vote

Article II

Using the powers of the office of President of the United States, Richard M. Nixon, in violation of his constitutional oath faithfully to execute the office of President of the United States and, to the best of his ability, preserve, protect, and defend the Constitution of the United States, and in disregard of his constitutional duty to take care that the laws be faithfully executed, has repeatedly engaged in conduct violating the constitutional rights of citizens, impairing the due and proper administration of justice and the conduct of lawful inquiries, or contravening the laws governing agencies of the executive branch and the purposes of these agencies.

This conduct has included one or more of the following:

1. He has, acting personally and through his subordinates and agents, endeavored to obtain from the Internal Revenue Service, in violation of the constitutional rights of citizens, confidential information contained in income tax returns for purposes not authorized by law, and to cause, in violation of the constitutional rights of citizens, income tax audits or other income tax investigations to be initiated or conducted in a discriminatory manner.
2. He misused the Federal Bureau of Investigation, the Secret Service, and other executive personnel, in violation or disregard of the constitutional rights of citizens, by directing or authorizing such agencies or personnel to conduct or continue electronic surveillance or other investigations for purposes unrelated to

national security, the enforcement of laws, or any other lawful function of his office; he did direct, authorize, or permit the use of information obtained thereby for purposes unrelated to national security, the enforcement of laws, or any other lawful function of his office; and he did direct the concealment of certain records made by the Federal Bureau of Investigation of electronic surveillance.

3. He has, acting personally and through his subordinates and agents, in violation or disregard of the constitutional rights of citizens, authorized and permitted to be maintained a secret investigative unit within the office of the President, financed in part with money derived from campaign contributions, which unlawfully utilized the resources of the Central Intelligence Agency, engaged in covert and unlawful activities, and attempted to prejudice the constitutional right of an accused to a fair trial.

4. He has failed to take care that the laws were faithfully executed by failing to act when he knew or had reason to know that his close subordinates endeavored to impede and frustrate lawful inquiries by duly constituted executive, judicial, and legislative entities concerning the unlawful entry into the headquarters of the Democratic National Committee, and the cover up thereof, and concerning other unlawful activities including those relating to the confirmation of Richard Kleindienst as Attorney General of the United States, the electronic surveillance of private citizens, the break-in into the offices of Dr. Lewis Fielding and the campaign financing practices of the Committee to Re-elect the President [sic].

5. In disregard of the rule of law, he knowingly misused the executive branch, including the Federal Bureau of Investigation, the Criminal Division, and the Office of Watergate Special Prosecution Force, of the Department of Justice, and the Central Intelligence Agency, in violation of his duty to take care that the laws be faithfully executed.

In all of this, Richard M. Nixon has acted in a manner contrary to his trust as President and subversive of constitutional government, to the great prejudice of the cause of law and justice and to the manifest injury of the people of the United States.

Wherefore Richard M. Nixon, by such conduct, warrants impeachment and trial, and removal from office.

—Adopted July 29 by a 28–10 vote

Article III

In his conduct of the office of President of the United States, Richard M. Nixon, contrary to his oath faithfully to execute the office of President of the United States and, to the best of his ability, preserve, protect, and defend the Constitution of the United States, and in violation of his constitutional duty to take care that the laws be faithfully executed, has failed without lawful cause of excuse to produce papers and things as directed by duly authorized subpoenas issued by the Committee on the Judiciary of the House of Representatives on April 11, 1974, May 15, 1974, May 30, 1974, and June 24, 1974, and willfully disobeyed such subpoenas. The subpoenaed papers and things were deemed necessary by the Committee in order to resolve by direct evidence fundamental, factual questions relating to Presidential direction, knowledge, or approval of actions demonstrated by other evidence to be substantial grounds for impeachment of the President. In refusing to produce these papers and things Richard M. Nixon, substituting his judgment as to what materials were necessary for the inquiry, interposed the powers of the Presidency against the lawful subpoenas of the House of Representatives, thereby assuming to himself functions and judgments necessary to the exercise of the sole power of impeachment vested by the Constitution in the House of Representatives.

In all of this, Richard M. Nixon has acted in a manner contrary to his trust as President and subversive of constitutional government, to the great prejudice of the cause of law and justice, and to the manifest injury of the people of the United States.

Wherefore, Richard M. Nixon by such conduct, warrants impeachment and trial, and removal from office.

—Adopted July 30 by a 21–17 vote

17

The Reagan Revolution

By the late 1970s the public mood in America had turned sour. Abroad the United States seemed on the defensive. During these years the Soviet Union expanded its military strength and extended its influence into Central America, West Africa, and Afghanistan. Meanwhile, in the wake of the 1973 Arab-Israeli War, the Organization of Petroleum Exporting Countries (OPEC) raised oil prices to levels that threatened to strangle the American economy. At home, the worst of the sixties turmoil was past, but crime, drugs, illegitimacy, divorce, sexual permissiveness, pornography, and other social problems lingered and indeed seemed to become worse.

The American economy also seemed sick. A chronic condition called "stagflation"—simultaneous price inflation and stagnant economic growth—had gripped the nation and would not yield. At the same time the United States seemed to be losing its competitive edge in the international economy. Japan, Germany, and other Asian and European nations had captured many of America's foreign customers as well as the American domestic market for cars, steel, clothing, cameras, and electronics goods.

Perceptions of decline and retreat reawakened a dormant conservative movement, which in 1980 triumphed with the presidential election of Ronald Reagan, the former Hollywood actor and recent governor of California.

The Reagan administration that came to power in January 1981 promised to reduce inflation, restore America's international prestige, unleash economic energies, and improve the nation's moral climate. The documents that follow touch on several aspects of this conservative movement that culminated in what has been called the "Reagan Revolution." You will encounter defenders as well as detractors of conservative policies and programs, and as usual you should thoughtfully consider their contending views. The final evaluation, however, as always, is yours to make.

17.1:   The New Right (1985, 1980, 1978)

The political right of the late 1970s and eighties was a composite movement. One strand derived from the individualistic conservatism that had coalesced around Barry Goldwater in 1964. Inspired by the frontier tradition, this brand was sustained and financed by self-made entrepreneurs from California, Texas, the mountain states, and the newly prosperous South.

The first selection is by James Watt, a Denver lawyer who made his reputation as a defender of western ranching, mining, and timber interests opposed to environmentalist federal land and resource policies. In 1981 Watt came to Washington as Ronald Reagan's first secretary of the interior and promptly created a furor by policies and pronouncements that emphasized exploiting rather than preserving federally owned natural resources. An unabashed conservative, in 1983 Watt was forced out of the administration.

What is Watt's central theme? Are his views new ones? Or have Americans always been suspicious of government? What sort of society would America be today if Watt's views had prevailed in the past? Are there any signs in this selection that Watt is willing to compromise with liberalism?

The second document represents another thread in 1980s conservatism: the new religious right. It is written by the Reverend Jerry Falwell, the pastor of the Thomas Road Baptist Church in Lynchburg, Virginia. A fundamentalist who believed in the "inerrancy" of the Bible and deplored the moral damage of weakening Christian faith, Falwell had attacked the social activism of Martin Luther King, Jr., and other clerical defenders of civil rights during the 1960s. By the end of the next decade, however, he had concluded that without the active intervention of traditional religion the country would go to the dogs—or to the sinners.

In 1979, in collaboration with a new breed of secular conservative activists, Falwell and other religious conservatives organized the Moral Majority to imprint their moral vision on American public life. The Moral Majority urged pious Americans to express their beliefs at the ballot box in order to bring the reprobate nation back to virtue. The 1980 defeat of liberal candidates for Congress opposed by the Moral Majority convinced many Americans that the religious right had become a formi-

dable political force.

The selection included here is from Falwell's Listen America!, *a 1980 book that conveys the spirit of his concerns. Falwell refers to "situation ethics" and "secular humanism." What are these, and why does he abhor them? Why does he urge the defeat of the Equal Rights Amendment? There is a strong patriotic theme in the excerpt from* Listen America! *Is there a logical connection between Falwell's religious faith and a passionately pro-America position? Can liberals be patriots too?*

The third selection incorporates still another theme of the new right revival of the 1980s: "supply-side" economics. A creation of Arthur Laffer, Robert Mundell, and other conservative economists, the new theory sought to explain, and proposed a remedy for, stagflation. The economy's poor performance, supply-siders claimed, was the result of high taxes, government deficit spending, and the excessive emphasis on consumption (demand), all of which discouraged enterprise and investment. Rather than worrying about insufficient demand, *they argued, the government should encourage a greater* supply *of goods and services by stimulating economic effort and increased investment through tax cuts. Higher investment and production would put money in the pockets of the public in the form of wages and dividends and indirectly increase demand as well. Not only would the economy rebound in the short run, but America would be better prepared for sustained long-term growth as well.*

One of the most eloquent supply-side publicists was Jude Wanniski, a conservative journalist who wrote for the Wall Street Journal. *The article excerpted here represents Arthur Laffer's ideas as interpreted by Wanniski. In what way is supply-side economic theory consistent with other conservative views? How were the supply-siders able to test their theories in practice during the Reagan administration? Did events confirm the value of the theories? Who gained and who lost by the application of supply-side economics to federal policies?*

Individual Freedom Made America Great

JAMES WATT

There is an intense battle raging in this land. It can be described in political terms, theological expressions or economic equations because it is being fought in the halls of government, in the churches and in the marketplace. Its outcome will determine how we and our children will be governed in the twenty-first century.

James Watt, *The Courage of a Conservative* (New York: Simon and Schuster, 1985), pp. 17–27.

The focus of the battle has become the dignity of the individual versus the domination of government. Will America have a society of giant bureaucratic institutions, in both the public and the private sector, institutions that will have increasing power to control the economic and social behavior of the individual? Or will we have a society that restores and respects the dignity of individuals, so that they can enjoy their spiritual freedom and political liberty?

Since its beginnings in the early 1960s, the modern conservative movement has been warning the American people that we are at a crossroads. A massive, powerful government bureaucracy egged on by selfish special-interest groups is encroaching on the rights of the individual.

The threats to our government, an experiment that commenced with the American Revolution of the 1770s, have a chilling similarity to events following more recent revolutions in other lands. Leaders in other countries have risen up to champion liberty and freedom, only to see the results of their blood and sacrifice lost through institutionalization of power. In place of their dreams stand ugly totalitarian states with centralized bureaucracies or even dictators squeezing the life out of their very own citizens.

Until now, the American experiment has shown amazing resilience. All around us, revolutions have come and gone, while, somehow, our purpose has survived. But the first signs of the erosion of liberty are all around us, even though they are discounted by some without much alarm.

The loss of individual liberty has usually begun by laws created, with the best of intentions, "in the name of the people" and for "the collective good." These are beguiling arguments—some people find them irresistible. "The world is not as simple as it was in the days of Washington or Lincoln," they tell us. "Some compromises may be necessary to address the problems of a modern age." But what has not changed is human nature, and what people will do with corrupting power when they have it.

As we look to the twenty-first century, America must make significant changes in the role and performance of government if we are to protect spiritual freedom, political liberty and the dignity of the individual. We conservatives must demonstrate the courage to face the challenge and to forge the changes. It will not be easy, but neither was the first step. When Thomas Jefferson declared independence from excessive government, he wrote, "For the support of this Declaration, with a firm reliance on the protection of divine Providence, we mutually pledge to each other our lives, our fortunes, and our sacred honor."

There is time to bring about change, and therefore, there is hope. Ironically, our best hope lies in the fact that our freedom has been eroding just long enough for us to have a record to study. We can begin to see where we are headed by taking a look at the winding trail behind us. . . .

The Rights of the Individual

. . . How have we, the American people, made our country greater than all others? Is it our free-enterprise system, which some say has triumphed so convincingly over the worldwide Socialist experiment? No. Immigrants were coming here long before America was rich or powerful. It was not the guarantee of riches that brought them. It was the guarantee of opportunity. They didn't want a handout, or even a hand. They simply wanted a chance.

A chance to do what? Economic opportunity was not the reason the Pilgrims came to Massachusetts or the Catholics to Maryland or the Quakers to Pennsylvania. They were seeking personal liberty and spiritual freedom. They were fleeing excessive government that in the name of "public good" was oppressing those with minority opinions. . . .

The motivation of those immigrants to the United States is the same motivation of conservatives today. It is the concern for the individual and his or her dignity. It is not a new concern. History tells us that mankind has always had a yearning for liberty that flows like a stream of life. From it comes the cry for the right of men and women to assemble together, to establish their own government, to work for whom they desire, to train their children as they wish, to provide for their own, to exercise their political liberty.

The individual frequently has found himself trapped by the will of government. Often it has been for the noblest of reasons that political liberty has been denied the individual. Sometimes the force of oppression was called the king, sometimes a dictator or warlord or czar, sometimes it was the Gestapo. But always it was excessive government.

The same history tells yet another story. Mankind has also had a yearning for another kind of freedom that also flows like a stream. That yearning is the desire to worship God, to join with others of like, precious faith, to develop their own doctrines and to train and educate their own children, to enjoy spiritual freedom. It is hard for twentieth-century youth reared in our now secularized society to appreciate how deeply rooted Western science, art and politics have been in religious faith. But history very clearly shows us how desperate the desire has been for spiritual freedom and how the struggle for it, too, has always been opposed by excessive government.

At one point in history, destiny provided that these two streams of life, political liberty and spiritual freedom, would come together in a mighty confluence called America. This combination, which permits pluralism, has made America great. It is these principles that still attract modern pilgrims like Alexander Solzhenitsyn. And it is the erosion of these principles that threatens our uniqueness. . . .

A Limited Role for Government

Then what is the conservative alternative? If government cannot solve all the problems of the people, who will? Shall we let the disadvantaged starve? Shall we allow confidence men to promote phony cures for cancer? Should all federal regulations be cut, all subsidies to the needy stopped? Should the federal government pull out and leave volunteer organizations, the states and local communities holding the bag for everything? Shall we return to the separatism of colonial America?

Of course not. Modern conservatives recognize that circumstances are different today from what they were in the 1770s. We would not repeal the Social Security system or eliminate welfare payments to the truly needy. We acknowledge that a kind of second revolution took place when, under Franklin Roosevelt, the federal government stepped in and took charge during the emergency of the Great Depression. We applaud the ability of a centralized government to respond quickly in a modern age when national problems arise. We applaud the federal government's role in helping to check racial discrimination, for example.

That is why I refer to our movement as the *modern* conservative movement. In America's past, we conservatives of today would hardly be considered conservative at all. We are conservative now about the degree of federal involvement. At best, we see excessive government as promoting a failed economic policy, financially defrauding the very disadvantaged people it had promised to help. At worst, we see excessive government as a threat to the spiritual freedom and individual liberty of its citizens.

Modern conservatives have not called for the dismantling of the entire government bureaucracy. But we have called for a serious pruning, and, far beyond any technical adjustment here or there, we are seeking to recapture the original American idea.

The modern conservative takes issue with the suggestion that the American system is flawed or corrupt and requires massive governmental intervention to right it. We have no romantic illusions about a worldwide Socialist movement that manifests itself in its newly formed governments with mass murders of millions, and in its older established governments with inefficient industry, creating products that don't work and shortages for its workers. Conservatives feel no compulsion to borrow economic solutions from countries that can't even supply their own people with basic needs. We believe in the original American idea of guaranteeing dignity for the individual through political liberty and spiritual freedom. We seek a counterrevolution to recapture the best of that idea.

A Question of Survival

America is at a crossroads. With each election, she is taking another step. We conservatives argue that her roots are good, that we can trust and should conserve the original idea. There is no other country with our spiritual freedom and individual liberty. Let the Swedes nationalize their banks to resolve a temporary economic crisis. Let the French government experiment with socialism and take ownership of its steel factories. Let the British tax their corporations at an 80 percent rate and socialize their medicine. Let the Cubans and Nicaraguans protect their peoples from the "evils of religion" and use government to fight—and, in the case of the Cubans, actually close—their churches and synagogues.

America is one of a kind. She should not be insecure and should not let her imperfections panic her into mimicking inferior models.

There was another special moment during that private dinner at the White House. Before the evening was over, we stopped in a narrow hall. President Reagan nodded solemnly toward a browned, frayed parchment framed on the wall. "Let me show you this, Jim," he said. "This is an original of the national anthem. It's in Francis Scott Key's own handwriting."

We chatted a moment about the history of "The Star-Spangled Banner," and then I told the president this story. A few years ago, I was attending an evening church service. Our pastor asked us to stand and sing the national anthem. As I stood with the congregation, I heard for probably the first time the meaning of the words I had sung so many times. As I came to the end of the first verse, I sang with gusto these words: "Oh, say does that Star-Spangled Banner yet wave/O'er the land of the free and the home of the brave?" Our national anthem ends with a question mark. I had never noticed it before. It is a question that must be answered, and answered again and again.

President Reagan was deeply moved by my story, and as I finished, his eyes misted. Neither of us said anything. Outside, on the South Lawn of the White House, illuminated by bright spotlights, the American flag was billowing in the wind. Over what kind of land is our flag waving? Is it a land of people who are free to exercise independent choice, or has their grip on freedom begun to slip? Is it waving over the home of people who are brave enough to face an unknown future without guarantees from the government? Brave enough to resist a foreign power whose weapons could hold the whole world hostage if it threatened to destroy mankind? Francis Scott Key's question must be answered for itself by each generation.

We Must Return to Traditional Religious Values

JERRY FALWELL

We must reverse the trend America finds herself in today. Young people between the ages of twenty-five and forty have been born and reared in a different world than Americans of years past. The television set has been their primary baby-sitter. From the television set they have learned situation ethics and immorality—they have learned a loss of respect for human life. They have learned to disrespect the family as God has established it. They have been educated in a public-school system that is permeated with secular humanism. They have been taught that the Bible is just another book of literature. They have been taught that there are no absolutes in our world today. They have been introduced to the drug culture. They have been reared by the family and by the public school in a society that is greatly void of discipline and character-building. These same young people have been reared under the influence of a government that has taught them socialism and welfarism. They have been taught to believe that the world owes them a living whether they work or not.

I believe that America was built on integrity, on faith in God, and on hard work. I do not believe that anyone has ever been successful in life without being willing to add that last ingredient—diligence or hard work. We now have second- and third-generation welfare recipients. Welfare is not always wrong. There are those who do need welfare, but we have reared a generation that understands neither the dignity nor the importance of work.

Every American who looks at the facts must share a deep concern and burden for our country. We are not unduly concerned when we say that there are some very dark clouds on America's horizon. I am not a pessimist, but it is indeed a time for truth. If Americans will face the truth, our nation can be turned around and can be saved from the evils and the destruction that have fallen upon every other nation that has turned its back on God.

There is no excuse for what is happening in our country. We must, from the highest office in the land right down to the shoe shine boy in the airport, have a return to biblical basics. If the Congress of our United States will take its stand on that which is right and wrong, and if our President, our judiciary system, and our state and local leaders will take their stand on holy living, we can turn this country around.

I personally feel that the home and the family are still held in reverence by the vast majority of the American public. I believe there is still a vast number of Americans who love their country, are patriotic, and are willing to sacrifice for her. I remember the time when it was positive to be patriotic, and as far as I am concerned, it still is. I remember as a boy, when the flag was raised, everyone stood proudly and put his hand upon his heart and pledged allegiance with gratitude. I remember when the band struck up "The Stars and Stripes Forever," we stood and goose pimples would run all over me. I remember when I was in elementary school during World War II, when every report from the other shores meant something to us. We were not out demonstrating against our boys who were dying in Europe and Asia. We were praying for them and thanking God for them and buying war bonds to help pay for the materials and artillery they needed to fight and win and come back.

I believe that Americans want to see this country come back to basics, back to values, back to biblical morality, back to sensibility, and back to patriotism. Americans are looking for leadership and guidance. It is fair to ask the question, "If 84 per cent of the American people still believe in morality, why is America having such internal problems?" We must look for the answer to the highest places in every level of government. We have a lack of leadership in America. But Americans have been lax in voting in and out of office the right and the wrong people.

My responsibility as a preacher of the Gospel is one of influence, not of control, and that is the responsibility of each individual citizen. Through the ballot box Americans must provide for strong moral leadership at every level. If our country will get back on the track in sensibility and moral sanity, the crises that I have herein mentioned will work out in the course of time and with God's blessings.

It is now time to take a stand on certain moral issues, and we can only stand if we have leaders. We must stand against the Equal Rights Amendment, the feminist revolution, and the homosexual revolution. We must have a revival in this country. . . .

As a preacher of the Gospel, I not only believe in prayer and preaching, I also believe in good citizenship. If a labor union in America has the right to organize and improve its working conditions, then I believe that the churches and the pastors, the priests, and the rabbis of America have a responsibility, not just the right, to see to it that the moral climate and conscience of Americans is such that this nation can be healed inwardly. If it is healed inwardly, then it will heal itself outwardly. . . .

Americans have been silent much too long. We have stood by and watched as American power and influence have been systematically weakened in every sphere of the world.

We are not a perfect nation, but we are still a free nation because we have the blessing of God upon us. We must continue to follow in a path that will ensure that blessing. . . .

Let us never forget that as our Constitution declares, we are endowed by our Creator with certain inalienable rights. It is only as we abide by those laws established by our Creator that He will continue to bless us with these rights. We are endowed our rights to freedom and liberty and the pursuit of happiness by the God who created man to be free and equal.

The hope of reversing the trends of decay in our republic now lies with the Christian public in America. We cannot expect help from the liberals. They certainly are not going to call our nation back to righteousness and neither are the pornographers, the smut peddlers, and those who are corrupting our youth. Moral Americans must be willing to put their reputations, their fortunes, and their very lives on the line for this great nation of ours. Would that we had the courage of our forefathers who knew the great responsibility that freedom carries with it. . . .

Our Founding Fathers separated church and state in function, but never intended to establish a government void of God. As is evidenced by our Constitution, good people in America must exert an influence and provide a conscience and climate of morality in which it is difficult to go wrong, not difficult for people to go right in America.

I am positive in my belief regarding the Constitution that God led in the development of that document, and as a result, we here in America have enjoyed 204 years of unparalleled freedom. The most positive people in the world are people who believe the Bible to be the Word of God. The Bible contains a positive message. It is a message written by 40 men over a period of approximately 1,500 years under divine inspiration. It is God's message of love, redemption, and deliverance for a fallen race. What could be more positive than the message of redemption in the Bible? But God will force

Himself upon no man. Each individual American must make His choice. . . .

Americans must no longer linger in ignorance and apathy. We cannot be silent about the sins that are destroying this nation. The choice is ours. We must turn America around or prepare for inevitable destruction. I am listening to the sounds that threaten to take away our liberties in America. And I have listened to God's admonitions and His direction—the only hopes of saving America. Are you listening too?

Taxes, Revenues, and the "Laffer Curve"

JUDE WANNISKI

As Arthur Laffer has noted, "There are always two tax rates that yield the same revenues." When an aide to President Gerald Ford asked him once to elaborate, Laffer (who is Professor of Business Economics at the University of Southern California) drew a simple curve to illustrate his point. The point, too, is simple enough—though, like so many simple points, it is also powerful in its implications.

When the tax rate is 100 percent, all production ceases in the money

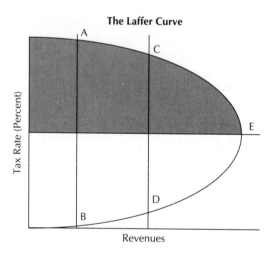

The Laffer Curve

economy (as distinct from the barter economy, which exists largely to escape taxation). People will not work in the money economy if all the fruits of their labors are confiscated by the government. And because production ceases, there is nothing for the 100-percent rate to confiscate, so government revenues are zero.

On the other hand, if the tax rate is zero, people can keep 100 percent of what they produce in the money economy. There is no governmental

Jude Wanniski, "Taxes, Revenues, and the 'Laffer Curve.'" Reprinted from *The Public Interest*, No. 50 (Winter 1978), pp. 3–16. © 1978 by National Affairs, Inc.

"wedge" between earnings and after-tax income, and thus no governmental barrier to production. Production is therefore maximized, and the output of the money economy is limited only by the desire of workers for leisure. But because the tax rate is zero, government revenues are again zero, and there can be no government. So at a 0-percent tax rate the economy is in a state of anarchy, and at a 100-percent tax rate the economy is functioning entirely through barter.

In between lies the curve. If the government reduces its rate to something less than 100 percent, say to point A, some segment of the barter economy will be able to gain so many efficiencies by being in the money economy that, even with near-confiscatory tax rates, after-tax production would still exceed that of the barter economy. Production will start up, and revenues will flow into the government treasury. By lowering the tax rate, we find an increase in revenues.

On the bottom end of the curve, the same thing is happening. If people feel that they need a minimal government and thus institute a low tax rate, some segment of the economy, finding that the marginal loss of income exceeds the efficiencies gained in the money economy, is shifted into either barter or leisure. But with that tax rate, revenues do flow into the government treasury. This is the situation at point B. Point A represents a very high tax rate and very low production. Point B represents a very low tax rate and very high production. Yet they both yield the same revenue to the government.

The same is true of points C and D. The government finds that by a further lowering of the tax rate, say from point A to point C, revenues increase with the further expansion of output. And by raising the tax rate, say from point B to point D, revenues also increase, by the same amount.

Revenues and production are maximized at point E. If, at point E, the government lowers the tax rate again, output will increase, but revenues will fall. And if, at point E, the tax rate is raised, both output and revenue will decline. The shaded area is *the prohibitive range for government,* where rates are unnecessarily high and can be reduced with gains in *both* output and revenue.

Tax Rates and Tax Revenues

The next important thing to observe is that, except for the 0-percent and 100-percent rates, there are no numbers along the "Laffer curve." Point E is not 50 percent, although it may be, but rather a variable number: *It is the point at which the electorate desires to be taxed.* At points B and D, the electorate desires more government goods and services and is willing—without reducing its productivity—to pay the higher rates consistent with the revenues at point E. And at points A and C, the electorate desires more private goods and services in the money economy, and wishes to pay the lower rates consistent with the revenues at point E. It is the task of the statesman to determine the location of point E, and follow its variations as closely as possible. . . .

Work vs. Productivity

The idea behind the "Laffer curve" is no doubt as old as civilization, but unfortunately politicians have always had trouble grasping it. In his essay, *Of Taxes*, written in 1756, David Hume pondered the problem:

> Exorbitant taxes, like extreme necessity, destroy industry by producing despair; and even before they reach this pitch, they raise the wages of the labourer and manufacturer, and heighten the price of all commodities. An attentive disinterested legislature will observe the point when the emolument ceases, and the prejudice begins. But as the contrary character is much more common, 'tis to be feared that taxes all over Europe are multiplying to such a degree as will entirely crush all art and industry; tho' perhaps, their first increase, together with other circumstances, might have contributed to the growth of these advantages.

The chief reason politicians and economists throughout history have failed to grasp the idea behind the "Laffer curve" is their confusion of work and productivity. Through both introspection and observation, the politician understands that when tax rates are raised, there is a tendency to work harder and longer to maintain after-tax income. What is not so apparent, because it requires analysis *at the margin*, is this: As taxes are raised, individuals in the system may indeed work harder, but their productivity declines. . . .

Imagine that there are three men who are skilled at building houses. If they work together, one works on the foundation, one on the frame, and the third on the roof. Together they can build three houses in three months. If they work separately, each building his own home, they need six months to build the three houses. If the tax rate on homebuilding is 49 percent, they will work together, since the government leaves them a small gain from their division of labor. But if the tax rate goes to 51 percent, they suffer a net loss because of their teamwork, and so they will work separately. When they were pooling their efforts, since they could produce six houses in the same time it would take them to build three houses working alone, the government was collecting revenues almost equivalent to the value of three completed homes. At the 51-percent tax rate, however, the government loses all the revenue, and the economy loses the production of the three extra homes that could have been built by their joint effort. . . .

The Politics of the "Laffer Curve"

The "Laffer curve" is a simple but exceedingly powerful analytical tool. In one way or another, all transactions, even the simplest, take place along it. The homely adage, "You can catch more flies with molasses than with vinegar," expresses the essence of the curve. But empires are built on the bottom of this simple curve and crushed against the top of it. The Caesars understood this, and so did Napoleon (up to a point) and the greatest of the Chinese emperors. The Founding Fathers of the United States knew it well; the arguments for union (in *The Federalist Papers*) made by [Alexander]

Hamilton, [James] Madison, and [John] Jay reveal an understanding of the notion. Until World War I—when progressive taxation was sharply increased to help finance it—the United States successfully remained out of the "prohibitive range."

In the 20th century, especially since World War I, there has been a constant struggle by all the nations of the world to get down the curve. The United States managed to do so in the 1920's, because Andrew Mellon understood the lessons of the "Laffer curve" for the domestic economy. . . .

The stock market crash of 1929 and the subsequent global depression occurred because Herbert Hoover unwittingly contracted the world economy with his high-tariff policies, which pushed the West, as an economic unit, up the "Laffer curve." Hoover compounded the problem in 1932 by raising personal tax rates almost up to the levels of 1920. . . .

The British empire was built on the lower end of the "Laffer curve" and dismantled on the upper end. The high wartime rates imposed to finance the Napoleonic wars were cut back sharply in 1816, despite warnings from "fiscal experts" that the high rates were needed to reduce the enormous public debt of £900 million. For the following 60 years, the British economy grew at an unprecedented pace, as a series of finance ministers used ever-expanding revenues to lower steadily the tax rates and tariffs.

In Britain, though, unlike the United States, there was no Mellon to risk lowering the extremely high tax rates imposed to finance World War I. As a result, the British economy struggled through the 1920's and 1930's. After World War II, the British government again made the mistake of not sufficiently lowering tax rates to spur individual initiative. Instead, the postwar Labour government concentrated on using tax policy for Keynesian objectives—i.e., increasing consumer demand to expand output. On October 23, 1945, tax rates were cut on lower-income brackets and surtaxes were added to the already high rates on the upper-income brackets. Taxes on higher incomes were increased, according to Chancellor of the Exchequer Hugh Dalton, in order to "continue that steady advance toward economic and social equality which we have made during the war and which the Government firmly intends to continue in peace."

From that day in 1945, there has been no concerted political voice in Britain arguing for a reduction of the high tax rates. Conservatives have supported and won tax reductions for business, especially investment-tax income credits. But while arguing for a reduction of the 83-percent rate on incomes above £20,000 (roughly $35,000 at current exchange rates) of earned income and the 98-percent rate on "unearned income" from investments, they have insisted that government *first* lower its spending, in order to permit the rate reductions. Somehow, the spending levels never can be cut. Only in the last several months of 1977 has Margaret Thatcher, the leader of the opposition Conservative Party, spoken of reducing the high tax rates as a way of expanding revenues.

In the United States, in September 1977, the Republic National Committee unanimously endorsed the plan of Representative Jack Kemp of

New York for cutting tax rates as a way of expanding revenues through increased business activity. This was the first time since 1953 that the GOP had embraced the concept of tax cuts! In contrast, the Democrats under President Kennedy sharply cut tax rates in 1962–64 (though making their case in Keynesian terms). The reductions successfully moved the United States economy down the "Laffer curve," expanding the economy and revenues.

It is crucial to Western economic expansion, peace, and prosperity that "conservative" parties move in this direction. They are, after all, traditionally in favor of income growth, with "liberals" providing the necessary political push for income redistribution. A welfare state is perfectly consistent with the "Laffer curve," and can function successfully along its lower range. But there must be income before there can be income redistribution. Most of the economic failures of this century can rightly be charged to the failure of conservatives to press for tax rates along the lower range of the "Laffer curve." Presidents Eisenhower, Nixon and Ford were timid in this crucial area of public policy. The Goldwater Republicans of 1963–64, in fact, emphatically opposed the Kennedy tax-rate cuts!

If, during the remainder of this decade, the United States and Great Britain demonstrate the power of the "Laffer curve" as an analytical tool, its use will spread, in the developing countries as well as the developed world. Politicians who understand the curve will find that they can defeat politicians who do not, other things being equal. Electorates all over the world always know when they are unnecessarily perched along the upper edge of the "Laffer curve," and will support political leaders who can bring them back down.

17.2:   The Liberals Hit Back (1982, 1981)

Needless to say, many Americans never accepted the views of the revived political right. Liberal and left-of-center publications and critics disliked virtually everything about the New Right and denounced the Reagan administration and its policies. The first selection is an attack from the political left by economist Robert L. Heilbroner on Reaganite economic policy that goes beyond objections to supply-side tax policies. What is Heilbroner really indicting? Are his characterizations of the prevailing socioeconomic system well taken? Is it fair to hold the Reagan administration, or conservatives generally, responsible for the failings that Heilbroner sees in American society in the 1980s?

The religious right also encountered opposition. Religious liberals objected to the theology as well as the social philosophy of the Moral Majority and of the Protestant fundamentalists who formed its core. In the second selection Robert McAfee Brown, a prominent Presbyterian minister and professor of religion at New York's liberal Union

Theological Seminary, takes issue with Falwell and his colleagues. What is the stated religious basis for Brown's disagreements with the Moral Majority? Do you think Brown is solely concerned with what the Bible teaches? In what way do his politics disagree with Falwell's? Why do the two clergymen reach such different social and political conclusions?

The third selection is an attack on Reagan's policies by liberal public interest attorney Mark Green. Written in early 1981, just as the first Reagan budget proposals were wending their way through Congress, the piece takes issue with the underlying premises of supply-side economic theories. What are Green's major objections to "Reaganomics"? Why does he call the Reagan program "Cowboy Economics"? What does he anticipate will happen if the Reagan proposals pass? Has time confirmed or refuted Green's predictions?

The Demand for the Supply-Side

ROBERT L. HEILBRONER

Supply-side economics has taken Washington by storm. Both a diagnosis and a prescription, supply-side economics comprises ideas about what is wrong with the economy and remedies to put it right. As its name would indicate, both diagnosis and prescription emphasize the actual production of goods and services rather than the buying of them. From this vantage point, supply-siders see our fundamental difficulties as constraints, mainly caused by taxes that deter productive effort, rather than as problems deriving from a lack of purchasing power. We catch a vision of the economy as a coiled spring held down by the weight of government. Remove the weight, and the spring will reveal its inherent force.

Most of the heated discussions about supply-side economics are concerned with how much tension the spring really has and how vigorously it will respond to the removal of various tax disincentives. I shall come back to these matters later. But it seems foolish to begin an appraisal of supply-side economics with debates about how far we must cut income taxes to achieve renewed growth, or how quickly inflation will be overcome by increased output. At the root of all supply-side remedies lie profoundly held if sometimes implicit convictions about the nature of the capitalist system itself. Since I am convinced that these views are wrong, I cannot get much exercised about the particular prescription on supply-side medicines. . . .

To turn to . . . strictly economic matters: supply-side economics puts forward two policy prescriptions. First, it advocates a substantial reduction in marginal tax rates, in order to create a burst of response. A response of

Robert L. Heilbroner, "The Demand for the Supply-Side," in Robert Fink, ed., *Supply-Side Economics: A Critical Appraisal* (Frederick, MD: University Publications of America, 1982), pp. 80–91. An imprint of Greenwood Publishing Group, Inc., Westport, CT. Reprinted with permission.

what? The supply-siders are convinced that more hours will be worked, that less effort will be diverted into the underground economy, that more risks will be taken. In a word, we will produce more, giving rise to more employment, and ultimately to a diminution of inflationary pressure.

Here everything hinges on the crucial matter of how individuals or firms respond to tax cuts. The fact of the matter is that we do not know very much about this problem. Worse, it is possible to construct two quite opposing, but equally convincing predictions. The supply-siders[1] see individuals using their tax bonanzas, such as the Kemp-Roth proposed reduction of taxes by 10 percent a year for three years, to add to their savings, or as a spur to more effort because more income will be kept. Skeptics see an entirely different picture. They see families reacting to a tax bonanza the way they react to all income increases: they will spend about 95 percent of it. They also see an increase in their after-tax incomes permitting a lot of people to give up moonlighting, overtime, or other distasteful tasks to which high taxes have driven them. Thus the skeptics see the impact of supply-side policies as boosting inflation far more than production. I number myself among the skeptics.

And what about the stimulus to production that firms will experience, as taxes are rolled back and onerous regulations repealed? In all likelihood there will be some response: the crucial question is how much. Again two views are plausible. One of them, exemplified by George Gilder's[2] stress on the creative efforts of individual entrepreneurs, sees a great burst of small business formation, not only creating jobs but providing the innovative zest needed to restore economic vitality. The other, more skeptical view looks to the great corporations that dominate so much of economic life and asks whether tax reductions or milder regulation will suffice to turn the automobile industry around, to reinvigorate the steel industry, to strengthen the transportation system, to solve the energy problem, and the like. Once again, I number myself among the skeptics.

Second, supply-siders want to roll back government, not merely to get it off our backs, but also because government is perceived as essentially a wasteful, not a productive, use of resources. This last is a very interesting contention. I would be the last to deny the presence of government waste: the MX missile system, the space shuttle, the tax subsidies to various upper-income groups, not to mention the petty cadging and occasional grand larceny among welfare clients. However, I want to call attention to a curious aspect of the question of waste. It is that there is no waste in the private sector. This is the case because all "wasteful" activities are eliminated by the market, like the famous Edsel. On the other hand, whatever survives the test of the market is not waste. The five giant buildings that will be erected between 53rd and 57th Streets along Madison Avenue are not waste, whatev-

---

[1] A supply-side measure introduced in Congress by Representative Jack Kemp of New York and Senator William Roth of Delaware to federal income taxes—ED.

[2] A conservative writer on social and economic themes—ED.

er chaos they create, unless they cannot be rented. The $100,000 Rolls Royce is not waste, assuming that it sells. There is not waste in the production of *anything* that sells, because the very act of purchase provides the justification for whatever resources have been used.

Clearly there are entirely different criteria for waste in the public and private domains. Suppose that the scrutiny usually directed at government were brought to bear on private output, and that each act of private production had to justify itself by the *noneconomic* criteria we apply to public output. Would we not find a great deal of waste in the private sphere? And suppose that the government limited its production to those things it could sell—pocket-sized missiles and saleable services of all kinds. Would not all waste disappear from the public sphere? This leads one to think about the meaning of the "waste" perceived from the supply side.

It leads one also to reflect on the ideological element within supply-side thinking. To be sure, all social orders have ideologies, and none could exist without them. Therefore societies never think of their prevailing views as being "ideological," but rather as expressing self-evident or natural truths. As [historian] Immanuel Wallerstein has acutely remarked, during most periods of history there is effectively only one class that is conscious of itself, and this dominant class sincerely expresses its own views as representing those of the entire society. Thus the senators of Rome, the lords of the manor, the monarchs of France and England, and the members of the Soviet elite all speak with unself-conscious assurance in the name of their societies. None feels itself to be a "privileged" class or thinks its views to be other than universal. . . .

The question to be pondered is why supply-side economics has attracted the worst ideology, and why it has dulled the sensibilities of the best ideologists. I am ashamed to say the one convincing reason that occurs to me: supply-side economics has as its immediate objective the improvement of the conditions of the rich. What bonanzas will result from the lowering of the high marginal rate on property income and on the reduction of the capital gains tax! I too rub my hands at the prospect. To be sure, like all policies, the *ultimate* objective of supply-side economics is the improvement of the condition of everyone. Just the same, I do not think supply-side economics would adduce quite the same fervor, or quite the same dulling of critical sensibilities, if its *immediate* aim were the improvement of the poor and its ultimate aim the bettering of the rich. Self-interest has extraordinary powers of persuasion. . . .

What is likely to happen over the next decade? Nothing. I say so from a profound skepticism about the efficacy of supply-side stimuli. But from a more history-laden point of view, I mean something different by "nothing." I mean that the slow, almost invisible trends of the past will continue to have their way, not because these trends have a life of their own but because they express the inner motions, the self-created dynamic of the system. I will mention only two of these trends:

1. *State-owned or state-dependent organizations will emerge as the leading agents of accumulation.* We are all familiar with the slow drift in the texture of the representative firm, from a single-product, single-plant, single-family enterprise to a multi-product, multi-plant, multi-national managerial bureaucracy. This has been the consequence of the continuing division of labor and of technologies of control which have brought concentration and centralization in virtually every field of human endeavor.

    This trend now seems likely to move to a new level of organizational size and strength by combining the capital-mobilizing and competition-buffering abilities of the state with the independence and drive of private management. Most capitalist nations today have public-private firms in airlines or airframes, in steel, automobiles, chemicals, and the like.

    Many of these public-private firms have been formed to prevent private bankruptcies. That in no way weakens my argument. But the Japanese present a more interesting case. Japan is evidently now preparing to enter the semiconductor industry on a public-private basis with one or two huge firms. That industry today is still dominated by the United States, where numerous businesses compete vigorously for market shares. The result, as Lester Thurow[3] has written, is that in the U.S. the market is likely to eliminate the losers, and the Japanese will thereafter eliminate the winners.

    Whether or not the Japanese "model" of public-private coordination can be exported, I would think that statist enterprise of some sort is very likely to be the form in which the accumulation of capital is carried on in the coming years.

2. As part of this statist movement, I would also expect to see the emergence of an ever more explicit reliance on national planning. This will assume two forms. One will be macroplanning for adequate employment, probably through government work programs, for acceptable price behavior through a network of controls and mandatory incomes policies, and for international buffers through protectionism. The other form of planning will be microplanning aimed at channeling labor and capital into socially advantageous uses and at coping with disruptive problems such as energy, urban decay, etc.

    It may be objected that planning does not "work," that we are now in retreat from it—a retreat led by supply-side economics. That depends on what one means by "work." As I see it, *no organizational system can smoothly combine the explosive technology, restless polity, and deadening work experience of contemporary industrial society.* This is as true for self-styled socialist societies as for capitalist ones. Hence I do not expect state capitalism to "work" particularly well, but I expect it to survive and to continue the function that is the driving force of capitalism—the accumulation of capital by means of wage labor.

    It is possible, of course, that ideological opposition may reverse this two-century-long trend toward centralization. Social orders sometimes refuse to adopt changes which, to outsiders, would preserve their regimes: one thinks of the refusal of the Roman senators to undertake land reform, or of the opposition of the French aristocracy to tax reform. To identify historical trends is not to deny social orders the right to commit suicide.

These considerations lead inescapably to the question of how long capitalism is likely to survive. I would think for quite a long while. No one can project an "indefinite" life span for capitalism. It is by its nature dynamic,

---

[3] Thurow is a liberal economist—ED.

and is constantly changing. Today it is pressing against the absorptive limits of the environment and thereby threatening the pace and scope of accumulation. Its moral cement, as I have remarked, is dissolving in its commercial ethic. It faces the contradictions of its antagonistic policy and economy, and the Laocoön-like struggles of its accumulation mechanics. Its broad movement today seems toward a bureaucratic statist regime. After that, who can tell?

Nonetheless, I do not see any immediate "end" of capitalism. Much of the world remains to be penetrated by its formidable mode of labor organization, its seductive technology, its intellectual brilliance. However decadent at its center, capitalism is today without a serious rival as an economic system, dangerous though the Soviet Union may be as a military rival.

This expectation of continued life seems all the more likely because, as I have just said, there is really nothing yet visible beyond capitalism. As an imaginable institutional arrangement, socialism has become a word almost without content. If it means the nationalization of industry or private-public planning, it can be seen—at least, so I suggest—as the extension of capitalism. As a deindustrialization of society it holds forth the specter of a catastrophic decline in living standards. As a vast extension of worker participation, it suffers from a complete lack of any economic and political institutions—or conception of such institutions—within which workers' autonomy could be expressed. In the underdeveloped world it is all too likely that socialist revolutions will usher in narrow, inefficient, and xenophobic regimes.

Hence there is little enthusiasm for socialism today, always excepting the burning desire of oppressed peoples or abused workers to throw off cruel or simply sclerotic regimes. After that, the realities of the industrial process, the impatient expectations of the masses, the contagion of Western ideas and goods must somehow be accommodated. The next stage of economic history, whatever its label, will not be a pleasant one. That supply-side economics, the darling and fad of conservative thought, imagines itself to be the vehicle of this next stage strikes me as an extraordinary fantasy. It is to confuse a small eddy, located in a few board rooms and academic centers, with the Gulf Stream of history.

The Need for a Moral Minority

ROBERT McAFEE BROWN

Some of you may have misread the title "The Need for a Moral Minority," and assumed that I was going to address the Moral Majority. I am going to make some references to the Moral Majority in the course of these remarks, but I do not want to concentrate exclusively on that movement. I particularly

Robert McAfee Brown, "The Need for a Moral Minority," in Herbert Vetter, ed., *Speak Out against the New Right* (Boston: Beacon Press, 1982), pp. 118–126.

do not want to have the Moral Majority setting my agenda, or our agendas, for the eighties. I think that agenda is somewhat politically naive and theologically un-Biblical; I will try to footnote that in a little while.

My overall concern is much more how we can relate religion and politics positively. If along the way we can learn some things from the Moral Majority, about how not to do it, I am willing to call that a gain.

This whole problem of a religious presence on the political scene which has been highlighted for us in this rather recent emergence of the theological right wing, the problem of religion of the political scene is illustrated for me by a comment from an anonymous 17th century writer, one of my favorite anonymous comments. This writer wrote: "I had rather see coming toward me a whole regiment with drawn swords, than one lone Calvinist convinced that he is doing the will of God." Now that statement illustrates both the glory and demonry of Calvinism, and by a not very difficult extension, the potential glory and potential demonry of all political involvement on the part of religiously minded persons. On the one hand, there is something immensely freeing and energizing about the feeling that one is doing God's will, and that the outcome of one's activity is therefore safe in God's hands. Such an attitude can liberate one to new kinds of courage, to immense risk taking, even to the point of death. . . .

But there can be a demonry as well in the invoking of God's support which we find exhibited when individuals or groups decide what they want to impose on others, and then claim divine sanction for it. This gives them carte blanche to do whatever they feel is necessary to stop their opponents since their opponents, being opposed to them, are clearly opposed to God as well, and do not finally deserve the right to speak or act or persuade, and Christians have often been guilty of this. The Crusades were an example, Christian anti-Semitism is another, and sometimes the Christian willingness to kill, whether in support of a Nazi ideology, or extreme nationalism, whether of the Russian or American variety, these are other instances that come to mind. And as I look at the current American religious scene, it is this tendency that seems to me in danger of characterizing this recently emerged religious right of which [the] Moral Majority is at least one very clear-cut example.

Mr. Falwell, Jerry Falwell, the leader of that movement, states that he knows just what is wrong with our country, and tells us: "God has called me to action. I have a divine mandate to go into the halls of Congress and fight for laws that will save America." As this position develops, it turns out that those who disagree with him are really by definition disagreeing with God, since he, and not they, have access to God's will. Liberals, for example, who Mr. Falwell abominates, are not just political liberals or theological liberals, they are godless liberals. They are the ones who must be removed from public office, since they are not only wrong, but evil. What we must have in office are God-fearing, Bible-believing Christians, which is bad news to Jews and secularists.

I do not for a moment challenge Mr. Falwell's right or anybody's right to get into the American political process, to work for change, to support candidates, urge people to vote and all the rest. That is the way the American system works, and the more people that are doing that, the better for the health of the system. And it would be a very perverse logic to claim that only people with whom I agree ought to be engaging in political activity and I want no part of such an argument. I have taken my own political stands in the past; I intend to keep doing so in the present and in the future, so can and should everyone, whether named Billy Graham or Bill Coffin, whether named Jerry Falwell or Robert Drinan.[1]

Furthermore, this emergence of the Radical Right on the political scene, means that there is one ancient battle we are not going to have to fight for a while. For the most of my adult life, at any rate, people on the theological right have been saying religion and politics do not mix. The rest of us have been saying, "They do too mix." And now, for better or for worse, that message has been heard.

The question is no longer, "Do religion and politics mix?" The question is simply, "What is the nature of the mix?" And it is the nature of the mix, as far as groups like [the] Moral Majority are concerned, that is increasingly concerning me, and even on some levels beginning to frighten me. Now let me say just enough about that kind of mix so that I can then set the stage in the latter part of these comments, for what seems to me a more appropriate alternative.

In Christian terms, and I think in terms with which all Jews could also agree, my real complaint about the Moral Majority's intrusion of the Bible into American politics, is that they are not biblical enough. I do not for a moment concede that they have the Bible on their side and that the rest of us are nothing but godless liberals or secular humanists which, in Mr. Falwell's lexicon, is very close to being either a Socialist or a Communist.

So let me illustrate that in two ways. First of all, it seems to me that the Moral Majority's biblically inspired political agenda involves a very selective, very partial, and therefore very distorted use of the Bible. They have isolated a set of concerns that they say get to the heart of what is wrong with America—homosexuality, abortion, and pornography. These are the things that are wrong and that are destroying our nation. What we need to do, what we need to be for, basically for prayer in public schools, and for more bombs. Jesus wants our kids to pray and he wants the Pentagon to be able to kill more people if necessary. I know that sounds a little crude, but I believe it is. I am not denying that there are moral dimensions involved in all those issues and that people can take different moral positions in response to them, but the notion that they represent what the Hebrew and Christian scriptures offer us as the key for understanding what is wrong with the world today, is one that strikes me as grotesque.

---

[1]Billy Graham, a conservative Protestant revivalist; William Sloane Coffin, a liberal Protestant minister; Robert Drinan, a liberal Catholic priest—ED.

Take the issue of homosexuality. If one turns to the scriptures as a whole, to try to come up with their central concerns, homosexuality is going to be very low on such a list even if indeed it makes the list at all. There are perhaps seven very ambiguous verses in the whole biblical canon that even allude to it and I will any day subordinate the minuscule import of those seven verses, isolated verses, to hundreds and hundreds of places where the scriptures are dealing over and over again with questions of social justice, the tendency of the rich to exploit the poor, the need for all of us to have a commitment to the hungry, the need for nations not to put their major trust in armaments, the concern for the sick, the recognition that all people are children of God, even if they are Russians or Cubans or Salvadoreans. The Moral Majority creates an agenda and then proceeds to impose that agenda on scripture by developing little strings of unrelated verses to give divine sanction to the position. As those who work with the Bible know, one can prove absolutely anything that way. You can make a biblical case for militarism or pacifism, nationalism or internationalism, for male dominance or for women's rights, though it is a bit more difficult with women's rights. One can make a case for capital punishment or for letting the prisoners go free. One can make a case for socialism or for capitalism, simply by selecting a few verses very carefully and ignoring all the others.

It seems clear to me that there are great and central overriding themes and concerns in the scriptures. You and I might have slightly different lists of what these themes would be, but there would be certain ones that simply could not be ignored if we were going to respond honestly to the text. There are huge sections, for example, on the dangers of national idolatry, that is to say, making the nation into God, accepting uncritically whatever we have to do as a nation against other nations.

Those major emphases stand in very sharp contrast to Mr. Falwell's assessment that we should have done whatever we needed to win in Vietnam because our national honor was at stake. That was the criterion and I submit that national honor is a criterion that the Bible unremittingly attacks. There are long sections in scripture dealing with the need to be concerned about the poor and the destitute. There are treatments of the "virus" of racism. There are many recognitions that those with wealth will always be tempted to act repressively against the poor and so on and so on. It is breathtaking that when one looks over the agendas of the Moral Majority there is absolutely no mention of such things, there is a total silence. We seem to be living in two different worlds, reading two different books. . . .

So let me now to conclude, suggest very briefly five characteristics that I think would be appropriate to the moral minority. . . .

First . . . the Bible does not talk about minorities as much as about remnants. Since the demise of . . . Constantinian Christianity[2] where Christians were running the show . . . this remnant posture has become both appropri-

---

[2] The emperor Constantine the Great in the fourth century A.D. made Christianity the supreme religion of the Roman world—ED.

ate and descriptive for Christians. We are a small percentage, a remnant, of the whole human family, particularly when we look at ourselves globally. . . .

[One remnant within the remnant might be to dissent from the prevailing views of local church establishments. Our model for this might be the circumstances of Latin America.] For centuries . . . the Catholic Church in Latin America was at the beck and call of the little group of the wealthy who had all the power, who had all the money, all the prestige. . . . But in recent years the churches have been getting away from that uncritical alliance with those in power [and speaking up and working for social justice]. . . .

Secondly . . . if we could break out of the kind of "culturally-conditioned" ways we have read the Bible, we could find it an explosive arsenal of material for creative change. . . . When the Bible talks about good news for the poor we immediately interpret that to mean the spiritually poor. . . . Now, I am sure that is part of what was meant, but it seems to me very clear what is also meant [is] that when Jesus is talking about the poor, he also meant the materially poor, the really impoverished, who do not have enough to ear, . . . who do not have enough power. . . .

The third thing the moral minority could stress, perhaps the most important thing in the time in which we live, would be the necessity of a global perspective. This world is now just too small to allow for anything else. And to look at the world simply in terms of what is good for the United States, is ultimately going to be self-defeating. To put the main stress and priority on more weapons, as the national debate is now suggesting, is truly likely to increase the likelihood that we will use them. . . .

That suggests a fourth thing the moral minority might become; it could become group in our society which is genuinely committed to the powerless and voiceless. . . .[T]he church . . . must be that place where the voiceless are empowered to speak on their own behalf, and are guaranteed a hearing. . . .

Fifth, and finally, a moral minority must . . . set its own agendas. . . . Our agendas must not be set by the Moral Majority movement. We must not fall into the trap of single-issue politics. . . . I find it kind of morally oppressive to be told, again and again, some kind of obsession about other people's sex life [sic] is the burning issue of the day, when the majority of the human family went to bed hungry every night or to be told to rally around getting prayers back into schools when millions of people are unable to find jobs, or get minimal help if they are unemployed and disadvantaged. . . . [T]he whole human family is hurting from the mad escalation of the arms race, the need for more equitable distribution of food, coming to terms with denials, both abroad and home, of basic human rights, such as education and medical care and jobs and all the rest.

I think we need to rally around these problems in a context which provides a forum for seeking the good of all, not just small segments of the population. We must try to present issues without demagoguery cheating. We must acknowledge that problems are complex and that simplistic solutions will be misleading and wrong, and acknowledge also that ambiguities abound not only within the positions of those with whom we disagree, but within our own positions as well. With some such way of engaging in political life, we might be able to create a moral minority that could propose convictions without arrogance but insight without absolutism, with commitment but without coercion and with democracy but without demagoguery.

Reagan's Cowboy Capitalism

MARK GREEN

With firmness and style, President Reagan has commandeered the rhetorical high ground by his "program for economic recovery." The phrases and concepts of Reaganomics—get government off our backs, tax cuts boost revenues and productivity, Federal spending and regulation are destroying our economy—are about as catchy as anything since Franklin D. Roosevelt took off after the "economic royalists."

But will his program work? And where is the evidence? These questions are crucial, for the President is apparently placing all the hopes of his administration in this single economic package. A dicey move, as Alexander Haig[1] would say. So far all we have is repetition and assertion. The more one vainly looks for statistical and analytic support, the more Jack Kemp[2] and Ronald Reagan seem to be economic Lysenkos,[3] rather than our new [John Maynard] Keynes and F.D.R.—the purveyors of a specious philosophy masking the real interests of corporatist ideology.

Let us take a closer look at the ten myths of the new Cowboy Capitalism:

- *Government Spending Is Too High.* Federal, state and local governments spend 34 percent of our gross national product. Only in Australia and Japan among industrial nations is there less spending of G.N.P. In France it is 40 percent; West Germany 42 percent; Britain 44 percent; the Netherlands 51 percent.
- *Federal Deficits Cause Inflation.* The cumulative Federal, state and local budget is balanced right now. Federal debt as a percentage of G.N.P. fell from 103.5 percent in 1946 to only 27.1 percent in 1979. Of the seven leading industrial countries, the United States had the lowest ratio of government deficits as a percentage of G.N.P.—1 percent in 1977–79, compared with 3 percent in West Germany and 6 percent in Japan, whose economies are far outperforming our own. The Congressional Budget Office has estimated that every $10 billion cut in Federal spending would reduce inflation by one-tenth of 1 percent.
- *America Has a Capital Shortage.* Conservative economist Pierre Rinfret testified in 1977 that the capital markets were glutted. The next year *Business Week* said of the oil industry, "The prospect of big pools of incoming cash presents industry strategists with a compelling need to find outlets for that cash." Indeed, accord-

Mark Green, "Reagan's Cowboy Capitalism," *The Nation*, March 7, 1981, pp. 258, 261.

[1] The newly appointed secretary of state—ED.

[2] Then a conservative Republican congressman from Buffalo, New York, Kemp was a disciple of Arthur Laffer and joint author of the first major supply-side proposal for drastic cuts in federal taxes to stimulate economic growth—ED.

[3] Trofim Lysenko was a Soviet agronomist of the 1930s who, contrary to the best science of the day, insisted on the inheritability of acquired characteristics among living things. The application of his theories damaged Soviet agriculture severely—ED.

ing to freemarket theory, which in other circumstances is devoutly followed by this Administration, there can't be a capital shortage: if there's a need and a market, the capital will be there; otherwise, not.

- *Investment Is Dangerously Low.* Director David Stockman of the Office of Management and Budget said the United States is "on the dangerous path of consuming its own capital and living off its own savings." Yet total investment (apart from housing) has risen from 9.5 percent of G.N.P. in 1950 to 9.6 percent in 1960, 10.5 percent in 1970 and 11.3 percent in 1980.

- *Individual Taxes Are Too High.* America ranks eleventh of twelve major industrial nations in the share of personal income taken by the tax collector. In this country it is 29 percent; in France, 39 percent; in West Germany and Britain, 37 percent, and in the Netherlands, 46 percent. In his book *The Zero-Sum Society,* Lester Thurow argues that "All our empirical studies show that our current taxes are far below the levels that create disincentives to work . . . highly progressive tax systems (much more progressive than the tax system now in place) do not seem to reduce work effort."

- *Corporate Taxes Are Too High.* In the Eisenhower years, receipts from corporate income taxes made up 20 percent of all Federal revenues; today they provide only 12 percent. According to the Congressional Joint Tax Committee, taxes on all capital contribute 43.5 percent of all revenues in Japan compared with 39.25 percent in the United States.

- *Lower Taxes Mean More Work, More Investment, More Revenues.* The Government Accounting Office concluded that $19 billion of investment tax credits in 1978 affected investment decisions very little. A recent study by the Treasury's Office of Tax Analysis found that big investment tax credits "buy little or no additional equipment." Business invests if there is a profit to be made, not because one of its costs is reduced. *Working Papers* editor Bob Kuttner has written, "Lowering taxes is just as likely to encourage people to substitute leisure for work," as to encourage more work and saving. According to Walter Heller, President Kennedy's chairman of the Council of Economic Advisers, "The notion that a tax cut's prompt demand stimulus—let alone its long-delayed supply stimulus— could generate enough revenue to pay for itself, unfortunately finds no support in the available statistical evidence."

- *Costs of Regulation Hurt Industry.* President Reagan said in 1976 Federal regulation of the auto industry cost $666 per car. Yet when the Federal auto safety agency asked car manufacturers how much the price would fall if there were no regulation, the answer was $80 per car. The President also estimated that all Federal regulation costs $120 billion a year in expenditures and "compliance costs," but $25 billion of that is Internal Revenue Service paperwork, which is hardly "regulation," as the term is commonly used. Only $32 billion is the kind of environmental and consumer regulation he so often attacks—or only 1 percent of G.N.P.

- *Our Society Is Too Egalitarian.* While the number of poor fell by half in the 1960s, poor people continued to make up about 11 percent of the total population throughout the 1970s. The "progressive" tax system in this country, according to economists Joseph Pechman and Benjamin Okner, is really "proportional," taking roughly the same percentage bite out of an income of $20,000 as it does out of $200,000. According to the O.E.C.D. (Organization for Economic Cooperation and Development) only France among democratic industrial nations has a greater income inequality than the United States. West Germany and Japan have more equality—and more productivity.

- *We're Worse Off.* President Reagan in his first economics address to the nation argued that "we're very much worse off" in 1980 than in 1960. But per capita income after taxes rose some 80 percent, from $2,709 to $4,567 (in constant 1972 dollars) during those twenty years.

Exactly what, then, stands behind the Republicans' economic ideology—other than thirty years of after-dinner speeches to business and conservative gatherings by the President? Unless "God is a Republican," as Prof. John Kenneth Galbraith has put it, a successful economic program simply cannot be based on such faulty premises. The program's impact on inflation and unemployment in the real world—not Mr. Reagan's winning smile and adroit delivery—will be the only barometer of success. By then, it may become apparent that, like the last Administration, this one is better at getting elected than at managing the economy.

18

The New Environmentalism

As we move through the last decade of the twentieth century, we can see that the Cold War's end will not free America of global concerns. If nothing else the 1991 Gulf War has made that clear. But it is also apparent that more of our attention and resources will have to be devoted to domestic matters and to the sort of peaceful international issues that the United States seldom had to consider in the past. None of these concerns and issues will be as vital as preserving the physical environment, for the air, the land, and the waters are the very foundations of human existence.

Our environmental worries are not new. The conservation-preservation movement of almost a century ago foreshadowed our present concerns. But the modern surge of environmentalism dates from the writings of Rachel Carson, whose 1962 book, *The Silent Spring,* describing the blighting effects of DDT and other pesticides, alerted millions to new environmental dangers.

Since then environmental awareness has blossomed into a worldwide consciousness of the delicate ecological balances of nature and humankind's dependence on those balances. During the 1960s the new concerns generated a flood of federal legislation designed to eliminate pollutants, protect the nation's air and waters, and preserve its natural heritage. Robust public interest in the environment coincided with the winding down of the Vietnam War and the demise of the New Left, and served as an alternative to campus protest for many idealistic young men and women. In their staging, their spirit, and their personnel, the rallies for the first Earth Day in 1970 resembled the antiwar demonstrations of the same era. Later in the decade, particularly in Europe, various "Green" parties would make environmental reform into a political force that challenged centrist as well as traditional left-wing parties.

In the following selections you will encounter a variety of environmentalist positions as well as critiques of the environmental movement. See if you can detect, behind the contending pronouncements and formulas, the fundamentally different views of humanity's proper relations with nature.

18.1:   The Ecology Ethic (1949, 1975, 1973)

Rachel Carson may be the source of the modern public's environmental fears, but the founder of the larger post–World War II ecological consciousness was Aldo Leopold, a naturalist who worked successively for the U.S. Forestry Service, the Arms and Ammunition Manufacturers' Institute,[1] and the University of Wisconsin. As a disciple of Gifford Pinchot, Leopold was initially a utilitarian conservationist who sought to advance the rational use of natural resources. He later moved beyond that position to defend the preservation of unspoiled nature and to insist that humans no more "owned" the land than they "owned" other human beings. The first selection in this chapter is from his book A Sand County Almanac, *published in 1949, just after his death, in which Leopold announced a new a "land ethic" of respect, even reverence, for nature coupled with a belief that humankind was merely a part of nature, not its lord and master.*

Does Leopold dismiss economic factors in considering how people should manage natural resources? In his view, what other factors must they take into account? Would Leopold's opinions be considered bold or radical today?

The second item is by Harvard professor George Wald, a Nobel Prize winner in biology and charter member of Friends of the Earth, an influential voice for environmental-ecological concerns. It is part of an address Wald delivered in 1975 to a conference in Switzerland on "The Limits to Medicine."

Wald speaks with a different voice from Leopold. Leopold is thoughtful and philosophical about the environment; Wald sounds a note of alarm at the environmental havoc that people have caused. And yet it is possible to see a connection between the ideas of the two men. What is that connection? On the other hand, there are differences. How can we explain them? What events that occurred in the intellectual, economic,

---

[1]Given the general linkage of modern environmentalism with liberal political causes, this connection is surprising. Yet those interested in game hunting have long sought to preserve the natural environment, for only if it survives will the animals they stalk survive. Theodore Roosevelt epitomizes this marriage between big game hunting and the wilderness preservation side of the environmental movement.

and political worlds between 1949 and 1975 might account for the differences in the tones of their statements? The Wald selection raises another question: Does an ecological consciousness imply a political viewpoint? Can you detect an implicit political position in Wald's remarks? If so, what is it? Is his political perspective common among those who view the environment as he does?

The third selection, on the critical environmental issue of nuclear energy, is by Ernst Schumacher. Author of Small Is Beautiful, *an influential book advocating limits on economic and population growth, the German-born Schumacher is one of many environmentalists who have warned of the grave dangers to human life posed by nuclear energy.*

His is a contribution to an important force behind the recent environmental movement: the health and safety fears of millions confronted with the power and mystery of modern technology. Are these fears exaggerated? Can we meet our energy needs if we abandon the nuclear option? What are some alternate energy choices? Would adopting alternative energy sources impose crippling costs on society? Have the antinuclear forces been effective in slowing the use of nuclear energy?

The Land Ethic

ALDO LEOPOLD

When god-like Odysseus returned from the wars in Troy, he hanged all on one rope a dozen slave-girls of his household whom he suspected of misbehavior during his absence.

This hanging involved no question of propriety. The girls were property. The disposal of property was then, as now, a matter of expediency, not of right and wrong.

Concepts of right and wrong were not lacking from Odysseus' Greece: witness the fidelity of his wife through the long years before at last his black-prowed galleys clove the wine-dark seas for home. The ethical structure of that day covered wives, but had not yet been extended to human chattels. During the three thousand years which have since elapsed, ethical criteria have been extended to many fields of conduct, with corresponding shrinkages in those judged by expediency only.

The Ethical Sequence

This extension of ethics, so far studied only by philosophers, is actually a process in ecological evolution. Its sequences may be described in ecological as well as in philosophical terms. An ethic, ecologically, is a limitation on

Aldo Leopold, "The Land Ethic," *A Sand County Almanac: With Other Essay from Round River* (New York: Oxford University Press, 1949), pp. 201–4, 223–6.

freedom of action in the struggle for existence. An ethic, philosophically, is a differentiation of social from anti-social conduct. These are two definitions of one thing. The thing has its origin in the tendency of interdependent individuals or groups to evolve modes of co-operation. The ecologist calls these symbioses. Politics and economics are advanced symbioses in which the original free-for-all competition has been replaced, in part, by co-operative mechanisms with an ethical content.

The complexity of co-operative mechanisms has increased with population density, and with the efficiency of tools. It was simpler, for example, to define the anti-social uses of sticks and stones in the days of the mastodons than of bullets and billboards in the age of motors.

The first ethics dealt with the relation between individuals; the Mosaic Decalogue is an example. Later accretions dealt with the relation between the individual and society. The Golden Rule tries to integrate the individual to society; democracy to integrate social organization to the individual.

There is as yet no ethic dealing with man's relation to land and to the animals and plants which grow upon it. Land, like Odysseus' slave-girls, is still property. The land-relation is still strictly economic, entailing privileges but not obligations.

The extension of ethics to this third element in human environment is, if I read the evidence correctly, an evolutionary possibility and an ecological necessity. It is the third step in a sequence. The first two have already been taken. Individual thinkers since the days of Ezekiel and Isaiah have asserted that the despoliation of land is not only inexpedient but wrong. Society, however, has not yet affirmed their belief. I regard the present conservation movement as the embryo of such an affirmation.

An ethic may be regarded as a mode of guidance for meeting ecological situations so new or intricate, or involving such deferred reactions, that the path of social expediency is not discernible to the average individual.
Animal instincts are modes of guidance for the individual in meeting such situations. Ethics are possibly a kind of community instinct in-the-making.

The Community Concept

All ethics so far evolved rest upon a single premise: that the individual is a member of a community of interdependent parts. His instincts prompt him to compete for his place in that community, but his ethics prompt him also to co-operate (perhaps in order that there may be a place to compete for).

The land ethic simply enlarges the boundaries of the community to include soils, waters, plants, and animals, or collectively, the land.

This sounds simple: do we not already sing our love for and obligation to the land of the free and the home of the brave? Yes, but just what and whom do we love? Certainly not the soil, which we are sending helter-skelter downriver. Certainly not the waters, which we assume have no function except to turn turbines, float barges, and carry off sewage. Certainly not the plants, of which we exterminate whole communities without batting an eye. Certainly not the animals, of which we have already extirpated many of the largest and most beautiful species. A land ethic of course cannot prevent the alteration, management, and use of these 'resources,' but it does affirm their right to continued existence, and, at least in spots, their continued existence in a natural state.

In short, a land ethic changes the role of *Homo sapiens* from conqueror of the land-community to plain member and citizen of it. It implies respect for his fellow-members, and also respect for the community as such.

The Outlook

It is inconceivable to me that an ethical relation to land can exist without love, respect, and admiration for land, and a high regard for its value. By value, I of course mean something far broader than mere economic value; I mean value in the philosophical sense.

Perhaps the most serious obstacle impeding the evolution of a land ethic is the fact that our educational and economic system is headed away from, rather than toward, an intense consciousness of land. Your true modern is separated from the land by many middlemen, and by innumerable physical gadgets. He has no vital relation to it; to him it is the space between cities on which crops grow. Turn him loose for a day on the land, and if the spot does not happen to be a golf links or a 'scenic' area, he is bored stiff. If crops could be raised by hydroponics instead of farming, it would suit him very well. Synthetic substitutes for wood, leather, wool, and other natural land products suit him better than the originals. In short, land is something he has 'outgrown.'

Almost equally serious as an obstacle to a land ethic is the attitude of the farmer for whom the land is still an adversary, or a taskmaster that keeps him in slavery. Theoretically, the mechanization of farming ought to cut the farmer's chains, but whether it really does is debatable.

One of the requisites for an ecological comprehension of land is an understanding of ecology, and this is by no means co-extensive with 'education'; in fact, much higher education seems deliberately to avoid ecological concepts. An understanding of ecology does not necessarily originate in courses bearing ecological labels; it is quite as likely to be labeled geography, botany, agronomy, history, or economics. This is as it should be, but whatever the label, ecological training is scarce.

The case for a land ethic would appear hopeless but for the minority which is in obvious revolt against these 'modern' trends.

The 'key-log' which must be moved to release the evolutionary process for an ethic is simply this: quit thinking about decent land-use as solely an economic problem. Examine each question in terms of what is ethically and esthetically right, as well as what is economically expedient. A thing is right when it tends to preserve the integrity, stability, and beauty of the biotic community. It is wrong when it tends otherwise.

It of course goes without saying that economic feasibility limits the tether of what can or cannot be done for land. It always has and it always will. The fallacy the economic determinists have tied around our collective neck, and which we now need to cast off, is the belief that economics determines *all* land-use. This is simply not true. An innumerable host of actions and attitudes, comprising perhaps the bulk of all land relations, is determined by the land-users' tastes and predilections, rather than by his purse. The bulk of all land relations hinges on investments of time, forethought, skill, and faith rather than on investments of cash. As a land-user thinketh, so is he.

I have purposely presented the land ethic as a product of social evolution because nothing so important as an ethic is ever `written.' Only the most superficial student of history supposes that Moses `wrote' the Decalogue; it evolved in the minds of a thinking community, and Moses wrote a tentative summary of it for a `seminar.' I say tentative because evolution never stops.

The evolution of a land ethic is an intellectual as well as emotional process. Conservation is paved with good intentions which prove to be futile, or even dangerous, because they are devoid of critical understanding either of the land, or of economic land-use. I think it is a truism that as the ethical frontier advances from the individual to the community, its intellectual content increases.

The mechanism of operation is the same for any ethic: social approbation for right actions; social disapproval for wrong actions.

By and large, our present problem is one of attitudes and implements. We are remodeling the Alhambra with a steam-shovel, and we are proud of our yardage. We shall hardly relinquish the shovel, which after all has many good points, but we are in need of gentler and more objective criteria for its successful use.

The Lethal Society[1]

GEORGE WALD

I've had the strange feeling in this meeting, listening to the papers on the limits of medicine, that they seem to disregard what I think is our major trouble. That is that we are talking about the limits of medicine in a highly lethal society, and indeed one that is threatening to die, perhaps soon. And that makes a special set of problems.

Why do I say a highly lethal society? Well, because no society in human history has cultivated the killing and destruction as has Western society under Christianity. It's a commentary on this that our Western world has been so shocked that India produced an atom bomb, a very small one by present standards. The shock was not in the atom bomb (we have lots of those, and big ones). The shock consisted in an atom bomb being produced

George Wald, "The Lethal Society," in Mary Lou Deventer, ed., *Earthworks: Ten Years on the Environmental Front* (San Francisco: Friends of the Earth, 1980), pp. 230–35.
[1]Illustrations deleted.

in the wrong place, by the wrong kind of nation. A Third World country has no business producing an atom bomb. . . .

My own nation, the United States, is now making three hydrogen warheads per day. The Soviet Union keeps pace with us. You must think of the limits of medicine, and how to humanize medicine, against the background of the production in my country of three hydrogen warheads per day.

It is not only atomic bombs we need to fear. Nuclear power, that enticing thing, in all its present forms threatens our future as a civilization and as people. . . .

Every nuclear reactor of any type now at work produces as a by-product plutonium 239, probably the most toxic substance known. One milligram inhaled is enough to kill a person within hours by massive fibrosis of the lungs. One microgram is likely eventually to cause lung or bone cancer. Also, this is the most convenient material out of which to make fission bombs. The "trigger" quantity, the quantity of plutonium 239 with which one can make an atom bomb, is *two kilograms*. You could carry that amount perfectly safely in a brown paper grocery bag. A plutonium 239 bomb of the explosive force of the bomb that leveled Hiroshima and killed 100,000 persons would take six to seven kilograms. You'd have to put that in a shopping bag. . . .

The Workplace Environment

I have not yet heard spoken of in this meeting a terrible problem. It is the danger of the workplace, the problem for workers to stay alive while making a living. I have heard several times here the auto referred to as a big killer of healthy persons. In the United States, the workplaces are at least as big a killer. We register about 22,000 deaths by industrial accident every year and 2.2 million disabling accidents. But those statistics don't touch the slow killing: the black lung of the coal mines; the brown lung that is produced by exposure to the dust of cotton and hemp and flax in the textile mills; the silicosis, asbestosis, and uranium poisoning, and the large number and variety of cancers associated with these conditions. None of these chronic conditions is in the statistics. And indeed, this kind of statistics is hard to come by, because the industry fights tooth and nail to keep them concealed. The reason is obvious. Every attempt to make the workplaces safer increases the cost of production; every alleged work injury represents an insurance or compensation cost. So it is in the interest of industry to conceal these disabilities. In the US, the only physicians who concern themselves with these disabilities, or who are available at the workplace, are almost without exception employed by the industry and make their reports to the industry, not to the workers. . . .

The whole of humanity now suffers from a series of exceedingly threatening new developments, all coming to a head at about the same time, close to the year 2000. I am one of those scientists—and believe me, it is no pleasure—who, trying as we will, hoping as we do that something in our view of things is wrong, still find it very difficult to see how the human race is to get itself much past the year 2000. So there isn't much time.

The Jolly Green Giant

Every few years one is told that [Thomas] Malthus was wrong: that he was "naive" in thinking that we might eventually overpopulate the globe relative to our food resources. The last event said to demonstrate that Malthus was wrong was the Green Revolution.[2]

In fact, the Green Revolution has a terrible contradiction at its core. The biggest single event in the history of life on this planet was the development of photosynthesis. That made us independent of the accumulation of organic molecules upon which life depended from its origin until—through photosynthesis, using the energy of sunlight—life could make its own organic molecules. Well, the Green Revolution has reversed this development by making us dependent again upon fossil organic molecules. It is a poor bargain. The total energy consumed by US agriculture per year is equivalent to more than 30 billion gallons of gasoline. This represents more than *five times the energy content of the food produced*. The Green Revolution means that we use fossil fuels produced by early ages of photosynthesis to promote present-day photosynthesis.

The Green Revolution rests upon huge amounts of synthetic fertilizers and synthetic pesticides and herbicides, all produced with fossil fuels—with coal and oil. That worked as long as coal and oil were cheap. But they no longer are cheap; and with that, much of the Green Revolution, particularly for the Third World, has gone bankrupt. . . .

The Cultivation of "Marginal Men"

Until recently, the intensifying food shortages in the world could be ascribed mainly to increase in population. To this a new element has been added, mainly within the last decade: a sudden large increase in the demand for meat—for beef and pork—in the developed nations. I was in Japan twice, six years apart, and was amazed by the change in Japanese dietary habits during that short period. This places an enormous burden upon the poorer and hungrier parts of the world, because making that meat strikes a very bad nutritional bargain. It takes about eight pounds of grain to make one pound of meat. The grain that might otherwise go to feeding a starving peasantry is instead fed to hogs and cattle to supply this enormously increased demand for meat in the affluent world. Dr. Georg Borgstrom has calculated that US livestock consume enough food materials to feed 1.3 billion persons and world livestock consume enough to feed 15 billion persons.

---

[2]The Green Revolution is a name given to a surge in agricultural productivity of the 1960s based on modern genetic science—ED.

Another development greatly aggravates these troubles. Most of human work used to be done with human muscles; but now, increasingly, it is done by machines—even in agriculture. Agriculture is rapidly going over from farming to agri-business. In my own country, 51 percent of the vegetables, 85 percent of the citrus fruits, 97 percent of the chickens, and 100 percent of the sugar cane are being produced by the same companies that make our aircraft, control our soil and coal, and run our transportation system. That kind of thing is happening all over the world. It is another aspect of the Green Revolution; and everywhere it is throwing people out of work. Unemployment is rising all over the world—and something much worse. It is not just that many persons are unemployed, which one thinks of as a temporary condition, but that there is no further use for them in the free-market economy. They are wanted neither as workers nor as consumers. They are not wanted at all. Their existence is looked on as an embarrassment—even as a potential threat, for they continue to demand food, clothing, and shelter. Even education. Robert MacNamara, in his report to the World Bank of September 21, 1970, referred to such superfluous persons as "marginal men." He estimated that there were then 500 million of them, that by 1980 there would be one billion, and by 1990, two billion. That would be close to half the world population. . . .

The Limits of Research

What are we to do? It is easy to say what is wrong, but how to make it right?

Our kind of person has one answer all prepared. Research. If people are hungry, set up a well-funded project on hunger. If our world is coming to an end, set up a well-funded Project Apocalypse.

As a research person, I should like to say something about this. Research is a fine thing. We never know enough about anything. But research must not be allowed to become a trap, a means of endlessly putting off action. And that's the way it is frequently being exploited. That's the way it is with the big industrial diseases, with pollution, with tobacco smoking and cancer. We are told that "all the facts are not yet in." How inane! All the facts are never in. Each of these situations changes as one studies it. So let's by all means have more research. But let us also act; let us do what is needed.

We already know enough to *begin* to cope with all the major problems that are now threatening human life and much of the rest of life on Earth. Our crisis is not a crisis of information; it is a crisis of decision, of policy.

Though we already know enough to begin to cope with all the major problems, I don't know one of those major problems that we could begin to cope with *while maximizing profits.* And I think that a society such as our own that puts the maximization of profits above all other considerations is thereby headed for destruction and is doomed. . . .

What we need is a reorganization of our society, a fundamental change in its direction, so as better to meet human needs, to fulfill human values, to humanize what is now increasingly alienating, to serve life rather than death.

To fulfill short-term goals for an increasingly narrow power structure, we are devastating the Earth; and the business of killing—armaments—is now by far the world's biggest business.. . . .

Toward a Non-Lethal Society

As I try to think in terms of a reorganization of society, it seems to me increasingly clear that the really significant journey to make is not to the moon, but to China. One sees things going on in China that are altogether surprising to middle-class persons who have grown up in our society. . . .With famine in much of the Third World, no Chinese is expected to starve this year. You don't have to take that from the Chinese or from me. Twenty American agricultural experts went over as a delegation a couple of months ago, and they came out saying that China seems well supplied with food— that the hunger prevalent in other parts of the Third World is not afflicting the Chinese. Then they said something more that has a wonderfully ironic twist: that the Chinese are not producing agricultural experts, and that unless they begin quickly to produce agricultural experts, they'll soon be in trouble! . . .

The only solutions for the problems I have spoken of are *political.* They must come out in the form of political power exercised by an aroused people who insist on taking their lives back into their own hands.

What we fondly call the free world is composed almost entirely (in its Third World components) of military dictatorships. That phrase, the free world, used to trouble me until I finally realized what it meant. The free world consists of those nations that get their armaments free from the US.

In our free world—perhaps you feel differently in Switzerland—the governments are not masters. . . .Then who are the masters? I think that our so-called free world is now wholly controlled by such multinational super-enterprises as General Motors, Exxon, the Chase Manhattan Bank, ITT, Royal Dutch Shell, and British Petroleum. . . .

I don't know myself where to turn politically. We don't have a politics in the United States at present that promises to go in the direction I think our society needs to go. That's no accident. We now sell and buy political candidates in exactly the same way we sell and buy toothpaste and soap. The same advertising methods are used, and the same people are paying for it. . . .

Our present society seems to me to have the following structure. In control is a very small power elite, in which is concentrated more power and wealth than ever before in human history. At the other end of the social scale is a great, faceless mass of workers—increasingly urban, and hence increasingly dependent on their employment. In between is the middle class to which we ourselves belong. It includes all government officials, high and low; all military and police officials; professors, journalists and clergymen; physicians and lawyers. The role laid out for it is to mediate between the power elite and the working masses; to keep the system running, if possible smoothly, but to keep it running at all costs; to rationalize the system's contradictions; to foster its acceptance through education, indoctrination, and religious exhortation; to fragment and dilute any opposition, and in the event of serious challenge, to control or crush it.

Conceivably, such a system could work to social advantage. At times and places in the past, it may have done so. But in recent history, it has turned destructive. It is leading our society rapidly toward disaster. In an obsessive pursuit of short-term profit and power, it threatens to bring an end to the human enterprise. And our role as the middle class, the role for which we are designed, trained, employed, and paid, is to help that to happen—to do what we can to smooth the way to that disaster.

But we do not have to accept that role. We have a choice. We can opt for life rather than death. Rather than serve the power elite in its present plunge toward destruction, we can turn the other way; we can *serve the people*.

The Energy Assumption

Urbanization and the availability of energy are closely related. The emergence of the first cities was closely associated with agricultural breakthroughs such as the harnessing of draft animals, the domestication of new agricultural plants, and the development of irrigation systems. In effect, these enabled humans to harness more energy for their own purposes—to capture more solar energy in plants or, in the case of draft animals, to convert otherwise unusable roughage into a form that could be used to increase the food supply. Important though these new energy sources were, the agricultural surpluses they made possible were never enough to support more than a small proportion of the population living away from the land. Indeed, as recently as 1800, only 2.2 percent of the population of Europe lived in cities of 100,000 or more.

The energy breakthrough that permitted much larger populations—even majorities—to live in cities was the discovery of fossil fuels, initially coal and later oil. The harnessing of fossil fuels to generate steam for industrial power gave birth to the industrial revolution, permitted the concentration of economic activity, and ushered in a new era of urbanization.

The large-scale migration of people from countryside to city required an abundance of energy. Cities require more energy to satisfy food, fuel, housing, and transport needs. Assuming no change in consumption levels, each person who moves from the countryside to the city raises world energy requirements.

With food, urbanization raises energy requirements on two fronts. As the urban population increases relative to the rural food-producing population, more energy is required in agriculture to generate this requisite food surplus. At the same time, more energy is needed to process the food and transport it to urban areas.

As more and more people move into the cities, each person remaining in agriculture must produce an ever-larger surplus. This, in turn, requires the broad substitution of mechanical energy for labor in food production. In a world where energy is becoming scarce and unemployment is rising, it makes little sense to continue this substitution in countries with large, unemployed rural populations.

It is customary to point with pride to the small percentage of the population living on the land in industrial nations such as the US, where 5 percent of the people provide food for the rest. This level of labor productivity in agriculture requires vast amounts of energy. Professor David Pimentel, writing in *Science* (November 2, 1973), illustrates how much. If the current four billion world population were to be fed at US consumption levels, using US energy-intensive agricultural production techniques, and "if *petroleum* were the only source of energy, and if we used *all* petroleum reserves solely to feed the world population, the 415-billion barrel reserve would last a mere 29 years."

Although the amounts required for food production are large, they are dwarfed by comparison with the amount of energy used to transport, process, and distribute food. Within the US, one-fourth of the energy used in the food system is used to produce food. Three-fourths of the total is used to transport, process, and distribute that same food.

Urbanization also increases energy requirements for waste disposal. At the village level, waste disposal is not a major problem. Organic wastes are returned to the soil to enrich it, an important and integral part of nature's nutrient cycles of phosphorus, sulfur, and nitrogen. In this way they contribute to the food supply. But once large numbers of people congregate in cities, waste may no longer be an asset. Indeed, efforts to safely dispose of it are often an additional drain on scarce energy resources.

The rapid urbanization of this century, so far, occurred during an era of cheap energy, an era which may be historically unique. Oil production has already peaked in some major producing countries, including the US. Production declines in other countries will follow. With the end of the petroleum age now clearly in sight, the world must turn to other forms of energy, forms which may, by their very natures, affect the pattern of human settlement.

Until recently, it was assumed that the world would move from the fossil fuel era into the nuclear age. After a quarter-century of experience with nuclear power, the world is beginning to have second thoughts about continuing down the nuclear path. Failure to devise any satisfactory techniques of waste disposal, the inevitable spread of nuclear weapons along with nuclear power, and the prospect of terrorist groups acquiring nuclear materials and weapons are all beginning to raise doubts in even the most sanguine of minds.

Beyond the seemingly insoluble waste disposal and security problems, the economics associated with nuclear power are becoming questionable. In 1975 there were 25 times as many nuclear reactors cancelled or deferred in the US as there were new orders placed. The industry is undoubtedly sick; the real question is whether or not it may be terminally ill.

The world may well move not from fossil fuel to nuclear, but toward growing reliance on solar energy. If the world moves toward a solar age, the population will need to be broadly distributed, for the simple reason that solar energy itself is broadly dispersed.

The Dangers of Nuclear Energy

ERNST SCHUMACHER

Of all the changes introduced by man into the household of nature, large-scale nuclear fission is undoubtedly the most dangerous and profound. As a result, ionising radiation has become the most serious agent of pollution of the environment and the greatest threat to man's survival on earth. The attention of the layman, not surprisingly, has been captured by the atom bomb, although there is at least a chance that it may never be used again. The danger to humanity created by the so-called peaceful users of atomic energy may be much greater.

A new dimension is given also by the fact that while man now can—and does—create radioactive elements, there is nothing he can do to reduce their radioactivity once he has created them. No chemical reaction, no physical interference, only the passage of time reduces the intensity of radiation once it has been set going. Carbon-14 has a half-life of 5900 years, which means that it takes nearly 6000 years for its radioactivity to decline to one-half of what it was before. The half-life of strontium-90 is twenty-eight years. But whatever the length of the half-life, some radiation continues almost indefinitely, and there is nothing that can be done about it, except to try and put the radioactive substance into a safe place.

But what is a safe place, let us say, for the enormous amounts of radioactive waste products created by nuclear reactors? No place on earth can be shown to be safe.

The most massive wastes are, of course, the nuclear reactors themselves after they have become unserviceable. There is a lot of discussion on the trivial economic question of whether they will last for twenty, twenty-five, or thirty years. No one discusses the humanly vital point that they cannot be dismantled and cannot be shifted but have to be left standing where they are, probably for centuries, perhaps for thousands of years, an active menace to all life, silently leaking radioactivity into air, water and soil. No one has considered the number and location of these satanic mills which will relentlessly accumulate. Earthquakes, of course, are not supposed to happen, nor wars, nor civil disturbances, nor riots like those that infested American cities. Disused nuclear power stations will stand as unsightly monuments to unquiet man's assumption that nothing but tranquility, from now on, stretches before him, or else—that the future counts as nothing compared with the slightest economic gain now.

Ernst Schumacher, "Production in Service to Life," in Hugh Nash, ed., *Progress As if Survival Mattered: A Handbook for a Conserver Society* (San Francisco: Friends of the Earth, 1981), pp. 236–37.

No degree of prosperity could justify the accumulation of large amounts of highly toxic substances which nobody knows how to make `safe' and which remain an incalculable danger to the whole of creation for historical or even geological ages. To do such a thing is a transgression against life itself, a transgression infinitely more serious than any crime ever perpetrated by man. The idea that a civilisation could sustain itself on the basis of such a transgression is an ethical, spiritual, and metaphysical monstrosity. It means conducting the economic affairs of man as if people really did not matter at all.

18.2:   The Critics (1971, 1988, 1970)

The contemporary environmental movement has had its detractors as well as its defenders. Its opponents have accused it of encouraging "ecoterrorists" who release mice and dogs from scientific laboratories to stop animal testing, drive spikes into trees to discourage lumbering, and cut power lines to sabotage nuclear energy reactors. They say it has fostered alarmists who exaggerate the dangers of technology and seek an impossible risk-free society. The new ecologists, they believe, often put abstract nature before human needs.

The first of the selections is by Richard Neuhaus, a Lutheran pastor [1] *who has written extensively on conservative social and political themes. Neuhaus is responding to a group of "Neo-Malthusian" environmentalists who, inspired by the eighteenth-century English economist Thomas Malthus, warned that human population growth, if unchecked, will soon exhaust the earth's resources and lead to mass poverty and even starvation. The Neo-Malthusians believe that the potential threat of demographic disaster justifies limiting economic growth and reducing resource exploitation.*

In what way does Neuhaus challenge the Neo-Malthusians? What principle does Neuhaus elevate above that of nature's sovereignty? Why might a Christian clergyman object to some of the views of environmentalists in general and of Neo-Malthusians in particular?

The second selection concerns the issue of risk. Environmentalists, as we have seen, tend to be skeptical of technology, believing it to be an expression of humankind's arrogant attitude toward nature and all too often dangerous to the environment and to human health. In the name of safety and protection of the environment they often favor keeping older technology and, indeed, replacing some modern technology with less

[1]Neuhaus later converted to Catholicism.

damaging preindustrial practices. Their opponents have at times accused them of using scare tactics to further their antitechnology ends.

In the document below a political scientist from the University of California at Berkeley, who does not share the antitechnology bias of some environmentalists, considers the question of how to assess the risk of a new product or technique realistically. What are Aaron Wildavsky's views of this issue? How does he link general economic growth with the ability of a society to reduce risks to health and nature?

The third selection is a critique of environmentalism from the political left. Reflecting the views of Ramparts *magazine, a radical publication founded in the 1960s, it was written on the occasion of the first Earth Day in the spring of 1970, at a time when the New Left was still a flourishing ideology. What are the editor's reservations about the environmental movement of the day? From a radical political perspective, is the assessment valid? Since 1970, have fears such as those expressed by the* Ramparts *editors been validated or refuted?*

People vs. Trees

RICHARD NEUHAUS

Because they agree that "not much time is available" many policy planners and promoters of survival are not inclined to wait for "the intricate processes and symbol-systems of whole societies" to take their course. At a highly secretive symposium in New York City, Professor Garrett Hardin[1] broke the question down into some simple propositions: Population + Prosperity = Pollution. "To reduce pollution, one must reduce either population or prosperity, and it is better to reduce population rather than prosperity." The American people—not to mention the people of the Third World—are not yet ready for the implications of this simple proposition. In the symposium, sponsored by the Population Council in May 1970, Hardin suggested that the implications must be slipped to the general public in small doses accompanied by a new understanding of what is moral and what is immoral. According to the report of the meeting, Hardin urged that "we should go lightly in encouraging rising expectations [among the poor] . . . for if everyone in the world had the same standard of living as do we, we would increase pollution by a factor of 20. . . . Therefore, it is a questionable morality to seek to increase the food supply. We should hesitate to make sacrifices locally for the betterment of the rest of the world."

Reprinted with the permission of Macmillan Publishing Company from *In Defense of People: Ecology and the Seduction of Radicalism* by Richard J. Neuhaus. Copyright © 1971 by Richard John Neuhaus.
[1]A professor of ecology at the University of California at Santa Barbara who warned of the dire consequences of excessive population growth—ED.

Proponents of "nature's rights" might ponder Hardin's resolution of the problem posed by someone suggesting that the redwood trees should be cut down in order to grow potatoes on that land and ship the potatoes to the victims of famine. "If the space required to grow four redwood trees could be devoted to growing food for one person, we should say directly and bluntly that four redwood trees are more important than a person." If this sounds callous, we are piously reminded that "We are guardians of the future, not owners of the trees, but trustees of the trees, trustees for the future. We are trustees of the grandchildren of the world, ours included." Oh yes, *ours* especially. Hardin acknowledges that the predictions of disaster that make such ethical transformations necessary may turn out to be wrong. In that case, we are assured, there is no great loss. "You can always produce more babies." The redwoods are irreplaceable.

Hardin, like Ehrlich,[2] is no ecological eccentric but is one of the movement's formative voices and has authored some of the more influential statements on population policy. Their views are echoed in an editorial in the February 1969 issue of *Bioscience:* "Because it creates a vicious cycle that compounds human suffering at a high rate, the provision of food to the malnourished populations of the world that cannot or will not take very substantial measures to control their own reproductive rates is inhuman, immoral, and irresponsible." Writing in the *New Republic,* Wayne Davis of the University of Kentucky, asserts, "It is time we faced our responsibilities. Those who call for increased food production in the world are asking that we make a grave problem still more grave. Responsible people must oppose any food distribution plan that is not tied to a program of birth control and a genuine effort to help the recipients break the poverty cycle." In its myriad forms, the logic of the "triage" solution is on the ascendancy. The long drum roll has begun for two-thirds of humanity. We are called to the banners of the rich, led by America, in righteous crusade against the wretched of the earth who will either surrender to our terms or die in their wretchedness. But please do not be misled. This is not the old warfare of nationalist pride, racial prejudice and the arrogance of power; this warfare, made possible by a revolution in values, is the battle of a new morality. It is human, it is responsible, and the poor who survive it will some day understand that we did only what was best for them.

The dispassionate observer of the present ecology movement cannot help but be struck by the ironies and contradictions coexisting under that one banner. Compassion and callousness, altruism and greed, world vision and nationalistic *hubris,* all join in what some presume to term the ultimate revolution, the revolution to end revolutions, the reordering of man's place in nature. It is as though, in the same movement and often within the same persons, the left hand refuses to know what the right hand is doing. The lit-

[2]Paul Ehrlich, a Stanford University biology professor and author of *The Population Bomb,* which warns about world population exceeding world resources—ED.

erature of the movement is marked by a moving reverence for "the seamless web of life," accompanied by a shocking indifference to the weaker and less convenient forms of human life and by an almost cavalier readiness to disrupt the carefully woven web of civility and humane values. Threatened forms of fauna and animal life are passionately protected while the threatened and oppressed forms of human existence are too often ignored. The insight of Abraham Heschel's[3] axiom, "The health of a society is measured by the protection it affords its weakest members," is applied to extra-human nature which must be preserved even at the expense of violating the axiom with regard to human society.

The language and its implicit value assumptions have infiltrated far beyond the ecology movement itself. Economist Robert Heilbroner speaks of "the most fearsome reality of all—a population that is still increasing like an uncontrollable cancer on the surface of the globe." An official and conservative Lutheran church periodical pronounces "every effort for social change is futile unless we first take realistic measures to reduce the earth's population." The printed programs for symphony orchestra concerts at Carnegie Hall have interspersed in their pages the little boxed cartoon of a round bomb (plant earth) with a lighted fuse and the legend, "The Population Bomb Keeps Ticking." It is no doubt a comforting thought for the affluent patrons of Carnegie Hall to believe that the world's inequities, so glaringly apparent when contrasted with Americans at the symphony, can be attributed not to economic and political injustice but to the evasively anonymous "population explosion." The cartoon reappears on matchbook covers at Marchi's, one of New York's more expensive restaurants. Remember the old-fashioned Thanksgiving dinner when in the saying of grace we were reminded of the hungry of the world? It made us uncomfortable about the lavishness of the meal, but it seemed only right to acknowledge the outrageous inequities in the distribution of the world's wealth, and no doubt some of us did then and there resolve to do something about righting the wrong. No longer need the edge of guilt impinge upon the enjoyment of our good fortune. We need not, indeed we should not, do anything about feeding the hungry. Such misguided compassion "can only make an already grave problem more grave." The fault lies not with the structure of American power that works so well to our advantage but with the heathen hordes who resist conversion to our enlightened policies whereby some of them may survive and, as Ehrlich says, "none represents a threat to the developed sections of the world." The fault lies not with our rapacity but with their fertility. On with the symphony; on with the feast; up America!

Ironies and contradictions abound among the gentle people of ecology's public springtime. Charles Lindbergh devotes his latter years to protecting the environment. In his *Wartime Journals* he describes flying over Nuremberg

---

[3]A professor of religion at Jewish Theological Seminary—ED.

after it had been devastated by allied bombing: "Pushing my head further out, I can see one spire of the cathedral, gutted but still beautiful, dimly silhouetted in the light. Above there are broken clouds, and the stars are coming. I feel surrounded by death. Only in the sky is there hope, only in that which man has never touched and which God forbid we ever will." He seems unaware that the death all around him came from the air, from the pristine sky of his poetic ardor. The sky is absolved of responsibility, as others absolve American power of any responsibility for the sufferings of the Third World. The sky, nature, is the illusion of innocence, so unlike the earth that has been tainted, corrupted, maggot-infested, by the archenemy People. The popular press views Lindbergh's devotion to conservationism as a balance to the opprobrium of his past sympathies for Nazi Germany. It is probably more accurate to see his inclinations and passions in dramatic continuity. It is apparent from his *Journals* that Lindbergh, guided by the lights of "nature's order," shared many of Hitler's views on inherently superior and inferior races. How natural that he should toward the end of his life turn away from the artificial contrivances of man and his politics and seek solace in the eternal verities of nature.

"Man is the measure of all things" was never entirely satisfying. But it is a thousand times preferable to "Nature is the measure of all things"—especially if by "Nature" one means everything apart from man. For the believer, man himself was measured in light of the transcendent and this enhanced his glory as cantor, caretaker and celebrant of the universe. From the Renaissance and Enlightenment, discovery and delight in mankind have emerged the values that have made Western civilization, with all its grievous faults, a reasonably tolerable form of the human condition. One does not wish to praise civilization too highly, lest he give false comfort to those responsible for its widespread injustices. At the same time, we dare not despise and reject the assumptions that have made possible whatever good there is in it. Undergirding these assumptions is the reverence and delight in humanity itself.

Are we now to reject Shakespeare's declaration of human dignity? "What a piece of work is a man! How noble in reason! how infinite in faculty! in form, in moving, how express and admirable! in action how like an angel! in apprehension how like a god! the beauty of the world! the paragon of animals!" We have been wearied by our failures and are now advised to conclude with Hamlet, "And, yet, to me, what is this quintessence of dust? man delights not me; no, nor woman neither. . . ." Shall we now accept Loren Eiseley's[4] view, so pervasive among those who write on ecology? "It is with the coming of man that a vast hole seems to open in nature, a vast black whirlpool spinning faster and faster, consuming flesh, stones, soil, minerals, sucking down the lightning, wrenching power from the atom, until the

---

[4]A prominent American anthropologist and writer on environmental issues—ED.

ancient sounds of nature are drowned in the cacophony of something which is no longer nature, something instead which is loose and knocking at the world's heart, something demonic and no longer planned—escaped, it may be—spewed out of nature, contending in a final giant's game against its master."

> *O Lord, our Lord,*
> *how majestic is thy name in all the earth!*
>
> *When I look at thy heavens, the work of thy fingers,*
> *the moon and the stars which thou hast established;*
> *what is man that thou art mindful of him,*
> *and the son of man that thou dost care for him?*
>
> *Yet thou hast made him little less than God,*
> *and dost crown him with glory and honor.*
> *Thou hast given him dominion over*
> *the works of thy hands;*
> *thou hast put all things under his feet,*
> *all sheep and oxen, and also the beasts of the field,*
> *the birds of the air, and the fish of the sea,*
> *whatever passes along the paths of the sea.*
>
> *O Lord, our Lord,*
> *how majestic is thy name in all the earth!*
>
> *Psalm 8, RSV*

Is it all a lie? Are we rather something unnatural, a hateful mutant, spewed out and rejected by the natural order, a cancer besmirching Spaceship Earth's green and pleasant land? Our vanity cries out to deny it. But it is not vanity alone that protests. There is the sure intuition that, for all our abuse of our dominion, God has no other instrument to divine and fulfill his work. There is the sure intuition that our failures do not excuse us from further duty. And there is the sure intuition that, if we learn to despise ourselves, we will shortly despise also our sisters and brothers; losing our nerve, we will become the victims of the few who seize the authority of nature's law to crush our proud illusions of human dignity.

The Principle of Uncertainty, the Axiom of Connectedness, and the Rule of Sacrifice[1]

AARON WILDAVSKY

Once we stop thinking of health and safety as qualities we already know how to achieve—and government's task being simply to choose what it confidently knows is life-enhancing, while rejecting what it already knows is life-deny-

---

Aaron Wildavsky, *Searching for Safety* (New Brunswick, NJ: Transaction Books, 1988), pp. 4–10.
[1]Footnotes deleted.

ing—the question of how to search for safety becomes paramount. Which set of principles, axioms, and rules, I ask, helps us discover how to reduce risk overall so that society as a whole becomes safer? Though no one can say for sure, my candidates in opening up the inquiry on risk and safety are: the principle of uncertainty, the axiom of connectedness, and the rule of sacrifice.

Dangers will arise; everyone agrees on that. Uncertainty about the consequences of present acts and about others as yet unforeseen cannot be reduced to zero. The principle of irreducible uncertainty is based not only on the self-evident premise that no one knows it all, but also on the slightly less obvious consideration that even as human beings act on their environment they are creating consequences of which they are as yet not fully aware. Although some uncertainties may be reduced under some circumstances, a modicum of uncertainty is a universal condition. Hence Kenneth Boulding writes about "irreducible uncertainties."

To the principle of uncertainty I wish to add another—the axiom of connectedness. This states that the good and the bad (safety and harm) are intertwined in the same acts and objects. There may be unalloyed goods (though I doubt it) but, if so, they are few and far between. Take the two principles together—uncertainty cannot be eliminated and damage cannot be avoided. This combination stipulates the conditions (old risks cannot be reduced without incurring new ones) under which the question of how to increase safety should be considered.

Suppose the things of this world, and the practices people follow, were all good or all bad in terms of securing safety. Then nothing would matter except to discover and choose the safe, and reject the dangerous. The end—securing safety—is given, and a decision rule exists for choosing among available means.

But life is not so straightforward. For the most part, safety and danger coexist in the same objects and practices. Under the right (or wrong) conditions, everything we need for life can also maim or kill: water can drown, food can poison, air can choke. Babies cannot be born without risk to the mother, nor can they grow to adulthood without facing innumerable dangers.

The trick is to discover not how to avoid risk, for this is impossible, but how to use risk to get more of the good and less of the bad. The search for safety is a balancing act. For if the axiom of connectedness holds, there is no choice that results in no harm. Merely minimizing danger to some people would not meet the safety criterion if it resulted in less safety for a larger number of other people than there otherwise would have been. If every act and every thing has harm for someone somewhere, indeed, if the safety we seek is ineluctably bound up with the danger that accompanies it, more harm than good may be done by efforts to avoid risk.

The principle of uncertainty and the axiom of connectedness can be generalized to all (including human) systems: each part of every system cannot be stable at the same time. Economist Burton Klein expresses the thought well:

> It is true, of course, that in an imaginary, unchanging world economies can be predictable both in the small and in the large: that is, they can survive simply by taking the classical law of supply and demand as a given. However, if an economic system is to make smooth adjustments in dealing with new circumstances—if it is to remain predictable in the large, so to speak—it must be able to adapt itself to new circumstances. In fact, what I mean by "dynamic" *is the ability of a person, a firm or an economy to adapt itself to new circumstances by generating new alternatives.* But, it should be apparent that if predictability in the small is defined as "microstability" and predictability in the large as "macrostability" neither an individual firm nor an entire economy can simultaneously conserve its micro and macrostability. Only in heaven can microstability be equated to macrostability. Here on earth, the greater the insistence on microstability—the greater the insistence on preserving a way of life—the lower will be its macrostability. Conversely, if a system is to enjoy a high degree of macrostability it must enjoy the ability to generate new alternatives, when confronted by necessity.

I will call this—the safety or macrostability of the whole being dependent upon the risk taking or instability of the parts—the "rule of sacrifice."

Does risk in the human context mean that specific individuals must give up their lives or limbs for a collective entity? No. It does mean that if the parts of a system are prevented from facing risks, the whole will become unable to adapt to new dangers. The concern with harming individuals for the benefit of the collective is warranted but misapplied. For harm is being done anyway; existing hazards are already taking their toll. The only real alternatives involve understanding the balance among those helped and hurt. Since there is no way of avoiding harm for everyone, the search for safety has to proceed on the understanding that the rule of sacrifice is inexorable: there can be no stable whole without some unstable parts.

Rival Strategies for Securing Safety

Assertions about risk should be treated as hypotheses. That is why I have decided to focus on the agreed objective—securing safety—rather than the disputed means. Is "taking no chances," for instance, conducive to safety? [Elsewhere in this book] I argue that it is not. Many predicted dangers have turned out to be exaggerated or nonexistent. Others are real, but the policies invoked merely shifted dangers from one place or people to another. Still other, worse dangers resulted because the products or practices protested against were replaced by more harmful substitutes. There are, to be sure, unanticipated consequences of technology that do more harm than good. But there are also . . . "unconsequent anticipations," i.e., predictions of unsafe events that never come to pass. When government acts to prevent all imaginable dangers, the costs associated with such predictions are no longer cheap. The cost is counted not only in money but also in damage done by those very preventive measures, and in harm that might have been mitigated had resources not been used up on unrealized risks.

Acting safely, it is said, requires rejection of risky things—chemicals, processes, apparatus—that could cause grave damage. Instead of making progress by trial and error, some proponents of safety propose a rule of allowing no trials without prior guarantees against harm. This across-the-board risk aversion actually increases danger, I shall argue, because in thus achieving "safety" the harm avoided is part and parcel of even larger, as yet unknown, benefits that will be forgone. By taking a narrow view—a certain thing does harm—instead of a broad perspective—what is the balance of harm and help here compared to alternatives—measures designed to increase safety can lead to an overall decrease. When a strategy of "no trials without prior guarantees against error" replaces "trial and error," the opportunity to take risks in order to achieve beneficial consequences is lost.

The risks stemming from trial and error should also be discounted by the "safety risks" that flow from trying to prevent damage. For if all things are potentially dangerous, merely giving a measure a safety label is no guarantee that it will not do harm. Rem Khokhlov, an eminent mountain climber and scientist, for instance, was also part of the Soviet political elite. When he suffered a pulmonary embolism during a training mission at 20,000 feet, a helicopter was sent for him, after which he was taken to Moscow for treatment. "It has been suggested to me by several Soviet friends," Peter Franken wrote in *Science,* "that Khokhlov's seniority in the Soviet system was partly responsible for his death in that it led to his being treated by physicians who were less familiar with this particular illness than was the medical community nearer the site of the accident."

Overwhelming evidence shows that the economic growth and technological advance arising from market competition have in the past two centuries been accompanied by dramatic improvements in health—large increases in longevity and decreases in sickness. One might expect a focus on profit to have led to neglect or even disregard of safety. Why, then, does society nevertheless usually end up healthier? Economists, so far as I know, have not turned their attention to the relationship between markets and safety: Does economic competition increase or decrease safety?

The positive association between market processes and economic wealth is well documented. "Richer Is Sicker Versus Richer Is Safer," the third chapter [of this book], begins by postulating another truth, just as well-established, though less well-publicized: human health is a function of economic wealth. Whether comparisons are made between nations or among people within them, wealthier is healthier. Why this is so, however, is not self-evident.

Disputes over the moral implications of economic costs as a consideration in regulation of risk (Should life be sacrificed to material gain?) do not make sense if health and wealth are positively related. In a wealth-health analysis, I ask whether a regulation or device or practice adds more to human safety than its cost subtracts from that safety.

The common wisdom is captured in the proverb "an ounce of prevention is worth a pound of cure." As is usually true with proverbs, however (he who hesitates is lost, but, look before you leap), they do not state the conditions of applicability. Cure may well be better than prevention if the former is feasible and the latter is not or if cure increases flexibility in dealing with future dangers while prevention induces rigidity.

Is it better to attempt to anticipate dangers before they occur or to inculcate a capacity to respond resiliently, i.e., to learn from experience to cope with untoward events? If seeking to anticipate dangers saps a system's energies without enabling it to guess right, for instance, then the system might end up without the benefits of either anticipation or resilience. And, further, if anticipation works well enough to suggest that stability is permanent, unexpected challenges may yet overwhelm the system. How, then, can society protect itself against unknown dangers?

Human beings can engage in prevention. They can plan. But how well? Planning depends on prediction, which presumes the elimination (or, at least, reduction) of surprise. I am not talking about minor (a small change in probabilities) but about major surprise, a change in kind, a change like acquired immune deficiency syndrome that central decision makers could not imagine might occur. Confusing quantitative surprise (where we surmise what might happen but not its probability) with qualitative surprise (where we have no idea of the kind of event) trivializes the problem of unexpected danger. If only "expected surprise" existed, there would be a lot less to worry about. Fire drills may protect against expected surprises, but not against the qualitatively unexpected.

How, then, might members of society develop defenses without knowing what might be in store for them? How might a society sample the unknown so as to get hints about future dangers before they become massive? One good question deserves another. Who has both the capacity and the incentive to undertake this strange sort of task? Who might so benefit from outguessing the future as to be willing to absorb the losses from what might be a high rate of failure? The larger and more centralized the organization that seeks to predict the future, the longer it will take to get agreement, the fewer hypotheses it can try, and the more costly each probe is likely to be. Instead of assuming that anticipation must be centralized, therefore, I would like to open up the possibility that safety might be improved by spreading the anticipatory function more widely throughout society.

Decentralized anticipation (numerous independent probes of an uncertain future) can achieve a greater degree of safety. Since innovations are introduced piecemeal as a result of these independent probes, a larger proportion of emergent dangers can be perceived early while each hazard is still localized and small. The ability of market competition to interrogate the unknown at a low cost to society, while simultaneously encouraging individuals to overcome adversity, has been underappreciated.

Anticipation and resilience, the broadest strategic alternatives for attempting to secure safety, subsume other strategies. Decentralized, rapidly moving trial and error contributes to a strategy of resilience. Centralized, slow-moving regulation of trials to prevent errors is essential to a strategy of anticipation. Are these strategies mutually exclusive, or can they be combined?

Why, the reader may well ask, are these strategies dichotomized into extremes instead of joined together? Obviously, the intelligent person would want to combine anticipation with resilience. Even though, in the end, a mixed strategy should be adopted, I think these large questions, with their polar-opposite alternatives, are good to ask.

Each extreme alternative has real advocates. The strategy of "no trials without prior guarantees against error" has substantial support; . . . it is written into law. The debate about whether the "no threshold effect" (a single molecule of a carcinogenic substance, some say, is enough to kill) should be used as the major criterion of regulatory choice is instructive in this regard.

But if we suppose, following Ronald Heiner's seminal essay on "The Origin of Predictable Behavior," that human uncertainty is deeper and more pervasive than has heretofore been thought, reliance on simple rules of thumb makes more sense. Has the individual on the verge of decision reached the right conclusion about both his objectives (or preferences) and/or the means for obtaining them? Perhaps he has the right preferences, but at the wrong time or for different conditions. Since the consequences of actions are so entangled—undoubtedly the product of diverse causes, some recent, the others long past—our decision maker cannot be at all certain about whether past solutions have worked or to what degree. Evolution proves survival, to be sure, but survival alone is hardly convincing evidence that the strategy itself was beneficial. The doctrine of "adverse selection" reminds us that organisms or practices may be selected because they inhere in desirable objects despite the fact that the item selected, were the truth known, is actually harmful.

Torn by uncertainty, decision makers place a high premium on reliability, i.e., on increasing the likelihood that a choice will work reasonably well under most conditions, though not necessarily exceptionally well under any. The chance that a given objective can be perfectly realized, Heiner argues, is exceedingly low compared to the probability of missing by so wide a margin that nothing is attained. Blame is reduced by reasonable success, not by failing to achieve perfection. The need for reassurance in an uncertain world, therefore, may lead to adopting a polar strategy—resilience or anticipation—even though neither is expected to work supremely well in every instance.

Also, mixed strategies are not always feasible; when a decision maker must choose a single strategy, therefore, it is desirable to estimate which one would yield the best overall results. It may be advantageous to start with one possible strategy, modifying it as circumstances warrant. The danger is less in beginning than in ending with a single strategy. Polarizing proposed solutions is largely a device that ultimately enables us to devise mixed strategies.

Editorial on Environmentalism

EDITORS OF *RAMPARTS*

The environment may well be the gut issue that can unify a polarized nation in the 1970's, writes Time magazine. The Hearst Press sees it as a movement "that could unite the generations." And the New York Times solemnly predicts that ecology "will replace Vietnam as the major issue with students."

The wishful thinking of a frightened Establishment? Perhaps. But the organizers of the officially-sanctioned April 22 Teach-In movement are doing their best to give life to the media's daydream about the co-optive potential of ecology. If they succeed, thousands of young people across the country will engage in a series of environmental extravaganzas, embellished to capture the excitement of the original Vietnam teach-ins, but structured to encourage the young to forsake the "less important issues" and enlist in a crusade to save the earth.

We think that any analogy between what is supposed to happen around April 22 and the organization of the Vietnam teach-ins is obscene. We think that the Environmental Teach-In apparatus is the first step in a con game that will do little more than abuse the environment even further. We do not think it will succeed.

The originators of the Vietnam teach-ins worked at great odds and against the lies and opposition of government, university administrations and the media. They raised their own money and had offices in student apartments or small storefronts. "Earth Day" came to life in the offices of Senator Gaylord Nelson, received blessings from Nixon's Department of Health, Education and Welfare, was funded by foundations, and has worked out of facilities lent by the Urban Coalition.

Vietnam protestors had to create their own reading lists, fact sheets and white papers; they had to work against the "expertise" of Southeast Asia scholars. The Environmental Teach-In comes prepackaged; a well-paid and well-staffed national office sends local organizers an official brochure which avoids mentioning the social and economic environment with which Mother Nature has to cope. Friends of the Earth (FOE) provides, through Ballantine Books, a semi-official "Environmental Handbook," which insists that saving the environment "transcends the other issues" and that we should in non-partisan fashion "support a man from any political party if he is a true Friend of the Earth."

Never mind if he's a racist. Don't worry about whether or not he supports American imperialism. This spring the Nixon Administration is busy undo-

Editors of *Ramparts*, *Eco-Catastrophe* (New York: Harper and Row, 1970), pp. vii–xii.

ing 15 years of struggle for school integration: the police continue to murder black people in the streets; the American judicial system is disintegrating and, in the eyes of the State, every radical has become a conspirator; the war machine in Washington has made clear its intention to stay in Vietnam indefinitely and to spread its war to Laos. All this—and the Teach-In organizers want to banish everything but environment to the back pages of our minds. They must be blind, or perverse, or both.

How can anyone in this dark springtime believe kind words—about environment or anything else—from the men in power? Once we might have been able to believe that because a President had embraced the civil rights issue, apartheid in the Deep South was dead. But such illusions can hardly be sustained any longer. The Open Housing Act, the chief legislative victory of those years, finds use this season only for its "H. Rap Brown Amendment"—the interstate travel ban on which the Justice Department hung the Chicago 7.

Lyndon Johnson promised that We Shall Overcome. Now Richard Nixon promises to clean up America. Even TV's "Laugh-In"[1] knows the punch-line: "If Nixon's War on Pollution is as successful as Johnson's War on Poverty, we're going to have an awful lot of dirty poor people around."

Haven't we learned after a decade of social struggle that major problems like Vietnam, Race, Poverty—now Environment—can't be packaged separately, each protected from contamination by "other issues"? Even the Kerner Commission[2] realized that white racism was systematic, structural and linked to economic and social institutions. Even the most determined skeptic has now been shown by the Nixon Administration that the Vietnam war was no honest mistake, but the result of a long history of American expansion into Asia and a long-term policy of subjecting poor nations to the imperatives of American investors. To understand why Washington has persisted in its genocidal war in Indo-China, don't look at the politicians who come and go; look at the structures of power and interest that remain.

Threats to the environment are no different. At their source is the same division of society—those with power against those without: the corporations, which organize for their own benefit, against the people whom they organize destructively.

Look at the values which galvanize energies and allocate resources in the business system: pursuit of money, enrichment of self, the exploitation of man—and of nature—to generate still more money. Is it surprising that a system seeking to turn everything into gold ends up turning everything into garbage? The market is master. Business makes money meeting consumer demands; it makes even more money creating new demands. More money is spent on advertising and sales promotion in America, on planned obsoles-

---

[1] A popular TV comedy program of the 1960s—ED.
[2] A Presidential Commission of the late 1960s that investigated the causes of ghetto rioting—ED.

cence and consumer manipulation, than on all education—public and private, elementary school through the university. This is pollution of the mind, and it has its own costs. Some students estimate that socially useless, ecologically disastrous waste products make up nearly half of the Gross National Product. Nixon has already predicted a 50 per cent increase in the GNP by 1980, ostensibly to finance new priorities like environmental reform. It would be better if he had questioned how much waste the dynamic American economy will have to produce in the next decade simply to clean up the waste of past decades.

Others, like the organizers of the National Teach-In, tell us that it is in the interest even of the corporate rich to clean up the environment. If all their customers are asphyxiated by air pollution, explain these optimists, business (and businessmen) would expire as well. By this same logic, the military-industrial complex should bar the ABM[3] from its cities, and the corporations, always eager to bring new consumers into the market, should make the war on poverty work. But no businessman, alone or with other businessmen, can change the tendencies of this ultimately ecocidal process unless he puts the system out of business. As long as society organizes production around the incentive to convert man's energies and nature's resources into profit, no planned, equable, ecologically balanced system of production can ever exist. Teach-ins which fail to confront this fact of life do worse than teach nothing. They obstruct knowledge and stand in the way of a solution. They join the struggle on the side which permits them truly to say—not of mankind, but of themselves—"We have found the enemy and he is us."

Perhaps the Teach-Ins could teach better if, instead of their present brochure, they distributed a full-page ad from Fortune's special environment issue. Sponsored by the New York State Department of Commerce, the ad pictures Governor Nelson Rockefeller inviting businessmen to come grow with New York. The pitch is simple: "Personal property of manufacturers is completely exempt from taxation in New York . . . During the past eleven years, there has not been one single new business tax in New York." Nowhere does the ad mention New York's long series of new *nonbusiness* taxes. In 11 years in office, Rocky has first imposed, then hiked a new state sales tax; quadrupled the cigarette tax; tripled the gasoline tax; and lowered the minimum income below which poor people are free of the state income tax. Businesses apparently aren't expected to care who subsidizes their growth. But the ad does want them to know that Governor Rockefeller, author of the "soak-the-poor program," considers "economic growth—a continuing expansion of the private economy—to be the indispensable ingredient of all progress."

Rockefeller doesn't say this only because he's a Rockefeller; he says it because he's Governor and every governor wants business to invest in his

---

[3]Anti-Ballistic Missile, a missile designed to shoot down attacking missiles. It was said to be an invitation to nuclear attacks—ED.

state. Private business accounts for 85 per cent of the GNP; it must be kept happy and expanding, or, short of revolution, there will be nothing for anyone at all. Regulation of business consequently can never be more than self-regulation, federal intervention into the business sector never more than federal intervention on behalf of the business sector.

But regulation is not the question. We simply don't need any more gross national product, any more unnecessary goods and factories. What we do need is a *redistribution* of existing real wealth, and a *reallocation* of society's resources. Everyone knows what this redistribution and reallocation should do; the crises of the last ten years have made it all so obvious: The poor must have adequate income, the cities must be rebuilt to fit human requirements, the environment must be de-polluted, the educational system must be vastly expanded, and social energies now poured into meaningless pursuits (like advertising and sales promotion) must be rechanneled into humanly edifying and creative activities.

We must, in short, junk the business system and its way of life, and create revolutionary new institutions to embody new goals—human and environmental.

All this sounds utopian. Well, utopias are relative. More utopian by far than revolution is the idea that the present society, dominated by business, can create lasting, meaningful reforms sufficient, for example, to permit mankind to survive the century.

At a recent "Survival Faire" in San Jose, California, ecology organizers bought a new car and buried it as a symbol of the task which they saw confronting ecology action groups. This was an indication of dangerous political naivete that must be overcome. To buy the car in the first place was to pay the criminal and strengthen him. But this act also pointed the finger of guilt at the consumer, who has only the choice of traveling to work by auto or walking 30 miles to work on the freeway. In opposition to this misdirected gesture of revolt, San Jose's black students angrily demanded that the car be raffled to provide defense funds for their brothers on trial. The blacks made their point very clearly. "Don't bury the car," their placard said, "bury the system."

In contrast to this Survival Faire, the week after the Conspiracy defendants were sentenced in Chicago, angry students razed the local branch of the Bank of America in Santa Barbara, California. The only bank in the Isla Vista youth ghetto, B of A had long treated young people as a class apart. It had opposed the grape strikers centered in Delano. It had supported, with branches in Saigon and Bangkok and with its leadership of the investment build-up in the Pacific, the American occupation of Southeast Asia. Two of its directors sit on the board of Union Oil, which had for so many months desecrated the once-beautiful beaches of Santa Barbara and destroyed their wildlife. Most important, as the branch manager explained to the press, it had been the major local symbol of capitalism and the business system.

Burning a bank is not the same as putting the banks and their system out of business. To do that, millions of people in this country will first have to wake up to the real source of their misery. The action in Santa Barbara, a community which has seen its environment destroyed by corporate greed, might spark that awakening. If it does, the students who burned the Bank of America in Santa Barbara will have done more to save the environment than all the Survival Faires and "Earth Day Teach-Ins" put together.